D0091798

AGE OF FRACTURE

AGE OF FRACTURE

Daniel T. Rodgers

THE BELKNAP PRESS OF
HARVARD UNIVERSITY PRESS
Cambridge, Massachusetts, and London, England

Copyright © 2011 by Daniel T. Rodgers
All rights reserved
Printed in the United States of America

First Harvard University Press paperback edition, 2012

Library of Congress Cataloging-in-Publication Data

Rodgers, Daniel T.
  Age of fracture / Daniel T. Rodgers.
    p. cm.
  Includes bibliographical references and index.
  ISBN 978-0-674-05744-9 (cloth : alk. paper)
  ISBN 978-0-674-06436-2 (pbk.)
    1. United States—Civilization—1970–. 2. Culture conflict—United States—History—
20th century. 3. Politics and culture—United States—History—20th century.
4. Individualism—United States—History—20th century. 5. United States—Social
conditions—1960–1980. 6. United States—Social conditions—1980–. 7. United States—
Economic conditions—1971–1981. 8. United States—Economic conditions—1981–2001.
9. United States—Intellectual life—20th century. 10. Popular culture—United States—
History—20th century. 11. Political culture—United States—History—20th century.
I. Title.
  E169.12.R587 2011
  973.91—dc22   2010028391

Once again, for Rene

Contents

Prologue

It's a war of ideas.

"There were words," Peggy Noonan wrote of her stint in the Reagan White House. "There were phrases: Personnel is policy and ideas have consequences and ideas drive politics and it's a war of ideas." People kept big books splayed open on their reading tables, she remembered: Paul Johnson's *Modern Times* and Jean-François Revel's *How Democracies Perish* on conservatives' tables; Paul Kennedy's *Rise and Fall of the Great Powers* and William Julius Wilson's *Truly Disadvantaged* on their liberal counterparts', had she seen them. The half-opened books were there so that their ideas and phrases could be soaked up and deployed in conversation and argument. They were there to display the kind of person their owners were. They were there as tokens in a multisided contest of arguments and social visions that ranged across the late twentieth century.[1]

"It's a war of ideas" was a particularly prominent slogan among conservatives. "It may not be with rockets and missiles, but it is a war nevertheless," Paul Weyrich, one of the architects of new right politics sounded the call to arms in the late 1970s. "It is a war of ideology, it's a war of ideas, it's a war about our way of life. And it has to be fought with the same intensity, I think, and dedication as you would fight a shooting war." Describing the Heritage Foundation's mission to a *Time* magazine reporter in 1986, the foundation's vice president leaned on the same language to explain, "We are the intellectual shock troops of the conservative revolution." When the free-market advocacy organization the Madison Group launched a newsletter in 1990, it titled its publication *Intellectual Ammunition*.[2] But the sense that ideas had far-reaching consequences, that the course of history could turn on framing and agenda setting, on struggles on the intangible fields of the mind, was not limited to conservatives. What was the nation itself, Bill Clinton asked a Georgetown University audience in 1995, but "an idea"? Not a product of experiment and social experience, as a common phrase from the 1950s had had it; not the amalgam of habits and institutions that was said to constitute the "American way" in another prominent Cold War expression. "America is an idea," Clinton insisted. "This country is an idea."[3]

Contests over ideas are, of course, no monopoly of the recent past. Political and social struggles have always turned not simply on the question of who should rule but also, and at least as consequentially, on what ideas of society and the self, morality and justice, should dominate. The rights of man, the indissoluble permanence of the Union, the prerogatives of property, the special world mission of the United States: they were all ideas laid across the messier realities of experience, helping to construct its character and possibilities, framing and polarizing its meanings. "What rules the world is ideas, because ideas define the way reality is perceived," Irving Kristol put the point in 1975.[4]

Still, if struggles over the intellectual construction of reality are inherent in all human societies, Kristol and his contemporaries were not wrong to sense that they took on new breadth and intensity in the last quarter of the twentieth century. Novel forms of intellectual production and dissemination—more politically oriented think tanks, new journals of scholarly debate and opinion, more argumentatively structured media—now began to move ideas more aggressively into circulation. More entrepreneurial university settings heightened the stakes of the intradisciplinary wars that fractured the law schools, the economics faculties, and the literature departments. Most striking of all was the range across which the intellectual assumptions that had defined the common sense of public intellectual life since the Second World War were challenged, dismantled, and formulated anew.

Those multisited battles and their consequences are the subject of this book. It is a history of the ways in which understandings of identity, society, economy, nation, and time were argued out in the last decades of the century, and how those struggles of books and mind changed the ways in which social reality itself would be imagined. It is not a story that falls into the neat left-right camps that the partisans of the "war of ideas" slogan imagined. But neither is it a tale of isolated arguments. Across the multiple fronts of ideational battle, from the speeches of presidents to books of social and cultural theory, conceptions of human nature that in the post–World War II era had been thick with context, social circumstance, institutions, and history gave way to conceptions of human nature that stressed choice, agency, performance, and desire. Strong metaphors of society were supplanted by weaker ones. Imagined collectivities shrank; notions of structure and power thinned out. Viewed by its acts of mind, the last quarter of the century was an era of disaggregation, a great age of fracture.

When it comes to the naming of ages, the cultural critic Stuart Hall writes, "What is important are the significant *breaks*—where old lines of thought are disrupted, older constellations displaced, and elements, old and new, are regrouped around a different set of premises and themes."[5] We are still learning to think of the last quarter of the twentieth century in this manner as a coherent period in the history of the United States. The journalists' and popular historians' propensity to punctuate by decades—1970s, 1980s, and 1990s, each with its own putative style, character, and decade-end summings up—interrupts the effort to map out longer narratives. Presidents and contending presidential administrations loom larger than life over the recent past, not the least the president that Peggy Noonan wrote for and venerated, Ronald Reagan. No other figure loomed larger on the political stage than Reagan or impressed his convictions and personality onto the political culture more forcefully. But too sharp a sense of break at Reagan's 1980 election simplifies and distorts. The decisive realignment election that political observers anticipated all through the period, waiting for the Republican party to sweep aside its rival as the Democratic party had so dramatically done in 1932, failed to take place.[6] Divided, not unitary, government was the rule in the last quarter of the century. Reagan's presidency was spent facing off against a Democratic House of Representatives, most of Clinton's against a Republican one. The age was not Reagan's in remotely the way that the 1930s were Roosevelt's. If we are to look for clearer historical fault lines, we must look elsewhere than to presidential elections.

Even the "1960s"—that explosive decade and a half in culture and politics that began with the sit-ins of black students in Greensboro and Nashville in 1960 in defiance of racial segregation and had barely lost its intensity by the time of the mass wave of antiwar protests in 1972 and the angry confrontation between white and black Bostonians over school integration in 1974—did not change the world as fully as its protagonists had hoped or its antagonists had feared. The upheavals of the 1960s etched a vivid trail of anger and memory. "The Sixties, I have come to believe, are something of a political Rorschach test," the editor Joseph Epstein wrote in what was already a truism by 1988. "Tell me what you think of that period, and I shall tell you what your politics are."[7] But for all the shock waves they set off in society and culture, and for all the ways in which their slogans could be found lodged in incongruously diverse places in later years, the social movements of the 1960s did not, in the end, set the forms into which the shaken pieces would be recast. The 1960s were a moment of break, but the regrouping around a different set of premises and themes, as Hall describes it, was the work of the era that followed.

The axis of that regrouping in the last quarter of the century was a reformulation, in idea and imagination, of concepts of "society." Strong readings of society had been one of the major intellectual projects of the middle decades of the twentieth century. In contrast to mid-nineteenth-century notions of the self as a free-standing, autonomous production of its own will and ambition, twentieth-century social thinkers had encircled the self with wider and wider rings of relations, structures, contexts, and institutions. Human beings were born into social norms, it was said. Their life chances were sorted out according to their place in the social structure; their very personalities took shape within the forces of socialization. Societies divided up people into castes and classes, even as they aggregated them under the pressure of the mass media and mass society's ways of life. The forces of history swept over them. Structuralist interpretations of society and culture of this sort ran hard through the big books of the postwar years: C. Wright Mills's *White Collar*, Hannah Arendt's *Origins of Totalitarianism*, and David Riesman's *Lonely Crowd*. They fueled the rise of social psychology, modal personality studies, social relations theory, functionalist and structuralist sociology, and projects of social modernization. They were absorbed into much of 1960s social thought, as rebels against the dominant culture resisted through the invention of countersolidarities and structural concepts of their own: the "system," the "movement," the "one-dimensional" entrapments of commercial cultural life.[8] Actual social life was never this tightly organized. Fissures and contradictions ran all through it. Still, to know the pressures of society on the self was, in mid-twentieth-century America, to speak within the bounds of the prevailing common sense of the matter.

But then in the last quarter of the century, through more and more domains of social thought and argument, the terms that had dominated post–World War II intellectual life began to fracture. One heard less about society, history, and power and more about individuals, contingency, and choice. The importance of economic institutions gave way to notions of flexible and instantly acting markets. History was said to accelerate into a multitude of almost instantaneously accessible possibilities. Identities became fluid and elective. Ideas of power thinned out and receded. In political and institutional fact and in social imagination, the 1930s, 1940s, and 1950s had been an era of consolidation. In the last quarter of the century, the dominant tendency of the age was toward disaggregation.

The terrain of this process was the field of ideas and perception, not, in the first instance, society itself. Toward the end of the era, in an argument that raced almost instantly through the sociology and political science seminars, Robert Putnam claimed that levels of civic association in the United States had, in sober fact, declined in the 1970s, 1980s, and 1990s. "Bowling Alone," he titled the phenomenon, in reference to the precipitous decline in weekly bowling leagues, but he meant by it something much deeper than shifts in recreational life. What worried Putnam was that more and more Americans bowling their way through modern life alone, without the voluntary associational support of neighbors and fellow citizens, threatened to deplete the fabric of civic trust and social capital that Tocqueville and others had thought so foundational to American life. When reworked and challenged by others, however, Putnam's data turned out to be messier than he had supposed. There were, indeed, fewer bowling leagues by the 1990s than before. Labor union membership had declined precipitously, falling to half its level when the age began. The supply of women eager for volunteer opportunities had been sharply diminished by the massive movement of women into the paid labor force after 1970. But other associations held their own or flourished. Volunteering rates among teenagers rose, megachurches boomed, and advocacy groups of all sorts grew dramatically.[9]

What characterized the age of fracture was not a literal thinning out of associational life. In an age of Oprah, MTV, and charismatic religious preaching, the agencies of socialization were different from before, but they were not discernibly weaker. Social structures persisted. What changed, across a multitude of fronts, were the ideas and metaphors capable of holding in focus the aggregate aspects of human life as opposed to its smaller, fluid, individual ones.

In accounting for the transformations in ideas and culture that reshaped the last quarter of the twentieth century, three sharply different explanations have been offered. The first posits a shift in the nation's core psyche and character. It was the "me decade," the journalist Tom Wolfe wrote famously in 1976: an age obsessed with self-referentiality. The nation, this line of reasoning argues, was caught up in an "age of greed," a new "culture of narcissism," a collapse of faith in public institutions, a pell-mell, selfish rush into a myriad of private lifestyle communities. The advice of the soon-to-be-imprisoned investor Ivan Boesky becomes, in this reading, the motto of the age: "Greed is all right, by the way," Boesky told the University of California business school's graduating class in 1986 in one of the most quoted snippets of the decade. "I want you to know that. I think greed is healthy."[10]

Selfishness there was aplenty in the age of fracture and new institutional ways in which the powers of money could be exercised and magnified. But the notion of a national mood or psyche is the illusion of writers and journalists hard-pressed by a deadline. Wolfe was struck by the ways in which the people he met talked not about wealth but obsessively about themselves, as if they had taken their psychoanalytic sessions public. Christopher Lasch, who made the "culture of narcissism" phrase famous, insisted that he had been misread to suggest that the nation had turned in on the self; what worried him, to the contrary, was that the intrusive therapeutic operations of late-capitalist society had made selves all but empty. Only a tiny sliver of the population actually lived in gated communities. To imagine a national mood across a society as diverse as the United States is to fall into the language of partisans of the time rather than to explain it.[11]

A second and more powerful explanation looks to changes in the institutions of intellectual life. In this reading of late-twentieth-century U.S. history, the key to the age was the conscious efforts of conservative intellectuals and their institutional sponsors to reshape not only the terms of political debate but the mechanics of intellectual production itself. By the late 1970s, Nixon's former secretary of the Treasury, the Wall Street investor William E. Simon, was urging that "the only thing that can save the Republican Party . . . is a counterintelligentsia," created by funneling funds to writers, journalists, and social scientists whose ideas had been frozen out of general circulation by the "dominant socialist-statist-collectivist orthodoxy" prevailing in the universities and the media.[12]

Within a decade, Simon's project had dramatically reshaped the production and dissemination of ideas. Older foundations, Simon's Olin Foundation in the lead, turned into conscious incubators of new conservative ideas, publicizing books and sponsoring authors, subsidizing student organizations and newspapers, and establishing university positions and programs for the promotion of ideas more favorable to business enterprise—all with the intent of changing the prevailing terms of debate. With corporate and entrepreneurial support, a global network of conservative think tanks proliferated to advance market-sympathetic ideas and speed their way aggressively into media and political debate. Journals and newspapers were floated on new conservative money. Publishers staked out claims in the newly politicized intellectual market, some playing one side of the intensifying war of ideas, others, like the Free Press, Basic Books, and the *New Republic,* playing both. In time, many of the leading figures in these new conservative institutions established themselves on the television cable news and talk shows, where argument flourished as a new form of sporting contest. By the end of the century, liberal funders and foundations that had once been more interested in sponsoring practical, on-the-ground ventures in social change than in books and press releases were actively playing at the idea-promotion game.[13]

The work of the conservative idea brokers changed the landscape of publication and intellectual argument. Their products will be visible in every one of the chapters to follow. Yet both sympathetic and critical observers of the counterintelligentsia project are inclined to overestimate its efficacy. In some areas—the law and economics movement in the legal faculties, the hardening terms of debate over policy toward the poor, the creation of the Federalist Society as a fraternity of like-minded law students and faculty, and the elaboration of a neoconservative foreign policy—the work of the conservative intellectual establishment was decisive. But extensive foundation funding for Richard Herrnstein's and Charles Murray's *Bell Curve* could not make its neo-eugenicism respectable or turn the *New Criterion* into a major scholarly journal. Heavily subsidized writers like Dinesh D'Souza rose and fell from grace. Many conservative public policy projects, despite weighty institutional backing, fell apart: monetarism in the early 1980s, the Social Security privatization project in the 1990s. The largest liberal foundations—Ford, Carnegie, and, by the mid-1980s, MacArthur—had far deeper pockets than the conservative ones. The budget of the liberal and centrist Brookings Institution was consistently larger than that of its conservative rival, the American Enterprise Institute.[14]

But more important, the era's key intellectual shifts cannot be pinned to any single part of the political spectrum. Ideas slipped across the conventional divisions of politics, often incongruously and unpredictably. Deregulation was a radical project before it became a conservative one. The first practical school voucher proposals were the work of liberal social scientists. The fracture of the social—though it took different terms and operated through different analytical languages—was, in the end, as much a product of left-leaning intellectuals as it was of the new intellectual right. The notion of a conservative age in American intellectual life, like the notion of Reagan's domination of the era's politics, harbors only half the truth.

A third family of explanations stresses not mood nor politics nor institutions of intellectual production but the deep structures of the late-capitalist economy. In this reading of the age, the precipitant of its cultural and intellectual transformations was the collapse of the high-wage, high-benefits "Fordist" economy that had dominated post–World War II American society. In the course of the economic crisis of the 1970s, profit margins were squeezed more intensely than before. Corporatist compromises between labor and management unraveled; manufacturers went abroad in search of cheaper labor; corporations hollowed themselves out by outsourcing all but a few core activities; production of goods and services moved from an inventory to a just-in-time basis. Fordism gave way to flexible accumulation, with its much shorter time horizons, much shallower institutional investments, and global extension. On this far-reaching change in structure, Fredric Jameson, David Harvey, and others have argued, the superstructures of "postmodern" culture changed to fit. Selves became more flexible and less unitary, time horizons shrank, artistic forms that had been radically separated in space and time collapsed into each other, attention moved from structures to surfaces. In the "cultural logic of late capitalism," as Jameson termed it, the structuralist assumptions of post–World War II social thought shattered and dissolved.[15]

This is an argument that must be taken seriously. Histories of the late twentieth century now routinely point to the Arab-Israeli War and Arab nations' oil boycott of 1973 as a critical hinge point in global economic history.[16] The subsequent shifts in the U.S. economy from production to finance, and from national to global scale, helped make just-in-time delivery of everything from computer chips to ideas part of the fabric of social life. Where everything circulated more rapidly, older understandings of social life in terms of institutions, solidarities, or the pressure of history could not help losing some of their force. Where the instruments of finance came ever closer to most Americans' lives—in pension stock funds, balloon-rate mortgages, leveraged buyouts, corporate restructuring, and plant closings—it was not surprising that the language of market economics should travel with them, seeping into new terrains of social imaginations.

Still, the notion that economic structures moved first, carrying ideas in their wake, does not adequately explain the age. Economies are rooted not only in structures of exchange but also, and just as fundamentally, in ideas, practices, norms, and conventions. The victory of the new models of market action that reconstituted economic theory for the age was already an accomplished fact by the end of the 1970s, well before anyone clearly discerned the new shape of the global economy. Arguments over selves and identities were not simply a reflex of the world's capital markets. What precipitates breaks and interruptions in social argument are not raw changes in social experience, which never translate automatically into mind. What matters are the processes by which the flux and tensions of experience are shaped into mental frames and pictures that, in the end, come to seem themselves natural and inevitable: ingrained in the very logic of things.

This book endeavors to tell a history of these acts of mind and imagination and the ways in which they changed America in the late twentieth century. It is not the narrative of a single movement of ideas that swept everything before it but an account of the ways in which contemporaries, working within the stock of ideas they possessed, tried to make sense of their times, and how through those very efforts—through argument and imagination, marginalization of some ideas and victories for others—the categories for social thinking were themselves remade. It is a story of the debates across a half-dozen fronts through which Americans tried to reimagine themselves and their society: the economic crisis of the 1970s, the new shape of finance capitalism and global markets, the struggle to hold identities stable where race and gender proved unnervingly divisive, the linguistic turn in culture in an age of commercial and malleable signifiers, the nature of freedom and obligation in a multicultural and increasingly unequal society, and the collapse of Communism. Social thought clustered on these and other problematics. These were the nubs on which issues were forced, assumptions shattered, ideas broached, categories naturalized, paradigms strained and reconstituted. No logic was already locked into them. Thinking in modern societies—that is to say, in the diverse and intellectually compartmentalized societies of modern times—is piecemeal, context-driven, occasional, and (even if the task is to unknot an intellectual puzzle) instrumental.

What crossed between these widely flung fronts of thought and argument was not a single, dominant idea—postmodern, new right, or neoliberal—but a contagion of metaphors. Intellectual models slipped across the normal divisions of intellectual life. Market ideas moved out of economics departments to become the new standard currency of the social sciences. Certain game theory set-pieces—the free-rider problem, the prisoner's dilemma, the tragedy of the commons—became fixtures of common sense. Fluid, partial notions of identity, worked out in painful debates among African-American and women's movement intellectuals, slipped into universal usage. Protean, spill-over words like "choice" were called upon to do more and more work in more and more diverse circumstances. In the process some words and phrases began to seem more natural than the rest—not similes or approximations but reality itself.

It was an age of such contagions. Arguments poached on parallel debates around them, reworking their claims and concepts—markets, identities, rights—for new occasions. For all the hyperspecialization of modern intellectual life, the boundaries between its arenas were always porous and open to raiding. To watch one traveling, versatile set of ideas lose value to another, across a diverse array of uses and arguments, is to see a historic intellectual shift in action.

Ideas moved first in the arena of economic debate. The modern concept of markets as fields of natural, optimizing, rational choice was not the dominant analytical language of post-1945 macroeconomics. The revival of market ideology was a product of attempts to rethink the core paradigms of economics during the global economic crisis of the 1970s: a product of contest, rivalry, paradigmatic exhaustion, and innovation that was to have profound effects on the social thought of the age. That contest, its key players, and its unexpected outcomes are the subject of Chapter 2. Reconceptualizations of power are the subject of Chapter 3. By definition, perfect markets operate free of coercion in a world of mutual consent. But the market models spilling out of the economics departments into the law schools and social science faculties in the 1970s and 1980s did not eliminate the need for concepts of power: where it was lodged, who held it, and how it worked in an age of investment capital. Drawing on new class theory or rational-choice models, on concepts of culture and hegemony, or on the long shadow cast by Michel Foucault's work, scholarly and popular writers struggled to find a language of power where power itself seemed to shift shapes so rapidly.

Chapters 4 and 5 turn to debates over identity. The first, on race and social memory, throws us into the ways in which arguments over the politics, obligations, and finally the very essence of race came into contest in the age of fracture. The era began with Alex Haley's sweeping historical account of kin and memory; it ended with race in question marks. Sisterhood, the subject of Chapter 5, disaggregated in much the same way, as conceptions of womanhood became more multiple and fractured, and gender and sexuality themselves were reconceived as performative and elective. If these were liberations, as in part they were, they proceeded against a background of pain: bitter struggles over the legacies of racism, angry separations, and, not least, the eruptive battle over certainties, with gender at its core, that came to be called the "culture wars."

Chapters 6 and 7 turn to conceptualizations of society and time. In the face of late-twentieth-century society's growing diversity and inequality, how strong a sense of mutual obligation was necessary to hold a national community together? That was a debate that drew in social theorists like John Rawls, libertarians like Robert Nozick, multiculturalism's advocates and enemies, the architects of the new welfare policy who essentially called off as a failure the 1960s war on poverty, and, not the least, those who, in the altered language of the age, called themselves conservatives. Finally, where choice and flux are imagined to prevail everywhere, history itself becomes increasingly malleable, flexible, and porous. One can imagine piercing through history: backward in time to read the original intention of the Constitution's drafters, or forward to imagine that the post-Communist nations could be spurred in a single leap into capitalism.

In these ways, piece by piece, as people tried to think their way through events and experiences using the shifting stock of categories at their disposal, the terrain of common sense shifted. Notions of power moved out of structures and into culture. Identities became intersectional and elective. Concepts of society fragmented. Time became penetrable. Even the slogans of the culture war's conservatives were caught up in the swirl of choice.

In these contexts, the language of twentieth-century politics took on new and unexpected patterns. Chapter 1 begins with the shifting formulas of presidential speech making in the age: its keywords, slogans, implicit rules, and gestures. In the late years of the Cold War, the rhetoric of politics was saturated with a historical and social urgency, a sense of obligations and sacrifice. But presidential speeches cannot escape the very dynamics of the ideas they hope to mobilize. When Ronald Reagan, unexpectedly and early in his term, lost the words for the Cold War, the event revealed more about the age of fracture than his speechwriters knew.

Beginning in a crisis of economic ideas, the age ended in crisis as well. When the shock of the destruction of the World Trade Center towers in

2001 broke into the new world of disaggregated ideas and concepts, it brought an instant reaction: a whirlwind of fear and anger, a resurgent nationalism, and a sense of fierce aggregate loyalties. And yet, even as the language and urgencies of the Cold War were revived, as neighborhoods were suddenly swathed in flags and bunting, large elements of the social thought of the last quarter of the twentieth century endured. Sorting out what changed and what survived in the America of the global war on terror is the task of the epilogue.

In a historical inquiry of this sort, it is impossible to deal with more than a fraction of the ideas in motion across an age. The generation and circulation of ideas are radically open processes. Ideas were made at every pore of society: in the back and forth of the radio talk shows, in the movies, in the *Cosby Show* and *Dallas* and *West Wing* scripts and those who hung week by week on them, in arguments at bars, lunchrooms, and workplaces, in churches, clubs, and classrooms. In every modern society there is a surfeit of ideas and claimants for primacy. Any one history can draw out only some of these, hoping to make sense out of a major part (but never the whole) of the terrain. In what follows I have been drawn to the fields where the heaviest public intellectual ammunition of the era was mobilized, where academic thought and public policy met with the sharpest implications for each other. This is, in that sense, a story of the big books that Peggy Noonan saw on display, the arguments in which they were deployed, the contexts in which they were shaped, the ways in which they refashioned the frames of public argument, and through that, reshaped the age itself.

A still more important limit to these pages is their scant attention to the parallel debates that swept across the world outside the United States. For all their distinctive American inflections, the arenas of twentieth-century social thought were global and transnational. French theory invaded U.S. literature departments. British think tanks spawned American affiliates. Debates over identity were global in scope. Arguments over economic and regulatory policy moved across the nations. Even behind the intellectual border walls of the Communist world, knots of discussants, reading groups, and strategists poured over the same issues—markets, history, society, identity, and power—that ran through the academic campuses of the United States. Although we will probe some of those connections and contrasts, a much fuller, global history of social thought and social argument in the last decades of the twentieth century cries out to be written.

In the meantime, rescuing a piece of that larger global story from the stereotypes and simplifications that are quickly wrapped around the recent past, making it safe and tidy for its boosters and critics alike, may be ambition enough for the book at hand. For us, living in the immediate slipstream of these intellectual events, in the ragged turbulence of argument and conviction they left behind, the question historians have asked for other, more distant times and places takes on a closer importance: how it was that a vocabulary of social thought unexpectedly became outmoded and passé, and another way of thinking, for an era, made claim to its place.

1

Losing the Words of the Cold War

We're not called upon to make that kind of sacrifice.

Kenneth Khachigian, notes of a conversation with Ronald Reagan

There had not always been so many words. Surrounding public figures with a nearly endless sea of rhetoric is an invention of the twentieth century. Presidents, in particular, once talked in public far less often than they do now. Thomas Jefferson's rule that presidents should communicate to Congress only in writing remained the norm until Woodrow Wilson broke it in 1913. Nineteenth-century presidents spoke to gatherings of the people at large, but they did so in a strikingly passive voice and not frequently. Jeffrey Tulis counted a total of about a thousand presidential speeches delivered over the course of the entire nineteenth century, almost the number that Jimmy Carter gave in his four years in office. Even in the twentieth century, the stream of words that presidents have issued has grown dramatically. Franklin Roosevelt gave less than three hundred speeches of all sorts during the New Deal's first term—vastly more than Lincoln (who gave seventy-eight) but far below the thousand-speeches-a-term rate that Reagan, G. W. H. Bush, and Clinton all chalked up. The modern talking presidency, drawing on the resources of an extensive staff of writers, idea generators, and message consultants, is a phenomenon of the post-1945 years.[1]

Presidents use their modern fount of words for many purposes. They use them to outline their policy proposals and to persuade Congress and the people of the wisdom of their chosen course of action. They use public words to mobilize their electoral base and corral the undecided voters. They use them ritually and ceremonially. But in the very course of the everyday acts of politics, presidents and their speechwriters cannot help mapping an inchoate theory of society and politics: an image of the nation as a collective entity over which they preside. Presidential speeches not only use public words for tactical ends, large and small, but also shape the public words of the day. They set into circulation mental pictures of society and its field of obligations. They articulate the nation and its promises. Even at its most formulaic and ritualized, when test groups pass judgment on slogans and sound bites and relays of writers work over one another's drafts, the modern rhetorical presidency offers a window into the stock of ideas, assumptions, and social metaphors that hold traction in their day.

In the generation after 1945, the assumptions that saturated the public talk of presidents were the terms of the Cold War. In language and setting, a sense of historically clashing structures dominated the presidential style. Urgency and obligation were its hallmarks. The Cold War political style clothed the events of the moment in high seriousness; it bound them into a drama of global struggle; it drew leaders and nation into tight and urgent relationships. It formed a way of articulating public life in which society, power, and history pressed down on individual lives as inescapably dense and weighty presences. Across the divide between the free and the Communist worlds two differently organized social systems confronted each other: not two world-spanning geopolitical powers, merely, but two antagonistic patterns of social roles and norms, two profoundly different ways of organizing political power and authority, two competing understandings of the long march of history. Freedom was at the center of Cold War political rhetoric, but within these urgent contexts, freedom was inescapably social and public. That was what John Kennedy meant in urging the nation "to seize the burden and the glory of freedom." That was what Barry Goldwater's speechwriters meant in 1964 in ringing their changes on the word: "*Freedom! Freedom*—made orderly . . . *Freedom—balanced* so that liberty, lacking order, will not become the license of the mob and of the jungle."[2] To act freely within these terms was to act not alone but within a larger fabric of relationships, purposes, obligations, and responsibilities.

In these emphases the rhetoric of the post-1945 presidencies repeated and amplified the dominant language of mid-twentieth-century social thought. The high urgencies of Cold War politics mirrored the theme of intense, agonistically difficult choice that ran through existentialist literature, neo-orthodox theology, and the theater stage. Its insistence on a world-shattering collision between social systems, mores, and "ways of life" put the language of sociology and social anthropology directly into mass, public play. Its sense of the long drag of history, the thickness with which the past overlaid and bore down on the present, was a college lecture hall truism. No simple generalization can adequately capture the complexity of post–World War II American social thought, or the dissent and dynamics that always roiled within it. From the cultural radicals of the late 1960s and early 1970s a more anarchic and libertarian strain was already bursting into the public forum, shaking nerves and certainties. But if there was a characteristic distinctive to social thought in the decades after 1945, marking it off from what preceded and followed it, it was the intensity with which the socially embedded, relational sides of existence framed ideas of the human condition. The freedom which hung so urgently in the balance in 1950s and 1960s America was ballasted by and contained within its complements: responsibility, destiny, justice, morality, and society.

This was the language that saturated the public talk of presidents when the 1970s began. But by the end of the 1980s the language and style of the Cold War presidency were clearly in eclipse. Freedom, once so tightly tied to its contexts of challenge and destiny, had become disembodied, unmoored, imagined. Themes of self-fashioning that had been incubated in the 1960s counterculture were fissuring through every domain of social thought. The nation disaggregated into a constellation of private acts. Among the unexamined ironies of the last decades of the century is that it was in the speeches of the oldest of the Cold Warriors, Ronald Reagan, that the words and gestures of the Cold War gave way, so unexpectedly, to something new.

Modern presidential oratory is a highly structured affair. The major speeches of a president—the Inaugural and State of the Union addresses in which the particularly heavy lifting of social articulation is performed and in which the trail of social thought is etched particularly clearly—proceed within scripts already half written, as if they were welded to massive subterranean templates of grammar and conviction. State of the Union messages report and propose, always in two parts, domestic and foreign. Inaugurals begin, profess continuity, and announce an era of renewal: a "new hope" (Truman), a "new purpose" (Johnson), "a new era" (Nixon), or, down to tautological bedrock, a "new beginning"—the phrase that Reagan's speechwriters swiped from Carter's, just as Carter's had swiped it from Nixon's.[3] Speechwriters learn their art by copying the work of other speechwriters in the way that Peggy Noonan, new to the Reagan speechwriting staff in 1984, set out to find the authentic presidential "sound" by reading the speeches of Franklin D. Roosevelt. The "grammar of the presidency," as Noonan called it, was the work of the speechwriters' continuous, creative recycling of the words and gestures of their predecessors.[4]

The key to that grammar in the post-1945 years was an urgent sense of history's demands. To talk in the presidential voice was to talk against a backdrop of crisis, danger, and trial. Presidents addressed their most important speeches to a world in peril: a "shaken earth" in its "season of stress" (Eisenhower), a nation in its "hour of maximum danger" (Kennedy), at its "time of testing" (Johnson).[5] In the contest with Communism, the urgencies turned intense and apocalyptic. "It is of the utmost importance that each of us understand the true nature of the struggle now taking place in the world," Eisenhower drew out the theme in 1955:

> It is not a struggle merely of economic theories, or of forms of government, or of military power. At issue is the true nature of man. Either man is the creature whom the Psalmist described as "a little lower than the angels" . . . or man is a soulless, animated machine to be enslaved, used and consumed by the state for its own glorification. It is, therefore, a struggle which goes to the roots of the human spirit, and its shadow falls across the long sweep of man's destiny.[6]

In this sustained crisis, the task of presidential leadership was to warn and awaken the American people. This was the axis on which presidential oratory recapitulated the forms of a Protestant sermon and on which the president assumed the preacher's part. The words that defined leadership, the Cold War presidents insisted, were uncomfortable words. "We sometimes chafe at the burden of our obligations, the complexity of our decisions, the agony of our choices," Kennedy had admonished the nation in his State of the Union message in 1962. "But there is no comfort or security for us in evasion, no solution in abdication, no relief in irresponsibility." Presidents were expected to know and to name, as Johnson put it in 1967, the "disorders that we must deal with . . . the frustrations that concern us . . . the anxieties we are called upon to resolve . . . the issues we must face with the agony that attends them."[7] As watchman on the walls of the republic, the president awakened the citizenry from its narrow contentments. As preacher, he called his nation to its better self, prescribed its obligations, enunciated its resolve, and blessed its endeavor. The sermonic turns of phrase that coursed through presidential oratory in the post-1945 years—"let us begin" (Kennedy), "let us resolve" (Johnson), "let us accept that high responsibility not as a burden, but gladly" (Nixon)—were emblematic of the relationship between the people and their presidential preacher.[8]

Of all the dangers against which presidents spoke after 1945, none called out stronger rhetorical effort than a weakening of public resolve. In the standing tension between "our common labor as a nation" (as Eisenhower put it) and the temptations of a purely private life, Cold War presidents spoke for the imperatives of public life. "America did not become great through softness and self-indulgence," Eisenhower warned. Greatness was achieved through devotion, courage, and fortitude, through "the utmost in the nation's resolution, wisdom, steadiness, and unremitting effort."[9] Here freedom's "burden" was clearest. To remain free required resistance to the allure of selfish comfort, the sirens' call of self-gratification. "This is no time of ease or rest," Eisenhower insisted in his Second Inaugural. "High will be its cost" in "toil" and "sacrifice" of the "labor to which we are called." John F. Kennedy's famous challenge "ask not what your country can do for you," his summons "to bear the burden of a long twilight struggle . . . against the common enemies of man," were cut from the same cloth.[10]

The upheavals of the 1960s overtly changed none of that. Nixon's speeches were filled with echoes of Kennedy's high rhetorical gestures polished anew. Talk of "crisis," "purpose," "responsibility," and the "honor" of responding to "our summons to greatness" propelled them. The unattached self was, as before, an object of high suspicion. Nixon's speechwriters piled up repetitions of the word "together" in heaps in his major speeches, as if the words themselves could bridge the raw social divisions that the wedge issues of race and the Vietnam War had cracked open in the late 1960s. Nixon, the constant political calculator and polarizing political force, went to the public in the self-abnegating language of his predecessors. "Until he has been part of a cause larger than himself, no man is truly whole," Nixon repeated the conventional rhetorical wisdom in his First Inaugural. "To go forward at all is to go forward together."[11]

The first breaks in the formula that joined freedom and obligation all but inseparably together began with Jimmy Carter. From the start he brought to the presidency a markedly different language shaped not only by his outside-Washington experience but, still more, by his immersion in Protestant evangelical culture. No president's inaugural address in a century had mentioned the Bible on which he had lain his hand to take the oath of office (it was Carter's mother's), much less the passage (Micah 6:8) to which he had had it opened. The idea of the nation as a gathered congregation of faith saturated Carter's rhetoric. He talked easily of the "common good" and the "beloved community." For all his experience as a naval officer and business owner, Carter was never comfortable in the high leadership style of Cold War political culture. In his low-church image of the presidency, the congregation held the nation's moral force; the president was the people's temporary servant.[12]

Carter brought all this into the presidency in 1977 in a flurry of populist symbols. He had campaigned on a promise of a government "as good as its people." His challenge, as he articulated it, was to stay as intimate with the people as a low-church preacher was with his flock. "You have given me a great responsibility," he pledged in his Inaugural: "to stay close to you, to be worthy or you, to exemplify what you are." The people's "sense of common purpose," he repeated the formula the next year, "towers over all our efforts here in Washington . . . as an inspiring beacon for all of us who are elected to serve." The antigovernment line that Carter articulated—"government cannot solve our problems, it can't set our goals, it cannot define our vision," he admonished in 1978—was premised on the assumption that the "new spirit among us all" ultimately mattered more than policies. The presidency, in passages like these, was merely a vessel for the nation's moral will and faith.[13]

But as Carter's administration collided with the economic ruptures that were to reshape the age, the new formulas strained and fell apart. The economic crises had begun in the last years of the Nixon administration. The runaway inflation of 1973–1974 had already ebbed by the time Carter took office in 1977; unemployment receded slowly in the first three Carter years. But by the end of the 1970s, the annual inflation rate had shot up all over again. The Soviet Union's invasion of Afghanistan and the shock to global oil production as revolution dried up Iran's oil exports set off tremors throughout the world. In the context of inflation, gas shortages, and renewed Cold War fears, as Carter strained to amass the political capital necessary to address the crises that beset the country, the high Cold War style flowed back into his speeches.

Already in his Inaugural address in 1977, Carter's belief in an "undiminished, ever-expanding American dream" had mixed uncertainly with his admonition that even the greatest of nations faced "limits." By his State of the Union message in 1979 Carter was warning of the unprecedented subtlety and complexity of the problems facing the nation. At the depths of the crisis over oil and economics that summer, as angry, bumper-to-bumper drivers queued up for gas in lines that seemed to snake on without end, Carter reached back to the Cold War tropes of crisis, commitment, and sacrifice. He had already invoked the crisis leadership of Lincoln, Roosevelt, and Truman. Now, in this time of "challenge," "pain," and "danger," he pledged to lead the people against the "fundamental threat" that the oil crisis posed to the "social and political fabric of America."[14]

The fight for independence from foreign oil was the nation's new moral equivalent of war, Carter urged. "Self-indulgence and consumption" had sapped the nation's will. Worship of material goods had emptied lives of meaning and eroded a sense of common purpose. Faith in the future was unraveling. But by joining hands and pledging themselves to a renewed faith and action, a united people could resist the path "that leads to fragmentation and self-interest." "On the battlefield of energy we can win for our nation a new confidence, and we can seize control again of our common destiny." The "malaise" speech, as it was quickly dubbed in the media, was later to be accounted a blunder: too pessimistic and too moralistic in tone. But the pollsters reported that Carter's approval ratings, which had sagged badly during the spring, shot up 11 points in its wake.[15]

Dedication, courage, responsibility, self-scrutiny, and sacrifice: these were the nouns that bore the burden of Cold War presidential rhetoric. The terms clustered together: freedom with responsibility and discipline; peril with wisdom, leadership, firmness, and resolve. The key words of political culture in the third quarter of the century were social, historical, and relational. Whatever the context of the moment, whatever the other voices straining to make themselves heard in the divided and contention-filled public sphere, this was the way presidents sounded.

Ronald Reagan knew those formulas intimately. He was virtually the last American president of the Cold War and the one whose career had been most shaped by its massive impress on politics and culture. Though, as he often joked during his presidential years, he was not quite as old as his audiences might imagine, Ronald Reagan's public career spanned the entirety of the Cold War struggle, from Yalta through *glasnost,* from the blacklists of 1940s Hollywood to the eve of the Soviet Union's disintegration. The words and assumptions of Cold War politics were ones he had lived with for a long time, a way of framing history and politics that came as naturally to him as the ease with which he felt the timing of a speech, or the way his speechwriters sprinkled his trademark word of hesitation, "well," throughout his addresses.

Reagan needed no tutoring in the rhetoric of the Cold War presidency. His basic speech of the early 1960s had fit hand in glove into its prevailing rhetorical structures. It broke the continuity of American history apart at the advent of international Communism. It espied a sea of surrounding terrors ("We are faced with the most evil enemy mankind has known in his long climb from the swamp to the stars"). It pleaded for vigilance ("freedom is never more than one generation away from extinction"). It encouraged inner discipline ("Will you resist the temptation to get a government handout for your community?"). If there was a distinctive thread in Reagan's prepresidential speeches it was the way they turned the Cold War's anxieties back on domestic politics—their displacement of the totalitarian nightmare from the world scene to the stealthy, creeping, insidious growth of government at home. "We'll adopt emergency 'temporary' totalitarian measures, until one day we'll awaken to find we have grown so much like the enemy that we no longer have any cause for conflict," Reagan warned in 1961. His tone was disturbing. He was more the nagging Jeremiah than he was Kennedy's trumpet-sounding Joshua. Still, in their urgencies, their Manichaean readings of history, and their zeal to waken the nation to a contest for total stakes, Reagan's basic speeches of the 1960s flowed down well-worn channels.[16]

Reagan's presidential speechwriters knew the grammar of the presidency equally well. They grasped for rhetorical continuity with a more eager hand than had any presidential speechwriters before them. Reagan's post-1980 addresses were virtually an American Bartlett's of pre-used materials, quoted or tacitly cannibalized from Washington, Franklin, Jefferson, Paine, Lincoln, Theodore and Franklin Roosevelt, Truman, Kennedy, and, not infrequently, his defeated antagonist Jimmy Carter. Kennedy's exhortation that we sail "with the tides of human freedom in our favor" was recycled by Reagan's speechwriters in a dozen different variations. Carter's boast in 1978, "It has been said that our best years are behind us. But I say again that America's best is still ahead," was remade to look as if it had been Reagan's all along.[17] At the Democratic party convention in 1976, Walter Mondale had turned to Carl Sandburg's words for inspiration: "I see America not in the setting sun of a black night of despair . . . I see America in the crimson light of a rising sun fresh from the burning, creative hand of God." Looking for something authentically Reaganesque, Reagan's speechwriters reused the identical lines in 1984.[18]

With the right occasion and the right speechwriter, the tropes that had dominated the mid-twentieth-century presidency would be reinvigorated, propelled by Reagan's exceptional ability to project his own inner confidence and conviction across the television screen. He would talk of the tides of history, the fabric of society, the vast empire of evil, the heavy responsibilities of freedom, and (in Franklin Roosevelt's words) our "rendezvous with destiny."[19] But those occasions grew rapidly fewer. Already in his years in the California governorship, a less hectoring tone had begun to shape some of his speeches, with more talk of dreams and possibilities. Ensconced in what Theodore Roosevelt once called the "bully pulpit" of the White House, terms like "crisis," "peril," and "sacrifice" slipped one by one out of Reagan's major speeches like dried winter leaves.

One catches the speed and direction of the transformation as early as his First Inaugural, when Reagan paused to tell the story of a World War I soldier, Martin Treptow. The story was mythic, not only in the liberties the speech took with the facts (Treptow's body lay in a Wisconsin cemetery, not in the Arlington hills on which the television cameras focused), but also in having been told in other versions many times before, most famously in Elbert Hubbard's stem-winding paean to Spanish-American War loyalty, "A Message to Garcia," in 1899. Treptow had been a small-town barber before taking up a post on the Western front—a figure ripped from his private concerns by perils that reached now even into small-town Arcadia. Dispatched to carry a message between battalions, Treptow was killed. His diary, recovered later, revealed a handwritten pledge: "I will fight cheerfully and do my utmost, as if the issue of the whole struggle depended on me alone."

Reagan read the words of that pledge, but then he plunged unexpectedly on, lest his listeners mistake the meaning of the story:

> The crisis we are facing today does not require of us the kind of sacrifice that Martin Treptow and so many thousands of others were called upon to make. It does require, however, our best effort and our willingness to believe in ourselves and to believe in our capacity to perform great deeds, to believe that together with God's help we can and will resolve the problems which now confront us. And after all, why shouldn't we believe that? We are Americans.

It was a remarkable passage in its head-spinning moves from Treptow's self-sacrifice to "our best effort," from his death to our confidence in ourselves. Treptow's part was to give his life; ours, as Reagan glossed the story, was simply to "believe" that deeds as great as Treptow's were possible. It was to be one of the last significant mentions of sacrifice in Reagan's major speeches.[20]

On the axis of "belief," Reagan's speechwriters broke up and recast the rhetorical formulas of Cold War political culture. The story of peril, leadership, and resolve was replaced by a different plot. This one moved from initial confidence to momentary despair (some say that "ours is a sick society"), finally to a "revolution of hope" restored. None of this was wholly new. "For we are a nation of believers," Lyndon Johnson had declared in 1965. "And we believe in ourselves." "We've always believed," Carter had pleaded, trying to brush past the pessimism he sensed in the nation at large in 1979. In no small part, the Reagan speechwriting office's investment in a politics of belief was Carter's gift. To contrast the present moment with the "era of paralyzing self-doubt," to proclaim that "America is back" and "standing tall," to insist that the electoral choice was a choice between "their government of pessimism, fear, and limits, or ours of hope, confidence, and growth," was to make sure that on every domestic political occasion Carter, though unnamed, would be indelibly remembered. The restoration-of-hope theme was a brilliantly opportunistic political-rhetorical maneuver.[21]

But no president before Reagan had invested belief itself with such extravagant power and possibilities. In Reagan's urgency-filled speeches of the 1960s and early 1970s the enemies were institutionally and sociologically palpable: the Kremlin and its "anti-heap of totalitarianism," the planners and welfare-state advocates, the forces of "anarchy and insurrection" on the Berkeley campus.[22] By the time Reagan entered the White House, freedom's nemesis had migrated into the psyche. Freedom's deepest enemy was pessimism: the mental undertow of doubt, the paralyzing specter of limits, the "cynic who's trying to tell us we're not going to get any better." From Carter's talk of hard choices, from Reagan's own early desire to talk of "controversial things," the theme of psychic restoration moved to center stage. "We are first; we are the best," Reagan told the nation in 1984. "How can we not believe in the greatness of America? . . . We're Americans."[23]

In these cheerleading motifs, Reagan's speechwriters retold the story of the American past. The doubts and inner divisions of the revolutionary era, the anguish of the Civil War, the stresses of twentieth-century social change were edited out. The story of a people "born unto trouble" but nevertheless "always becoming, trying, probing, falling, resting, and trying again," as Lyndon Johnson had put the American story, was reconstructed as a country of timeless confidence, in which past and present met on a field of eternally positive thinking. At the close of the Constitutional Convention in 1787, Benjamin Franklin had told some of those near him that through the long days of the convention and through "the vicissitudes of my hopes and fears," he had looked at the half sun painted on the back of the president's chair without being able to tell whether it was rising or setting. Now, at last, he had "the happiness to know" that it was a rising sun. "Well, you can bet it's rising," Reagan glossed the story in his State of the Union message in 1987, "because, my fellow citizens, America isn't finished. Her best days have just begun." In acts of historical revisionism like this, the American experiment was straightened out on the axis of enduring optimism.[24]

Still more striking was Reagan's embrace of Tom Paine, the radical whom he brought into the sacred circle of American history in a way that Paine had never been embraced in life. The consummate late-eighteenth-century international revolutionary whose works were a favorite of the Communist reprint presses, the man whom Theodore Roosevelt had once called a "filthy little atheist," Paine was a powerful source for Reagan. "We have it in our power to begin the world over again"—"that stupendously dumb statement by Tom Paine," as George Will termed it, that slap in the face of continuity and tradition, that radically unconservative statement of human hubris—was virtually the whole of Reagan's Paine. But it was all he needed, just as the phrase from one of the early twentieth century's most prominent intellectual socialists and free-love advocates—"all that is and has been is but the twilight of the dawn"—was all Reagan's speechwriters needed of H. G. Wells. Searching for the right quotation to end his speech to the National Association of Evangelicals in 1983, Reagan gave them the cosmic optimism of American history's most radical Deist, Paine.[25]

Under the new terms of the Reagan presidency, the older layers of rhetoric endured, to be pressed into the breach of other emergencies. Reagan pitched the necessity of military aid to the Nicaraguan *contras* as an exact replay of Harry Truman's commitment of assistance to Communist-beleaguered Greece and Turkey at the Cold War's onset in 1947. In the aftermath of the assault on the U.S. marines stationed in Beirut in 1983, his speeches were charged with appeals to firmness, courage, patience, and responsibility. "We have found the will. We have held fast to the faith," Reagan reassured a London audience in 1988 in the familiar language of Cold War resolve.[26] On the White House speechwriting staff, the most consistent champion of the older rhetoric of crisis, resolve, and leadership was Anthony Dolan: protégé of William Buckley, Catholic, and articulately conservative. It was he who, given the National Association of Evangelicals speech that no one else thought important in 1983, succeeded in injecting into it the "evil empire" phrase he had floated, only to be overruled, some months before. He put explicit confession of faith in higher law and the efficacy of prayer into Reagan's Guildhall address in London in 1988. For Reagan's commencement address at Notre Dame in 1981, Dolan remembered writing "this big thing about how the Western heritage of spiritual values would make a mockery of the values held by the Soviet Union—our spiritual values compared to the squalor of Soviet ideology."[27]

There is no indication in Reagan's extensive handwritten emendations

of his speechwriters' work that he hesitated over most of these reinfu-
sions from the past. As the drafts upon drafts of the major speeches now
housed in the Reagan Presidential Library show, Reagan was a meticu-
lous editor of his own words. After 1981 he rarely offered much initial
guidance to his speechwriters, but he went over the final products in detail: condensing, rewording, adding a paragraph or two, and smoothing
the final text with the skill of a seasoned line editor. The Martin Treptow
story and its oddly undercutting moral ("we're not called upon to make
that kind of sacrifice") were both his own insertion.[28] He did not balk at
Dolan's "evil empire" reference. Whatever nerves it rattled in 1983, the
phrase, with its attack on the forces of Godless "totalitarian darkness"
and their unwitting pawns in the nuclear freeze movement, was consid-
erably milder than Eisenhower's typical references to Soviet Communism, with its overweening desire to "enslave," its regimented atheism,
and its relentless "chariot of expansion." It was, for that matter, much
tamer than Reagan's own speech to the American Conservative Union six
years earlier, in which the cinematic center had not simply been the
Soviet Union itself but Communism's "terrifying, enormous blackness,"
"huge, sprawling, inconceivably immense," slithering across the globe.[29]
Throughout the friendship with Gorbachev that grew so rapidly after
1986, Reagan's speeches continued their attacks on the brutalities of the
Soviet system.

But after its first use in 1983, the "evil empire" virtually disappeared
from Reagan's speeches, edited out by Dolan's rivals in the interests of
other agendas. It was Reagan himself who struck out Dolan's lines about
the spiritual superiority of the West for his Notre Dame address. Where
Dolan had proposed ending the Second Inaugural with a call to pass on
the dream of freedom "to a troubled but waiting and hopeful world,"
Reagan kept the phrase but deleted the uncomfortable word "troubled."
At Notre Dame, he did not quote Dolan's hero, Whittaker Chambers, as
Dolan had hoped; he told his audience how it had felt to play Knute
Rockne's story in the movies.[30]

All presidential speechwriting is fraught with contest. "Each speech was a
battle in a never-ending war," Peggy Noonan remembered, each metaphor a hard-fought skirmish in the continuous struggle over policies and
politics that marked the speechwriting process during Reagan's adminis-

tration.[31] Rival versions of the most important speeches streamed out of the Reagan speechwriting office, together with anguished memos pleading for their adoption. Still, over the long haul, for all the shifting and intensely fought lines of battle, the older rhetorical formulas were overrun by the newer, softer, less demanding ones. Only near the end of his time in office, besieged by criticism of his arms trade with Iran, did Reagan lead off a State of the Union address with the foreign affairs section, where the language of duty and steadfastness had its natural home. On the domestic front in the early 1980s, through the first hard years of recession, one can find calls to "courage," "patience," and "strength." "No one pretends that the way ahead will be easy," Reagan warned in this vein in 1982. But appeals of this sort quickly moved out of Reagan's heavy-duty, mass-audience speeches. By the mid-1980s, the familiar Cold War rhetoric, heavy with collective imperatives and presences, had given way to simple ego boosting. "Twilight? Twilight?" he told the Republican party convention in 1988: "Not in America. . . . That's not possible. . . . Here it's a sunrise every day."[32]

The eclipse of words thick with a sense of society, history, and responsibility by the new rhetoric of psychic optimism was abetted by the new focus-group techniques that had begun to move in a big way into Republican campaign management strategies in the 1980 contest. In a typical session, a group of one or two dozen people, each gripping a handheld response device, viewed the precast of an advertisement or listened to the draft of a speech. When they heard a phrase they liked, they squeezed, and an analyzer correlated the phrase, the images, and the squeezes together. They squeezed eagerly when they heard the words "reach," "free," and "America." They squeezed on positive terms. They did not like hearing worrisome words such as Afghanistan, Angola, Cambodia, or Nicaragua.[33] Whether because of these electro-psychic tabulations of the public's hunger for optimism, or the more intuitive judgments of the speech vetters, or the influence of the cadre of libertarians on the White House staff, references to collective obligations dried up in Reagan's speeches. In a particularly shrewd comparison of Carter's and Reagan's emotional rhetoric, Haig Bosmajian noted the highly charged words that carried the burden in Reagan's and Carter's inaugural addresses. Common to them both were freedom, faith, confidence, glory, liberty, love, and strength. The list of terms unique to Reagan's inaugurals, however, reads like a handbook of self-actualizing psychology: alive, big-hearted, courageous, daring, dynamic, forward, liberate, progress, robust, reborn, vibrant.[34]

None of this was necessitated by the moment—not even by the antigovernment animus that Reagan's election instantiated in the White House. Reagan's friend and ally Margaret Thatcher was, like Reagan, a convert to Friedrich von Hayek's strictures against creeping, liberty-destroying statism. She worked just as hard on her major speeches as Reagan did, arguing into the night with her speechwriting staff in a way that the much more distant Reagan never did. In the process, phrases from the new, oddly unconservative American conservatism occasionally slipped into Thatcher's vocabulary. "Can we not believe in ourselves?" she asked her fellow Tories in this Reaganesque vein in 1981. But freedom in Thatcher's speech was never unqualified, and it was rarely actually free. "There are many difficult things about freedom; it does not give you safety; it creates moral dilemmas; it requires self-discipline; it imposes great responsibilities," she cautioned in 1978, the year before she ascended to the position of prime minister. If there was a key word in Thatcher's public speech it was "responsibility." She quoted not the radical Tom Paine but Rudyard Kipling, poet laureate of striving, burden-bearing, imperial England. "What I am working for is a free and responsible society," Thatcher urged. In these times of "difficulties," "testing," and "sacrifices," "let us stand together and do our duty."[35]

The theme that soared in Reagan's rhetoric, by contrast, was that ultimate state of boundlessness: dreaming. Nothing captured so well the eclipse of the Cold War vocabulary of peril, endurance, leadership, and courage than the way Reagan's public speech turned more and more frequently not merely on the need for confidence but on the possibility of slipping free from limitations altogether. The most striking employment of the "dream" motif was the series of transitions that climaxed Reagan's address to Congress on his program for economic recovery in the spring of 1981. From a somewhat tedious restatement of the terms of his tax and budget proposals, Reagan moved suddenly to remind his television audience of the recent space shuttle launch (the *Columbia* "started us dreaming again"), thence to a snippet from Carl Sandburg ("The republic is a dream. Nothing happens unless first a dream"), on to a claim for the national distinctiveness of dreaming ("that's what makes us, as Americans, different"), until his tax and budget cuts were enveloped in an aura of boundless optimism. "All we need to begin with is a dream that we can do better than before. All we need to have is faith, and that dream will come true."[36]

In its report in 1980, the blue-ribbon President's Commission for a National Agenda for the 1980s, stocked with distinguished business and civic leaders, had warned that the reigning motif of the decade would be the "hard choices" that lay ahead for Americans—the tradeoffs that could not be avoided where unlimited claims clashed with limited resources. But in Reagan's America-dreaming sequences of the mid-1980s there was no hard thorn of sacrifice, no tradeoff in choice. "In this land of dreams fulfilled, where great dreams may be imagined, nothing is impossible, no victory is beyond our reach, no glory will ever be too great."[37]

Dreaming was limitless. It was cut loose from the past. It was, in the language of focus group analysts, a pro-word, a button-pusher. Even as the sharply critical shots at totalitarianism continued, the face of the nation's enemies was reconstructed. They were no longer the masters of the Kremlin; now they were the doubters, the qualifiers, the realists without vision. "Let us begin by challenging our conventional wisdom," Reagan urged in his State of the Union address in 1985. "There are no constraints on the human mind, no walls around the human spirit, no barriers to our progress except those we ourselves erect."[38]

The rhetoric was familiar, but not from politics or from conservatism. Into the network of associations with the term "freedom," Reagan and his speechwriters drew the language of the self-actualization psychology handbooks of the 1970s, the Jonathan Livingston Seagull phrases, the Esalen notion of freedom, the slogans of the 1960s cultural radicals. Tony Dolan, clinging to an older understanding of conservatism, would insist years later that "what Reagan is about [is] a rejection of the modernist notion that man is sovereign."[39] But there was nothing perilous or fragile in the new rhetoric of freedom, as there had been in Reagan's speeches of the 1960s, when freedom had been never more than a generation away from extinction. There was no need for overcoming, no manacles to be broken, no trial to be endured, no pause in the face of higher law. As Meg Greenfield noted at the time, Reagan "is the first president in years who has, at least so far, failed to cultivate the image of crisis and ordeal and almost unbearable testing."[40] To dream, to reach, to sing, to break loose, to fly as high and as far as the imagination would carry you, to be all you might be: under the skin of the familiar words, the notion of freedom was enchanted. It was privatized and personalized, bent in on itself in the very enunciation of its limitlessness.

As the vocabulary shifted, as phrases of the counterculture leaked into the rhetoric of conservatism, the way Reagan acted the presidential part changed as well. Nowhere had the line between the rituals of church and state been more blurred in the post-1945 years than in the way in which presidential speech making capitalized on the forms of Protestant preaching. The resemblance ran much deeper than the references to God sprinkled heavily throughout presidential speeches or the benedictory forms with which they closed. Adaptation of sermonic authority and sermonic cadence was integral to the high presidential style. The people gathered together—preacher and congregation—to hear their civic creed reaffirmed, their mandate of leadership accepted, and their duties made clear. The pulpit rose above the pews. The words that came from it bound the people and their president together and made sacred the responsibilities of both.

On particular occasions, Reagan's speechwriters gave him a statement of faith to confess. But just as the terms of crisis and resolve receded from Reagan's vocabulary, so he slipped out of the preacher's role and pulpit. He did not speak in church syntax with the modifying clauses piled up at the front of his sentences, the hortatory verbs ("let us," "grant us"), and the Biblical references. He served not as the nation's better conscience or (as Carter tried, however ineffectually, to be) as its revivalist. His distinctive rhetorical field was the story of America. His métier was that of the program host: the president as the nation's off-camera narrator.

The point is true literally as well as figuratively. Reagan's speechwriters were the first to exploit to the full the possibilities of removing the president from the center of the camera's eye. Toward the end of his First Inaugural address, Reagan turned from the guiding principles of his foreign policy, through a short paragraph telegraphing his support for school prayer, suddenly to the view of the city from the West Front of the Capitol. The metamorphosis from president to tour guide proceeded without a hiccup: "Directly in front of me, the monument to a monumental man, George Washington. . . . Off to one side, the stately memorial to Thomas Jefferson." Beyond, the Lincoln Memorial and Arlington National Cemetery. Primed with advance copies, CBS cameramen obediently swung to the narration. Peggy Noonan's description of the making of Reagan's Normandy address on the fortieth anniversary of D-Day evokes the film-making imagination that flourished in the White House communications office. The words came to her, she later reported, "cinematically." Reagan would say, "'These are the boys of Pointe du Hoc,'" and "that's when the cameras would start to turn and the President would say, 'These are the men who took the cliffs.' And suddenly you were going to look at these faces—I'm getting choked up—of these seventy-year-old guys, and you'd be very moved."[41]

Even when the cameras stayed fixed on Reagan, his scripts worked on cinematic rather than sermonic principles. Standing within the Capitol during his Second Inaugural, he told the nation, "we see and hear again the echoes of our past: a general falls to his knees in the hard snow of Valley Forge; a lonely President paces the darkened halls and ponders his struggle to preserve the Union; the men of the Alamo call out encouragement to each other; a settler pushes west and sings a song, and the song echoes out forever and fills the unknowing air. It is the American song." Some of the central figures on Reagan's speechwriting staff dismissed these passages as mere "rubbish" and "schmaltz," even as they took their turns at larding them in between the hard-fought policy points of his major addresses. But poeticized and visually immediate narration of this sort was as indispensable a part of Reagan's presidential persona as the eloquent call to arms was to Kennedy or the plain-speaking radio chat to Franklin Roosevelt. The long narration with which Reagan's 1984 convention acceptance speech concluded, in which he described the journey of the Olympic torch across the continent, carried by toddlers, teenagers, and grandmothers in wheelchairs, passing crowds that burst into spontaneous song, was out of the same mold. The preacher left the church and settled in a porch chair to tell the nation's story, making word-pictures in the air.[42]

If this momentary disappearance from the camera's eye came more easily to Reagan because he knew the role of program host from his years with *General Electric Theater*, it represented nonetheless a remarkable reimagining of the presidential role. Carter had sprinkled his speeches heavily with the word "I." ("I promise you that I will lead our fight.")

Reagan, by contrast, effortlessly blended his self into his story of America. He did not stand outside the present moment, challenging its premises, as he had in the 1960s. He retold an American story that was already embodied in fact, and from which, as its narrator and speaking voice, he was inextricable. He claimed no special knowledge, no expertise, no special qualities of leadership beyond embodiment of the public's common sense. As Kathleen Jamieson observed: "Reagan does not reside at the center of his discourse."[43]

This cinematic dissolve of the president into the people, this relinquishing of overt authority, goes a long way toward explaining the resilience of Reagan's popularity. It was to become one the stories woven around Reagan that he was an extraordinarily loved president: the most popular occupant of the White House, according to some versions of the tale, since polling data began in the 1940s. In fact, by most of the available measures, he was not an exceptionally popular president. His highest approval rating, 71 percent, was three points below Carter's highest rating. (At their peak, Eisenhower [77 percent], Kennedy [83 percent], Johnson [79 percent], and both Bushes [89 percent] were all rated much higher.) Reagan's lowest approval rating, 35 percent, at the depths of the recession of the early 1980s, was a point below the worst that the hapless Gerald Ford achieved. Reagan's reelection in 1984 was, like Johnson's reelection in 1964 and Nixon's reelection in 1972, one of the landslide victories of postwar politics. But measured by the percentage of his months in office (61 percent) during which he polled a positive approval rating, Reagan ranks just about in the middle of post–World War II presidents. Coming into office on the heels of four presidencies that ended disastrously—Johnson's in civil turmoil, Nixon's in disgrace, Ford's and Carter's in defeat—Reagan stands taller than life, an embodiment of the restoration theme. Measured against that of Eisenhower, who fell only twice below 50 percent in his approval ratings, and that of Kennedy, who never fell below the 50 percent mark at all, Reagan's popularity was unremarkable.[44]

The distinctive point about Reagan was not his popularity per se but the way his popularity was produced. In an outline for the 1984 campaign, Richard Darman, then White House assistant chief of staff, advised: "*Paint RR as the personification of all that is right with or heroized by America.* Leave Mondale in a position where an attack on Reagan is tantamount to an attack on America's idealized image of itself—*where a vote against Reagan is in some subliminal sense, a vote against mythic 'America.'*"[45] Reagan amassed affection by distancing himself from his often polarizing policies, by blending his self and his story-telling voice into the fabric of everyday dreams and aspirations, by dissolving the distance between people and president. Abdicating the high presidential style, he let mountains of responsibility roll off his and his listeners' shoulders.

Getting himself out of the way was key to Reagan's gestures. Restoration was his primary rhetorical act. He gave the nation's freedoms and its future promise back to "the people." It was their seamless history that he painted in verbal miniatures, their hopes he claimed to enunciate. Reagan performed the part of identification with the people far more effortlessly and with vastly less inner contradiction than did his rival, the populist Carter, despite Carter's sweaters, suitcases, and Mr. Rogers–derived props of neighborliness. Carter and his advisers, struggling to read the minds and the anguish of the people, worried through a relationship that Reagan simply took for granted. "Just three words," Reagan told the nation's children in his State of the Union address of 1987, contained the whole secret of America: "We the people."[46]

Reagan's commitment to these lines was unswerving. Kenneth Khachigian, called in to work on the 1987 State of the Union message, heard the "We the people" motif from Reagan himself, and wrote it into the speech with the excitement of adding a new and "perfect Reagan touch." In fact it had been part of Reagan's core stock of phrases since at least the mid-1960s. In Reagan's mind the anecdote paired with the words was always the same. In other countries, governments told the people what to do. In contrast, "Our revolution is the first to say the people are the masters and government is their servant."[47]

To insist on the concrete reality of "the people" was, for Reagan and conservative Republicans, an essential precondition to the act of wedging the government and the people apart into sharply antagonistic political fields. The division was old in Reagan's rhetoric. "Already the hour is late," he had warned in 1964. "Government has laid its hand on health, housing, farming, industry, commerce, education . . ." For the Constitution's drafters, the phrase "We the People" had been a legitimating device: a means to give moral and political foundation to a stronger national government. In Reagan's speeches, the same words were refashioned to distance the natural, spontaneous acts of the people from the work of those they elected to be their representatives.[48]

Reagan was not the first of the post-1945 presidents to run on an anti-government program. "Government cannot solve our problems," had been Carter's line in the 1970s; "it can't set our goals, it cannot define our vision." Carter's populist rhetoric, however, had strained toward healing. Alienation underlay these formulas as strongly as antagonism underlay Reagan's. We "have seen our Government grow far from us. . . almost become like a foreign country, so strange and distant," Carter lamented in his 1978 State of the Union message. He talked easily of humility, mercy, justice, spirit, trust, wisdom, community, and "common purpose." "It is time for us to join hands in America," he urged in his energy crisis address.[49] Reagan's talk of government and the people, by contrast, pushed toward severance. His goal was to rearrange the verbal system such that government was not the agent, embodiment, or reflection of the people. Rather, government was the people's antagonist, the limiter of their limitlessness. The twin pillars of his domestic policy—tax cutting and corporate and environmental deregulation—flowed directly from those premises.

But to devolve power to the people required that the people themselves be made visible. They needed words and representation. The terms in which Reagan referred to the people were instinctively expansive and inclusive. He was the last president to preside over the common audience that television network news had made, where a single voice could be imagined to speak to and for the nation. The gray, muffled prose of an Eric Sevareid and the mannered but reassuring avuncularisms of a Walter Cronkite were already under challenge in 1980. The pioneer of argumentative television, where panelists faced off like wrestling team opponents to parry, declaim, interrupt, and shout, *Agronsky and Company,* had been launched in late 1969. *The McLaughlin Group,* a favorite of Reagan's, heated up the formula in 1982, from which it was quickly and widely cloned. Radio, with its smaller niche audience always more argumentative than television, turned up the volume of dispute sharply with the arrival of Howard Stern and, by 1988, Rush Limbaugh. But Reagan still

presided over an America in which public speech was not yet systematically polarized, and the notion of the "people" was not yet a mere verbal
fig leaf covering the fact of permanent political campaign.[50]

At times, Reagan's speechwriters slipped into something close to
Franklin Roosevelt's image of the people as a broad occupational phalanx: workers, farmers, and businessmen bound together by bands of
economic interdependence. "We the people," Reagan limned them in
1981: "neighbors and friends, shopkeepers and laborers, farmers and
craftsmen." But Reagan's word-pictures of the people almost never
showed them working together, their energy and talent joined in a common action. As Benjamin Barber, one of the first to pick up this sub-
surface theme, wrote of "the people singing" sequence in Reagan's Second Inaugural in 1985: "The speech lauds 'We the People,' but its heroes
are men alone . . . In the President's script, Washington leans on no comrades in arms, Lincoln consults no cabinet . . . a single settler is conjured
for us—his family wagon and the long train of Conestogas that must
surely have accompanied it are kept out of sight (and out of mind)." In
Reagan's very celebrations of the people, the plural noun tended to slip
away, to skitter toward the singular.[51]

The impulse to disaggregate and individualize the people took still
more prominent symbolic form in the so-called heroes in the balcony
segment of his State of the Union messages. Reagan did not inaugurate
the practice of calling forward an individual's special deeds in a major
state address. He was the first, however, to take the inherently public
occasion of a report on the nation from the chief of one branch of government to the heads of another and dissolve it, toward the end, into a mon-
tage of individual faces. Heroes, volunteers, teenagers with dreams, returned prisoners of war were gathered in the halls of Congress, where
Reagan, stepping out of the camera's eye once more, would introduce
them one by one. In 1963, John Kennedy had read the names of three
American soldiers killed in Cuba, South Korea, and Vietnam. But here
they now were in the flesh, where the applause, the acts of individual accomplishment, and the guest-program tableau all redounded to the administration's acclaim. The first three heroes in the balconies appeared in
Reagan's State of the Union address in 1982; five more appeared in 1984,
two in 1985, four in 1986.

Reagan was fond of saying that his political opponents saw people only as members of groups; his party, to the contrary, saw the people of America as individuals.[52] In fact, no set of Americans was ever chosen with a keener grasp of interest group politics than were Reagan's heroes in the balconies. A charitable black woman reassured Reagan's audience that the president had not forgotten the poor; a Hispanic medic drew sympathy for the Grenada invasion; a returned prisoner of war appealed to the patriotic electorate; a teenager whose experiment had been lost in the *Challenger* explosion lobbied silently for the high frontier of space; the two business figures on the list, a black female advertising executive and a Cuban refugee entrepreneur, spoke to the aspiration of minority business owners.

But the collective calculations of politics brooked no mention. Introduced by the presidential program host, the constituent atoms of the people stood up, for their moment in the camera's eye, one by one. Reagan asked viewers, not to imitate them or to rise to the challenge they set, but only to applaud them, to believe that their acts were possible. "We the people," as a collective entity, tacitly disaggregated under the touch.

Acting the Cold War part was a different matter, of course, from speaking its lines. Reagan was a more cautious Cold Warrior than his pre–Vietnam War predecessors had been. He preferred surrogates—*contras* in Nicaragua, Jonas Savimbi's UNITA rebels in Angola, the anti-Soviet *mujahideen* in Afghanistan—to direct military intervention. He preferred to spend defense dollars than to risk military casualties or long-term military entanglements. The much-touted invasion of Grenada was the sort of act that U.S. presidents had ordered frequently in the Caribbean in the 1910s and 1920s, without much apology or much political fanfare. On the other side of the balance, Reagan's massive additions to the defense budget, even at the cost of the ballooning deficit, his insistence on funding for the Strategic Defense Initiative and on the deployment of a new generation of missiles in Europe, at the risk of destabilizing the nuclear standoff, and his deep, instinctual sense of embattlement with a resurgently aggressive Soviet Union on fronts across the world were acts fully within the Cold War frame. Reagan was far too little the Cold Warrior for his critics on the Committee on the Present Danger, who (even before Reagan's friendship with Gorbachev began to ripen) had written openly of their "anguish" at his weakness and penchant for wishful thinking. For his critics on the left, Reagan was far too much the Cold Warrior. Still, there is no doubt that Reagan saw himself, like the Cold War presidents before him, as the leader of a nation locked in a continuing, vigilance-demanding, globally diffused war with the heirs of the Communist Revolution.[53]

Reagan did not lose that war. What he lost were its words and its rhetorical gestures, its collectively enacted rituals of urgency, the language of obligation and responsibility that had been its inextricable attachment. In his major addresses, those were eclipsed by different terms; structures gave way to cameos, destiny to infinite possibilities, the preacher's voice to that of the family storyteller's. In the place of the style that had reigned since the 1940s, he offered a less urgent and commanding presidency, a seamless and tension-drained sense of time, a set of dreams and narratives in the place of old-style demands and certainties, a vision of freedom without obstacles or limits, a vocabulary of public words not abandoned but quietly individualized and privatized, a populism whose representation of the people dissolved society into pieces.

By the end of the 1980s, the new style had become a common coin of rhetorical politics. At the Democratic party convention of 1992, though Clinton pitched his "new covenant" in the sermonic language of the past, the most striking theme was the omnipresence of the personal story. Tom Harkin told the tale of his mother's emigration from Slovenia, Lena Guerrero told the story of her mother's labor picking cotton, Paul Tsongas talked about his cancer and his mother's tuberculosis, Clinton related (not for the first time) the life story that had begun in Hope, Arkansas. Heroes of ordinary life told their stories: a mother whose infant had died of AIDS from a transfusion of contaminated blood, a couple who had lost their health insurance, and a machinist laid off after twenty years of work, who spoke via satellite television. Pain abounded, personalized, individualized, made empathetic, and so did dreams. But the "hard choices" of the party's 1980 convention rhetoric, the need for "courage" and steadfastness, the recognition (as Clinton himself had put it then) that "we are in a time of transition, a difficult and painful time from which no one can escape the burden and no one can avoid a responsibility to play a part," had quietly been omitted.[54]

The new ingredients that flowed into political language came from many sources. The motifs in Reagan's public speeches were patched together from the optimistic 1940s movies that Reagan loved, from the counterculture and the psychic self-empowerment literature of the 1960s and 1970s, from a populist backlash against the experts and against the oil-crisis engendered talk of limits, from a new libertarian strain in the conservative coalition, and from the market confidence of the sun belt entrepreneurs prominent in the Reagan Republican coalition. But in ways beyond either Reagan's or his speechwriters' knowing, Reagan's post–Cold War style was connected to intellectual trends that ramified out far from the Reagan White House, often articulated by persons who would have denied any connection with the figure who by 1981 held the presidential stage.

No one has ever persuasively described Ronald Reagan as an intellectual. He was instead, as Margaret Thatcher described herself, a "conviction" politician. Reagan cared passionately about his commitments, just as he cared passionately about the rhetoric of persuasion. He had written out his own speeches longhand for years before he acquired a staff to write them for him. He read voraciously, although, like many readers, he preferred to read things he already agreed with rather than those he didn't. But though a set of powerful ideas framed his understanding of the world, he had no interest in the play of argument, the nuances of a concept, the passion for inquiry that are the marks of the modern intellectual. The academic debates of the day were for him largely a foreign country.

And yet in the enchanted, disembedded, psychically involuted sense of freedom that slipped into Reagan's speeches, in the disaggregation of "We the people" into balconies of individual heroes, in the celebration of the limitless possibilities of self and change, there were more parallels with the intellectual dynamics of the age than many observers recognized at the time. The realm of free, spontaneous action that Reagan celebrated mirrored the way in which the economists began to reimagine the spheres of exchange as self-acting, naturally regulating markets. The recession of the social echoed the shrinking prestige of sociology, which had ridden the crest of the social movements of the 1960s. Concepts of power became more subtle, more intangibly imagined, and harder to pin down. Identity loomed larger than ever before: not as a collective given, now, but as a field of malleability and self-fashioning. The categories of race, class, and gender, after sweeping into academic discourse in the early 1980s, turned less distinct, disaggregated into subcategories and intersections of categories, or slipped into quotation marks. Historians talked less of structure and more of narratives and consciousness—if not of the end of history and the disappearance of its powerful dialectical pincers altogether. As the force seeped out of the older, mid-twentieth-century ways of imagining society, talk of freedom did not diminish. But its meanings changed. Individualized and privatized, released of its larger burdens, freedom was cut loose from the burdens and responsibilities that had once so closely accompanied it.

No single event precipitated this sea change in ideas and social metaphors. Reagan's words did not call the new world of social thought into being. But they caught, in mid-course, a movement of ideas and arguments. In losing the words of the Cold War, Reagan helped articulate some of the broader intellectual dynamics of the times—even if it was not in the way he might have imagined or that we, pulling an old phrase like the "evil empire" like a well-thumbed thread out of the novel pattern, have been inclined to remember.

2

The Rediscovery of the Market

"Market" is one of the most overworked and imprecise words in economics.
James Tobin, *"Are New Classical Models Plausible Enough to Guide Policy?"*

The term "macroeconomic" will simply disappear from use.
Robert Lucas, Models of Business Cycles

In an age when words took on magical properties, no word flew higher or assumed a greater aura of enchantment than "market." It meant not only the affairs of Wall Street and its sister hubs of global exchange, swelling by the late 1980s with new wealth for those lucky enough to have a foothold in them. The term "market" that insinuated itself into more and more realms of social thought meant something much more modest than the financial markets' churning, and, at the same time, something much more universal and audacious. It stood for a way of thinking about society with a myriad of self-generated actions for its engine and optimization as its natural and spontaneous outcome. It was the analogue to Reagan's heroes in the balconies, a disaggregation of society and its troubling collective presence and demands into an array of consenting, voluntarily acting individual pieces. "You know, there really is something magic about the marketplace when it's free to operate," Reagan told the nation in early 1982 as the motif of limitless dreams was swelling in his speeches. "As the song says, 'This could be the start of something big.'"[1]

"Something big" was a corny touch. Still, not in a century, not since the late-nineteenth-century vogue of Charles Darwin's *Origin of Species,* had the idea of the beneficent results of competition cut so broad a swath through public and academic discourses or been called upon to do and explain so much. Conservatives, who had so often worried about the amorality of markets where everything could be put up for sale, rediscovered markets' moral and spiritual foundations. Left and right critics of managed capitalism, turning back the page on one of the progressive era's major innovations, took up the cause of market deregulation. Liberal economists, who in the 1960s had imagined steering the macroeconomy through the turbulence of the business cycle, now warned of the futility of opposing market forces. Let the fundamental economic laws be thwarted, they cautioned, and "the market strikes back."[2] In the universities, the analytical tools of microeconomics were employed to extend models of utility-maximizing behavior into virtually every quirk and cranny of human life. Lawyers talked knowingly of Pareto optimality and the Coase theorem; philosophers and political theorists debated analytical models of rational choice. In more and more contexts and in answer to a broader and broader range of questions, one heard now that "the market decides."

The "market" at the center of these debates was a distinctly abstract concept. Business interests in the 1940s and 1950s, crusading to defend themselves from their critics on the left and in the labor movement, had championed the rights of management and the productive powers of the free enterprise "system."[3] They had put the modern, efficient corporation at the symbolic core of mid-twentieth-century capitalism. By contrast, the "market" that came into vogue in the 1970s floated virtually free of institutional or corporate presence. It was not simply an instrumental device, good for certain purposes, clumsily made for others. Whereas governments, it was said, moved by coercion and deliberative politics stumbled through concession and compromise, the market was held out as the realm of freedom, choice, and reason. The market was "a form of unanimous consent arrangement," the chair of Jimmy Carter's Council of Economic Advisers, Charles Schultze, put the new orthodoxy. No change occurred in the market, it was said, but that it left society more efficient than before and every active party to the transaction better off.[4] Self-equilibrating, instantaneous in its sensitivities and global in its reach, gathering the wants of myriad individuals into its system of price signals in a perpetual plebiscite of desires, the ideal market marked off the sphere of exchange as a separate world, perfectionist in its possibilities.

That so many voices should have been drawn to the language of economic analysis in an age whipsawed by economic crisis and structural economic change was hardly a surprise. From the painful intersection of unemployment and price inflation, the destabilization of the giant, blue-chip corporations, and the flight of high-wage jobs in the 1970s to the Wall Street boom of the late 1980s, the corporate takeover dramas, and the new hegemony of finance capital, economic news was, more than ever, general news. Stock-invested pension funds made everyman and everywoman a player in the finance markets.

The puzzle of the age is not that economic concepts moved into the center of social debate; the riddle is that so abstract and idealized an idea of efficient market action should have arisen amid so much real-world market imperfection. From the sudden worldwide ratcheting up of global oil prices during the Arab-Israeli War of 1973 through the energy crisis of Carter's last years in office, the first part of the age was a period of extraordinary turmoil in the economic markets. By the end of the 1970s the U.S. economy had experienced inflation rates higher than at any time since 1946 and unemployment rates unequalled since the early 1940s. The nation's largest city, New York, and its tenth largest industrial firm, Chrysler, both stumbled into near bankruptcy. The so-called misery index, produced by adding the rates of inflation and unemployment, was a political ploy when Carter invented it in the 1976 presidential campaign to highlight the Ford administration's economic record, but it was real enough to take hold in the public's imagination. It averaged 7 percent during the Kennedy-Johnson years. It averaged 16 percent during Carter's presidency.

Economically, the first half of the 1980s was not much better. Put forcefully into deflationary gear by action of the Federal Reserve in late 1979, the economy veered into its sharpest recession since the 1930s Depression. In April 1982, just as Reagan was celebrating the magic of markets, the Department of Labor announced a monthly unemployment rate higher than any in the 1970s; it would climb past 10 percent by September before it came back, in mid-1984, to the level it had registered when Reagan took office. For many of the world's economies, recovery came still more slowly. The 1980s was a lost decade for the economies of Latin America after the massive debt structure created by international commercial bankers in the 1970s collapsed in the wake of the Mexican government's default of 1982. The European economies that had steered through the inflationary pressures of the 1970s better than the U.S. economy found themselves with stubbornly high unemployment levels in the decade that followed. Growth came back in the U.S. economy (and more slowly elsewhere): an unprecedented "Great Expansion," as Robert Collins calls it, that would carry forward, virtually uninterrupted, for over twenty years. Global integration of markets and communication proceeded at a pace unimaginable when discussion of the future of transnational corporations had first seriously begun in the 1970s. By the early 1990s, bookshelves were awash in popular accounts of an altogether new age of global capitalism, where the personal computer and satellite-transmitted telephone and television signals had virtually annihilated place, and information and investments now moved instantaneously around the world.[5]

But the emergence of the market as the dominant social metaphor of the age was not a product of the later years of the era, the years of sustained American economic growth and global integration. It was made in the chaotic economic turmoil of the 1970s. Intellectually the process was virtually complete by the time Ronald Reagan took office in 1981. The puzzle of the era's enchantment of the market idea is that it was born not out of success but out of such striking market failure.

A contrived paradox, a reader may object, for clearly many of the core ideas in the resurgent talk of markets in the 1970s United States were old. The concept of a "natural" system of "invisibly" ordered exchange was Adam Smith's long before Friedrich von Hayek or Milton Friedman repopularized it. And yet in subtle and deeply consequential ways the ideal of the market that emerged from the economic confusions of the 1970s—more abstract and decontextualized, employable over a much broader range of human actions—was newer than it superficially appeared. Smith had not opened *The Wealth of Nations* in a London market, amid the din of bargainers' cries and the spectacle of goods laid out for sale; he had opened it, in a chapter on the productive gains achieved through the division of labor, in a pin factory. For Smith and his successors, the focus of economic science was on the production, not the exchange, of wealth. That was the question that opened virtually every English-language economics textbook of the last three quarters of the nineteenth century: how the three great factors of production—land, labor, and capital—worked together to generate wealth, and how that wealth, in turn, was distributed through three great "classes of the community" (as David Ricardo called them), landowners, capital investors, and laborers. Atomistic as classical political economy appeared to its critics, its very premises sustained a certain sociological and institutional realism, a sense of power and aggregates that persisted even through the height of nineteenth-century individualism.[6]

It was the marginalists of the late nineteenth century who brought something much closer to the modern idea of the market into the center of economic analysis. It was they who turned the core issue from the aggregate production of wealth to the satisfaction of wants, as a myriad of anonymous, disaggregated sellers and purchasers sought each other out through the pricing signals of the economy. It was they who made a pair of intersecting lines on a two-axis diagram into the great visual-conceptual engine of economics pedagogy, unforgettable to even the rankest beginner in a modern economics course, and in so doing helped to inject the notion of equilibrium into the very definition of a market. And yet a fully abstracted mathematical understanding of markets did not yet dominate economics. Even Alfred Marshall, whose *Principles of Economics* of 1890 consolidated the introduction of marginalism into English-language economics, still wrote of markets as physical extensions of familiar city marketplaces—even though the crying of wares might now be done by telegraphed bids and price lists streaming across much larger trade regions.[7] As late as the 1940s, the economist Robert Solow writes, recollecting his introduction to the craft, a student in an up-to-date university economics program absorbed a pluralistic, socially imbedded understanding of markets; one learned to think intuitively of different "kinds of goods, kinds of industries, kinds of labor."[8]

The analytical revolution of the 1950s swept away the older descriptive and institutionalist economics that Solow could still remember and enthroned mathematical reasoning in its place.[9] Paul Samuelson, the young MIT economist most responsible for synthesizing John Maynard Keynes's analysis of business-cycle dynamics into a general system of economics, was himself one of the brightest and most influential of the new economic modelers. His *Economics* of 1948 was to be one of the most extraordinary textbook successes of the century; forty years later Joseph Stiglitz could write that current economics textbooks were still, by and large, "clones of the one great textbook written in this century, Samuelson's."[10]

Yet to crack an economics textbook in the Samuelson mold was to enter a world in which markets were extremely powerful but always imperfect. Into the 1970s, economics textbooks still retained separate chapters for the consideration of agricultural economics and labor economics, which were deemed different enough from markets in the abstract to require their own analytically distinctive treatment. Labor relations received a separate chapter in Samuelson's edition of 1961; so did capitalism's Marxian alternatives.

At the high-status end of the profession, where Keynes's conceptual revolution had been focused, markets were all about imperfection. The macroeconomy, as it first began to be called in the 1940s, was the arena where market inadequacies and public governance met. Stabilizing the aggregate economy's cycles of growth and contraction was, for every economist working in the prevailing neo-Keynesian mold, macroeconomics' work. In the "mixed economy" of the postwar years, macroeconomics gave public policy managers the conceptual and practical tools to even out the volatility inherent in the productive capacities and energies of market capitalism. Macroeconomics' importance was reflected in the textbook convention that macroeconomics should be introduced first, and only later, many chapters on, the approximately realized world of "perfect markets" where the abstract rules of the price system worked.

Textbook publishers, to be sure, learned to color code their chapters to accommodate teachers who preferred to teach the microeconomics of firms and prices first. But Samuelson himself had no doubts about the conceptual order of economics' new realms. Only in conditions of economic stability and relatively full employment, Samuelson advised generations of undergraduates, did the supply-and-demand equilibria work in their textbook simplicity. In times of "substantial unemployment" economics entered a "topsy-turvy wonderland" where the commonsense rules of economic relations ran backward or failed to run at all. Even in ordinary economic times, students needed to understand the "fallacy of composition"—to realize that the laws of aggregate, social economic behavior were often distinctly different from individually modeled economic action. At an extremely high level of abstraction, to be sure, where the Arrow-Debreu theories of "general equilibrium" applied, economies were always in balance. But those theorems were the product of "some heroically abstract assumptions," Samuelson cautioned; their models of systemwide stability were "not a picture of the real world as we know it." Macroeconomics provided the stabilizing condition for the microeconomic price system to work. That was why for the next thirty years, even in politically conservative textbooks, macroeconomics came first.[11]

Through the 1960s, the neo-Keynesian assumptions codified in Samuelson's *Economics* dominated the textbooks, the discipline, and the policy discourse. They gave a generation of postwar economic advisers a powerful confidence in the possibilities of macroeconomic management. In the mid-1960s, Arthur Okun of Lyndon Johnson's Council of Economic Advisers remembered, neo-Keynesian economists "were riding about as high a crest of esteem and respect" as economists had ever received.[12] Within another fifteen years, however, both axioms and confidence were rapidly melting away. In place of lessons in the "fallacy of composition," textbook authors were working hard to erase the Samuelson-era distinction between social and individual action and to set macroeconomics on microeconomic foundations. Economic models of perfect price adjustment were an academic growth industry. In political discourse, Samuelson's mixed economy had fallen into sharply distinct parts: markets and government, rhetorically at polar opposites from each other.

Like Adam Smith's pin factory, these were metaphors all. The timeless, placeless, self-equilibrating register of individual preferences that was now more and more often being called "the market" was an abstraction, as complex and intricately manipulable a figure of speech as any of the neologisms in the Keynesian vocabulary. But metaphors are not idle. They "think for us," Donald McCloskey writes.[13] By the end of the 1970s, a new idea of the market, cut free from the institutional and sociological relationships constitutive of earlier economic analysis—from Ricardo's great economic "classes," from Marshall's tangibly imagined Manchester cotton exchange, from Samuelson's government macroeconomic stabilizers—was being called on to do unprecedented amounts of thinking. Under the skin of an old word, something quite new had indeed emerged.

The shift began with strains in the old system of ideas, though not where observers at the time anticipated them. At the back of their minds all economists knew that the macro- and microparts of economic science were not theoretically well integrated, that the aggregate economic data and big computerized forecasting models upon which macroeconomic

analysis depended were analytically remote from the microeconomic behavior of individual economic actors. But the vulnerable point of the system turned out to be not the aggregate demand and investment functions
at neo-Keynesianism's core but a recent add-on, a historical extrapolation never fitted out with terribly strong theoretical support called the
Phillips curve. The origins of the Phillips curve lay in an inductive study
of British wage-price data for the period 1861–1957 which seemed to
show that yearly shifts in unemployment and inflation could be mapped
along a smooth tradeoff curve, higher inflation rates "buying" lower unemployment levels and vice versa. Broached in 1958 and quickly repli-
cated with post–World War II U.S. data, Phillips's long-term historical
tendency was translated into a short-term economic rule in the Samuelson textbook in 1961, and from there into a tool for macroeconomic policy making, just as Kennedy-era confidence in economic management
for full-capacity employment was reaching its peak.[14]

Through 1969, as the Johnson-Kennedy economists tried to regulate
the inflation-unemployment tradeoff, the economic data complied with
the Phillips curve. And then, in the event that, more than any other,
structured the economic controversies of the 1970s, the expected relationship fell apart into theoretical chaos. Joblessness rates rose through
the politically sensitive threshold of 5 percent and stuck there, while inflation rates, rather than receding to accustomed recession levels, shot up
during the oil producers' price shock of 1973–1974, fell back, and then
rose precipitously all over again in 1979–1980. The Phillips data danced
wildly across the economists' graphs.[15] The expected patterns of the business cycle seemed to disintegrate, its phases colliding into one another in
the phenomenon Americans called "stagflation," and the British, caught
up in an even sharper version of the same troubles, called "slumpflation."

In the face of these anomalies, there was an extraordinary flailing
about for measures of macroeconomic control. Richard Nixon, turning
his back on a century of Republican party policy, instituted emergency
across-the-board wage and price controls in the summer of 1971, adopt-
ing a course outsiders and public opinion pollsters had been urging for
months. Gerald Ford convened a special "town meeting" of the nation's
leading civic and economic figures in hopes that they could talk their
way to a solution. Then, for good measure, he asked all Americans to
send him a list of the ten things they themselves were going to do to help

lick inflation. Administrations struggled to persuade union and corporate leaders to stay within voluntary wage and price increase guidelines, despite the consistent ineffectualness of the effort. Throughout the nervous search for economic policy in the 1970s, virtually all the politically viable programs assumed that restoring economic stability was a task of conscious social and institutional compromise. Republican and Democratic administrations alike took it as a matter of course that big labor and big business both deserved a place on the wage and price control boards. As for the public, approval of wage and price controls (sometimes by a narrow margin, sometimes by a wide one) was a constant of the decade; as late as June 1979, a majority of those polled still endorsed them.[16]

But the core problem was not the achievement of a viable political compromise, heroically difficult as that might have been, given the sharply different ways in which high unemployment and high inflation cut through the population. The deeper problem was the collapse of economic predictability. Gerald Ford, who had opened his administration in August 1974 calling inflation the nation's "public enemy number one," came back to Congress five months later to press for a quick tax cut to stave off what his advisers now feared was a looming recession. The slump that Carter's economic advisers predicted when he submitted his economic stimulus program to Congress in February 1977 had turned into an unanticipated reburst of inflation by April, when he suddenly withdrew it.

Macroeconomics in the post–World War II years had tied its prestige to predictive economic models, but their analytical capacity had gone awry. The price movement of the past year "was the most extraordinary in almost a generation," the Council of Economic Advisers reported in 1974; its explanation, the council lamely confessed, "confounded the Council and most other economists alike." The field of macroeconomics itself was in a state of "total chaos," the discipline's most closely watched theorist, the University of Chicago's Robert Lucas, was publicly declaring by 1979. "Nobody has any answers he is confident of," the sociologist Daniel Bell told a *Washington Post* reporter. Even Samuelson was to write of the "failure of any paradigm to deliver the goods."[17]

The economic crisis of the 1970s was, in short, not merely a crisis in management. It was also, and at least as painfully, a crisis in ideas and intellectual authority. An extremely confident analytical system had failed to explain or to make sense of the unexpected. In time, after the economy emerged from the recessionary wringer of 1980–1983, something like the Phillips curve would return. The Reagan tax cuts of the early 1980s, it would be said, ultimately functioned as a Keynesian demand stimulus, just as the textbooks might have predicted. Conventional macroeconomics did not predict dramatically wrong. What was devastating to the reigning models was that none of their architects knew why they mispredicted.

As the economy unraveled and textbook economic certainties of the 1960s frayed out into confusion and qualification, a new set of claimants pressed into the controversy, battling for recruits and influence, vying to define an alternative theoretical frame for economic analysis. In the circumstances, it was not surprising that many of them should have entailed radically simpler models of society than beleaguered neo-Keynesianism or that they should have hitched their promises to more automatically working processes than the frustrated efforts of the councils of economic advisers. The idea of the self-acting market was ultimately to be borne along on both assumptions.

Of the contenders for Keynesianism's place, monetarism seemed to loom the largest in the 1970s. Until it, too, fell apart in an implosion of its practical and theoretical promises in the early 1980s, it served as a highly effective exploiter of the economic and conceptual troubles of the 1970s and, though it was not itself a very coherent expression of the new market ideas, as a practical rallying point for those who desired one.

The University of Chicago's economics department, where monetarism was born, had been the most important American university holdout against the neo-Keynesian revolution in economic theory. By the 1960s and early 1970s it had gathered the most important cluster of internal exiles to be found in the discipline: George Stigler, Gary Becker, Milton Friedman, and Robert Lucas in the economics department; Aaron Director, Ronald Coase, and Richard Posner in the law school. Milton Friedman's role was not to dominate the department; its emphasis on classical price theory was set long before Friedman arrived on its faculty in 1946, fresh from labors on wartime tax policy. But even in this circle of strong personalities, Friedman was the University of Chicago circle's most forceful politicizer.[18]

Monetarism, as Friedman framed it, was essentially a policy idea trailing a much weaker theory behind it. Beginning as a restatement of an older quantity theory of money, it was given its modern form on the basis of Milton Friedman and Anna Schwartz's historical correlation of movements in money and prices in the United States since the Civil War. Recasting historical experience as predictive law (just as Samuelson was doing at almost precisely the same time with the Phillips curve), Friedman extracted monetarism's policy claim: that the cause of changes in the overall price structure was to be found solely in shifts in the growth rate of the volume of circulating money. In this radically simplified model of aggregate economic behavior, state, society, and institutions all shrank into insignificance within a black box that translated money inputs directly into price outputs. To those who objected to this heroic analytical simplification, Friedman countered that the positive test of economic theory lay strictly in its predictive capacities, not in the superficial realism of its assumptions. Fully developed monetarism was by no means as unsophisticated as it often publicly appeared, but Friedman, a tireless combatant in the policy wars, was his own eager and terrible simplifier. He gave monetarism a mantra—"inflation is always and everywhere a monetary phenomenon"—and a panacea for economic stability: a money-growth rule for central bankers of 3–5 percent a year.[19]

Within the monetarist "counter-revolution," as Friedman was calling his attack on Keynesian business-cycle analysis by 1970, the relationship between monetarist policy and market ideology was, from the beginning, complex. Monetarism was built from economic aggregates down, not up from the microeconomic foundations of individual choice. Focused almost entirely on Federal Reserve Board rule making, its macroeconomics was in its own way as state-centered as Keynes's or Samuelson's, as Friedrich von Hayek, among others, observed. In his social politics, on the other hand, Friedman was a libertarian, unfailingly confident of the processes of society once they were released from government control, and an ingenious promoter of the abilities of markets to revolve questions of social choice. School vouchers, social security privatization, a negative income tax for the poor, and constitutional limitations on government spending were all ideas he helped set in motion and, with boundless energy, worked to publicize.[20]

Critics often pointed out that the two halves of Friedman's project did not cohere very tightly. For all Friedman's unrelenting criticism of governmental policy as the root cause of economic distress ("Inflation is entirely made in Washington—and nowhere else," he was to charge in 1980), he never seriously proposed abolishing the Federal Reserve, though the logic of his libertarian politics seemed inexorably to lead there, and to letting the financial markets simply work things out.[21] At some basic level, rules preoccupied Friedman more than markets did. Let governments abdicate their discretionary, managerial powers, let them set aside ambitions for social and economic fine-tuning and do their essential work by clear and automatically functioning systems, and markets would do the rest. That social scientists possessed the capacity to deduce the rules of social optimization but not the capacity to administer them might have seemed, in another context, an odd sort of confidence. But as it was, Friedman used his scholarly prestige in monetary theory to give his libertarian opinions an air of economic certainty that he was not at all shy to exploit.

Given monetarism's organized base at the University of Chicago, Friedman's long and easy relationship with politically conservative money, ready access to the media (by 1966 he had landed a berth alongside Paul Samuelson as a regular *Newsweek* columnist), and a public message whose simplicity contrasted strikingly with the qualifications around it, monetarism was an idea with many institutional advantages. Still, without the heating up of inflation, Friedman's prominence on the national scene in the 1970s is all but inconceivable. In a widely circulated analysis in late 1967, when the economic policy establishment still thought full employment an achievable goal of macroeconomic policy making, Friedman had proposed that every attempt to stimulate the economy beyond its "natural rate" of unemployment (or nonaccelerating inflation rate of unemployment, as others would rename it) dissipated not simply into inflation but into accelerating and destabilizing inflation. The precisely managed economy, he seemed analytically to show, could produce only artificially ignited inflation. When the general price level took off between 1967 and 1970, Friedman suddenly stood out as a seer in a kingdom of the blind.[22]

The checking of hyperinflation in Chile by a cadre of University of Chicago–trained economists in the late 1970s provided a second, highly publicized coup for monetarism. Latin America had long been a center of historical and institutionalist economics, which combined to encourage a major state presence in the economy—as protector of domestic markets against external competition, as state entrepreneur and promoter of economic development, and as a buffer for the peasant majorities against the unshielded effects of the price system. When the socialist president Salvador Allende's government was violently overthrown in a military coup in 1973 amid economic turmoil and triple-digit inflation, the ruling generals first turned to the established Chilean economists. But in 1975 they gave over economic management to a cadre of University of Chicago–trained economists who had constructed an "exile" faculty of their own at the Catholic University of Chile. Over the next seven years, "the Chicago boys," as they were known in the Chilean press, used the military's power to work a dramatic transformation of the Chilean economy: shrinking the size of the public sector, slashing economic controls, privatizing the major state industries, eliminating agricultural subsidies, privatizing social security, and sharply restricting labor union rights. Economic inequality grew, but hyperinflation gradually receded. The University of Chicago economists did not hesitate to take credit for the work of their Chilean disciples; Friedman himself gave his blessing to their work in a heavily publicized speaking tour in Chile in 1975.[23]

Monetarism achieved an even greater victory in the late 1970s by capturing the minds of British conservatives. Monetarism's first champions in the United Kingdom were the organizers of the Institute of Economic Affairs, a privately funded player in the global war of ideas. Monetarism was picked up by some of Britain's most prominent economic journalists in 1973–1974, when oil price shocks pushed British inflation rates into double digits. Whipsawed by money and labor pressures, British governments, like their U.S. counterparts, cast about for ad hoc economic measures that continuously fell apart beneath them. By 1975, a year in which the annual inflation rate in Britain reached 24 percent and the year in which Margaret Thatcher seized the leadership of the Conservative party, Keith Joseph, the party's most ambitious intellectual, had publicly committed himself to the simpler tenets of monetarism, carrying Thatcher, still his pupil in economic matters, along with him.[24]

Promising to cure inflation, monetarism relentlessly focused attention on it. In response to monetarist pressure, Federal Reserve officials began announcing money-supply targets in 1975, which, in turn, immediately took on economic consequence in the calculations of private financial managers. In conservative political circles it became common to pair the socially disastrous consequences of the Great Inflation of the 1970s with the Great Depression of the 1930s and to implicate it in everything from the revolution in sexual mores to the scandals of political corruption. Within the economics profession itself, monetarism was never nearly as strong, even at inflation's height, as it appeared in the news headlines and business columns. In a poll of six hundred professional American economists published in 1979, only 14 percent "generally agreed" with the core Friedmanite position that the Federal Reserve Board should be instructed to increase the money supply at a fixed rate.[25] But as the Phillips curve crumpled and the standard economic forecasting programs misfired, as the policy managers struggled to demonstrate that they were in charge of an economy whose dynamics they professed they no longer understood, as the abandonment of international currency agreements injected a new instability into the global economy, and as the quarrel intensified over who should bear the social and economic costs of the high unemployment–high inflation complex, monetarism's public stature swelled apace.

Monetarism offered a strikingly simple rule for hard times: let the money supply be prudently managed and markets would provide the rest. But when its victory came at the decade's very end, monetarism's reign turned out to be brief and highly turbulent. Margaret Thatcher committed Britain to a monetarist course when she assumed the prime ministership in May 1979; in the fall Carter's new Federal Reserve chair, Paul Volcker, followed suit. Though they effectively snuffed out the inflationary pressures, the process turned out to be disastrous for monetarist practice and theory alike. Between 1979 and 1983, as monetary authorities in both countries did their best to steer by money-supply targets alone, rather than by the usual, eclectic basket of economic indicators, the smooth deflationary landing that the leading monetarists had predicted turned into a classic business-cycle collapse. Squeezed by record interest rates and unemployment levels higher than at any time since the end of the Great Depression, inflation finally tumbled. But even as the general market contraction wrung inflation out of the economies, monetarism's predictive capacities were falling apart. Not only did the relationship between price level and money supply fail to behave predictably under the short-run pressure. Destabilized by the ingenuity of the financial markets in spinning off new money forms, the quantity of money proved impossible to measure. Volcker's Federal Reserve Board abandoned one of its aggregate targets in early 1981 and "temporarily" deemphasized another in October 1982, by which point it was clear in every regard except explicit public announcements that it had returned to discretion and rules of thumb. After a similarly futile chase after a reliable and controllable money measure, Thatcher's ministers publicly threw in the towel in 1986.[26]

Through these controversies Friedman insisted that monetarism, mishandled by its executors, had never really had a proper trial. What most economists took from the experience, however, was the death knell of rule-monetarism: that aggregate money in exchange in modern societies was in practice beyond a central bank's power to estimate, control, or even effectively define.[27] With that, much of the rest of monetarism's larger intellectual structure fell apart. His *Free to Choose* series on PBS in 1980, organized by a former McGovern Democrat and funded by conservative donors, gave Friedman one more highly prominent stage on which to preach his now-familiar compound of aggregate money rules and libertarian politics.[28] But by the mid-1980s, monetarism no longer drew new recruits among economists; even at the University of Chicago, graduate students in economics told interviewers that "people [here] do not look to Friedman's models and try to solve them or work with them."[29]

Monetarism, in short, turned out to be a bulldozer that could raze a building but could not erect one. A powerful collector of anti-Keynesian sentiments, monetarism did a great deal to delegitimize the conventional economic wisdom, to break down the case for macroeconomic fine-tuning, and ultimately to transfer business-cycle management from Congress and the Council of Economic Advisers to Volcker's heirs at the Federal Reserve. Friedman's idea of a "natural rate" of unemployment endured in the economics profession as a standing reminder of the limits of macroeconomic management. The "full employment" dreams that liberals had nurtured from 1946 through the Humphrey-Hawkins Full Employment Act of 1978 were among its most important casualties. The term had all but disappeared from economic theory by the mid-1980s.

But the heavy-weight paradigm battle between monetarism and Keynesianism that was expected to define the era petered out without conclusion.

In retrospect the more consequential struggles over ideas and paradigms took place elsewhere: in the economic retooling of the lawyers, in
the universities, and finally in the recapturing of optimism by a new cluster of "supply-side" market populists. Each was shaped by the same inflationary anxieties that fueled the rise and fall of monetarism's fortunes.
Each drew on the power of simple ideas in hard and confusing times.

The first of these transformations was the infusion of market models into
the law. Law had always been at the foundation of market exchange, setting its rules and property claims, but lawyers had not always known
much about economics. Outside specialized enclaves such as antitrust
law, their professional discourse had run toward narratives of justice,
property, rights, and blame—stories thick in particulars, institutions, and
social circumstances. Their domain was the field of dispute adjudication,
not economic maximization. By the late 1970s, however, courses in the
price system had become a booming enterprise in the law schools, and a
new rhetoric of costs and efficiency was bearing down hard on antitrust
judgments, liability law, and, most dramatically, regulatory policy—re-
shaping them all on models of highly idealized markets.

These intellectual shifts in the law were the product of several sources.
One was the growing hold of the distinctive antitrust doctrine that had
been taught at the University of Chicago since the early 1950s and that
emphasized price and efficiency—rather than firm size or market share,
as antitrust doctrine since the 1930s had had it—as the market's un-
ambiguous register of monopoly control. Bigness itself worked no economic injury if it were the product of naturally created efficiencies, those
schooled in the University of Chicago antitrust doctrine argued. It was
the little players in collusion with the government—price-fixing lawyers,
union plumbers, medallion taxi drivers, and their like—who were much
more likely to try to rig the markets. Spread by the appointment of increasing numbers of economists to the staffs of the Justice Department
and the Federal Trade Commission and incorporated into federal jurisprudence, price-grounded antitrust doctrine had effectively won the day
by the time Reagan took office.[30]

The single most important text in what came to be called the law and economics movement, however, was a piece published in a fledgling University of Chicago journal in 1960: Ronald Coase's article "The Problem of Social Cost."[31] As the Coase tale was told and retold in the law schools in the 1970s, law students were instructed to imagine a farmer and a rancher working adjacent lands. The rancher's cattle, straying into the farmer's fields, trampled the farmer's grain. The farmer brought suit for damages in court, and the lawyers told the judge complicated stories of blame and responsibility while the judge tried to decide for one side or the other. The analytical surprise Coase inserted into this familiar tort-law story was that if the judge were to keep the economic good of society in mind, it didn't matter which way he decided. For if the judge decided in the farmer's favor, and if there were no costs or obstacles to impede the farmer and the rancher from further bargaining as soon as they left the courtroom, then the rancher had every economic incentive to lessen his liability by paying the farmer to leave some of his closely abutting land fallow. And if the judge decided in the rancher's favor, the farmer had every incentive to lessen his losses by offering the rancher a bonus to run fewer cattle. Either way, Coase demonstrated, the bargain they struck would not only leave each party better off than would be the case under any of the standard legal doctrines at the judge's disposal; it would also leave society better off by maximizing the total product produced—counting the value of the crops and cattle together and subtracting the total expenses the farmer and the rancher each incurred.

The Coase theorem, as others soon named it, was a powerful analytical story, couched in arithmetic that a fifth grader could follow and generalizable across virtually any instance of externalized cost and damage. In all such cases, Coase urged, it was beside the point, as an economist construed it, to ask who was to blame. A noxious factory did no harm without neighbors; the law's traditional narratives of responsibility only confused that kernel of reciprocity. If it cost the polluters more in total to abate a nuisance than it would have cost society to buy out the objecting neighbors so that they could move elsewhere, then the socially efficient answer was that the neighbors should leave and the stink should stay, just as they would if the parties had been left to themselves to bargain their way to an economically optimal resolution. In a world of zero transaction costs, the path of private market transactions, the path of least aggregate social cost, and the optional allocation of society's resources were precisely the same.

The actual field of the lawyer-economists' most interesting work, Coase himself was quick to caution, lay in circumstances much more complex than this, filled with disparities in information, institutional constraints, widely dispersed damages, and severe difficulties in sustained collective action. Summarizing his work on the occasion of his award of the Nobel Prize in Economics in 1991, Coase downplayed his famous "theorem" as a mere thought experiment on the way to much more important issues of the structure of the firms and legal regimes in which economic exchange took place.[32] But for all Coase's subsequent resistance to simple readings of his work, the concept of the social good he introduced into the law was powerfully simple. The social good was a maximization problem in aggregate market value: crops and cattle, property values and pollution-abatement costs, not, he had been candid enough to say, any close assessment of who stood best to bear the pain of the compromise or how unequally matched their resources might have been at the outset.

An outlier in the legal literature in the 1960s, Coase's essay took off in the 1970s as a conceptual formula by which large parts of law's most contested terrain could be reimagined not as questions of harm and restitution but as questions of market efficiency. The most influential of the Coase-influenced texts was Richard Posner's *Economic Analysis of Law,* which ran through a stunningly eclectic array of legal issues—from liability and nuisance law to the justice of widows' dowers to the logic of the common law itself—to argue that in every case the equitable answer lay in following out which course maximized the aggregate social wealth, measured by the prices economic actors put on it. "Can the idea of 'justice' . . . be deduced from the economist's idea of efficiency?" Posner asked, in a rhetorical question that became the hinge of law and economics classroom teaching.[33]

The "yes" of the law's new economizers was, from the beginning, controversial in the law faculties. Critics attacked Posner's equation of social value with willingness and ability to pay—such that polluting a rich man's air counted as a heavier social cost than polluting a poor man's, since it lowered the rich man's property value more. They criticized law and economics' animus against deliberative, political means of social choice, its indifference to power, and its translation of justice into a pure maximization problem on behalf of an abstraction, "society," so that whenever the gainers gained more in aggregate from a judgment or statute than the losers' aggregate losses one could say that society was better off, without bothering to consider who the winners and the losers actually were. "Maximum wealth, badly distributed, does not lead to maximum happiness," Posner's leading rival in the economic analysis of the law, Guido Calabresi, was writing by 1982.[34] But in a count made at the end of the 1990s of the most cited law writers of the second half of the twentieth century, Posner swept the field with a lead over his nearest rivals of almost two to one.[35]

One of the key factors in the success of the law and economics project was its attractiveness to the new conservative money that began to funnel into the production of ideas in the 1970s. By the early 1980s, William E. Simon's Olin Foundation was carrying an extraordinary weight of the law and economics teaching at the nation's leading law schools—underwriting the salaries of its teachers, subsidizing its journals and lecture series, and paying special scholarships to students taking its courses. The new conservative foundations also financed the summer "camps" in law and economics, organized by Henry Manne, corporation law scholar and a long-time colleague of Milton Friedman in the antistatist Mont Pelerin Society, to which scores of judges, congressional aides, and law professors came in the 1970s and 1980s to retrain themselves in price theory and microeconomic analysis. Copies of Friedman's *Capitalism and Freedom* served as graduation prizes.[36]

But the 1970s boom in law and economics cannot be explained only by its external funders. Nor, as the prominence of Calabresi and other liberals in the effort to apply economic analysis to the law showed, was its appeal confined to business sympathizers and political conservatives. In the wake of the explosive growth of the law and litigation into new domains of consumer protection and product liability, health and environmental regulation, class-action suits and public interest law, where the law's case-by-case rhetoric seemed less and less to comprehend the issues or to offer any larger, socially adequate resolution, law and economics operated as a compelling instrument of simplification. The leading tort law textbook of 1971 warned students that at first glance the cases they would consider would likely appear entirely unrelated to each other and that the central theme of tort law was "difficult to put into words"; only then did it venture to lead apprentice lawyers through the intricate subdivisions of negligence and the balancing acts by which the social interest might be restored.[37] The language of costs clarified. "No one likes to be at sea with a vague statutory word that seems to leave every decision at the discretion of the judge," the future Supreme Court justice Stephen Breyer was writing by the early 1980s; "the body of economic principle . . . offers objectivity—terra firma—upon which we can base decisions."[38]

The most dramatic instance of the new authority of market models came in public utility law. Public utility regulation had been one of the primary legislative achievements of early-twentieth-century progressives. Alarmed by the predatory power of railroads and utility monopolies, they had forced the price decisions of "natural monopolies" to pass through the judgment of public commissioners. But the regulatory system had been a beleaguered domain for some time. It had been criticized from the right for interfering with business autonomy and, from the 1960s on, criticized even more systematically from the political left as a system of captive government agencies that pliantly did whatever the regulated industries wanted. Long before a serious conservative deregulatory movement took the field, the idea of genuinely disinterested public utility regulation had been thoroughly hollowed out by its radical critics.[39]

Still, had Alfred Kahn moved from the Cornell economics department to the chairmanship of the New York Public Service Commission at any other time than 1974, the context might well have swallowed him up. But with the oil price escalation and the new environmentalist movement destabilizing every long-term power-industry calculation, Kahn succeeded in forcing the state's utilities through a wringer of marginal cost theory. When services were not priced at their actual marginal costs— when electricity consumers paid the same for a unit of electricity at peak summer demand as they did in the slack winter season, or when purchasers of long-distance calls paid more than their service cost and local callers paid less—the price system sent out distorted signals, Kahn insisted; utilities overbuilt plants, certain classes of customers unknowingly subsidized others, aggregate costs rose, and economic resources were wasted. "I do not want . . . to fall [from regulation] into the opposite error of simply substituting the cliché 'leave it to the market,'" Kahn was to write.

But to a great extent his achievement was exactly that: to force upon regulated industries as marketlike a set of rules as his staff of lawyer-economists could devise.[40]

That it might be in the public interest to "distort" the market by subsidizing certain customers or to allocate resources in a democracy by criteria other than cost and market price or even economic efficiency was an open question, of course. But to the extent that the inflation of the mid-1970s could be construed as the piling of thousands of incremental wastes and inefficiencies onto the aggregate cost structure, the drive to remake the rule of law on the model of the market was buoyed by the spiraling price index. It was never as clear as it sometimes seemed that regulation was, in fact, a major factor in the decade's accelerating prices. Murray Weidenbaum's estimate that regulation cost the American economy $100 billion a year circulated widely through conservative circles, but most economists recognized it as a rhetorically exaggerated guess.[41] In the shipwreck of the macroeconomic paradigms, however, regulatory reform became a kind of analytical refuge for policy-oriented economists. At the domestic "summit meeting" on inflation convened by Gerald Ford in the fall of 1974, the panel of invited economics experts divided over every macroeconomic question before it. It could not agree on whether monetary policy was too loose or too tight, whether wage and price controls should be continued or dismantled, or even whether the nation's most pressing problem was inflation or unemployment. Determined to bring a note of professional clarity out of this cacophony, Arthur Okun helped engineer a face-saving consensus on a list of twenty-two modest efficiency and deregulatory reforms which, with varying degrees of enthusiasm, the panelists hoped would "improve the pricing and cost performance of the economy."[42] As with monetarism, deregulation's fortunes were inextricably bound to the inflationary context.

To galvanize the economists' second thoughts about regulation, the lawyers' new interest in markets, and the public's anxiety over inflation into a general movement for regulatory dismantlement took a single, dramatic case, and the airlines provided it. The instance was easy, singular, and well known among economists. Insulated from price competition with one another, protected from upstart competitors by federal regulators, the major carriers had been content to make their assured profits and let the average American ride a bus. In search of a consumer interest issue in 1975, Senator Edward Kennedy took up the topic of airline pricing in hearings orchestrated by Stephen Breyer, fresh from teaching antitrust law at Harvard. The effort attracted an extremely broad coalition of allies from Milton Friedman to the corporations' critic Ralph Nader. Seeking a consumer advocacy issue of his own, Jimmy Carter brought Kahn to the Civil Aeronautics Board in 1977 to oversee airline price reform. The next year, without waiting for Kahn's reforms fully to take hold, Congress abolished airline price regulation altogether.

With airline deregulation, the singular case became, almost overnight, the general model. In 1979, Breyer was still writing about the need for careful, case-by-case analysis of regulatory policy, matching industry specifics to a wide array of procompetitive policy alternatives.[43] But the power of a generalized idea of automatically working market efficiency ran stronger than Breyer's institutionalist realism. When in the first year of airline price reform, airline fares fell and profits rose, deregulation became, in Martha Derthick and Paul Quirk's words, a "policy fashion," "a buzzword and bandwagon." Between 1979 and 1982, trucking, long-distance bus transport, rail transport, telecommunications, oil, and savings and loan institutions were all substantially removed from regulatory controls.[44] The results were much more mixed (and in some cases, much more costly) than the advocates of wholesale deregulation anticipated. In telecommunications, where cornucopias of new technologies were poised to take advantage of deregulation, the range of consumer options was dramatically expanded. In the savings and loan industry, where the pinch of economic pressure was intense and dishonest operators moved swiftly into the vacuum created by regulatory neglect, the results were disastrous.

Like all legislative fads, deregulation eventually ran out of steam. In environmental policy, employment of market solutions made very little headway, despite the early interest of one of the key environmental lobbying groups, the Environmental Defense Fund. Not until the 1990s were the first significant market-trading systems in pollution employed in federal environmental law, though economists had been insisting on the superiority of pollution markets and pollution taxes over controls since the 1970s. Much of the energy of deregulation turned offshore, as International Monetary Fund and World Bank economists wrote liberalization of economic controls into their preconditions for structural adjustment loans. At home, in the law school reviews, law and economics–based contributions slowly tapered off after their high point in 1980–1981, when, according to one study, they had accounted for a third of all the articles published.[45]

But if the practical effects of the shift from law to markets were mixed, the intellectual victory was deeper and more enduring. Even the authors of liberal college economics textbooks now routinely began their description of how to think like an economist with set-piece explanations of the economic inefficiencies of regulation. At the law schools and public policy programs, fluency in economic reasoning became a virtually inescapable mark of professional competence. Where law and economics teaching took hold, the proposition that the free play of private interests might better promote maximum social well-being than could the active management of regulators and lawyers moved closer and closer to the default assumption. In its very simplifications, it filled a yearning for clarity that the older, more complex pictures of society could not. Through a conjunction of policy fads and intellectual quandaries played out against the decade's uncertain, inflationary context, in short, a new deference to market dispositions of crops and cattle, tort damages and corporate size, air fares and energy prices had shifted the law's ideological center.

The era's second critical shift in the prestige of market models and metaphors took place within the academic study of economics itself. Obscured by the widely reported conflicts between monetarists and neo-Keynesians, the more lasting event was an effort to turn away from macroeconomics' aggregate categories and try to rethink economics altogether from microeconomic principles outward. Couched initially in terms of time expectations, it ultimately went to the heart of the sociological assumptions imbedded in the Samuelson-era synthesis. Whereas the most prominent practitioners of law and economics undertook to replace a historical-institutional sense of society with a precise and arithmetized conception of economic efficiency, the new intellectual movements in economics pushed to its limits the extent to which society could be analytically dissolved altogether into its individual, utility-maximizing parts.

The idea of human behavior as a system of maximizing rules and calculations was hardly new, of course. In the late 1950s and 1960s, at the high tide of postwar interdisciplinary social science, a small group of theorizers not shy about their imperial ambitions had begun to apply economistic models across broader and broader ranges of human activities. Where sociology met economics, the University of Chicago's Gary Becker proposed maximization models for a wide variety of behavior—fertility, housework, criminality, and the use of time—that had resisted economic modeling before. In political analysis, Anthony Downs and others began to suggest that legislative behavior could be better understood as an arena for the maximization of the individual utilities of politicians than as a search for a phantom public interest. Game theory moved out of Defense Department circles into philosophy departments, where certain set-pieces—the "prisoner's dilemma," the "tragedy of the commons," the "free-rider problem"—acquired a status as paradigmatically central as Coase's corn and cattle. To all these, the word "rational" began to adhere. For the most ambitious players in the field, indeed, there was nothing other than rational, optimizing behavior. All the "irrationalities" that psychoanalysts had relegated to the unconscious, that anthropologists had relegated to "culture," and that historians had ascribed to mysterious shifts in "values," Becker was arguing by 1976, could be more compellingly explained by shifts in costs played out against stable preferences.[46]

As integral as microeconomic propositions of this sort were to the background assumptions of professional economists, however, they had not played a particularly prominent role in the high-status, macroeconomic wing of the profession, tied as it was to aggregate economic indicators and complex computer modeling. It was a commonplace in the discipline to regret that macroeconomic and microeconomic analyses were not more tightly integrated. But it was only when the macroeconomic models' predictive capacities began to fall apart in the 1970s that a group of insurgent theorists went back to the macro-micro split to ask if the discipline's paradigmatic disarray did not have its roots there.

The most important endeavor in this regard was the "rational expectations" movement that spun out of Robert Lucas's work at Carnegie Mellon University and the University of Chicago in the early 1970s. The conceptual core of rational expectations was simple. Economic actors did not simply react to economic information; rather, Lucas maintained, they learned to anticipate economic actions, decoding the rules of thumb of other economic actors and foreseeing their line of action. Yet if the point was simple, the practical and theoretical consequences were not. Milton

Friedman had already suggested in general terms that anticipation of further inflation radically destabilized the policy makers' capacity for containing it. In 1972, in the elegant mathematics which became a mark of the movement, Lucas proposed that in monetary policy only truly unanticipated changes—decisions that successfully fooled and misled economic actors—actually made a difference in aggregate economic behavior. By the late 1970s, economic theorists were locked in a highly sophisticated argument over whether macroeconomic management was possible at all—whether any act of fiscal or monetary steering was effectual once the foresighted calculations of economic actors had been fully taken into account.[47]

Their rebellion launched so boldly, the rational expectations dissidents were soon in full press against the dominant neo-Keynesian establishment, competing for students, funding, and theoretical elegance. To raise the "Lucas critique" was to demand to know which regime of long-term anticipations an economic proposition incorporated, and it proved a low-cost way to derail a lot of freight. The reigning economic forecasting models, built on nonanticipating hypotheses of economic action, were "useless," it was said. The "entire meaningless vocabulary associated with full employment, phrases like potential output, full capacity, slack, and so on," was fatally flawed as well, Lucas urged. The Phillips curve's misfiring was, by this judgment, only the visible tip of a much more massive conceptual failure to take time anticipation seriously. Lucas's taunt that "Keynesian economics is dead" and that there was not a serious Keynesian under age forty were fighting words, not an accurate description of the profession. But by the time the financial press discovered the rational expectationist controversy at the end of the 1970s, it had shaken economic analysis at its very center.[48]

Under the rhetorical heat and status competition, serious intellectual issues were at stake. Most visible was a contest about time. To the rational expectationists, the assumptions built into Keynesian macroeconomics seemed fatally static. Incorporating game theory into the economics of individual action, they proposed to "dynamicize" economics—replacing its myopic and reactive modal actors, capable of being lured by the surprise of a price shift or tax cut into quick but ultimately counterproductive economic action, with much cleverer, long-term calculators. The rational expectationists' treatment of time was one of several ways in which they absorbed the economic experience of the 1970s. The economic actors at their models' center were skilled inflation managers: not the producers of the classical economists' imagination, not even Marshall's cotton dealers minding the telegraph at Manchester, but lightning calculators and instant discounters of time, able to work out a life-earnings function on the way to the savings bank, to project with ease the comparative returns of the new global investment instruments coming ever more rapidly on line, or to see through the illusion of a tax cut that someone, sometime, would have to pay back. Rational expectations was economics for an inflationary decade, when the time-dependency of value was a lesson of day-to-day experience.

Integral to these arguments about time, however, was also an argument about markets and equilibrium. For if economic actors really anticipated, as the rational expectationists suggested, discounting in advance the actions of the state economic managers, folding time into their utility calculations, then the systemic slips and friction, the liquidity traps and "sticky" wages, all the structural macroeconomic imperfections that lay at the foundation of the Keynesian interpretation of the business cycle dissolved into an illusion of the theorists. The market that rational expectationist actors would make was an auction market, not unlike the stock market that was now playing such a larger practical and symbolic role in economic life: a place of extraordinarily quick response and instant clearing, where prices, wages, and demand moved with frictionless ease and the optimizing equations were always efficiently at work. In Lucas's mind, information costs kept the perfect equilibration from occurring. But others in the rational expectations camp came closer to insisting that perfect markets were a realistic description of the actual economy than economists had in a century.

Ultimately, the conflict between Lucas and his critics was a conflict about society. Intent on constructing a post-Keynesian, postmanagerial economics for inflationary times, the rational expectations economists let what Samuelson had called "the fallacy of composition" evaporate as irrelevant. Friedman (whose money rule Lucas was ready to defend on pragmatic grounds) had put stabilization of the aggregate money supply at economics' center; Posner and Coase had made an imperative out of aggregate wealth and "total product." But in rational expectations economics, social aggregates virtually vanished. In the Lucas-influenced models, where the behavior of a "representative agent" stood in for the whole, the Northwestern University economist Robert J. Gordon wrote, "one could move back and forth between the individual agent and the aggregate economy simply by adding or removing 'I' subscripts" without ever stumbling over a coordination or aggregation problem. A graduate student in economics at Lucas's University of Chicago in the mid-1980s put the point more baldly: "The macroeconomics [that we learn] here is very much like microeconomics. We work on individual levels and sum it up." Were the rational expectations project to succeed, Robert Lucas himself urged in 1985, "the term 'macroeconomic' will simply disappear from use." The split between macro- and microanalysis, the discipline's false step of the 1940s, would be allowed to heal. Economics would be rebuilt from the individual actor out, a seamless unfolding of strategic games and "rational" choices.[49]

In the end, the victory was not as simple nor as complete as Lucas envisioned it. Having raised the internal theory wars to a fever pitch by the early 1980s, the anti-Keynesian counterrevolution began to falter. The wrenching effects of the Volcker deflation caught the rational expectationist vanguard by surprise—many of whom had allowed themselves to imagine that genuinely rational actors would see through the game so quickly as to make the transition to a stable price regime all but painless. Lucas won the Nobel Prize in economics in 1995, but his own effort to devise a general business-cycle theory alternative to Keynes's eluded him. The policy-ineffectualness hypothesis, broached in 1975–1976, broke down. The fight for graduate students, which had tipped so strongly toward rational expectations' novelty and mathematical elegance, evened out.[50] By the late 1990s, among the most closely watched parts of the discipline was the new field of behavioral economics, situated at the intersection of psychology and microeconomics, where the limits of economic rationality were the point of study. In the term Herbert Simon had coined in the 1950s, rationality was now more and more often said to be "bounded." Economic actors made decisions by rules of thumb; they systematically misestimated; they satisfied rather than maximized; they did not always play games by selfishly optimizing rules. A new institutional economics also began to take shape, with transaction costs, firm structures, and information imperfections at its core.[51]

But despite these trends, the conceptual frame in economics had clearly shifted. By the time the macro wars had begun to ease in the late 1980s into an array of blends and compromises, the macroeconomists' indifference to the microeconomics of individual action had been swept away, and theorists of every sort were working hard to place economics on the foundations of individual, "choice-theoretic" behavior. What made the "new Keynesians" (Gregory Mankiw, George Akerlof, Joseph Stiglitz, and Ben Bernanke, among them) the hottest players in the macro field in the late 1980s and 1990s was their ability to generate explanations for Keynesian-scale macroeconomic friction out of the cumulative effects of small individual variations from perfectly rational economic behavior. Employers, they suggested, were reluctant to risk diluting the loyalty of their employees by cutting wages at the first signs of a softening labor market; sellers were reluctant to incur the cost of reposting their entire price menu in instantaneous response to the market's signals; asymmetries in the information available to economic actors were pervasive. The instabilities of the macroeconomy did not reside, as the Samuelson-era textbooks had described it, in an analytical world of its own; models of perfect competition, modestly and cleverly adjusted, could explain them all.[52]

The simpler pictures of the economy that Friedman and Lucas had dreamed of finding dissolved into an ad hoc collection of smaller puzzles and ingeniously modeled solutions. At the same time, Samuelson-era macroeconomics dissolved as well. There were still defenders of the utility of the IS/LM relationship that Samuelson had made famous. But as economics emerged from the disciplinary crisis of the 1970s and early 1980s, its focus was no longer on systemwide stabilization or the interplay of aggregates. Economics was about the complex play of optimizing behavior—a thought experiment that began with individuals and the exchanges they made. Even the "new Keynesians," James Tobin grumbled in 1993, could not stomach large-scale, institutional reasons for market failures. "They suspect that individual irrationalities are lurking somewhere in the theory."[53] The discipline's embedded theoretical frame now belonged to microeconomics: a choice-theoretic universe of myriad near-rational actors. Lucas's confidence that macroeconomics as the Samuelson generation had known it would disappear turned out, when the theory wars finally subsided, to hold an important kernel of truth.

The third group of figures responsible for reviving the rhetoric of the market, the prophets of "supply-side" economics, were products of very different social contexts than were the university-based law professors or the economic theorists. They were a small group of publicists and autodidacts with their center at the *Wall Street Journal*, who in the turmoil of the paradigms, the yearning for conceptual simplicity, and the eroding confidence in macroeconomic management, succeeded in gaining the ear of the Republican party and a president with a weakness for optimism.

Between those who sold the Republican majority on a massive tax cut in 1981 and the professional critics of Keynesianism there were deep rifts and rivalries. A striking number of the leading organizers of the "supply-side" movement were economic innocents: Robert Bartley, who assumed direction of the editorial page of the *Wall Street Journal* in 1972 with ambitions to make it (as he did) the most sharply conservative editorial page in mainstream journalism; Jude Wanniski, the flamboyant journalist who was Bartley's first associate editor; George Gilder, the self-taught sociobiologist; Jack Kemp, the maverick congressman eager to put a populist face on the Republican party; and Irving Kristol, dean of neoconservative journalism and matchmaker to the new conservative foundations. Robert Lucas dismissed the linchpin of supply-side economics—the Kemp-Roth bill calling for a 30 percent across-the-board cut in federal individual income tax rates—as a "crackpot proposal." Friedman endorsed Kemp-Roth as a tactical brake on government spending but kept his distance from the supply-siders' rationale. Supply-sider Arthur Laffer, in turn, ridiculed monetarism with a napkin diagram, asking how the tiny little box that was M1 could possibly control an aggregate money quantity so much larger.[54]

The gulf between the supply-side popularizers and the economics profession's liberal wing was even vaster. In the most widely read liberal statement of economic policy in 1980, *The Zero-Sum Society,* Lester Thurow argued that what made the major problems facing the late-1970s U.S. economy (inflation, dependency on foreign oil, slow economic growth, over-regulation) difficult to fix was not the challenge of prescribing their solutions. It was that, in an economy of limits, every one of those solutions required that some sector of the population accept a significant reduction in its standard of living. Whatever gimmickry there was in Thurow's title, it caught the long-standing strain of pessimism in the mainstream economics tradition: the reflexive self-reminders that theirs was the science of tradeoffs and scarcity, that whatever the free lunch being hawked at the moment might be, it was never really free.[55] The achievement of the supply-side amateurs was to recapture the ground of optimism: to make the idea of the market synonymous with boundlessness.

At the outset, drawn together by issues of international currency stability, the supply-side publicists were anti-Keynesian more by conservative reflex than by analysis. Keynes had scoffed at Say's law, the early-nineteenth-century proposition that there could be no "general glut" of goods beyond the markets' capacity to consume. Like Keynes's political antagonists before them, the *Wall Street Journal* circle adopted Say's law as a statement of faith. "Supply creates its own demand" was the supply-side circle's free translation. Economically, it was a meaningless slogan, but it came to stand for a wholesale dissent from the project of steering the economy by manipulation of aggregate demand; a conviction that the goal of economic policy should be promotion of the conditions of investment, work effort, and business growth (the "supply side," they called it); and, finally, a confidence that the key brake to supply-side growth was the marginal personal income tax rate. Release that restraint, and the magic of markets would pull the economy out of all the rest of its troubles.[56]

It was not hard to locate a constituency for a general solicitousness for the "supply side" of the 1970s economy. A corporate lobby for business tax reduction had been gathering muscle since 1975, when the major business lobbying associations began holding regular strategic planning meetings in Washington, D.C. The American Council for Capital Formation, revitalized by the lobbyist Charls Walker in 1975, pressed for capital gains tax reductions. Through the American Enterprise Institute, the Harvard economist Martin Feldstein was finding a broad audience for his studies of the effects of capital gains and social security taxes on the long-term prospects for adequate capital formation.[57] At the grassroots, a new populist constituency, angry at the rising prices, added to the voices calling for tax reduction. Property taxes—subject to the whims of unanticipated reassessment schedules, sudden shifts in tax incidence, and the strains of inflation-fueled paper values—were its flashpoint. The first major grassroots property tax revolt was California's Proposition 13 victory in the summer of 1978, precipitated by clumsy reassessment policies in the Los Angeles region. By 1980, as the antitax rhetoric and organizational experience developed in California spread through the deeply troubled economy, tax-limitation movements had won victories in six more states.[58]

The federal income tax, by contrast, had not been the focus of a powerfully organized lobby. The National Tax Limitation Committee looked to constitutional limits on federal spending as its logical next step, not cuts in federal income taxes. The wealthy had long ago made their peace with high marginal tax rates through tax shelters and income-shielding devices. In Congress, a concern for inflationary "bracket creep" had begun to thread its way into tax bill debates, but the big issue was the balance between federal revenues and expenditures, on which the Republican party record on strict fiscal discipline remained strong. When the Kemp-Roth bill to slash federal income tax rates by 30 percent was introduced in 1978, proponents were able to line up a core of favorable witnesses, including a handful of maverick academic economists, two former Council of Economic Advisers chairs, and Alan Greenspan, then a private investment consultant. Feldstein filed a terse and studiedly neutral statement. But most of the business economists were skeptical. A "most dangerous . . . experiment," the Chamber of Commerce's head called it; "irresponsible and demagogic," First Boston Corporation's managing director cautioned. Not even Kemp-Roth's backers testified at the bill's hearings that it would set off an economic renaissance. What most of Kemp-Roth's supporters envisioned in the summer of 1978, rather, was a kind of jujitsu politics in which, in cutting off Congress's revenue stream, the voters would force a correspondingly drastic shrinkage in federal spending. To most of the business economists this was an act of "economic brinkmanship," and, risk managers by profession, they resisted.[59]

The task of organizing the tax resentments of the late 1970s behind the project of a massive cut in federal income taxes was, in short, no small project. Layers of conservative practice and conviction stood in the way. The *Wall Street Journal* group had no patience with the Republican party's traditional commitment to making spending cuts first. Jack Kemp heralded a new era of "dynamic" economic thinking that would leave behind the "static" balanced-budget thinking of the past. Laffer was famously sure that almost any tax cut would pay for itself, though almost no other professional economists agreed with him. The achievement of "the boys who cried Nirvana," as the *Boston Globe*'s David Warsh called them, was to force the tax cut bill past this impasse by inventing a new rhetoric of populist market optimism.[60]

Two writers figured essentially in this task. The first, Jude Wanniski, was the supply-side movement's Henry George, a self-taught economic publicist of one idea. Economics was so simple, he wrote, that children knew its essentials from infancy. Think of a coconut gatherer and a fisherman on a Pacific island trading goods with each other, and ask if either would work so hard if some agency were to reach in from outside to seize the last hour's worth of fish and coconuts. This was *The Way the World Works:* a society of economic nomads living in a world composed purely of individual labor and individual exchange. Drive the "wedge" of taxation into this system and people stopped working or slipped off the books into the barter economy. Release the wedge throughout the nations of the world, Wanniski wrote, and work and savings efforts would rebound and global peace and unimagined prosperity would bloom.[61]

Whereas Wanniski was the supply-side movement's gifted simplifier and panacea salesman, George Gilder, whose *Wealth and Poverty* shot onto the best-seller lists in early 1981, was its Walt Whitman, celebrator of the entrepreneurial future that tax cuts would bring. An even more marginal figure than Wanniski, Gilder was sure that the argument for diminishing returns was wrong and that the application of mathematics to economic enterprise from the early nineteenth century forward distorted the matter entirely. The idea of society as a zero-sum game, he wrote, "strikes at the living heart of democratic capitalism." Classical economics' fatal mistake, he wrote, had been to emphasize the static intersection of supply-and-demand curves rather than "the turbulent process of launching new enterprise." Tax cuts were not about greed, Gilder insisted, but about altruism. They were about the nurture of a new entrepreneurial "economy of faith," ready to leap from every innovator's imagination into economic reality if only the "doggedly obstruct[ive]" practices of government would get out of the way.[62]

These efforts to channel the economic resentments of the late 1970s into a vision of a reindividualized economy, hurtling on toward a limitless future, would have been bootless without institutions and patrons. Kristol opened the pages of *The Public Interest* to Wanniski's exposition of the Laffer curve in the winter of 1978 and helped Wanniski obtain a berth at the American Enterprise Institute. The Smith Richardson Foundation provided grants to enable both Wanniski and Gilder to finish their books.

Kemp and Bartley gave *The Way the World Works* a major boost in new right political circles and the nationally syndicated conservative newspaper columns. Their biggest catch was the prime optimist of 1980, Ronald Reagan, who made sure that a copy of *Wealth and Poverty* was presented to each of his new cabinet members. In the winter of 1981, as the administration's economists struggled to produce forecasts capable of integrating tax cuts on the Kemp-Roth scale into an economically plausible future, and the Treasury economists and the Council of Economic Advisers' economists were unable to agree on a coherent budget rationale, Gilder, the economic naïf, was commissioned to write the introductory section of the administration's *Program for Economic Recovery.* Although in the end Gilder's preface was not used, it was a telling story. In a pinch during the fierce debates over budget cuts in the winter and spring of 1981, when an unavoidable tradeoff reached the president for decision, Reagan's instinct was to believe that the economy, its entrepreneurial spirit unleashed by the new tax cuts, would surely bring in more revenue than his experts imagined.[63]

The supply-side publicists' accomplishment was broader than simply the capture of the president. The supply-siders spoke to a widespread public weariness with being hectored with hard choices and uncertain forecasts. They gave voice to a rising distrust in the capacities of public management. At bottom, they capitalized on the same circumstances that fueled all the new market thinking of the decade: the paradigmatic collapse at professional economics' center, the vulnerable record of the nation's economic managers and therefore the vulnerable record of governmental policy itself, the narrowing down of institutional society into word-pictures of isolated individuals, the hunger for self-administering economic rules, and the rising stock of simple ideas. Except for the setting into which it erupted, the supply-side case would hardly have gained a hearing in the op-ed pages and the congressional staff debates. In Gilder's purpled prose, Wanniski's "wedge," and the new president's vow to release the wellsprings of faith, work, and investment, the decade's revival of market ideology was yoked to a new optimism and a new constituency.

The frontier did not open up, of course, quite as Gilder imagined it. The linchpin of supply-side economics, the Laffer prediction that the income tax cuts would pay for themselves in a spurt of economic growth, did not materialize. Squeezed into recession by the Federal Reserve, the economy did not begin its cyclical recovery until 1983—by which point the annual federal deficit, which had once been the *bête noire* of Republican conservatives, had mushroomed to two and a half times its pre–tax cut levels. The unemployment rate did not fall back to its 1970 level until 1997. The cruelest betrayals of the supply-siders' predictions were in the two areas in which they were most confident of change: work effort, which grew only modestly, and domestic savings rates, which, despite the lessening of the federal tax "wedge," fell after 1981.[64]

But politically and ideologically, assumptions had changed. The Democratic party, abandoning its late-1970s hope for full employment legislation, turned to more modest plans for targeted industrial promotion and job retraining, and then, abandoning that, settled finally under Clinton for a program of North American free trade, a favorable investment climate, and tax credits for the working poor.[65] The Republicans, once the party of strictly balanced budgets, abandoned their past in favor of a new tax-cut populism. On the global stage, the promarket policies flowing out of Reagan's United States and Thatcher's Britain were already rippling outward through the agencies of international economic management. At the World Bank, where Robert McNamara had forcefully steered policies toward poverty alleviation and public sector development in the 1970s, his successors in the early 1980s, the banker A. W. Clausen and the chief economist Anne Krueger, were much more alarmed by "government failure" than by market failures. In alliance with neoliberal forces elsewhere, World Bank and International Monetary Fund managers now set lending conditions that routinely included privatization of public enterprises, trade deregulation, reduction of price subsidies, and relaxation of limits on foreign investments.[66]

Accelerated by the U.S. production of foreign graduate-trained economists, the universalistic rational-actor models of the graduate economics seminars diffused across large parts of the world economy. The term "monoeconomics" that Albert Hirschman coined for the phenomenon downplayed the sectors of resistance to the new "Washington consensus." But the notion that the path to growth for developing economies might be distinctly different from the guidelines for fully developed economies (an axiom of the developmental economics that Hirschman had helped elaborate) had all but evaporated. By 1983–1984, when under intense pressure from investors both the Mexican and the French governments abandoned their state-led economic policies, the near global dominance of the new political economy was clear. Faith in the wisdom and efficiency of markets, disdain for big government taxation, spending, and regulation, reverence for a globalized world of flexible labor pools, free trade and free-floating capital: this was now, despite the remaining holdouts, the world's dominant economic ideology.[67]

Markets transmitted economic desires and facilitated the production of wealth; in the newly regnant metaphors of the 1990s they did still more. At the beginning of the era, writing in one of the mid-1970s' most important books of social theory, *The Cultural Contradictions of Capitalism,* Daniel Bell had argued that the enormous productive capacities of markets went hand in hand with their destabilization of the very habits of bourgeois thrift and self-discipline on which capitalism itself depended. In the same vein, Bell's collaborator on *The Public Interest,* Irving Kristol, offered capitalism two cheers, not more, in the mid-1970s. Earlier still, Friedrich von Hayek had worried that the masses were becoming "strangers to the rules of the market," less and less imbued with its discipline and values.[68] By the 1990s, however, the dominant strain emphasized the naturalness and boundless freedom of markets. More efficiently than elections and representative government, they accomplished what theorists had imagined democracy to do. "Markets are voting machines; they function by taking referenda," Citibank's Walter Wriston wrote in 1992; they give "power to the people." Heralding the new global economy, Thomas Friedman wrote that markets had "turned the whole world into a parliamentary system," where "people vote every hour, every day." Unlike deliberative politics, markets were the realm of freedom. Loosed from institutions and power, they silently did their work: optimizing, signaling, making tangible the domain of choice.[69]

This was not the way markets had always been conceived. Varied and imperfect, sites of tradeoffs and compromise, markets had been imagined as indispensable to society, not as a metaphor for society as a whole. But from the temporary collapse of the Phillips curve and the monetarists' relentless exposure of the breakdown in the predictive capacity of Keynesian macroeconomics, to the unanticipated conjunctions of University of Chicago law and economics with the efficiency concerns of an inflationary era; to the rational expectationists' seizure of the implications of inflationary time and behavior; to the supply-side populists' success in channeling an inflation-fueled tax revolt into a federal income tax cut, a series of conjunctions between ideas, economic circumstances, and patrons had joined to push a newly abstracted and idealized concept of "the market" into the center of social and economic analysis.

Most novel about the new market metaphors was their detachment from history and institutions and from questions of power. As the market grew more abstract, society thinned out into highly reduced microeconomic mental pictures: Gilder's heroically independent entrepreneurs, Lucas's forward-looking utility maximizers, Wanniski's fish and coconut traders, the Coase theorem's rancher and farmer maximizing the public good as they stood on the courthouse steps. To imagine the market now was to imagine a socially detached array of economic actors, free to choose and optimize, unconstrained by power or inequalities, governed not by their common deliberative action but only by the impersonal laws of the market.

The new metaphors of markets and society were a heuristic myth, of course: a model of ideal action. Their "choice-theoretic" model of social relations had occupied a place somewhere toward the back of virtually every introductory university-level economics textbook in the 1970s, in the microeconomic section where abstract models of perfect competition were explicated. But in inducting students into the frame of economic analysis, the real-world complexities of the aggregate, institution-thick, "mixed" state-and-private economy had come first. As late as 1988, publishers resisted proposals to turn the formula around. Four years later, however, there was hardly a textbook publisher, even the publishers of so consciously liberal a textbook as Joseph Stiglitz's *Economics*, that was not scrambling to reverse the frame and put students' introduction to the idea of perfect competition first. The "fallacy of composition" fell out of the introductory economics courses.[70] In a series of elaborations and qualifications of the idea of perfect competition the rest of economic science now unfolded.

Nineteen ninety-two was the year in which the Samuelson textbook, its market share slipping and its once predominant command over the pedagogy of the subject eroded, turned its chapter order inside out and opened with microeconomics. The publishers advertised the "leitmotif" of the new edition as the "rediscovery of the market."[71]

3
The Search for Power

Power is everywhere; not because it embraces everything, but because it comes from everywhere.

Michel Foucault, The History of Sexuality

Power (whatever that much-used term means) . . .

Joseph Stiglitz, "Post Walrasian and Post Marxian Economics"

When John Kenneth Galbraith rose to deliver the presidential address of the American Economic Association in 1972, the angular Harvard professor and supremely self-confident adviser to presidents was arguably the most famous living economist in America. From *The Affluent Society* in 1958 to *The New Industrial State* in 1967, his critical accounts of capitalism's tendencies to underfund social goods and concentrate corporate control had been fixtures on the best-seller lists. Galbraith's thirteen-part BBC television series on the workings of capitalism in 1977 was to help goad the production of Milton Friedman's counterassertion of 1980, the PBS series *Free to Choose,* an iconic statement of the new market ideology.

An intellectual maverick among economists even at the height of his popular influence, Galbraith was a lightning rod for disciplinary resentments of many sorts. In an age of mathematical model building, he was a consciously old-fashioned institutionalist. He was deliberately out of step in the 1970s in defending the case for wage and price controls in season and out and for suggesting that the large business firms that dominated the modern economy lived in a world of administered prices and advertising-generated demand that had nothing seriously to do with his colleagues' idealized notion of markets. But Galbraith's theme in 1972 was not simply the ability of the largest corporations to dominate markets, politics, and desires. Failing to recognize power, he charged, economists failed to comprehend the institutional inequalities that pervaded economic life. "In eliding power," economics "destroys its relation with the real world." It "becomes, however unconsciously, a part of an arrangement by which the citizen or student is kept from seeing how he is, or will be, governed."[1]

It was an intemperate speech, delivered with Olympian scorn. By the end of the decade, the profession had responded by effectively reading Galbraith out of the ranks of serious economists. In the post-Samuelson universe, economics was about efficiencies and equilibriums, not power. It could incorporate a wide array of information costs and asymmetries. But power was not in its vocabulary. "Power has proved to be a disappointing concept," Oliver Williamson, the profession's leading neo-institutionalist, put the consensus view in 1993. "Power (whatever that much-used term means)," the neo-Keynesian Joseph Stiglitz reinforced the point on the eve of his appointment to the Clinton administration's Council of Economic Advisers.[2] In the models of market action that economists were elaborating with more and more intellectual confidence, concepts of domination and power receded to the margins—if, indeed, as Stiglitz's remark left open between its hanging parentheses, they retained any serious meaning at all.

Manifestly easy to feel, power is notoriously hard to describe and measure. It is both a category of domination—the means and institutions through which the will of some overrides the desires of others—and a category of inequality and differences in scale—a measure of the unequal capacities of wealth or influence or organizational resources that make domination possible. Power underlines the elements of coercion in social exchange: the monopolization of resources, the distortion of desire, the pinch of necessity, the coercion of consent, the extraction of obedience. The economists' reigning model of exchange stressed, to the contrary, the voluntary character of the act: without a sense of themselves as better off now with the results than they were before, no bargainers would come to agreement. The very definition of economic exchange constructed it as a realm of freedom.

But if power slipped out of the economists' categories, there were others ready to take on the task of finding an understanding of power adequate to the times. Political scientists, sociologists, historians, anthropologists, and popular forecasters of the future all wrestled intensively with the question. The outcome of their debates converged on no simple conclusion. In the discipline of political science, the search for an analytical language of power led toward tighter and tighter embrace of the rational-actor models flowing out of the economics departments. Among historians, the same search led to a virtual abandonment of the terrain of economics for new worlds of culture. Political conservatives, steeped in opposition to Marxian notions of history, reinvented and redeployed a Marx-derived language of class. Scholars on the left all but deserted class analysis to follow the ways in which power pervaded language, symbols, and consciousness. The futurologists, who had begun with a pervasive sense of constraint, abandoned the language of power altogether.

Down some of these winding paths, power fragmented, its bloc categories fracturing into smaller, individually situated micropolitical acts. Down others, power grew more diffuse, pervasive, and subtle. But in either case, the dominant languages for power grew thinner, less concentrated, and more difficult to grasp. The struggle for an adequate language of power was to prove much more difficult than Galbraith, preaching a message of institutional scale and domination to a deeply resistant economics profession, had imagined.

The age had begun with a sharp and insistent sense of power. The social movements of the 1960s had set new languages and new consciousnesses of power spinning across the political landscape. The radical movements raised power to an organizing slogan of the streets: Black Power, women's power, student power, Power to the People! In the contest between insurgent power from below and the vested power of the economic and political interests at the top, as activists on the left imagined it, history's fate would be decided.

Environmentalists in the early 1970s talked of power in different but equally insistent ways: as a corset of constraints that could not be violated over the long haul without disastrous consequences. The most widely read statement of the theme of resource exhaustion was *The Limits to Growth,* an early experiment in computer-modeled social extrapolation in 1972 whose Malthusian conclusions seemed to show a relentlessly expanding world population at the limits of its food and natural resources, indeed at the limits of economic growth itself.[3] Most pessimistic of all the early 1970s readings of the future was the economist Robert Heilbroner's meditations on the human prospect, originally published as a very long piece in the *New York Review of Books* in 1974, where Heilbroner mapped out a frightening scenario of global population explosion, the exhaustion and pollution of natural resources, and a proliferation of nuclear weapons and subnuclear warfare as nations found themselves unable to work their way out of their internal inequities and social tensions through rising economic growth.[4]

The recession of radical politics and the breaking of the stagflation crisis eased the apocalyptic readings of the early 1970s. But power persisted. Big government endured, resistant to the dreams of those in the Reagan coalition who had imagined that they might radically whittle it down in scale. New voting blocs appeared (new Christian right moral conservatives, blue-collar Reaganites, nascent greens, and consumerists) and older ones disintegrated, but bloc and interest-group voting remained the rule of politics.

The most striking change on the institutional landscape that Galbraith had surveyed was the movement of power from the megacorporations—the tightly integrated, market-dominating institutions that Galbraith had anatomized in *The New Industrial State*—to investment capital. The most famous businessman in America in the early 1980s was Lee Iacocca, the supremely confident auto industry veteran who had pulled Chrysler back from near bankruptcy in the hard times of the late 1970s. But an economy dominated by old-line corporate managers like Iacocca was already giving way to one dominated by brokers and deal makers, start-up entrepreneurs and venture capitalists, bond traders and arbitrageurs who dealt not in factories and mass-production goods but in capital itself. The first billion-dollar leveraged corporate buyout deal was closed in 1982. By the end of the 1980s, hostile and nonhostile corporate takeovers had profoundly altered the structures of business life. Firms and investors bought up other firms (or bought out their own), loaded them up with massive new debt, recirculated their assets through the booming high-risk bond market, managed them more leanly, or carved them into saleable pieces and spun them off, in a burst of mergers and acquisitions unequalled since the 1890s. Corporate managers who had once pegged their ambitions to corporate size, product, and workforce loyalty suddenly found themselves in the target sights of those who focused exclusively on share price and investor return. Capitalism's ceaseless, eternally churning processes of "creative destruction," as Joseph Schumpeter had called them, returned to the field of post–World War II corporate "Fordism" with a vengeance.

Against the often heated outcry against corporate raiding and trading, against the excesses of Wall Street and the hyperaggressiveness of its players, business school economists were quick to wrap the acquisitions and merger boom in the now dominant language of their discipline. The megatrades were, by their very nature, not bids for power but products of the markets' natural tendencies toward constantly greater efficiencies. Corporate managers who rested on ample reserves of capital padded their companies' expenses with unnecessary frills, they argued; grown flabby on profits, managers failed to hold a hard line against growing payrolls and higher labor costs. By contrast, highly leveraged debt loads released locked-up capital for better uses; the insistent need for high income to make good on that debt made managers more disciplined and more cost conscious; with their compensation repegged to the share price of their firms, managers' once divided allegiances were focused and simplified. In all these ways, economists rushed in to naturalize the shifts in business practice and structures and to ease them out of the moral categories of aggressors, greed, and victims.[5]

Still, power remained. The new regime of more aggressive and quickly acting investment capital, the financialization of management decisions, the precipitous rise and fall of corporate entities, the offshoring of production, and the decline of labor union membership: all this formed the new institutional backdrop on which the search for an adequate language of power would take place. It did not, in itself, dictate that it would be so hard to find.

The dominant reading of power in mid-twentieth-century America had been interest-group pluralism. On the fields of economy and politics, it was said, the best organized social interests competed ceaselessly for influence. Big business, big labor, and big government were the heaviest of the clashing interest groups. But there were many others with claims to extract from politics: old and entrenched ethnic elites, new immigrant voters and their political machines, regional and sectional interests, small business owners, agricultural and mining interests, commercial and manufacturing groups, professionals and bureaucrats, in a constantly shifting configuration of organized social and economic interests. To the question *Who Governs?*—as Robert Dahl in 1961 had titled the most widely influential study of authority, influence, and power of the post–World War II years—the dominant answer in postwar political science was that many social players did.[6] Multiplicity made democracy work: a field of competition so crowded, and the polity's sites of authority so multiple, that no single interest or interlocking set of interests, no power elite or ruling class, was capable of monopolizing it all. Even in the politics of a middle-sized city, like the New Haven that Dahl had studied, different social and economic groups prevailed in different arenas, checked and balanced by counterconfigurations of power. The genius of modern democratic societies, the pluralists argued, was not that they had found a way to disaggregate interest groups or to abolish power. It was, rather, that in setting power against power, interests against interests, they had constructed a balance of competing and countervailing forces whose very tensions kept the system whole.

That benign reading of fragmented power began to fray in the intensified social and political conflicts of the 1960s. As Americans of all sorts began to imagine that they were on the losing end of power struggles that had suddenly gone out of control, harder theories of domination flourished. Behind the overt processes of democratic politics, one now heard, lay hidden concentrations of power: cabals of backroom elites, webs of influence, an all-pervasive "system," new forms of class domination. On the left was a new interest in a line of argument that had run through dissident, Trotskyite Marxism focused on the bureaucratic-managerial class that, wresting power from the owners of money and property, was said now to manage and direct the key institutions of late-twentieth-century capitalism. A parallel line of analysis focused on the power of the experts and professionals who increasingly dominated the twentieth-century "therapeutic state": the doctors, psychiatrists, counselors, educators, and social relations experts whose baleful effects Christopher Lasch excoriated in *Culture of Narcissism*. The idea of a "new class" of managers and professionals, organized outside and beyond the original class categories of Marxism, played around both groups.[7]

What was unexpected in the history of "new class" theory was not that it should have risen out of the new interest in Marxist social analysis of the late 1960s left but, rather, its sudden, eager embrace by thinkers and

publicists on the political right. Rarely used in conservative rhetoric before 1970, it soon burst out everywhere. Irving Kristol injected it into his
op-ed pages at the *Wall Street Journal.* Robert Bork, Reagan's unsuccessful
Supreme Court nominee, blamed the sabotage of his appointment on the
forces of the new class. Attorney General Edwin Meese singled out the
new class for its thoroughgoing antagonism to the values of everyday
American citizens. A special section on new class theory made its way
into James Q. Wilson's American government textbook. "A spectre is
haunting the Western world," the conservative sociologist Peter Berger
reiterated the famous opening line of the *Communist Manifesto* in 1978:
"the spectre of the New Class."[8]

The spread of new class analysis among conservative intellectuals, for
whom denial of structural class divisions of any sort had long been an axiom of social thought, was partly the work of one-time radicals moving
right. James Burnham, the former Trotskyite whose *Managerial Revolution*
had provided 1940s readers with one of the formative statements of the
theory of bureaucratic-managerial domination, helped infuse a version of
the new class concept into William F. Buckley's *National Review,* where he
had become a regular writer in the 1950s. Irving Kristol moved from a
youthful immersion in Trotskyite politics to become the leading voice of
intellectual neoconservatism in the 1970s. *Commentary*'s Norman Podhoretz and the American Enterprise Institute's Michael Novak were refu-
gees from the 1960s left, bringing with them some of its verbal tics and
analytical style.

But there was more than mere displacement in the vogue of new class
analysis on the right. The subjects at the theory's center were no longer
the corporate managers of Burnham's early formulation. What conservative new class theorists put in their place was modern society's still larger
array of knowledge and symbolic workers: professionals, educators, cultural producers, and technocrats. Their surprising susceptibility to left
and liberal ideas in the 1960s had not been a passing fad, writers in the
new class vein argued. Rather, as rootless players in the system of production, owning neither property nor labor but only their skill in the manipulation of symbols, they had congealed as a class structurally hostile to
capitalism. The environmental and consumer movements, the welfare
state, the adversary culture and its denigration of bourgeois values, the
new permissiveness that saturated the media ("members of the new class

do not 'control' the media," Kristol wrote; "they *are* the media") were all bundled together as manifestations of the new class's interest.[9]

Above all, the new class found its interests in the big and growing state. Recognizing the weakness of its economic position, Kristol wrote in 1975, "the 'new class' . . . tries always to supersede economics by politics— an activity in which *it* is most competent—since it has the talents and implicit authority to shape public opinion on all larger issues." Symbols were its means of production, and capture of the state power was the object of its class interest. "What wealth is to a capitalist, what organization is to an old-style political boss, what manpower is to the trade unionist, words are to the new class," the neoconservative Jeane Kirkpatrick wrote. Colonizing big government, the professions, and the media, the new word workers sought relentlessly to expand their class base by undermining civil society's natural processes and the market's prestige, by exaggerating social problems so there would be more need for government-sponsored experts and professionals to rush in and set them right. At every opportunity they sought to expand the role of the state and in the process "to run the United States," as William Rusher put it in the *National Review,* "for the benefit of interests (notably their own, and those of a huge welfare constituency) conformable to that world view." The relentless expansion of the modern state apparatus, in these readings of politics, was not an adjustment to an increasingly complex society; it was a triumph of new class interest.[10]

Some of those close to neoconservative intellectual circles were not so easily convinced. Daniel Bell, Kristol's early colleague at *The Public Interest* and the sociologist who had done more than any other to point to the rise of the knowledge industry as one of the profound social events of the late twentieth century, found the new class a "muddled concept." It confused description of a mentality, he objected, with description of a tangibly rooted socioeconomic class. Burnham himself thought the term encompassed a rather "harum scarum crowd."[11] Others noted that the most rapid growth among knowledge workers in the postwar United States had not been among adversary intellectuals but among engineers and natural scientists, doctors and medical workers, lawyers in solo or corporate practice, economists and statisticians—few of them in government employment and most of them comfortably resident in the Republican party. Still other critics pointed out that Ronald Reagan, who from his radio days forward had lived and worked completely within the manipulation of symbols, was a perfect new class man—as, for that matter, were conservatives like Kristol himself, enmeshed in the project of developing what in strict class-analytical terms should have been impossible, a conservative counterintelligentsia of knowledge and symbol workers whose ideology ran at cross purposes to its class interests. By the early 1990s, Peter Berger had begun to suspect that the notion of a "quasi-Marxist class struggle" between the new class and the bourgeoisie had been mistaken in the light of subsequent blends of persons and values.[12]

But for all its limitations, the new class idea for two decades carried powerful intellectual traction. It packaged conservative resentments against the growth of state power in a language that seemed to carry sociological heft. It sharpened interest-group theory's emphasis on politics as a field of battle between structurally antagonistic interests. It explained what seemed otherwise so counterintuitive, the susceptibility to radical politics of some of the most well-educated of the 1960s young. It made plausible the strength of liberal voices in the universities and the media. It gave voice to an intuitive sense, running below conservative talk of the primacy of ideas, of the determinative effects of social position and of economic interests. Repeated with every tick of the "new class" phrase, a stripped-down Marx, a powerful sense of social aggregates, and a straightforward understanding of the relationship among class interests, power, and culture found its way incongruously into the rhetoric of modern American conservatism.

Alongside new class theory ran a second conservative reading of power, this one rooted not in dissident Marxism but in game theory and microeconomics. More precisely articulated than "new class" theory, it soon saturated the academic study of politics. Dispensing with aggregates, it bore down on the dynamics of self-interested individual political action, remapping the world of politics and legislative action as a field of individual preference-satisfying behavior. Power moves were everywhere in the economic analysis of politics. But what propelled those moves were not the needs of the bloc interest groups, as the pluralists had imagined it, or interests of a new knowledge class, but the microphysics of individual political action.

Given the imperializing ambitions of the age's economic theorists, their quickness to see preference-satisfying behavior everywhere, and their ingenuity at modeling it, it was hardly surprising that the dynamics of political behavior should have attracted the attention of economic modelers. As it happened, the pioneers in the economic analysis of politics were heavily weighted with figures deeply distrustful of politics and the state. Since the early 1960s William Riker at the University of Rochester had been using game theory models to analyze voting and legislative behavior as complex, advantage-seeking strategy games. At Virginia Polytechnic University, James Buchanan applied University of Chicago–style market-exchange theory to model the systematic propensity for legislatures operating under simple majority rules to overproduce public goods. Mancur Olson, a politically more ambiguous figure than the others, took apart the very idea of stable collective-interest formations by asking what individual calculus of gain could possibly induce individuals to offer dues and commitments to a trade association or a labor union. Free riding on whatever benefits others might extract was the cheaper strategy, Olson reasoned, and its distortions were pervasive. Behind all of these works stood the civic actor and legislator as calculator and self-interestedly "rational" actor, sniffing out advantages, cycling through tactically shifting alliances, extracting goods and resources from the political system, burdening collective action with private ends, maximizing reelection chances by carefully calibrated policy positioning.[13]

The new analysts of the microfoundations of politics brought the conservative strain in their politics to bear in their deeply pessimistic reading of the results. The favored strategic games in rational-actor models of politics—the prisoner's dilemma, Olson's free-rider problem, Garrett Hardin's tragedy of the commons, where existence of a free resource meant that no one had a stake in preventing that resource from being exhausted—all yielded, by their implacable logic, suboptimal results. At the most aggressive edge of the rational-actor models, in "public choice" political science, as Buchanan and Riker called their approach, politics was about nothing but suboptimalities. Legislators, it was said, cared only for their short-term individual interests. Legislative voting produced no consistent outcomes. Strapped to the "impossibility theorem" that Kenneth Arrow had posited years earlier to explain why under certain conditions different preference rankings could not be unambiguously aggregated, voting produced no majority will. Majoritarianism yielded, to the contrary, only "a fundamental and inescapable arbitrariness," as Riker put it, an endless, chaotic play of logrolling and vote cycling as factions won and lost control of the agenda. Given a different ordering of the sequence of votes, it could be shown, radically different results would come from the original preferences of legislators. Social movements, beset with free riders interested only in their own advantages, had no choice but to lobby for direct and narrow benefits to keep their members from melting away. "Rents"—the Buchanan group's covering term for every form of government-protected economic advantage—were pervasive. Still worse than rents themselves was pervasive "rent seeking," as Anne Krueger, who was to give the idea a powerful practical edge as the World Bank's chief economist in the 1980s, called it: the consuming, societywide, resource-squandering quest for government favors. To pass from the domains of economics to politics in the public-choice models was to pass from a market world in which self-interested behavior worked naturally for the good into a topsy-turvy world in which self-interest spawned endemic inefficiencies and capricious outcomes.[14]

Under the weight of these analyses the idea of governance as an expression of the public good all but evaporated. Riker and Buchanan were explicit in their methodological individualism. Phrases like "the will of the people" or "what society wants," Riker insisted, were meaningless and misleading figures of speech. In what Buchanan called the sciences of human choice, "the basic units are choosing, active behaving persons rather than organic units such as parties, provinces, or nations." The public interest was a mask. Government failure was endemic. The majority will was an unstable phantom. Impelled by these presuppositions, public-choice scholars pushed hard for schemes to limit the scope of political and government action and to restrict the action of majorities. Buchanan spent the last part of his career, like a latter-day John C. Calhoun, absorbed in countermajoritarian constitutional theory. Riker looked to tighter restrictions on legislatures by the courts. Even Olson urged that for economic growth and prosperity only stable property rights ultimately mattered.[15] "New class" theory gave conservatives a structural explanation for why they felt so marginalized in the early 1970s. In the application of interest-maximizing individual behavior to politics, by contrast, the aggregates did not clash, as they had for Berger and Kristol, but fractured out into myriad individual pieces.

Marginal to the discipline of political science in the 1960s, rational-actor models of political behavior, conceived from the microfoundations of calculated individual behavior up, swept into the universities in the next two decades. Rational-choice theory's ascendancy in the 1970s and 1980s was "meteoric," the political theorist Rogers Smith writes. "From the mid-1970s on, virtually all the nation's leading [political science] departments competed vigorously to recruit the leading scholars in rational choice." The percentage of articles based on rational-choice analyses in the discipline's flagship journal shot up from 5 percent in the 1960s to 33 percent by the mid-1980s. By the end of the 1990s, it was clear that the ascendant paradigm in political science departments had become the study of the microphysics of advantage with the individual at its methodological core.[16]

As rational-choice political science went mainstream, much of its earlier political coloring fell away. Model making was a game that people of all political persuasions could play; even Marxism, as Jon Elster undertook to demonstrate, could be reconstituted on the foundations of methodological individualism.[17] But even as the new model makers fanned out across the discipline, a certain pessimism about the possibilities of governance endured, absorbed from the disaggregative forces of the age. The withdrawal of voters from the polls as voter turnout declined through the 1970s and 1980s, the rise in individual ticket splitting among the voters who persisted, and the crowding of the field by single-issue advocacy and fundraising groups all reinforced the new models of voting as self-interested and cost-conscious action. The weakening of party discipline after the reforms of the early 1970s, the new frequency of governments in which the executive and legislative branches were controlled by rival parties, the diffusion of power to legislative committees and individual incumbents all mapped a new politics in which gamesmanship was endemic. Bluffs, gridlock, symbolic maneuvering, legislation under the threat of veto, legislation stuffed with particular goods for particular players: under the conditions of more open voter choice and volatility, these, more than ever before, were the inside games of politics. Modeling those actions with the mathematical and formal elegance that was its hallmark, the new political science turned from politics' external fields of socioeconomic interests and ideology to its messy internal games and processes. The very method of rational-choice analysis reflected the conditions it sought to illuminate.[18]

Other schools of political science, although they were hard-pressed for resources, did not disappear. With the slogan of "bringing the state back in," a cohort of political sociologists sought to turn the focus of attention to the ways in which the capacities of the state for public action structured the choices that governments made. Practical politicians stressed the renewal of collective ideological passions, which, by the mid-1990s on the conservative side of politics, had reinvigorated party discipline. Most of the era's introductory American government textbooks, sticking to the tested formulas of the past, gave beginning students barely a hint of the new game-theoretical work.[19] But on the research side of the discipline, the dominant trend was toward the microeconomic analysis of politics. In a field that had been distinguished by its attention to aggregates—the people, the public good, the dynamics of elites, the power of interests, the needs of the masses—the very aggregates themselves splintered. Power-seeking saturated the new analytical world of politics. It mapped a more pessimistic and harder-edged arena of action and counteraction than the interest-group pluralists had been able to conceive. But in the new models of politics, domination—the subjection of groups to the will of others—all but slipped out of the categories of analysis. As the egoistic, calculating, preference-optimizing, rational-actor models once distinctive to the economics faculties moved into the stock-in-trade of academic political science, the search for power disaggregated into a field of microplayers.

Even sociology by the end of the period felt the disaggregating pressures. Choice had never been a key word in the sociologist's vocabulary. The discipline's very understanding of the socialization of desire and the social nature of the self worked to undermine notions of an autonomous, preference-calculating self. Economics, it was sometimes said, explained choices; sociology explained why individuals had no choices to make. Certainly no other academic discipline had so large a stake in the macro categories of explanation: the power of collective norms and pressures of social conformity, the functional needs of society, and the systemwide effects of social strain.[20]

The most important conduit of rational choice into sociology, James Coleman, remembered in this context being "a Durkheimian from graduate school on." His major undertaking of the 1960s had been a massive quantitative study of school achievement, showing that the social backgrounds of students and the social composition of schools played a far larger role in students' learning success than did any calculation of individual effort. In his book *Power and the Structure of Society* in 1974, Coleman had written eloquently about the rise of the new giant corporate entities and the widespread feelings of powerlessness they evoked. But co-teaching an interdisciplinary seminar with Gary Becker at the University of Chicago in the 1980s, Coleman shifted analytical gears, setting out to construct a unified theory for sociology from the purposeful, preference-maximizing individual actor outward. Too much social theory consisted of "chanting old mantras and invoking nineteenth-century theorists," he objected. Social theory's holistic analyses "float at the system level without recourse to the actors whose actions generate that system." Rational choice and methodological individualism presented, in contrast, the "one paradigm that offers the promise of bringing greater theoretical unity" and clarity to the social sciences.[21]

Coleman's *magnum opus* of 1990, *Foundations of Social Theory,* with its three-hundred-page section on the "mathematics of social action," stuffed with the equations, matrixes, and Edgewood boxes familiar from economics and rational choice political science, was not the era's only contender for a new synthetic vision for sociology. In Britain, Anthony Giddens elaborated a theoretical intermediation between social structures and individual action that he called "structuration." In France, Pierre Bourdieu remapped social action in terms of power-saturated fields and "habitus."[22] Even Coleman insisted on the importance of power. But from a socially and institutionally imbedded phenomenon, power, like every category in Coleman's scheme, slipped down to its actor-centered microfoundations. Power was a trait, a possession, not a social relationship, as Coleman glossed it. It was the value of all the resources an actor controlled on the fields of social exchange. William Riker had set the pattern in 1973, positing power as an index measure of each individual legislator's capacity to exert influence over other legislators. The search for power's social face—in the monopolization of social resources, the giantism of institutions, the pressure of interest groups, the rise of new class antagonists—came down to a measure of individual capacities.[23]

For liberal and left intellectuals, the search for power took a strikingly different course from the one that led to new class theory or the microphysics of politics. They, too, began with a sense of big, contending aggregates locked in battle for social domination. Whereas conservative readings of power fragmented into calculi of individual choice, left readings kept alive the social dimensions of power. But as liberal and left intellectuals moved past the interest-group pluralists' straightforward, street-wise understandings of power—*Who Gets What, When, How?* as Harold Lasswell had posed the question—to unmask power's more hidden faces, their readings diffused.[24] Power grew less tangible, less material, more pervasive, more elusive until, in some widespread readings of power, it became all but impossible to trace or pin down.

The left intellectuals' quest had begun with a burst of confidence. Fueled by the social movements of the late 1960s, Marxian frameworks that had been all but taboo in the 1950s sprang into currency in the social sciences. Not since the 1930s had categories drawn from Marx had so large a force in American intellectual circles. A particularly revealing site was the new social history that was gathering force among left and liberal historians in the early 1970s. The project of recovering the historical "agency" of common people propelled peasants, workers, women, slaves, bread rioters, labor organizers, midwives, seamstresses, sailors, the multitudinous subjects of colonization, domination, and empire into the history books. New areas of history opened up: village studies, social mobility studies, gender studies, studies of households and production sites. A new American working-class history was integral to that project. Digging into the underside of American economic history, a generation of younger labor historians, many of whom had themselves been swept up in new left politics in the 1960s, began to recover a long, crisis-strewn history of struggle from below, as workers fought back against the new regimes of work, the arbitrary power of employers, and the injustices and inequities of everyday life. By the very terms of their project, they wrote the categories of class and domination into the core of American history.[25]

If there was a book that loomed over this work and shaped it by the power of its ideas and passions, it was E. P. Thompson's *Making of the English Working Class*. A huge, sprawling narrative of English working-class life in the late eighteenth and early nineteenth centuries, it cast an influence over the new history of the working class that, especially after the publication of an American paperback edition in 1966, is hard to exaggerate. Thompson's story was the story of a class in the making. From the first stirrings of London radicals in the early years of the French Revolution through the devastating disruptions of the work customs and livelihoods of artisans and craft workers, Thompson undertook to show how a new consciousness of class had taken hold among English working people. Out of the labors of handloom weavers, pamphleteers, Luddites, and chapel preachers—but, above all, out of experience itself—was forged a collective sense of self: "an identity of interests as between themselves, and as against their rulers and employers." Before socialism, before the spread of the factory system, long before the organization of the Labour Party, a class had brought its own self into being.[26]

All the new American labor historians read *The Making of the English Working Class,* and most of them worked, in one way or another, within the field of force it cast. Class had no predesigned shape in Thompson's scheme, no singular ideological language. Against more determinist Marxist readings of history, which saw class conflict as the virtually automatic result of revolutions in systems of production, Thompson insisted on the active, contingent, historical element of class formation. "The working class did not rise like the sun at an appointed time," his opening page famously announced. Being "present at its own making," it did not need to wait for conditions approved post facto by the Second International or the Comintern.[27]

The liberating effect of these moves on the new American social historians was profound. Thompson's pages had reached out beyond the traditional sources of labor history to embrace (as the historian William Sewell put it) "popular political and religious traditions, workshop rituals, backroom insurrectionary conspiracies, popular ballads, millenarian preaching, anonymous threatening letters, Methodist hymns, dog fights, trade festivals, country dances, strike fund subscription lists, beggars' tricks, artisans' houses of call, the iconography of trade banners, farmers' account books, weavers' gardens, and so on in endless profusion."[28] In like fashion, the new historians of the American working class moved out beyond the labor unions and radical political movements to trace resistance to the new regimes of wage labor and market exchange in a immense variety of keys: not only in strikes, demonstrations, and picket lines but also in recalcitrant customs, autonomous cultures, rituals of working-class manliness, and solidarities of neighborhood and family. The overt language of that resistance sometimes took the form of artisan radicalism; at other times, defense of autonomous manhood, populist anger at the hidden cabals of power, or CIO industrial unionism. Rejecting suggestions that there was only one historical path to class formation and that the American experience was an exception to it, historians showed, in a wealth of detail, that power had organized itself along the axes of class, even in America.[29]

When the mantra "race, class, and gender" came into currency in the history departments at the end of the 1970s, in short, the term "class" seemed to be one of the least problematic parts of it. But just at the moment when new class theorizing was solidifying among conservative intellectuals, the analytical language of class on the left was unexpectedly starting to fall apart. Part of the difficulty stemmed from the very multitudinousness of the social history project in its American setting. Bringing hitherto invisible working people into history's pages unveiled myriad stories of action and resistance, but consolidating those stories, as Thompson had, into a single narrative of class formation proved a daunting project. Reconstituted with each new massive influx of rural workers—African slaves, Irish peasants, Mexican *braceros,* and multitudes of others—the American working class seemed never to be "made" but to be always simultaneously in different phases of its development.

Worse, it was a class historically at odds with its own self—starkly divided (like American society itself) along lines of race, gender, region, religion, and ethnicity. The California workingmen's movement of the 1850s had its origins in fierce opposition to Chinese immigrant labor competition. Defense of the privileges of whiteness ran as a constant thread through labor movement history. Even the socialists at the turn of the century imagined a separate (and far from equal) labor sphere for women.[30] A sense of "an identity of interests as between themselves, and as against their rulers and employers," as Thompson had put it, was historically only one of the axes on which a working class had been organized in the United States, and not always the most salient one. By 1984, when a conference of leading historians called to work out a common paradigm for the new labor history fell apart in a fog of misunderstandings and collisions over the interplay of class, race, and gender in working-class history, it was clear that the category of class was not easily going to hold the historians' search for power. The struggle to preserve customs and values in the face of a dominant economic elite lay ev-

erywhere in the historical record, one of the conference's organizers concluded; but the manner of that resistance dissolved into an "eclectic pattern of behavior and belief that defied any attempt to identify a coherent
vision or purpose among working people."[31]

The still knottier issue at the DeKalb conference in 1984, however, was
a category that, putatively softer and more ephemeral than the others,
cropped up everywhere in the debate, and that was "culture." Between
class positions, interests, and power lay not simply ideologies, or superstructures of ideas (as orthodox Marxists had thought of them) but also, it
was said, something much more malleable, pervasive, elusive, and yet,
paradoxically, power-saturated. Thompson himself had been instrumental in injecting the concept of culture into the new labor history. "The
making of the working class is a fact of political and cultural, as much as
of economic, history," he had written. "It was not the spontaneous generation of the factory-system. Nor should we think of an external force—
the 'industrial revolution'—working on some nondescript undifferentiated raw material of humanity, and turning it out at the other end as a
'fresh race of human beings.'" The nascent English working class had experienced its economic dislocation and political repression through the
cultural traditions it already possessed: the moral economy of the villages,
the egalitarian traditions embedded in religious dissent, memories of a
just price and customs of the trade, and the new revolutionary talk of the
rights of free-born Englishmen. It was in mobilizing these older cultural
resources to bring its own experience to consciousness that "the working
class made itself as much as it was made."[32]

These were fighting words for British Marxists, and they drew Thompson into a series of heated polemics between the materialist claims of
structure and softer claims of experience and culture.[33] Among the younger American labor historians, however, the embrace of "culturalism"
was quick and enthusiastic. It formed an outlet for the politics of consciousness that had run so strongly through the new left, the civil rights
movement, and early feminism. Culture gave historical "agency" to the
common folk of history, who had so little else to offer. Scholars of
African-American life were already deep into explorations of the ways in
which culture and consciousness had kept personhood alive during the
torment of slavery: the ways in which folklore, tales, rituals, customs, the
coded language of song, and religious experience had created a sense of

nation and community even among the most thoroughly dispossessed.[34] Culture gave history's forgotten people the resources for resistance and agency.

But if culture was a conduit for power, it was a conduit that could be just as effectively used from the top down as from the bottom up. Political theorists like Steven Lukes and Murray Edelman were already worrying the question of power's culturally veiled faces. They manifest themselves in the strikingly different ability of groups and persons to articulate their needs and desires—not only to get their claims onto the agendas of social action but even to bring them to expression in the first place. Language and political spectacle, rather than fostering collective action, could construct mass quiescence.[35] Radical culture critics had been bringing the same critique to bear on the institutions of mass culture industry since the 1930s.

What gave a new analytical frame to the idea of the powers of culture in the early 1970s was the publication of extracts from the prison notebooks of the Italian Marxist Antonio Gramsci, hitherto almost entirely unknown in English. Written in fragments between 1929 and 1933 in language coded enough to circumvent the scrutiny of Mussolini's jailers, their concern was to release Marxism from the weight of its materialist and historical determinism, to reimagine society as in a state of continuous struggle between its hegemonic and emergent historical blocs, in which the organization of self-directed labor institutions and critical consciousness were key to the working class's successful seizure of power. As Gramsci's mass of writings was redacted and translated for American readers, however, Gramsci's theories of revolution were tacitly subordinated to the threads in the prison notebooks in which he had reflected on the opposite question: How do the rulers rule? By domination through violence and the coercive powers of the state, surely. But also and still more pervasively, Gramsci reflected, by the less choate power of "hegemony."[36]

As the British labor historian Gwynn Williams put it, in what was to become the single most quoted English-language paraphrase of Gramsci, hegemony was "an order in which a certain way of life and thought is dominant, in which one concept of reality is infused throughout society in all its institutional and private manifestations, informing with its spirit all taste, morality, customs, religious and political principles, and all social relations, particularly in their intellectual and moral connotation." Hegemony was the power of the dominant class not only to impose its social categories on others but also, and still more, to make its systems of meaning come to seem the natural order of things, so that by insensibly absorbing that order the many consented to the domination of the few.[37]

Worked out by a revolutionary in a prison cell, the concept of cultural hegemony came into American history attached, ironically, to the most reactionary of regimes, the slave South. The conduit for this already extracted Gramsci to the United States was the historian Eugene Genovese. The most prominent Marxist historian of his generation, he had already worked in the material history of slavery; in the 1990s, as he began moving further and further to the political right, he was to focus on the intellectual history of the Southern master class. But when Genovese's *Roll, Jordan, Roll: The World the Slaves Made,* a massive study of master-slave relations in the antebellum South, appeared in 1974, its focus was on the power of culture. Even as the slave owners built their rule on coercion and enforced it by the brutality of the lash and sale, Genovese argued, slave masters knew that their power had to be founded on more than this. It rested, ultimately, on their ability to diffuse throughout plantation society a sense of a paternal relationship between masters and slaves so strong that, even as slaves rejected and resisted it, they could not escape it.[38]

The heroism of the slaves lay not in their production of an autonomous culture, Genovese insisted, and he ridiculed the sentimentality of those who imagined it might be so. The heroism of the slaves was to take the terms of planter paternalism and press them as hard as they could: to bargain for reciprocal favors, to pin the masters to the terms of reciprocity that their claims of rule implied, to wrest from the masters' paternalism the masters' recognition of the slaves' own humanity. Within a system of hegemony as tight as this, accommodation and resistance could not be pried apart. "Accommodation itself breathed a critical spirit . . . and often embraced its apparent opposite—resistance," Genovese wrote. At the same time, the slaves' very strategies for survival and resistance "enmeshed them in a web of paternalistic relationships which sustained the slaveholders' regime."[39] The world that the slaves made opposed the masters' world at myriad points, but, nevertheless, it was made within that world's dominant "concept of reality." *Roll, Jordan, Roll,* it was quickly recognized, was in almost every way the great American counterpart to Thompson's *Making of the English Working Class* in its massive scale and the reach of its imagination, the eloquence of its prose, and the intensity of its politics. But it differed in one major respect: whereas Thompson had shown how culture could be the resource of the oppressed, Genovese had shown how, in the most subtle and penetrating ways, culture could be simultaneously, and even more importantly, the tool of domination.

The Gramsci that Genovese brought home to the slave South occasioned no small measure of skepticism and dismay among historians on the left. The leading labor historian Herbert Gutman dismissed *Roll, Jordan, Roll* as "functionalist"—preoccupied with the world the masters' fantasies had made, not with the real experience and, still less, the real historical agency of the slaves.[40] In a symposium on the "powers of historical pessimism" in the late 1980s, most of the labor historian participants were still resistant to the idea that Gramsci, the revolutionary strategist, should now be called in as a kind of coroner for an "inquest into the blasted hopes of the past."[41] But for all the unease it generated and for all the unanswered questions it raised—whether the mark of cultural hegemony was to be found in its power to mute the expression of contrary opinion, or to sweep up every expression of opposition into its own terms, or simply to strand its subjects immobilized in a state of contradictory consciousness—the term quickly become part of the toolbox of historical analysis. Even Thompson, turning to the ways in which the eighteenth-century English gentry sustained its power as its economic bases were crumbling, took up the line of argument. "To say that [ruling class control] was 'cultural' is not to say that it was immaterial, too fragile for analysis, insubstantial. . . . but to prepare for analysis at the points at which it should be made: into the images of power and authority, the popular mentalities of subordination."[42]

That Gramsci-provoked concern with "the popular mentalities of subordination" by the mid-1980s haunted the project of an American working-class history that was already fracturing out under pressure from historians of race and gender. Reagan's and Thatcher's abilities to peel away part of the labor vote from the Democratic and Labor parties, the steady decline in U.S. labor union membership, and the shrinking of the progressive political coalitions all took a toll on the confidence with which a history of the making of an American working class had begun. Stuart Hall's characterization of Thatcherism could have been written by any number of his American counterparts: "Far from one whole unified class outlook being locked in permanent struggle with the class outlook of an opposing class, we are obliged to explain an ideology [Thatcherism] that has effectively penetrated, fractured, and fragmented the territory of the dominated classes."[43] As the concept of class proved a more fragile vessel than had been imagined, as the efforts to recover the agency of history's common folk fragmented, as the political solidarities of the present partially dissolved, and as management of symbolic politics grew increasingly sophisticated, the domain of culture seemed to loom increasingly large.

The dominant language of power on the intellectual right was straightforward and economistic; on the left, where simple notions of base and superstructure might have been expected, the language of power had over the course of a decade and a half become less distinct and material, more vested in culture and consciousness, more contradictory and pessimistic.

While the new labor historians struggled to come to terms with the powers of culture, others were racing through what was soon being called the "cultural turn" in the social sciences with a sense of sheer intellectual excitement. One aspect of that turn was the positing of "languages" as ideologically charged systems of meaning. The concept was most forcefully launched in J. G. A. Pocock's immensely influential reading of the history of the American Revolution as a running battle not only between rival social blocs but also between rival language systems: a "civic republican" language of virtue and the common good, on the one hand, and, opposed to it at every turn, a language of individually possessed rights and counterbalanced interests. In England Thompson's heirs in the new British labor history began to argue that language was no transparent register of social experience but a thing of structure and power in its own right. Language "is an independent non-referential system," Gareth Stedman Jones was writing by 1980. It "set[s] the limits of what can be thought or apprehended at a given time."[44]

The still more influential turn in the late 1970s and early 1980s, however, was not toward linguistic structuralism but toward the looser categories of symbolic anthropology. The key figure here was the anthropologist and gifted essayist Clifford Geertz. In the same way that Thompson and Genovese fought their way out of the structures of orthodox Marxism to their readings of history, Geertz was a refugee from, and always in quarrel with, more determinative systems of social analysis. He had begun working within the structures of modernization theory, Marxism's liberal counterpart, trying to comprehend, and nudge forward, the prospects for sustained economic growth in the village and peasant societies of Indonesia.[45] But in the mid-1960s he began to set aside the social science language of structure and development for the ethnographic and literary threads that had been present in anthropology from its travel and encounter narratives forward. Not to explain distant societies but to "read" them; not to stretch them on the frames of analytical social science's categories but to try to unpack their socially performed meanings: this was interpretive anthropology's "foundational" departure from the past. To do ethnography, Geertz wrote, was to find oneself faced with "a multiplicity of complex conceptual structures, many of them superimposed upon or knotted into one another, which are at once strange, irregular, and inexplicit." It was like trying to read "a manuscript—foreign, faded, full of ellipses, incoherencies, suspicious emendations, and tendentious commentaries."[46]

In contrast to the imperial pose of the structuralist social sciences, there was something compellingly modest in Geertz's redescription of the work of anthropology. One guessed at meanings, knowing that one's "most telling assertions are [the] most tremulously based," that the more deeply cultural analysis goes "the less complete it is." Cutting culture down to size, the Geertzian move was to take an event, a recurrent ritual, like the betting play at a Balinese cockfight that his most widely read essay made famous, and, weaving reportage and academic concepts so artfully into "thick description" of the event-as-text that they could not be pried apart, "draw large conclusions from small but very densely textured facts." But as Geertz brushed by rival ways of reading societies—as systems of production and exchange, systems of authority and behavioral rules, systems of social differentiation and inequality, structures of cosmic belief and ideology—the audacity of Geertz's "foundational critique" of anthropology could not be missed. There were no structural foundations in Geertz's system: nothing but a play of texts, meanings, and semiotics all the way down.[47]

These were controversial claims among anthropologists, who proceeded to fight intensely over them.[48] But with the publication of the hauntingly evocative essays of *The Interpretation of Cultures* in 1973, the influence of Geertz's work ramified out through the interpretative social sciences. Turning their backs on the data sets and regression analyses of macrosociology, younger sociologists went local and ethnographical. In historical studies, analyses of carnivals, court day rituals, cat massacres, pardon tales, etiquette forms, civic processions, and courting customs—"history in the ethnographic grain," Robert Darnton termed it—burst into books and articles, many of which had been incubated in conversations with Geertz or in his seminar on symbolic anthropology at the Institute for Advanced Study.[49]

The structural social history that the editors of the *Journal of Interdisciplinary History* anticipated in 1981 in a reburst of economic history, historical demography, and quantitative history gave way, instead, to local stories, to colorful and particular events. That turn away from institutions and structures—the "thinning of the social," William Sewell called it—was the product of many dynamics. Some of the cultural turn was driven by a desire among historians and social anthropologists to flex their narrative and literary muscles, to think of their craft in terms of texts, stories, and readings. Another part stemmed from the way in which, once one had broached the idea of the symbolic construction of experience, the core evidence of the social sciences became itself an object of culturalist interpretation. If census returns were a text rather than simple reflections of social reality, if the very categories of social inventory were products of cultural construction, as Joan Scott showed with the categories of labor in nineteenth-century France, whose terms were no more stable than language itself, then all the aggregate compilations and correlations made from them came under a shadow of suspicion. Yet what fueled the cultural turn, most surely, was the fact that for a generation that had grown up in the wake of the media revolution of the post–World War II era, in a sea of texts and meanings, amid a symbolic bombardment that was now part and parcel even of politics, the notion that culture floated insubstantially on top of more basic structures of economic or demographic power made less and less intuitive sense. Power lay in meanings, in the very ability of a cultural form to give shape to the welter of experience, to spin reality into its forms.[50]

Not many of those who took the cultural turn put it precisely that way, but when Geertz himself at the end of the 1970s turned directly to questions of power, domination, and authority it was to virtually dissolve the distinction between power and thought. Precolonial Bali, the site of Geertz's inquiry, was a society saturated with power relations: between villagers and lords, between warring petty rulers, between the taxed and the tax takers. To the Marxist historian Karl August Wittfogel, it was a society whose dependence on central irrigation sucked power upstream into a form of "hydraulic" despotism. Turning to those structures in *Negara: The Theatre State,* in 1980, Geertz did not dismiss the play of power. If at the middle and bottom levels of society it was much more fragmented than others had seen it, at the top of Balinese society the ritual displays of the court—their grand, hours-long, symbolically laden cremation ceremonies, attended by tens of thousands of spectators—radiated power with burnished clarity. But as Geertz unpacked what he called "the semiotic aspects of the state," it was to dissolve any distinction between power and meaning, domination and display. The state did not exist behind the mask of its theater. It was itself its mask. The state existed as a "theatre designed to express a view of the ultimate nature of reality . . . theatre to present an ontology and by presenting it, to make it happen— to make it actual." To try to comprehend precolonial Bali as a system of coercion and resource extraction, masks and exploitation—"the great simple" to which modern Western political theory clings, Geertz wrote— was to misunderstand it utterly. Classical Bali comprised "an alternative conception of what politics is about and what power comes to. A structure of action, now bloody, now ceremonious, the negara was also, and as such, a structure of thought."[51]

The orphic sentences that Geertz's critics found maddening in his writing rolled out in *Negara.* "The real is as imagined as the imaginary." "Power was not allocated from the top, it culminated from the bottom." "Pomp served power, not power pomp."[52] All the way down Geertz's new lines most anthropologists and historians were not willing to follow.[53] But the cultural turn, the rise of thick description and the interest in reading reality as a text, was not simply a mark of a new analytical fad, or a device with which to fish for new readers, or a loss of nerve for social science history. It represented a new sense of how power was formed and exercised: not only in structures of class and society, and not only in the dominant classes' ability to make their view of the world seem inevitable and natural, but in meaning itself, in the very tremulous stuff of culture.

These tensions in liberal and left intellectual circles as writers strained to hold in focus the social dimensions of power even as power, in their hands, became less and less material, were made particularly visible in the American attraction to the figure who was to become most closely attached to the concept of power by the 1980s: the French philosopher and historian Michel Foucault. Like many of the influences that were to come to the United States from France, Foucault entered through a kind of time warp. He was essentially a figure of the 1960s; by the time he emerged as an intellectual superstar, lecturing to overpacked crowds at the University of California at Berkeley and elsewhere in the early 1980s, his major writings (*Folie et déraison*, 1961; *Les Mots et les choses*, 1966; *L'Archéologie du savoir*, 1969; *Surveiller et punir*, 1975; and the first volume of *Histoire de la sexualité*, 1976) were already well behind him.[54] There was nothing stable in Foucault's quest to trace out the workings of power or the shifting terms into which he tried, from moment to moment, to contain it. But in that quest and its reverberations in the United States, the difficulty of finding a language for power adequate to the era came acutely into focus.

Foucault's work began with institutions; prisons and their analogues were, in one way or another, his lifelong obsession. His first big book, *Madness and Civilization*, opened by evoking late medieval Europe's leprosariums: thousands of institutions of segregation and confinement, vacant now that leprosy had largely disappeared from Europe, but waiting, "soliciting with strange incantations a new incarnation of disease, another grimace of terror, renewed rites of purification and exclusion." Waiting, in short, for those who were going to be classified as the insane. From the end of the seventeenth century until Philippe Pinel ordered the chains chiseled off the mad at the Asylum of Bicêtre in the 1790s, Foucault wrote, a "great confinement" of the insane had swept through Europe. Driven out of the villages, the mad were simultaneously driven out of the imagination, as the men of reason labored to drive a wedge between madness and rationality, as if those two, inextricably linked and haunted by each other, belonged to altogether different forms of being. Only when that act was complete, only when the insane had been so thoroughly enwrapped in the rational language of the diseased, the abnormal, and the Other, that their imprisonment was certain, Foucault argued, did the physical chains on the fools and madmen fall away and the great confinement become redundant.[55]

The anti-Enlightenment stance of *Madness and Civilization* was to be a constant in Foucault's writing through each of his shifts in subject and analytical vocabulary. From imprisoning institutions he swung next to the prison house of language, just as linguistic structuralism was cresting in France in the mid-1960s. Like the unchaining of the mad at Bicêtre, Foucault argued, the Enlightenment had freed its human subjects only to recontain them within its logics and systems of classification. The discourses of the new human sciences cast their web over every aspect of humanity. Discourse classified, regulated, divided, and archived; it created the very "subject positions" out of which its subjects spoke.[56]

Breaking off his studies in discourses, Foucault turned back to the history of institutions. In *Discipline and Punish: The Birth of the Prison* (1975), bodies, practices, and (for the first time) power moved into Foucault's analytical center. Once, he wrote, power had been in the grip of sovereigns. In the king's name, the bodies of criminals had been torn apart on the rack; confessions had been violently extracted and retribution exacted. But since the end of the eighteenth century power had no longer tortured and dismembered bodies; it now normalized and surveyed. Like the army, the hospital, the school, and the factory, the prison refabricated its human material. It broke down and reengineered the human body, drilled and habituated its movements and its behavior. The construction of the "case," the inscription on the body of certain norms of propriety and health, the constant supervisory "gaze" under which the new human subjects were disciplined—these were the practices of power. Power's object was not obedience but, rather, something more insidious: the drilled and docile human body, "the disciplinary individual," "normal" and "knowable man."[57]

Even as American readers labored to assimilate Foucault's description of the prison into late-1960s critiques of institutions of "social control," however, Foucault's mind was already moving elsewhere, away from institutions altogether. Power was manifest not only in the disciplining of bodies, he now urged in essays and interviews, but also in the technologies of knowledge and the regimes of truth that power created. Power of this sort did not radiate out from an administrative center. The word "governmentality" entered into Foucault's vocabulary to signify the ways in which the new disciplinary regimes pervaded civil society, "penetrated [it] through and through with disciplinary mechanisms," "invested" (like parasites) its sites and practices. It was a mistake to think that individuals stood outside of these ever more widely diffused effects of power to be repressed or coerced by it. "The individual is not to be conceived of as a sort of elementary nucleus, a primitive atom, a multiple and inert material on which power comes to fasten or against which it happens to strike, and in so doing subdues or crushes individuals. In fact, it is already one of the prime effects of power that certain bodies, certain gestures, certain discourses, certain desires, come to be identified and constituted as individuals." The very self was a product of "power-knowledge," constituted in the discourses and practices of identification: subjectified and subjugated in the very same act.[58]

By Foucault's last writings, power had seeped out of sites and structures until it was everywhere. When he turned to write of "biopower" and the infinitely complex regulations and self-regulations of sexuality that Foucault saw at its heart, it was to refuse all the older vertical understandings of power. Power was present throughout—insidious, "capillary" in its effects, inserting itself into the actions, the discourses, "the very grain of individuals." It came from "everywhere," from below as well as from above, produced and circulated through every point. Power was "not something that is acquired, seized, or shared." "Let us not look for the headquarters that presides over its rationality . . . [nor] the caste which governs, nor the groups which control the state apparatus, nor those who make the most important economics decisions." There was no exteriority to power: even the points of resistance that were everywhere, formed "in the same place as power" itself, were not outside it.[59]

From the first, Foucault's readings of power evoked strongly critical reactions among American intellectuals. Reviewing *Discipline and Punish* in 1978, Clifford Geertz objected to its unrelenting pessimism, to the way in which each moment of apparent progress led only to new forms of unfreedom, like stairways in an Escher drawing that folded back upon themselves. Even those sympathetic to Foucault's critical project recoiled at his apparent undermining of all normative fixed points. In an exchange with Noam Chomsky in 1971 in which the two found much common ground in their readings of the "oppressions" of the modern age, Foucault had refused entirely to engage with Chomsky's discussion of the principles of "justice," which Foucault (to Chomsky's bewilderment) dismissed as of no analytical help at all.[60]

Foucault's notoriously difficult prose, full of abstractions and neologisms, constantly shifting categories, its clauses and synonyms piled up impenetrably into one another, added to the obstacles. Power shifted shapes in his writings. "Foucault calls too many different sorts of things power," the political theorist Nancy Fraser wrote in frustration at the point at which Foucault ultimately arrived. The literary critic Edward Said had been one of the first to adopt Foucault's concept of the imprisonments of discourse. In his powerful and provocative book *Orientalism* in 1978, Said had mapped the unspoken rules of Western writing about the Orient to show the ways in which its conventions, tropes, and descriptions had become absorbed into the very technology by which the region was studied, imperialized, and dominated. But Said, too, worried that in his last books "Foucault's use of power moves around too much, swallows up every obstacle in its path (resistances to it, the class and economic bases that refresh and fuel it, the reserves it builds up)." It obliterated intention, conflict, and agency. "In human history," Said wrote, "there is always something beyond the reach of dominating systems, no matter how deeply they saturate society, and this is obviously what makes change possible."[61]

And yet, despite their critics and difficulties, Foucault's books and essays were texts with which every interpreter of modern society had to contend. In 1996 *Contemporary Sociology* published its pick of the ten most influential books of the previous twenty-five years. Said's *Orientalism,* Geertz's *Interpretation of Cultures,* and Foucault's *Discipline and Punish* were all on the list.[62] Foucault's ability to cross into American academic culture was partly a product of the skill of his English-language decoders and the persistence of his American publisher, Pantheon Books. It was also partly a result of the very difficulty of the Foucauldian vocabulary, which, like the model-making demands of rational-choice political science, acted as a magnet for young scholars eager to accumulate intellectual capital.

If Foucault's accounts of insidious and inescapable power gained traction, however, it was also because there was something discernibly recognizable in them. By the end of the 1970s, the normalizing professions *were* ubiquitous, ensconced not only in institutions (hospitals, schools, social work, and psychiatry) but in the very self-scrutiny of the babycare book and diet manual. The acts of classification and investigation that were the mode of science *were* also processes of control, which not only categorized the self but also helped profoundly to constitute it. The ubiquitous practices through which subjectivities were structured *were* as clear an articulation of power as the organized interest groups and power blocs that had once been taken as power's primary manifestation. When in the late 1980s and early 1990s a growing number of American intellectuals took up Foucault, pushing past his exaggerations, opacities, and obscurities to write about governmentality, the microphysics of power, or power-knowledge, about decentered and disembedded power, there were not only losses of analytical clarity but gains as well.

Yet ultimately Foucault's readings of power entered the scene across an intellectual terrain prepared by the earlier dematerializations of power. "Culture" was not in Foucault's vocabulary; power was to be found not in consciousness or ideology, he insisted, but in tactics and strategy. But in their rejection of structures, their disaggregation of power, their stress on the power/knowledge juncture, Foucauldian readings of power entered a field already primed to receive them. Those who worked within Foucault's vocabulary were never more than a minority among the social scientists. Empirical studies of social structures, interest groups, institutions, influence, and money all persisted. The hard as well as the soft faces of power remained. But the seriousness with which Foucault was taken up in America—to be read, imitated, rebutted, or qualified—meshed with the larger tendency toward subtler and more insidious understandings of power. Foucault's flight from the linguistic structuralism, Geertz's quarrel with structural anthropology, and the new labor historians' flight from base-superstructure formulas were, in that sense, of the same piece.

What then was power? The class theorists on the left and the right had imagined power instantiated in the material structures of class. The neo-Gramscians had imagined it hanging, like a veil over the eyes of the many, in the dominant class's construction of reality. Geertz and the cultural historians had vested it in rituals and theaters of meaning. The rational-choice political scientists had located power in the strategies and resources of individual actors. With the transit of Foucault's work and reputation into English came a much subtler language of power in all its minute and capillary workings. Power had moved decisively into the spheres of culture, ideas, everyday practices, science. But if power relations were everywhere and saturated everything, not only investing individual subjects but producing them, if power were indistinguishable from resistance, incapable of being held by any identifiable group or institution, unlinked in any sense to "agency," had not the long, complex search for power's ever more subtle faces succeeded, at last, in finding nothing at all?

The debates over power were not resolved at the era's end. The often knotted intellectual exchanges between the theorists of power had no popular textbooks to disseminate them: no Milton Friedman or John Kenneth Galbraith to bring them to a larger audience. But a register of sorts could be found in the books of social forecasting that poured out of the general publishing houses as the age moved on. They had carried a sharply pessimistic streak in the early 1970s. Exhaustion of physical and cultural resources was a haunting theme, as the heavy-industry phase of human history came up against the vise of external constraints. Difficult choices were a standing motif. Even the systems analyst Herman Kahn, who was to weigh in strongly against the Malthusian forecasts of *The Limits to Growth*, had added a chapter to his own book *The Year 2000*, outlining a half dozen more realistically possible "Twenty-First Century Nightmares."[63] The prospects for domination did not overshadow these readings of the future. Their preoccupations were, for the most part, more elemental: the imbalance of population and global resources, the threats of war, the acquisition of adequate social expertise. But when it came to the power of circumstances, the futurists of the early 1970s saw its presence everywhere.

In the midst of this debate about circumstances, power, and human frailty was one partial outlier: Alvin Toffler's *Future Shock* of 1970. Toffler, like Irving Kristol and Daniel Bell, had been steeped in enough radical sociology in the 1940s to know the power of structures. He had written for the labor union press and then on labor relations for *Fortune* magazine before setting out with his wife, Heidi, as a freelance author and futurist in the mid-1960s. *Future Shock* was a loosely connected set of inquiries into what Toffler saw as a society swept up in accelerated, historically unprecedented change. As the future collided into the present, transience was the rule. It was manifest in the throwaway goods of modern societies, the career-switching and lifestyle shopping of "modular man," the corporations' bypassing of rigid organizational charts in favor of temporary task forces, and the trend toward serial, temporary marriage.

In a wealth of anecdote that shot *Future Shock* onto the best-seller lists, Toffler piled on the signs of "the death of permanence." But there were, nonetheless, stark "limits" in Toffler's vision of the future: the limited capacity of people to absorb endlessly accelerating change, the psychic overload of headlong social transition. "Change is life itself," he wrote. "But change rampant, change unguided and unrestrained, accelerated change overwhelming not only man's physical defenses but his decisional processes—such change is the enemy of life." *Future Shock*'s cautionary conclusion may not have grabbed readers' attention as strongly as Toffler's accounts of disposable paper wedding dresses, rentable children, and transient marriage, but he clearly meant it seriously. Technological change needed to be regulated, democratically debated, and collectively managed if the negative consequences of future shock (malaise, neuroses, free-floating violence, and dizzying disorientation) were not to overwhelm its subjects.[64]

Catapulted into fame by *Future Shock,* Toffler came back to its themes in a second huge best-seller in 1980: *The Third Wave.* Despite the economic shocks of the intervening decade, the energy crisis, and the eruption of new social issues into party politics, Toffler's vision remained much the same as before. Everywhere permanence was breaking down. The hierarchies of industrial society were crumbling. The computer was dissolving the factories. The media were de-massifying. Nations were becoming less and less relevant. Diversity and choice were multiplying. For those still living in the era of high industrialization, the third wave of the new postindustrial civilization had broken over their heads in a confused and eddied mass. "Super struggle," the "mental maelstrom," the "frenzy of nations"—Toffler still played with neon headlines on the shock and perils of change. But this time the focus was not on limits or on the collective management of change. It was on hope: on the new flexibilities to be anticipated as the great historic structures of power and circumstance all dissolved at once.[65]

In the book that cashed in most successfully on the social forecasting market, there was hardly a whisper of power or domination at all. John Naisbitt's *Megatrends* of 1982 stayed on the top-ten best-selling nonfiction book list for a year, compared with *The Third Wave*'s twenty-six weeks. In bullet points and punchy prose, it broadcast the tropes Toffler and others had popularized: the transition from an industry-based to a knowledge-based society, from hierarchical structures to networks, from centralized corporate decision making to smaller, more entrepreneurial units, from representative government to participatory governance. "The computer will smash the pyramid," Naisbitt promised. "The participatory corporation" was at hand. "From a narrow either/or society with a limited range of personal choices, we are exploding into a free-wheeling multiple-option society." The pessimists were wrong; the limits-talk of the 1970s had fastened on an illusion. Structures were smashed. As Naisbitt summed up the lessons of futurism a decade later: "The great unifying theme at the conclusion of the twentieth century is the triumph of the individual."[66]

It would be hard to exaggerate the contrast between the conclusions to which popular social forecasting had come and the knotted and winding debates over power that had taken place in the universities. In public choice theory, democratic governance was deeply problematic; individuals were players in games shot through with suboptimal outcomes. For the futurologists, democracy sprang naturally out of the network society, and individuals were society's new sovereigns. In Foucault's readings of power, discourses circulated with terrifying effect; for the futurologists, information democratized and liberated. Academic readings of power, on both the right and the left, sustained a strongly pessimistic thread. By the 1980s, the popular futurologists were selling an intoxicating hope. The chasm between these strains could not have been wider.

And yet, as the decade's search for power was drawn away from the old-fashioned terms of interest-group politics, as both Marxist and non-Marxist understandings of big social structures lost their force, as those who studied power turned increasingly to power's smaller and actor-centered dimensions, or to its less tangible forms and symbolic manifestations, receding from grasp even as its consequences inflated, the common thread in the two patterns could not be missed. Power fragmented and diffused; as its means became more subtle, its social dimensions grew thinner and more difficult to define. The terms for power that had been available as the era began became less graspable, less easy to employ. Power remained as it always does: instantiated in institutions, inequalities, and constraints. But the search for words and analytics for power and domination, which began so confidently, seemed ultimately to have found fragments, traces, and infinitely receding horizons.

ble of bewildering appropriations, crossovers, and choices. Rap, with its heavy load of angry, black, urban authenticity, caught on in the teen cultures of white suburbs. At white rallies in defense of the Confederate flag, observers spotted T-shirts on black power themes: "You Wear Your X and I'll Wear Mine." Younger black writers celebrated the in-between, "mulatto" character of black arts and music as the "New Black Aesthetic."[83] At the same time, the marks of race were also deeply static. The Rodney King riots, the sustained race-loyalties in voting, the endurance of race-marked inequalities and subordination, the starkly different sympathies of the black and white Americans who followed the O. J. Simpson trial, the continued pull of the idea of a black cultural nation, the power of racial-political entrepreneurs on both sides of the black-white division, all spoke to deep, sustained structures of history, power, and culture.

In all these ways, race did not in the least disappear. But despite the social weight bearing down upon its categories, they had nonetheless changed. The fissures within African-American society—always large—were more sharply configured than before. The efforts "of black intellectuals, artists, and leaders to impose provisional order on the perplexing and chaotic politics of racial identity," as Michael Eric Dyson put it, intensified.[84] Most striking was the way in which, through every facet of the arguments over race, the claims of the past had become more attenuated. Wilson's claim for the declining significance of race was an argument not only about society but also about sharp historic discontinuity. In the "color-blind society" project, amnesia was a conscious strategy, undertaken in conviction that the present's dues to the past had already been fully paid. The positioning of race in quotation marks both pointed to race's social and historic origins and slipped consciousness of those sources into a certain marginality.

"Identities are the names we give to the different ways we are positioned by, and position ourselves in, the narratives of the past," Stuart Hall wrote.[85] But from *Roots'* vividly imagined braid of memory and racial solidarity in the mid-1970s to the "post-essentialist" formulations of the early 1990s, the growth of more complex understandings of identity was also the retreat of history. A culture reshaped in the choices and present-moment preoccupations of a market-saturated society had transposed the frame of argument. In a liberation that was also the age's deficit, a certain loss of memory had occurred.

5
Gender and Certainty

Precisely because "female" no longer appears to be a stable notion, its meaning is as troubled and unfixed as "woman."

Judith Butler, Gender Trouble

Vulgar relativism is an invisible gas, odorless, deadly, that is now polluting every free society on earth.

Michael Novak, Awakening from Nihilism

In the early 1990s, when his bristly Afro and oversized glasses made his face, staring intently from the cover of *Race Matters*, a familiar feature of the bookstores, Cornel West was asked to compare his reading of race with the Afrocentrism of Molefi Kete Asante, who was also in the news at the time. The two agreed, West replied, in their critiques of white supremacy and in the stress they put on the importance of self-respect among people of African descent. But there they parted. Asante posited a unified field of African culture that is "alien to me," West said. "For him, notions of a solid and centered identity are positive. I revel in fluidity, in improvisation, in the highly complicated and paradoxical. . . . I begin with radical cultural hybridity, an improvisational New World sensibility. . . . I'm not for a solid anything."[1]

It was a quick exchange, but like the debates over fluid markets and decentered power, it carried more than casual significance. Choice, provisionality, and impermanence; a sense of the diffuse and penetrating yet unstable powers of culture; an impatience with the backward pull of history—these were the emergent intellectual themes of the age. The new terms joined the older frames of social thought in incongruous conjunctions. West the jazz-talking social democrat, Toffler the ex-Marxist business consultant, Reagan the Tom Paine–quoting bearer of the Cold War's legacy: for different purposes, each found himself dipping into the new era's common bank of metaphors.

And yet the emergent thread that ran in such intricate patterns through the era's debates was, at the same time, the point of deepest cultural contention. To release and destabilize not merely goods and fashions but "everything"—tradition, certainties, truth itself—was, for other Americans, a source of fear and outrage. Not until 1991, when James Davison Hunter's book *Culture Wars* put the title phrase on every op-ed page, did that unease acquire a general name.[2] For the next decade the term served as a banner for partisans, a verbal crutch for journalists, and the focus of a flourishing industry among academics seeking to explain its novelty and dynamics. In fact, cultural wars in which highly polarized moral values flooded into partisan politics had a long history in the American past. But that did not make their effect in the age of fracture any less important. They helped to mobilize conservative churchgoing Americans into new alliances and new political battles. They split university faculties into feuding intellectual camps. They stoked strident school board contests. They made the fortunes of best-selling books. Across the last quarter of the twentieth century, the emergent talk of fluidity and choice grew in tandem with contrary desires for centers and certainties, each drawing on the other's energy.

The culture war, the war "for the soul of America," as the conservative television commentator Pat Buchanan was to call it at the Republican National Convention in 1992, was a contest across a broad range of issues.[3] It was a battle over schools and school prayer, over the reach of federal regulation into local affairs, over "secular humanism" and presentiments of cosmic war, over the effects of immigration and the recuperation of a religious language of patriotism. It was a struggle over literary theory: over the stability of language, the determinacy of principles, and the relationship between signs and things. It was a contest over schoolbooks and word lists, over canons and university course requirements. It was, James Davison Hunter argued, a battle over the very foundations of morality: between those who thought of ethics as adaptive, progressive, and socially constructed and those who thought of morals as fixed, timeless, and non-negotiable.

But above all, in ways that historians of these culture clashes have only begun to realize, it was a battle over women's acts and women's and men's natures. Of all the certainties whose cracking seemed to culturally conservative Americans most threatening, the destabilization of gender roles and gender certainties set off the sharpest tremors.

The modern feminists' struggle for new terrains of freedom, their crusade to radically enlarge the arenas for women's actions and desires, was just moving into high gear when the age began. Born in the social and cultural struggles of the 1960s, the movement to liberate women from the gender constraints of the mid-twentieth century unsettled every facet of social life and social debate. Feminists fought to make space for women's authentic voice, to release it from its external and internalized censors. They shattered a raft of gendered social barriers in the economy, politics, and culture. They added important dimensions to the analysis of domination and power. Their example helped foster a parallel rethinking of men's inner nature—and indeed, of assumptions of gendered and sexual nature altogether. In all, they destabilized with power and effect.

As the age began, very few feminists imagined that the challenge to gendered norms and modes of domination might ultimately destabilize the category of woman itself. The turn that many leading feminist intellectuals were to take in the 1990s, abandoning visions of a common sisterhood for more fractured readings of womanhood and more pessimistic readings of culture and power, seemed barely in the cards in the early 1970s. The alliance that some of them were to make with poststructuralist French theory, as they sought to unmask the deep workings of gendered power, was not yet on the horizon. Nor was the bigger battle over flux and certainty, norms and "nihilism," that was to spin out from these contests across both popular and academic culture. Yet as these struggles for voice unfolded, the women's movement and the culture wars were to be inextricably bound together. In complicated ways, they were parts of the same story.

The era's debates over women took place amid a cascade of changes in women's lives. Most striking was the massive restructuring of the paid labor force. Between 1970 and 1980 the labor force absorbed six million mothers of infant and school-age children, as women left full-time family- and housekeeping, whose confinements and frustrations had been the focus of Betty Friedan's savage critique in *The Feminine Mystique* in 1963, and took up waged and salaried work. The destabilization of marriage was another striking manifestation of change, as age of marriage rose, codes of sexual reticence cracked open, and the divorce rate skyrocketed, peaking in 1979 at two and a half times its mid-1950s level.

Drawing on the momentum of the legislative victories of the civil rights movement, gender inequalities that had long been fixed in the law were dismantled in a rush of court decisions and legislative changes in the late 1960s and early 1970s.[4]

In this context of upheaval and change, the ambitions of those who spoke for the revitalized feminist movement of the early 1970s ran deep. Like the campaign for racial rights and freedoms, feminists' aspirations for change were, from the beginning, shot through with practical and ideological divisions. And yet for all the inner tensions of feminism in the 1970s, certain powerfully integrative intellectual threads ran through it. The concept of patriarchy, feminism's contribution to structuralist under-standings of power, was one of them. Exactly how patriarchy arose and how it was maintained was a point of controversy in the books that pro-pelled the idea into feminism's social-structural vocabulary in the late 1960s and early 1970s. For some, it was a labor system rooted in men's expropriation of women's unpaid family labor; for others it was a sys-tem through which men gained domination over women's reproductive powers by trading women as commodities in marriage and kinship ex-changes; for still others, it was a system of outright physical domination constituted in rape and sexual violence. Whatever its roots, however, pa-triarchy was a globe-spanning system of power that could not be re-duced to Marxist understandings of class, or understood as simply the grip of ancient tradition, or comprehended through mere social-role the-ory. Muscling into other analytics of power, it recast power's structural faces into the era's new race/class/gender formula.[5]

Upon the bodies of women, feminists argued, patriarchal power pressed not only the domination of men but also the socially constructed straightjacket of gender. Gender, as feminist intellectuals elaborated the term, was not biology. Gender was a prison house of roles and expecta-tions, ways of feeling, experiencing, and behaving that arrayed itself as natural and pseudo-biological. As such, it constrained possibilities not only for action but also for desire itself. Gender not only constrained choice; it produced "people who claim to choose what they are supposed to want, and claim to want what they have."[6]

To extricate women from these confinements, feminists in the early 1970s drew heavily on the work of bringing the hidden transcripts of women's experience into the open. Consciousness raising was their method of discovery. Joining together to tell stories of their private lives, women found themselves startled and inspired by the common threads they discovered in what they imagined to be their peculiar circumstances. Consciousness raising made the personal collective and political. It gave the idea of "experience" a powerful place in the 1970s women's movement. It shaped what feminist organizers thought of as woman's voice, liberated from the pressures of gender that had suppressed and distorted it. In the process it made solidarities: sisterhood where (it was said) only fragmented, male-identified, household-isolated, and family-absorbed women had existed before.[7]

The hopes that feminists invested in constructing a voice in which the word "we" could encompass all women, despite their differences, can hardly be exaggerated. In literature, Elaine Showalter called for literary criticism that would set aside the "androcentric" critical tradition that men had forged (disguising their own partial experience as normative) and create a feminist critical tradition grounded in "the questions that come from *our* experience." The poet Adrienne Rich wrote lyrically of a gathering of women across the globe that was transforming politics, sexuality, work, and intimacy: "Today women are talking to each other, recovering an oral culture, telling our life-stories, reading aloud to one another the books that have moved and healed us, analyzing the language that has lied about us, reading our own words aloud and to each other," seeking "to name and found a culture of our own."[8] In one of the most widely read women's studies books of the age, Carol Gilligan took on cognitive psychology's reigning claim that the only path to moral growth was the path that led from infant selfishness to abstract and lawlike moral reasoning—a dominantly male pattern that men had falsely imagined as universal. There was a path to moral development, more commonly traversed by women, Gilligan argued, that spoke "in a different voice," a voice rooted in "the feminine experience and construction of social reality" which foregrounded relationships, obligations, and care.[9] Through all these formulations of the feminist "we," the difference of all women from all men ran as a powerful thread. Women's difference flowed from a "female culture of emotion, intuition, love, [and] personal relationships," as a radical Detroit women's collective manifesto had put it in 1971, in a solidarity waiting to be consciously born.[10]

For some activists, feminism's new sense of voice, patriarchal power, and sisterhood flowed into a cultural and sexual identification of women with women that represented the movement at its most vital and intense. Lesbianism had had a long but largely closeted history; now it burst forth openly within feminism. Adrienne Rich was a particularly visible evangelist of the new language of a women-indentified "we," celebrating a broad array of "forms of primary intensity between and among women, including the sharing of a rich inner life, the bonding against male tyranny, the giving and receiving of practical and political support."[11] "Difference" feminism, this was called by its critics, who thought that in cutting off potential alliances with men, in creating an archipelago of women-only spaces, "difference" feminists were only cooperating in their own marginalization—imagining liberation to lie in embracing the stereotypes of nurture and care that had so long tacitly imprisoned them.[12] Still, the most influential books of the 1970s and early 1980s women's movement weighed in heavily on the side of the common threads in women's experience and their differences from men: Carol Gilligan's *In a Different Voice* (1982), Mary Daly's *Beyond God the Father* (1973), and Adrienne Rich's *Of Woman Born* (1976).[13]

Beneath these aspirations, beneath "the dream of a common language" among women, as Rich termed it, ran the realities of division and contention. At the cutting intellectual edges of feminism, women's writing collectives dueled with manifestoes and countermanifestoes. Caucuses organized and split apart, vied with each other over members, tactics, programs, and interpretations of the struggle. Minimalists with their eye on concrete legal changes clashed with maximalists, eager to transform the culture of patriarchy from the ground up; within both camps the tension between a desire to build up the identity of woman and the need to tear down the confining category of "woman" recurred, in a fissure that, in Ann Snitow's words, "runs, twisting and turning, right through [feminist] movement history."[14]

The complexity of gender politics' terrain was further exacerbated by the countermobilization of women who felt their social standing and ethics assaulted by the new feminism. Politically they had been barely visible when the campaign to codify women's legal equality in an Equal Rights Amendment (ERA) had sailed through its congressional endorsement in 1972. Phyllis Schlafly, the writer and organizer on the Cold War Catholic right who was to become the most visible spokesperson for the new counterfeminist politics, was still almost wholly absorbed in mobilizing awareness of the Soviet threat when the 1970s began. The ERA initiative, however, galvanized Schlafly to shift her energies to the new sexual-cultural front. Her Stop ERA, drawing on Schlafly's extensive contacts and mailing lists, leapt into the fray in 1972 in one of the first demonstrations of new right politics. Statehouse ratification battles over the ERA drew in other morally traditional women, often mobilized through their churches. Fueled by nightmare scenarios of the ERA's legal and practical effects, the counterfeminist campaign did not significantly diminish the ERA's popularity in the polls. But by 1974, after two years of initial victories in the states, ratifications abruptly slowed as legislators backed off, nervously, from what had now become a site of controversy.[15]

From the beginning, then, internal and external dissension shaped the context of late-twentieth-century feminism. Still, when the national women's movement organizations, with congressional support, turned their energies to a mammoth convention to celebrate the International Women's Year in 1977, and in the process spur the Equal Rights Amendment to its final victory, their sense of confidence could not be missed. The national women's conference brought some 20,000 delegates, observers, and reporters to Houston in a mood of high optimism to make (as the organizers put it) a "life-changing and history-changing event." Rosalynn Carter, the wife of the sitting Democratic president, Betty Ford, the wife of his Republican predecessor, and Coretta Scott King, the widow of the civil rights' martyr, joined relays of torch runners and thousands of delegates in reaffirming their endorsement of the ERA. With only three states left to ratify the amendment, its ultimate passage seemed to the Houston delegates unstoppable. Already the convention majority was pressing beyond the ERA with resolutions calling for comprehensive child care, full employment, new visibility for women in the government and the arts, national health insurance with special provisions for women's health needs, and a serious intervention against violence inflicted on women and children. Throughout the developed and underdeveloped world the delegates envisioned new women's movements pressing back against the forces of militarization and exploitation.[16]

Across town in Houston, the Stop ERA forces assembled a mammoth counterconvention of their own. There "pro-family" women rallied to protest the "radical feminist" threat they felt in the official national women's conference—the congressionally authorized "Marxist/lesbian" circus, as Beverly LaHaye styled it. There were many anti-ERA women in several of the state delegations at the national women's conference as well, where they kept up a strenuous floor fight before finally walking out to join the other conservative women across town. Among the dozens of planks the majority voted down was an amendment to the convention's resolution on education offered by a Nebraska delegate. In its escalating phrases, the proposal caught something of the larger moral-political controversies already in the air. The schools, it urged, should be required to teach "respect for a republican form of government, the free enterprise system, parents, all authorities, and absolute values of right and wrong."[17]

Within the feminist majority at Houston, other potential disruptions of sisterhood were on display. Actively seeking delegates from racial minority backgrounds, the Houston organizers opened up their scripts to interruption by dissident voices, by women who did not necessarily see women's issues, allegiances, and identities in the same terms as the white, well-educated women who dominated the organizing committees. In the giant exhibit hall, feminist affinity groups of all sorts put their aspirations on display.

And yet, shot through as it was with tensions and oppositions, the project of holding feminism's contending ideas and elements together still seemed possible in 1977. In a gesture of solidarity with lesbian feminists, the Houston delegates endorsed a plank calling for an end to discrimination on the basis of sexual preference. Even Betty Friedan, who had fought off the sexual-preference issue as a distraction from women's core needs for well-paying work and legal equality, endorsed the statement. Laboring deep into the night, the black, Hispanic, Indian, and Asian/Pacific women delegates rewrote and radically expanded the "minority" women's plank. The next morning, in a moment of intense emotion, the delegates voted overwhelmingly to embrace the minority women's statement. Women's claims to equality and women's claims to a culture and experience of their own could still be fused in 1977. Sisterhood, as the delegates' witness made clear, could be palpably felt. The project of finding voice and solidarity took heroic work; it did not flow automatically out of women's being. But for most of the Houston delegates in 1977, voice and solidarity still seemed achievable.

Ten years later, the dream of a common language for women had virtually disappeared. The essentialist assumptions of the 1970s women's movement lay under deep feminist suspicion. Confidence in an emerging global sisterhood had given way to smaller, more splintered movements. The very categories that had framed feminist analyses of society and self yielded to challenge. On the ground of day-to-day opportunities for women, the loss of confidence was less noticeable. The daughters of 1970s feminist activists took for granted rights—entry into jobs and political office, admission into universities and medical schools, protection against domestic violence and overt wage discrimination—that their mothers had scarcely imagined. But feminist intellectuals found it harder and harder to frame the questions of experience and power that been so urgent only a few years before: to speak in woman's voice, to represent her experience, or even to say what woman was.

Feminism's intellectual remaking after the end of the 1970s was partly a story of political stalemate and opposition. Ratification of the ERA, which had seemed a foregone conclusion to most public opinion pollsters, was blocked in the outstanding states, one by one, by the newly mobilized counterfeminist organizations. When the extended ratification deadline for the ERA elapsed in 1982, feminism's broadest common plank gave way. Repudiating a platform tradition that went back to 1940, the Republican National Convention dropped its support of the ERA in 1980; the same convention endorsed an anti-abortion plank, the first ever to appear in any political party's platform. The news magazines of the mid-1980s were full of talk of a new "postfeminist" mood among women—a revived emotional absorption in families and motherhood and a reluctance to embrace "feminism" as a label for one's own concerns. The 1980s, in Snitow's words, were feminism's years of "frustration, retrenchment, defeat and sorrow."[18]

But the stronger forces that strained the concept of sisterhood came not from defeat—which was far from total, as much of the substance of the ERA moved, without constitutional amendment, into law and practice—but from the growing difficulty of holding the feminist alliance together. One mark of the strain was the opening up of the fissures of race and ethnic difference that had been held together with such high emotion at Houston. The contrast between the experiences of the white suburban and college women who set the tone of the early 1970s women's movement and the experiences that working-class, African-American, and immigrant women brought to the women's movement was not merely a matter of difference. The deeper injury, it was increasingly said, lay in white feminists' unspoken, casual use of the women's "we." It lay in their suggestion that their own experience was general, unmarked by color; that there was a single, tacitly white, women's history and women's voice waiting to be found. The same unspoken assumption by which men thought of their experience as universal and normal—as simply the human experience—infused the thought of white feminists, their critics objected, who imagined their experience as representative and universal: as the condition of woman.

The challenge was not new, but it now spilled over into virtually every women's forum. "I see a lot of people who think because we are women that in fact all of our issues are the same. And that is erroneous," the African-American feminist and musician Bernice Reagon told a women's gathering in 1977. "We are separated by class, race, and all of those things put a strong stamp on us. . . . Every time you see a woman you are looking at a human being who is like you in only one respect, but may be totally different from you in three or four others." In the writings of Audre Lorde, bell hooks, and Alice Walker, in the Kitchen Table Press's collections of the powerful and eloquent voices of black women writers *(Home Girls)* and women writers of color *(This Bridge Called My Back),* the conversation held together at Houston broke into fragments. The search for the common grounds of women's experience increasingly fell apart into more particular experiences.[19]

The increasingly vocal challenge to the category of women along lines of race and ethnicity was one way the dream of common sisterhood came under new strain. The other was a painful split over sexual desire and commercial pornography that, in different terms, damaged the essentialist assumptions of 1970s feminism. That men exploited the bodies of women by framing, objectifying, and eroticizing them for their own pleasure and domination had been a common early theme in feminist conversations. When Catharine MacKinnon and Andrea Dworkin put that assumption into high theory and practice in the late 1970s, arguing that sexual objectification was the opening through which male domination, sexualized hatred, and violence inexorably flowed, there was nothing altogether unexpected in the project. But their determination to put into law not only new sexual harassment codes but also antipornography statutes, and their readiness to work with cultural conservatives to achieve that end, clashed head on with the belief of others in the movement who saw sexual expression as integral to feminism.[20]

The conflict came to a head at the 1982 Barnard College conference on the "politics of sexuality" as speakers defended the multiple possibilities of women's sexual pleasures, including domination and even pain, while antipornography feminists picketed the conference in a sense of outrage that feminists could fall into the traps that male sexual desire had laid for them. Charges of betrayal and disloyalty flew from both sides. At stake was not only the willingness of antipornography feminists to cooperate with the moral conservatives who had just successfully torpedoed passage of the ERA; not only the assumption, expressed through much of lesbian women's culture that women's sexual nature was essentially gentler and more relationally grounded than men's. What was also and still more painfully at stake was whether one could speak of women's nature at all if, when it came to sex and bodies, women's desires were just as diverse as men's.[21]

As differences triggered consciousness of still other differences in a cascade of disaggregations, the sharing of private experiences that had been, since the late 1960s, the women's movement's distinctive organizing technique now seemed only to exaggerate the difficulty. Writer Mary Louise Adams remembered how moved she had felt at a feminist gathering when one by one the participants had identified themselves as a married, heterosexual, African-American feminist; a white, married, childless, middle-class, suburban, college-educated, professional feminist; and so on until, as the list of qualifying adjectives grew longer, more precise, and more varied, she began to worry that the common noun, woman, might simply disappear. Anticipating sisterhood and solidarity, anticipating differences from men but not differences from within, feminism was not prepared, Wendy Brown writes, for the "cacophony" that its own practice produced. As for "'we,' that embarrassing macro-binary constraint from the days of units and solidarity," the Australian writer Meaghan Morris wondered in 1979, "whatever is to be done with 'we'?

How many disparate and displacing 'you's' and 'I's' are being dispossessed?" No one had written more eloquently of women's common language than the poet Adrienne Rich. By 1984, however, she had come to think that her notion of the "universal shadow of patriarchy" falling in the same way across the globe was a mistake, an unconscious expression of her own social, national, and racial location. In dreaming of global sisterhood, she wrote, the "problem was that we did not know whom we meant when we said 'we.'"[22]

In mainstream writing, the rhetoric of a culture common to all women endured. Ideas of women's nature mixed in dozens of different forms, from romance fiction, to Deborah Tannen's popular decoding of the gendered rules of men's and women's conversation, to the *Men Are from Mars, Women Are from Venus* publishing phenomenon of the 1990s.[23] Among feminist intellectuals, however, one heard more frequent references to the "non-innocence of the category 'woman,'" the strategic uses of essentialist categories, the combination of "both the violence and the necessity of a feminist 'we.'"[24] The possibility of imagining a common history or a timeless patriarchy stretching across time and space became less and less persuasive.[25] The women's movement had radically destabilized the cultural and social meaning of the term "woman," wresting it from its powerfully lodged locations in post–World War II culture and infusing it with new possibilities. The certainties of an era's gender norms had been radically challenged. Now, as the terms became more pluralized and controversial, the destabilization project itself became less clear and certain.

In this new, more fractured, less optimistic context, as feminist intellectuals took up the old questions of domination and power, their emphases changed. The social-structural approaches of the early 1970s receded; the attempts to write a feminist counterpart to Marx's *Capital* grew uncommon; the term "patriarchy," criticized as crudely totalizing of women's histories and experiences, was less often used. As the legal barriers to women's realm of actions fell away only to leave men on top throughout most of the dominant institutions of the economy and the polity, the quest for understandings of gendered power turned toward power's more intangible, more insinuating, and more abstract manifestations. One available analytical path led through Thompson, Geertz, Gramsci, and Hall toward anthropology, ethnography, and culture. The move that caught up many of the most prominent feminist intellectuals, however, was in many ways more unsettling and audacious: to interrogate the very language in which culture and experience itself were already prescribed and prepackaged.

The gendered structures of language had been a prominent theme in feminist thought since the movement's beginning. Man is "One," Simone de Beauvoir had famously written in *The Second Sex* in 1949: woman is invariably "the Other." He is essential and universal; she is relative and partial.[26] Worlds of power flowed out of those half-hidden premises. But if words had always engaged feminist thinkers, in the 1980s, as women intellectuals began to find an institutional foothold in the universities, most importantly in the literature departments, some of them began to ask if the reasons for gender inequality's endurance were not to be found in the very terms and discourses that carried "masculine" and "feminine" into everyday usage, reproducing them in all their varied but always dichotomous and unequal pairings. Drawing on poststructuralist theories of language incubated in Paris, the most audacious new feminist intellectuals were in the end to leave every gender certainty shaken.

For feminists interested in the deep power of words, Paris, to be sure, was not the only site where models were to be found. Another site was the elite American law schools, where a group of left-minded scholars, upset by the ways in which post–Warren Court justices were using increasingly formalistic reasoning to reach increasingly conservative political ends, had begun to challenge the category of legal "principle." Critical legal studies, the movement was called. Run out any legal rule or principle to its full implications in the real world of cases, the "crits" argued, and one ran ultimately into such a maze of contradictions and exceptions that the rule soon disappeared as an authoritative guide. Any principle, ingeniously enough pursued, could reach any predetermined destination—and so could its opposite principle. Showing the ultimate indeterminacy behind the mask of reasoning from principle—and how that indeterminacy enabled judges simply to pick whatever outcome they desired and disguise it behind a formalistic smokescreen—was called "trashing" in the law schools. There were both flamboyant examples of it, as exemplified by Harvard's Duncan Kennedy, and quieter lines of approach. Either way, the thrust of critical legal studies was, in the words of Yale Law School's Robert Gordon, to unmask the hidden arbitrariness of the law's language: "to expose belief structures that claim that things as they are must necessarily be the way they are."[27]

A more general impulse toward the same end of category deconstruction came from a cohort of Paris philosophers whose work began to be translated and read in the United States in the late 1970s. "Poststructuralist" was the term that stuck to them. In contrast to the pyramids of structural relationships that Claude Lévi-Strauss and others in the 1950s and 1960s had mapped onto mind and myth, a post-1968 generation of French philosophers had become consumed with what they saw as the inherent slipperiness between sign and thing. Signs, they pointed out, were arbitrary, indefinite, and unstable. They acquired their meaning by relationship with other signs: the regress, through an inexhaustible chain of binary oppositions, was infinite. Whereas Geertz, rebelling against structuralist anthropology, had taken up the study of "meaning," the preoccupation of the poststructuralist philosophers was with texts and discourses. Words ran over everything, in constantly circulating patterns of contending and unstable significations. There was no autonomous author behind them: that was poststructuralism's borrowing from structuralism itself. There was no "I" behind any text or gesture that was not already the product, through the circulating, self-referencing system of signs, of other borrowed texts and gestures.

Through this play of texts and signs ran, it was said, a kind of power: not the power of intention (authors being "dead"), or socially constituted systems of meaning, or the forces of social production (there being no way to pierce the surfaces of language, as Gramsci might have hoped, to grasp something more real underneath), or the pervasive disciplinary power toward which Foucault's mind was tending, but a power lodged in the hierarchical oppositions that formed the very stuff of language. Nature/culture, mind/body, inner/outer, male/female. In these overtly neutral binaries, one of the terms of difference was inevitably promoted at the expense of the other, made normal or natural in the very act of excluding, marginalizing, or making supplemental the other. Dominance and erasure ran all through what Jacques Derrida called the "violent hierarchies" of language, naturalizing what was arbitrary, disguising the dependence of the privileged term on the one it suppressed. "Postmodernism," with which poststructuralism was sometimes conflated, was an understanding of contemporary culture that stressed its decentered, fragmentary, surface-obsessed, patchwork character. In the hands of critics like Fredric Jameson, postmodernism was a Schumpeterian reading of culture, in which the market forces of commodification and creative destruction left nothing, even identity, stable. Poststructuralism began from the opposite premise: the extraordinary capacity of language to disguise and control the radical instability at language's heart. Poststructuralism offered not a theory about language's already existing order but, in Joan W. Scott's words, "a theory about how categories are constructed to appear closed or fixed when they are not."[28]

As the new languages of interpretation began to find footholds and practitioners, there was not much at first to attract the women just coming in numbers into the American university faculties. The macho intellectual style of critical legal studies' practitioners combined with skepticism about every legal abstraction, including the rights talk so integral to post–World War II feminism, to make them doubly difficult allies for many feminists. Apart from a small Paris group of renegade women disciples of the psychoanalytical theorist Jacques Lacan, whose notion of escaping the phallocentric power of language by writing directly from the body seemed to many American feminists only to be another route back to feminism's discredited "essentialism," the French poststructuralists showed almost no tangible interest in women's issues. The first Americans to absorb and proselytize their work were members of the male-dominated English faculties at Johns Hopkins and Yale, where Derrida became a regular visitor in the 1970s.

The Yale English department was to become a center for a style of reading in which the object was to find those places in the text where the language skidded into a point of undecidability and impasse, where the slippage and play of differences undid themselves and their instabilities were revealed, where the secondary term could be unmasked as preliminary to the first and the hierarchy momentarily reversed. The interpretive language of "deconstruction" (as Derrida had named it) was arcane and extremely difficult for neophytes. It encouraged heroic leaps of imagination between the texts and authors (Nietzsche, Foucault, Lacan, Freud, Heidegger, Barthes, Saussure, Lyotard, and Kristeva, among others) that Americans bundled together, often indifferent to the sharply articulated differences and incongruities among them, as the domain of "Theory."

The very difficulty of the new interpretive readings added to the status of those who acquired the codes and facility. In a university system that was moving toward more entrepreneurial and market forms, where administrators competed more and more heavily to be on the cutting edge of market trends, "theory" was a powerful commodity for the department and the academic entrepreneurs who could lay claim to it. But not many women were immediately attracted to the game. The reporter whom the *New York Times Magazine* sent in the mid-1980s to bring back an account of the new trends in literature did not have a sophisticated reading of the landscape; he might have gone to Duke, where Henry Louis Gates, Stanley Fish, and Barbara Herrnstein Smith were soon to converge, or to Harvard or the University of Pittsburgh, where Barbara Johnson and Gayatri Spivak were teaching, but what he brought back was a tale of five powerfully eccentric old men at Yale.[29]

But already the gender pattern had started to turn. "Around 1981," as Jane Gallop was to remember it, the year of Reagan's inauguration, the year before the ERA's ratification deadline expired, the year in which the first reports of gay men dying from an unknown virus began to circulate, the signs of feminist interest in the new theories of language began to multiply. Like most dates in the history of ideas, it was at best approximate. Gayatri Spivak's translation and explication of Derrida's *On Grammatology* had come out in 1976. The first widely available translation of Lacan's feminist revisers was published in 1980. Four years later, at the DeKalb conference on the future of labor history, Mari Jo Buhle was trying to think through the consequences of Hélène Cixous's aphorism: "Everything is word, everything is only word." None of the male labor historians at the conference seemed to have any understanding of what she was talking about.[30]

By the late 1980s, however, debates over poststructuralism were spilling out into all the major feminist reviews. On the one side was the plea (stated now with new respect for internal differences) for a language that would tap into women's experiences and empower women's voices; on the other, a caution that what women imagined to be their resources of language were, to the contrary, mazes of already formed discourses and verbal binaries. What passed as women's experience was in fact a set of fragmented and potentially unstable "subject positions." Experience itself, the political theorist Wendy Brown wrote, was "linguistically contained, socially constructed, discursively mediated, and never just individually 'had.'"[31]

The trajectory of one of the pivotal figures in these unfolding arguments, the historian Joan W. Scott, was particularly revealing of intellectual feminism's rapidly shifting ground. Scott had been a prominent player in the social history movement of the 1970s, coauthoring one of the pioneering studies of ordinary European women's work and family labor. Now, moving to the directorship of the Pembroke Center for Teaching and Research on Women at Brown University in 1981, she found herself plunged from social history's vocabulary into conversations steeped in philosophy and literary theory, Foucault's discourses, and Derrida's unstable texts. Trying to understand how gender inequalities could have persisted despite massive historical changes in the social structures beneath them, she turned to the hidden hierarchies of discourse.[32]

The categories of gender were not neutral, Scott had begun to write by 1986; they were not simply reflective of underlying social forces. The significations of gender were themselves the field in which power was articulated. Putting the point to practical use three years later, she entered the controversy over the decade's most important legal test of gender discrimination in employment, in which the Sears Corporation had been sued for promoting too few of its women staff to commission sales positions. In a brilliant deconstruction of the exchange that had taken place in the court, Scott argued that what was fundamentally at stake was neither the practices of the Sears managers (who clearly had promoted far fewer women to commission sales positions than they might have) nor the ambitions of women to take on high-pressure sales (which the Sears management, citing history, claimed had never been as strong as men's). What was at stake, Scott argued, was the binary opposition that stuck like a burr in the justices' mind. Were women "equal" to men or were they "different"? Were they just like men (which none of the expert witnesses in the trial had been interested in defending) and, in consequence, to be treated equally to men? Or were they different from men, and was it therefore natural to treat them differently/unequally? The false oppositions between the metacategories, constructed out of nothing but their own linguistic relationships, hung over the trial from beginning to end and framed its outcome, Scott argued. Without breaking apart those bi-nary oppositions, without disrupting the power and contradictions vested in the very categories of gendered identity, she insisted, there was no es-cape.[33]

If that meant that women recognized themselves as inextricable from the discourses in which their selves and experiences were constructed, so much the better. Instead of asking women to find their authentic voice, Scott wrote in 1992,

> it makes more sense to teach our students and tell ourselves that identi-ties are historically conferred, that the conferral is ambiguous (though it works precisely and necessarily by imposing a false clarity), that subjects are produced through multiple identifications, some of which become politically salient for a time in certain contexts, and that the project of history is not to reify identity but to understand its production as an on-going process of differentiation, relentless in its repetition, but also . . . subject to redefinition, resistance and change.

The turn upon the categories of early-1970s feminism—identity, experi-ence, action, agency—was all but total.[34]

From the outset there were angry, often anguished feminist voices of dissent. It was said that feminist deconstruction was saturated with jar-gon and rhetorical power moves; that it bought into a game and into an analytical voice that was dominated by men; that it encouraged the hawking of more and more abstract theoretical commodities that were less and less related to actual lives and literatures; that the best it could of-fer women was the fleeting experience of the undecidability of a text; that it dismissed the possibility of woman as a stable and unified subject; and that it erased all possibilities for human agency. Critics worried that the rereading of social experience as only the play of (internally contra-dictory and hence continuously regulated) categories deflected attention from the real terrain of power. They worried that the collapse of social re-lations into linguistic ones left no room for the grassroots social move-ment organizing that 1970s feminists had prized: that all that would be left would be a carnival of words.[35] Caught in the middle of these debates in a special issue of *Feminist Studies* in 1988, Leslie Rabine was not alone in confessing to her "profound and often enraged sense of insoluble ambiv-alence toward deconstruction."[36]

For all the strains and anguish it produced, however, poststructuralism meshed with the occupational shift that brought women intellectuals from the unstable worlds of activism and freelance writing into university positions. The language of "theory" gave women newly entering the graduate schools and literature departments an intellectual claim, a language of textual virtuosity, a voice that could not be dismissed as closeted in the identity politics of a women's studies program. As political feminism stalled in the 1980s, the turn to language gave feminist intellectuals a surrogate field of tasks and actions, codes to crack, texts to unmask. Using the institutional resources available to them (journals, conferences, academic presses), they, in turn, played a major role in the rise of theory in the university literature departments. Above all, in its pessimism, poststructuralism offered a new kind of power—not to speak as women (and in the process reinforce the very categories of women's subordination) but to destabilize the ways in which "female" was submerged, made marginal to, and always under the domination of "male." "If 'woman' is just an empty category, then why am I afraid to walk alone at night?" Laura Lee Downs demanded. To which Sharon Marcus replied that the deepest injury in rape was not something that was taken from women, however brutally; it was the way in which the very discourse of sexual assault constructed and preserved women as weaker, violable, and vulnerable. Until that script was broken, "it makes us into things to be taken."[37]

To all these trends the AIDS crisis, which swept through the 1980s in a tornado of death, fear, denial, and grief, gave a powerful acceleration. The terms in which the crisis entered public debate were an object lesson in the binary hierarchies of language: straight/gay, healthy/diseased, moral/immoral, normal/abnormal. Employment of any of these terms automatically triggered all the others: sympathy itself only encoded homosexuality's abnormality. Enraged at the dying of gay men and the slowness with which the epidemic was addressed, gay activists in the ACT UP and "queer nation" movements of the 1980s and early 1990s abandoned efforts to harness public compassion through linkages that only reaffirmed homosexuality's marginality and exclusion (disease/misfortune/abnormality/pity) and challenged the normal/queer binary at the heart of the matter. They made the contradictions and impasses of the culture's text into vivid political theater. Before the AIDS crisis, there had been very little affinity between the gay men's and the lesbian women's movements. Now, brokered by a common concern with the discourses of "normality," some feminists reached out in alliance. The turn to Paris-originated "theory" in 1980s America was, in queer theory as in feminism, a move on the axis of sexuality and gender.[38]

The book that brought these trends together was Judith Butler's *Gender Trouble: Feminism and the Subversion of Identity* (1990). Eclipsing Carol Gilligan's *In a Different Voice,* and written in a radically different register from Gilligan's account of female moral endowments, Butler's *Gender Trouble* was to be the most cited book in feminist theory of the 1990s. Butler's knotty and difficult argument began by repudiating altogether the notion of a voice, an identity, an "I" behind the play of discursive practices. "The feminist 'we' is always and only a phantasmatic construction," Butler wrote. Gender was the repetition of certain rule-bound stylized performative acts. There were only scripts, nothing outside and beyond them: "It is clearly not the case that 'I' preside over the positions that have constituted me, shuffling through them instrumentally, casting some aside, incorporating others, although some of my activities may take that form. The 'I' who would select between them is always already constituted by them."[39] And yet, for Butler as for other poststructuralists, the closure of the epistemic system was illusory. The erasures and suppressions were incomplete; the moments of undecidability (as the deconstructionists had called them) lay already buried in the performative scripts. At those points of internal contradiction, the scripts of gender lay potentially open for disruption, parody, or subversion.

From these rereadings of gender's troubles, two alternatives proceeded. One, infused with Foucaultian pessimism, reaffirmed the power of language in even more totalizing terms than before. Women spoke from the subject position that constituted them. They acted the scripts in which they were themselves "performatively constituted." The other path led toward exuberant disruption: parody, script inversions, camp, the gender-bending performances of a Madonna or a "queer nation" demonstration. Even the discourses constituent of the self, "the very power regimes which constitute us," Butler wrote, were "open to resignification, redeployment, subversive citation from within." Transgression, subversion, interruption: these were poststructuralist feminism's new politics.[40]

Either way—whether one imagined gender as a complex field of subject positions or as a fluid and contradictory set of regulatory scripts open for refusal and disruption—at the cutting edge of feminist theory there was no longer anything certain about gender. Feminist theorists in the late 1980s wrote of identity as "fluctuating," as "multiple, shifting, and often self-contradictory," as "fragmented and decentered." "That 'women' is indeterminate and impossible is no cause for lament," the British feminist and literary critic Denise Riley urged in 1988. Not on any illusory fixed ground but "on such shifting sands feminism must stand and sway." For those who remembered the dominant frames of feminist argument in the 1970s, there was reason for alarm. Jane Flax recalled the tensions at a women's conference on postmodernity in 1990 as more highly charged than anything she had seen since the late 1960s.[41] Without the possibility of a coherent self, how was liberation possible? With all larger categories reduced to fragments, was there anything left but individualistic politics? But to the new cohort of writers who announced themselves as feminism's "third wave" in the 1990s, hybridity and contradiction, a messy interplay of all manner of differences, formed women's only conceivable starting point.[42]

There was no essence. Seeking to liberate women's authentic selves from the gender roles that corseted them, the women's movement of the 1970s had itself been shaken by the unruly multiplicity of women's voices that had spilled into the public arena. Now at its elite intellectual edges, every bit of women's ontological certainty was being held up for question. The project of destabilizing the certainties of gender had been itself multiply destabilized.

The effects of all these movements in feminist thought and politics flowed quickly into the larger culture. The first and most important reaction from morally conservative women was distress at the challenge that early 1970s feminism posed to older norms of womanhood. The Stop ERA movement was the initial collector of that cultural backlash, filled with runaway scenarios of women drafted on the front lines of the military, women's labor-protection laws repealed, alimony abolished, women's ability to collect child support from men denied, marriage thrown open to all comers, and unisex bathrooms roamed by whoever happened to walk in. Proponents of the ERA read a long-deferred promise of equality in its mandate that "equality of rights under the law shall not be denied or abridged by the United States or by any State on account of sex." Their conservative opponents read into it the abolition of gender differences altogether.[43]

For other moral conservatives, the movement of gay and lesbian activists into constitutional-legal politics was their rallying point. The pop singer Anita Bryant's "Save Our Children" crusade was a particularly visible manifestation of this response, launched in 1977 in reaction to enactment by Miami's county council of an ordinance prohibiting discrimination on the basis of sexual orientation. Both the antifeminist and the antihomosexual strands came together in 1980 when the Carter administration, hoping to deepen its political appeal to women voters, launched an elaborately choreographed White House Conference on Families, designed to listen more closely to women's concerns. Veterans of the ERA opposition sprang into action at the state and regional preconferences with a highly committed grass roots organization and sense of mission already in place. They had a counteragenda ready: replacement of the administration's vague and elastic term "families" by commitment to "the family" as persons related by blood, adoption, or heterosexual marriage; defense of the rights of parents to raise, discipline, and educate their children free of federal intervention; defeat of the ERA; an end to sex education in the schools; and a prohibition against federal funding for abortion, divorce services, homosexual "rights" promotion, or any degradation of women's role as homemakers. The tactics that were to characterize the new Christian right in the next decade—skillful use of mailing lists, active church networks, and media publicity, together with a rhetoric of urgent and polarized moral choices—had their first run in these efforts to hold the norms of womanhood and gender fixed and certain. At the "Pro-Family Conference" held to compete with the official families conference in Long Beach, California, in 1980, the women organizers noted their pleasure at seeing the invited men—Jerry Falwell, Jesse Helms, and others—finally step up to the plate.[44]

The other critically important mobilizing issue in the emergent culture wars was the Supreme Court's affirmation of women's abortion rights in early and mid-term pregnancy in *Roe v. Wade* in 1973. The justices who decided *Roe v. Wade* with only two dissenting votes had little anticipation that it would become the lightning rod for the era's most polarized and agonized political-moral debate. The alarm and opposition of the Catholic

Church, to be sure, was clear from the beginning. It had been lobbying strenuously to block liberalization of abortion legislation at the state level since the 1960s, convinced that the result of easing access to abortion meant brutal violation of moral and natural law. Now, with that state-level effort stymied and fearful that a more tepid response might only dissipate its effects in the way that the Church's doctrinal opposition to birth control had lost authority over much of the Catholic laity, the Church plunged into national politics. Within two years of the Supreme Court decision, the Conference of Catholic Bishops had approved a political plan to organize a prolife lobby in every congressional district and press hard in them all for reversal of *Roe v. Wade*.[45]

Protestant moral conservatives were significantly slower to take up the anti-abortion cause. Reagan, who as governor of California in 1967 had reluctantly approved a measure decriminalizing abortion in cases where a panel of doctors declared a woman's physical or moral health at risk, rarely spoke about the issue in the 1970s. Jerry Falwell did not preach his first sermon on abortion until 1978, five years after the court decision.[46] The first "direct-action" abortion clinic blockaders were Catholics, as were the publicists who made the ultrasound images of tiny fetal hands and feet that became central to the visual shock case against abortion; so were the congressmen who introduced the first measures to cut off public funding for abortions, and so were most of the 1970s anti-abortion movement's rank-and-file activists. But like the anti-ERA movement, which soon expanded beyond the Catholic conservative circles in which Schlafly moved to bring in highly mobilized Protestants, the anti-abortion campaign crossed over into the evangelical Protestant churches. Abortion was not yet the primary issue in the White House Conference on Families battles in 1980; it was placed in the third plank in the "Pro-family statement of principles" which the conservative delegates prepared, bundled into a general statement on children's rights. By the mid-1980s, however, with the mass abortion clinic blockades of Operation Rescue rising toward a peak, the rights and wrongs of abortion had moved into the epicenter of the culture wars.[47]

Part of what gave these crusades their element of surprise was that they tapped groups that had historically been cautious about entering the fray of politics and the public pulpits that others monopolized. In a political culture that as late as the 1950s had been riven with anti-Catholicism,

both intellectual and populist, the Roman Catholic hierarchy had historically played a defensive part, seeking to hold its believers together against
the hostile forces of the majority Protestant culture. To be Catholic was to
be bound not only by special moral rules (large families, meatless Fridays)
and spiritual obligations (confession, the Latin Mass), but by a network of
intellectual formations (parochial schools and Catholic universities, a distinctly Catholic canon, and natural law reasoning) that stood visibly apart
from the world of the Protestant, Jewish, and secular intellectuals who
dominated the public and elite private universities. Preaching to the nation was a task that mainstream Protestants moralists assumed easily, as if
it were their natural role and responsibility. Sensing the risks, Catholics,
by and large, did not.[48]

The determination of the Catholic Church to propel itself into a national political fight over abortion reflected, in part, a socially more se-
cure Church, with a membership that was, for the first time, on average
better educated, wealthier, and more politically engaged than the average
American Protestant. It also reflected a more confident and assertive hierarchy. The Pastoral Plan for Pro-Life Activities was only the beginning of
a decade of highly public pronouncements on controversial public questions through which the leadership sought to claim a position as moral
conscience to the nation that had been almost exclusively Protestant before. The bishops' pastoral letter in 1983 on nuclear war, condemning the
strategy of mutual assured nuclear destruction as immoral and unjusti-
fied; their statement in *Economic Justice for All* in 1986 that the current
level of economic inequality in the United States was morally "unacceptable" and that the ultimate test of economic policy was not economic
growth in itself but its impact "on the poor and the vulnerable"; their opposition to the Reagan administration's military intervention in Central
America—all of which proceeded through publicly circulated drafts and
open, often highly contentious, discussion—were the signs of a minority
religious culture finding a newly assertive voice.[49]

The same could be said of the conservative evangelical Protestants who
turned toward politics in the 1970s. Evangelical—a term of self-identity
that a very broad range of Protestants accepted—was never their proper
name. They were Bible-quoting and Bible-carrying Protestants, many of
them (like the Moral Majority's founders, Jerry Falwell and Tim LaHaye)
fundamentalists in their literal understanding of the Biblical word. They

were people of Bible institutes rather than the established seminaries, and of independent churches, loosely affiliated and often preacher-owned, rather than the mainline denominations. Though their most common term for themselves was simply "Christian," they had been people on the Protestant margins. Whereas the mainstream Protestant churches had long played an active role in politics, they had since the 1920s been highly skeptical of politics and the worldly alliances it entailed. Billy Graham, whose compromises others had criticized, had been a notable exception. By and large, they kept their distance within an inward-looking cultural and intellectual ghetto of their own, stocked with church schools and Christian home-school curricula, Christian bookstores and publishing houses, Bible camps, and radio and television stations.[50]

The entry of these once-marginal Protestants into politics came, like that of post–Vatican II American Catholics, from a new sense of power. No general religious revival occurred in this period; the numbers of those describing themselves as active churchgoers remained virtually unchanged. But as older, established churches lost members by the millions to newer, theologically simpler, and more emotionally and relationally intense churches, a dramatic reshuffling of membership took place. The highly public religiosity of Jimmy Carter, so much in contrast to the religious coolness of his predecessors, added to the sense of confidence spawned by the new religious television outlets and megachurches. The first public opinion poll to ask Americans if they felt they had been "born again" religiously was released in 1976. Add the born-again Christians that the question enumerated to the morally conservative Catholics, and "there are millions of us—and only a handful of them," LaHaye wrote in his Christian bookstore best-seller, *Battle for the Mind,* in 1980. Lynchburg, Virginia, pastor Jerry Falwell had already been flirting with politics through alliance with Anita Bryant's anti–gay rights campaign and his own patriotic "I Love America" rallies when he was approached by a cadre of Republican party activists and encouraged to form what they called, in an overconfident reading of the Gallup results, the Moral Majority. A decade later, the churchgoers who had once been most skeptical about the efficacy of politics had established themselves as a major and intensely committed voting bloc in the Republican party coalition.[51]

As they moved from the margins to what they hoped would be a new center, the new Christian right activists brought with them a rhetoric of high moral warfare. "We are born into a war zone where the forces of God do battle with the forces of evil," Falwell urged his flock. Randall Terry's abortion clinic blockades, despite Terry's appeal to the direct-action legacy of Martin Luther King, were steeped in military rhetoric: "Warriors fight to win! Warriors are prepared to die." "If we are truly committed to Jesus Christ," Concerned Women for America's Beverly LaHaye wrote, "we have no other alternative but to wage warfare against those who would destroy our children, our families, our religious liberties."[52]

And yet just as important as the militant and apocalyptic tone was the shift in voice and presence. Insular subcultures that had not presumed to command the stage pushed to the center, spilled into the public square, claimed the authority to speak others' parts and seized others' microphones. "When members of groups we do not expect to hear from begin to speak, their voices appear too loud, out of place, inappropriate, excessive," the law professor Katharine Bartlett notes; "the noise is deafening." Bartlett was thinking about the agitation that spread in the wake of feminists' first outspokenness. Others made the same point about the open speech of gays. But it was also true, ironically, of gays' and feminists' most alarmist opponents.[53]

As the newly assertive social formations jostled for place on the public stage, competing for voice, talking in certainties and moral absolutes, contests over sexuality and gender ran all across the lines of battle. Catholic opposition to abortion was inextricable from Catholic intellectual understanding of the purposes and nature of women's reproductive capacities. By the early 1980s, progressive Catholics, fearful that the publicity generated by the Church's anti-abortion campaign threatened to narrow perceptions of Catholic moral teaching down to a single note, were working hard to stitch the abortion issue into what Cardinal Joseph Bernardin called a "seamless garment of life" that ran from the protection of the helpless and the unborn to a comprehensive program of human rights and social justice. But to the Catholic anti-abortion activists whom investigators interviewed in the 1970s, the heart of the matter was the nature of womanhood. They talked of women's need to accept their essential natures and bear with grace the burdens life imposed on them. They identified with the weak and helpless and recoiled from their opponents' quest (as they saw it) to bear only the perfect and perfectly wanted child. They took pregnancy and childbearing, with all its costs to their autonomy, as an integral and natural part of womanhood.[54]

For many of the most outspoken Protestants in the anti-abortion movement, the issue turned much more immediately on the control of women's sexuality. A sense of sex's anarchic, disruptive power ran all through the newly vocal conservative Protestantism. That was what lay behind the counterfeminists' shock at the demonstrations of lesbian pride they had seen at Houston; behind their conviction that homosexuals preyed on the young, twisting children's undisciplined sexual energies toward perversion. It lay behind their anger at pornography and the husbands who, emotionally abandoning their wives, fell for it; behind their fear for the sexual purity of their daughters if sex were talked about in sex education classrooms, or if abortion, without even parental notification, gave erring daughters an escape from the consequences of their sexual acts. Masculinity was endangered, too. A sense of faltering manhood helped to fuel concern that Americans had grown disastrously weak; that homosexuality would run rampant among men if tolerated and made public; that men were ceding their responsibilities to discipline children to others; that feminist ideas, insinuating their way into the culture of ordinary housewives, blurring gender lines and reversing gender roles, were already sapping the powers of husbands.[55]

Other issues wound through these, adding flammables to the culture wars. Women who were skeptical of the ERA worried that it would set men free of family obligations and leave women still more vulnerable than before. They resented the self-absorption they thought they saw in the single, childless, professional women in organized feminism's ranks. Others felt themselves deeply vulnerable vis-à-vis school and state officials, the evolution-talking teachers, the child abuse police, and the "secular humanists" who wanted to build what seemed to them a novel and alien wall between church and state. The Cold War issues that had been the entry point for many moral conservatives remained acute and quickly ignited. Desire to take back the nation to an old-stock European and Christian past ran hard just below the surface. Conservative moral-political entrepreneurs mobilized along all these fronts. But the most conspicuous and unifying single thread through the new moral-political contests was that of sexuality and gender.

Let gender roles slip, and every other certainty threatened to give way. By nature (as Catholic conservatives tended to put it) or by Biblical rule (for conservative Protestants) the difference between men and women was timeless and fundamental. The word "difference" ran through these arguments as passionately as it ran through "difference" feminism. "Abortion is of crucial importance because it negates the one irrefutable difference between men and women," an anti-abortion activist told the anthropologist Faye Ginsburg. "It symbolically destroys the precious essence of womanliness—nurturance." Men and women possessed different needs, emotions, natures, and purposes. "Society can be good or depraved, civilized or uncivilized," an anti-ERA flyer argued. "It either possesses order or chaos depending on the degree in which the male and female sex roles are accepted or rejected."[56] That was why the plural in the White House Conference on Families threatened, why, even as women's economic roles went through a wringer of change, the effort to stabilize women's essential nature mattered so deeply.

Holding ideas of gender fixed was key to the preservation of larger structures of certainties against the threat of slippage. Rosemary Thomson, one of the coordinators of the moral conservative forces at the White House Conference on Families, told the Minneapolis gathering: "Briefly, there are two philosophies—those who hold to the world views of traditional moral values, who believe in God, moral absolutes, right and wrong," on the one side and, on the other, the "chaos" of relativism. "I've standards that don't change based on the Scriptures," a fundamentalist woman told the sociologist who interviewed her: "I have moral absolutes. The majority of the population doesn't even think they exist."[57]

The effort to hold change at bay did not, in fact, prove easy. Families in the churches on the Protestant margins, sociologists showed, were just as vulnerable as others not only to the economic pressures drawing women into wage labor but also to the rising rates of divorce and separation. Though they might have refused the analogy, the religious seekers who left their families' denominations for the churches that had once been on the Protestant margins circulated through them in an open, highly competitive market of communities and identities. Blends and hybridities were a fact of religious identity. The organizations mobilized for culture war—the Moral Majority, the Christian Coalition—rose and fell in spectacular arcs as members and donors cycled through them. The structural circumstances of mobilization along the Protestant margins—splintered churches, heavy dependence on television, mass-mail appeals, and small-donor contributions, and uneasiness about the potential corruption of political engagement itself—meant that the movement was always crumbling, always fragile, always rebounding, always fracturing institutionally.[58]

Dissent was present as well. Both the Catholic and the evangelical Protestant churches were home to internal feminist minorities. A group of almost one hundred Catholics, many of them nuns, signed a full-page ad in the *New York Times* dissenting from the Church's abortion stand in 1984. Two years later the Evangelical Women's Caucus split apart on the question of civil rights protections for gays.[59] Attitudes toward abortion were resitant to change; but on gay rights and feminism, public opinion polls in the 1980s and 1990s found a population growing less polarized despite the alarms and calls to battle, rather than more so.[60]

Amid these crosscurrents, the keepers of the faiths struggled to define and hold gender certainties in place. The Conference of Catholic Bishops labored for five years on a pastoral letter on the status of women, finally issuing a draft in 1988 that foregrounded women's voices and condemned the sin of "sexism." But at the end of a process that had been strained throughout by divisions within the American Church and Vatican and pressures from beyond them, the final letter was never promulgated.[61] The Bible-quoting Protestant churches, in contrast, were awash in gender and family governance guidelines and handbooks. For almost all of them, the injunction of women's "submission" and "obedience" was the bedrock of gender certainty. "Our home is definitely not run like a democracy, and I can't find any place in the Bible where God says it should be so," Anita Bryant's husband wrote in *Raising God's Children*. Swift, clear discipline of children, so that the futility of their willful attempts to upset the family "chain of command" was firmly imprinted on them, was a staple of conservative Protestant child-rearing manuals. Men's "headship" of their families and women's "submission" to their leadership were Biblically fixed. Upset the vertical chain that rose, link above link, from the family upward to God, and everything else was thrown into chaos.[62]

And yet, even this proved hard to state with simple clarity. Against the

experience of evangelical women who often found themselves not repressed but inspired to special spiritual gifts by the separate social spaces
that many of the Bible-quoting churches gave to women, the leading
conservative evangelical Protestant writers on gender struggled toward
more complex intellectual formulas. Men were to exert "loving, humble headship" but not "domination" in their families, the widely circulated Danvers Statement urged in the late 1980s; women were to give
"intelligent willing and joyful submission" but not "servility." Outside
the home, John Piper and Wayne Grudem's almost 600-page gloss on the
Danvers Statement advised in 1991, women might assume leadership of
men (in a tactfully supervised work group that included men, for example), but not in ways that might undermine their manhood (as a woman
umpire in a man's baseball game surely would). A husband, for his part,
was to be a "humble, self-denying, upbuilding, happy spiritual leader,"
cultivating "tenderness and strength, a pattern of initiative and a listening ear." "We are adrift in a sea of confusion over sex roles," Piper and
Grudem worried. But nowhere was the drift more visible than in the way
in which, in their efforts to set things straight, the traditional languages of
masculine and feminine reversed and trespassed on each other.[63]

For Protestants of the Biblical word, escape from interpretation was,
in the end, as impossible as it was for the poststructuralist literary critics. Those seeking to make the leap from margins to center would have
agreed (had they known the phrase) that man and woman were ultimately subject positions within a sacred text. They lived in a world of
competing textual explications. Piper and Grudem included a long appendix that struggled to stabilize the meaning of the term *kephale* ("head")
against variant interpretations of it. Conservative church women, studies
showed, engaged in constant, creative, adaptive readings of their understanding of submission. The conservative Protestant protagonists of
the culture wars found themselves caught up precisely in the culture
they feared: sacralizing, refashioning, fusing, and appropriating the transient fads and products of "postmodernity" even as they tried to ward
them off. There were Christian rock and roll bands and, in time, heavy
metal, reggae, and hip-hop bands. There were sex manuals and sexual-
enhancement videos for Christian married couples. There were theme
parks and fashion products to let conservative evangelical Americans par-
ticipate in the whirling market of consumer goods.[64]

Where the boundaries were in flux and so much flooded over them, it was not surprising that certainty was as much a desire as a fact. As Susan Harding shrewdly noted of the Moral Majority's members, they were not absolutists so much as they were persons with the "rhetorical capacity and will to frame new and internally diverse cultural positions as 'eternal absolutes.'"[65] They were constructors of certainties, participants in a culture of foundational desires. But that was enough. Colliding with changes in sexual ideas and mores, their hunger for voice and stable ground had wedged open an angry, anxious debate down all the fault lines of gender.

"Do you hear what they're saying?" the Duke University literary critic Stanley Fish caught the accents of the moment in 1994. "Words have no intrinsic meaning, values are relative, rationality is a social construct, everything is political."[66] The poststructuralist turn in the academy had not been an issue for those who first rallied against the ERA or joined the picket lines at an abortion clinic. What shocked them were the potential consequences of women's new claims to rights and choices, not the later attempts of feminist intellectuals to break out of the prison house of language. But as debates over poststructuralism heated up in the universities, as the new theoretical imports from Paris spilled over into broader academic circuits, the rhetoric of a "culture war" moved out of the gender trenches where it had begun into more general intellectual polemics. By the time James Davison Hunter put the term "culture wars" into general circulation in 1991, it had expanded into a description of a general conflict between competing philosophies. "Orthodox" and "progressive" moral visions, Hunter called them. As conservative intellectuals elaborated the culture wars theme, however, the choice became less and less a conflict between different moral positions or different ways of balancing competing ethical claims and more a choice between "virtue" and "nihilism"—between having morals and having none at all.

"Nihilism," the sharpest of the new fighting words, was a holdover from the late 1960s. It had come into common critical use amid the intense student unrest over the war in Vietnam, the burning of inner-city African-American neighborhoods, the street battles with police, and the revolutionary manifestoes. Now, though the culture and campuses were vastly calmer than before, the term gained a second life. The book that contributed more than any other to its new currency, Allan Bloom's unexpected bestseller of 1987, *The Closing of the American Mind*, was also a voice out of the past. An intense teacher who (like his own mentor in the history of political philosophy, Leo Strauss) made life-long devotees of his seminar students, Bloom was a survivor of the 1960s campus wars. He had published an essay in 1967 on the unpreparedness of undergraduates' minds and the chaotic state of university teaching whose themes he now recycled in 1987 as a report on the current state of academic mores. He agonized over the passing of the 1950s universities and the eclipse of the Great Books curriculum that some of them had then embraced. He lamented the sexual anarchy of rock and roll, as if it had just broken down popular culture's door, and (in language typical of early 1960s campuses) the "moral relativism" of the young. Almost twenty years after the fact, he retold the story of militant African-American students' takeover of Cornell's Willard Straight Hall in 1969 as if it were still a current event.[67]

Unlike the economic conservatives, Bloom did not paint an idealized world of choice. Preoccupied with fashioning their selves and values, unwilling to be jolted out of their own self-referential experiences, college students, he worried, "shrivel up within the confines of the present and material *I*." To explain how the search for personal styles and values had eclipsed the pursuit of truth and nature, Bloom took readers (as he had taken generations of students) through a heroic excursion in intellectual history, from Socrates to Heidegger, to show how the great wrong turn toward value relativism had happened. "Nihilism, American Style" he called the intellectual heart of his book, though virtually none of the figures he touched on were Americans. His intellectual history climaxed with Nietzsche. He lamented feminism's rebellion against "nature" but, except for Margaret Mead, mentioned no feminists. The Paris poststructuralists barely got a passing comment.[68]

And yet it was anxiety about the feminist and poststructuralist invasion of the universities that, more than anything else, accounted for *Closing*'s mass reception. For conservative intellectuals fearful of the strange interpretive languages coming out of the humanities departments, worried about challenges to the Great Books canon from women writers and writers of color, nostalgic for remembered seminar talk of the nature of "man" and the meaning of the good life, Bloom's erudite defense of the idea of timeless things that were true by nature struck an extremely powerful chord. That the writer himself was hardly a conventional conservative—an atheist and aesthete, a homosexual closeted behind *Closing*'s lament that student sexuality no longer flowed in its natural course toward marriage, a teacher who wanted nothing more than to "liberate" his students through serious encounter with truly great minds from the banal ideas that their parents and peers had stuffed into them—all this mattered less than his message.[69] His dense, demanding intellectual history was less important to the book's reception than was the stark rhetorical choice he posed: between the quest to discern the essential nature of "man," on the one hand, and nihilism's mindless destructiveness on the other.

By the early 1990s, that Bloom-inflected polarity was in circulation throughout the conservative side of the culture wars. It ran through William Bennett's *De-Valuing of America*, Gertrude Himmelfarb's *De-Moralization of Society*, Lynne Cheney's *Telling the Truth*, and Michael Novak's *Awakening from Nihilism*. It framed the charge, by Roger Kimball and Dinesh D'Souza and others, that deconstruction was simply a new guise for Marxism, advanced by now-tenured radicals to sap, by different means, the moral foundations of American society. It inflamed the controversy over the discovery that one of the leading Yale deconstructionists had collaborated as a young writer in Nazi-occupied Belgium in the production of anti-Semitic propaganda. William Bennett organized a whole library of virtue-inculcating readings: examples of moral heroism as an alternative to the moral relativism in the culture at large and the mere morals discussions of school values-clarification classes.[70]

"Nihilism," Novak wrote, was the "cultural peril" that would stalk the twenty-first century. To the Nixon administration lawyer turned prison evangelist Charles Colson, the defining character of the present-day crisis was "the collapse of truth": the closeness of contemporary American culture to the "Nietzschean abyss." The blockbuster history of the twentieth century that Peggy Noonan saw on every staffer's desk in the Reagan White House, by the Catholic conservative author Paul Johnson, opened with "an unguided world adrift in a relativistic universe."[71]

Leave the ground of moral reasoning where things were fixed in nature for a world of choices, contexts, and competing perspectives, the argument went, and all that was left was the play of power and identity politics. If poststructuralist claims about the deep binaries seated in language needed confirmation, they might have found it here. To stake one's claims in certainties was to frame the alternative as an abyss of nothing-ness. Encounter with truth, on the one hand: the quicksands of rela-tivism on the other. The antonyms framed and polarized the debate. Threaded through them (as through essentialist feminist arguments about womanhood) ran a hope of extracting certain claims from the fray of politics and dispute: setting something essential about the nature of man or woman on the shelf, as it were, beyond the touch of argument.

"'Relativism,'" the philosopher Richard Rorty laced into Bloom's an-tonyms, "is the view that every belief on a certain topic, or perhaps about *any* topic, is as good as every other. No one holds this view. Except for the occasional cooperative freshman, one cannot find anybody who says that two incompatible opinions on an important topic are equally good." The "relativist . . . is just one of the Platonist or Kantian philosopher's imagi-nary playmates, inhabiting the same realm of fantasy as the solipsist, the skeptic, and the moral nihilist."[72]

Rorty, "the man who killed the truth," as the BBC was to profile him, wrote from experience. The most widely read antifoundationalist philos-opher of the era, he had made his own way around the linguistic turn in the 1970s. Cutting his ties to conventional analytical philosophy, he had begun to write more and more skeptically about philosophy's ability to mirror any of the truths of logic or of nature. Nietzsche, Dewey, and Heidegger were right, Rorty wrote, in their "repudiation of the very idea of anything—mind or matter, self or world—having an intrinsic nature to be expressed or represented." Doing philosophy for Rorty was akin to do-ing poetry, engaging in conversation, telling stories, not questing for "The One Right Description" of "how things really are."[73]

Rorty was ostensibly Bloom's perfect antagonist. On the left, Rorty's self-professed "social democratic" sympathies were criticized as too pri-vatistic and aesthetic, too wrapped up in the play of language and rede-scription, his understanding of history and society too ephemeral and lib-ertarian.[74] But even Rorty was not an amoralist. The hard work of ethical life was done not in the abstract but in the concrete and the particular, he insisted: in arguments over wages and health care, he wrote, not in de-bates about the commodification of labor or the underlying nature of "man." "Solidarity has to be constructed out of little pieces, rather than found already waiting, in the form of an ur-language which all of us rec-ognize when we hear it." Moral life was made, not found. "That something is fair or meritorious is not determined above the fray but within the fray," Stanley Fish wrote in the antifoundationalist vein: "it means that [we] must argue, thrash it out, present bodies of evidence to one another and to relevant audiences, try to change one another's minds." To choose *against* ethics, Fish argued, is to "stand free of any local network of beliefs, assumptions, purposes, [and] obligations," and that "is not an option for human beings."[75]

Critics of the essentialist strain in early 1970s feminism had made the same point. The end of an unproblematic "we" meant that women needed to turn to alliances, to move beyond feelings and experience-statements, beyond transgression and disruption, to the work of persuasion and argument. But in the escalation of terms, the panic over sexuality and certainty, and the fear of a literary tradition undermined by an arcane vocabulary and an infinite regress of meaning, the binary oppositions carried more decibels. Texts and truths were stable or they were nothing at all.

What one might have more accurately read from the furious, unfolding arguments that became the culture wars was how, in a world of instabilities, polarities could be constructed out of the very contingencies of experience. The political philosopher Jodi Dean writes that

> early on it seemed as if the nineties were going to be the "we" decade [but] as it turned out, no one really knew who "we" were. At home, lesbians and gay men struggled to decide if "we queers" included bisexuals and the transgendered. Feminists worried that any notion of "we women" would end up essentialist, excluding lesbians, women of color, or the differently abled. The myriad groups classified as "Hispanic" grappled with the problem of finding any inclusionary identity category. . . . Situated at the borders and intersections of the "we," people with multiple identifications experimented with notions like "world-traveling," "hybridity," and "the new mestiza."[76]

All these identities were set in prescribed discourses and fragmented subject positions. They were, simultaneously, open and unstable, multiple, disruptive.

Every solidarity, the period showed, was open to fissuring. The most distinctive voices of the 1990s writing on "identity" wrote about the messiness of its characteristics. Constructed by discourses which it in turn subverted, it was always contingent and precarious. What the sociologists found in the population at large, when they probed below the poll results, was a maze of compromises, tensions, divisions, alarms, accusations, tolerances, ambivalences, and uncertainties. But when gender roles had been shaken in the 1970s, when the women's movement had challenged the scripts and speaking parts, everything had seemed to sway. New languages of theory emerged, barely translatable into everyday speech. New groups jostled for place and voice on the public stage. Certainties—even the idea of certainty itself—were shaken and reclaimed. It had not felt like fracture. It had felt like war.

6

The Little Platoons of Society

Is it possible that we could become citizens again and together seek the
common good in the post-industrial, post-modern age?

Robert Bellah, Habits of the Heart

At the Falwell rallies for a moral America at the height of
the culture wars, flags were everywhere. Flags draped the arena walls;
the "I Love America Singers," dressed in red, white, and blue, positioned
themselves before a row of flags; audiences waved miniature flags like
the motion of a tricolored sea. Since the mid-1960s, flags had been the
symbolic centerpiece of the culture wars. They had been carried, waved,
burned, painted on hard hats, and stenciled on T-shirts. The bicentennial
in 1976 brought out flags by the hundreds of thousands. There were said
to be ten thousand on display in Washington, D.C., alone that Fourth of
July. A monster flag four hundred feet long, heralded as the largest in the
world, was unfurled on the Mall by a crew of one hundred on Flag Day
1983. Three years later President Reagan proclaimed 1986 the year of
the flag.[1]

The flag was a partisan rallying point, a weapon in the culture wars.
But like the term "we" that wound its way so prominently through presidential speech making, the flag was also a symbol of common ties and obligations. Even in an age of fracture, it made visible the claims and ambitions that the nation as a whole embodied. Like Reagan's retelling of a
mythic American story running from Valley Forge to the trenches of the
Meuse, like the phrase that Tony Dolan worked so hard to sprinkle into
Reagan's speeches in homage to "this kindly, pleasant, greening land
called America," the flag was a vessel for ideals that went beyond identity, self, and markets. It carried aspirations for a common culture and a

common set of public values: for vestment of the term "American" with something more than partisan and partial meaning. It is a commonplace of contemporary writing that the intensified global economic relations of the post-1973 era, and the flood of goods and media influences that they set in motion, did not diminish nationalism around the world but rather helped fuel patriotism's resurgence. With its "America is back" cheerleading, the United States was no exception.

But if the flag stood for aspirations for a common national culture, it also symbolized the nation's claims on the individuals who composed it. It condensed into an image the obligations that citizenship in the nation required: its demands for loyalty and affection, its webs of mutual obligation and support, its taxes and military service, its requirements of sacrifice for the common good. Across the grain of market individualism and fiercely held individual rights, the flag stood for the collective imperatives of the whole, the claims of each for all. How much inequality could a nation tolerate? How much internal division into smaller communities of value could it endure? How much allegiance to the will of its majorities could it demand? The flag was a highly malleable presence. You could burn it in an angry hope of bringing the real America back to its senses. You could salute it at an antigovernment tax-revolt rally. You could fly it over sports stadiums and car dealerships. But whatever its uses, that flag was a collectivist presence, a vessel for whatever sense of society the vast, diverse United States of the late twentieth century might hold.

Debate over which ideas of society might endure in an age of fracture took place across a multitude of stages, from the era's big books of political theory to its policy arguments over poverty and education. Some of it was broached in the abstract, in rival descriptions of the nature of a just society. Some of it turned on questions of equality and obligation that were sharply intensified in the new war over poverty that broke out in the 1980s. Some of it bore down on questions of cultural diversity, in arguments over schools that spilled out from issues of curriculum and toleration to questions of the public character of public education—if indeed there was anything public about education at all. Through all these venues and across lines that often confounded the simple divisions of the culture wars, Americans asked themselves what sort of moral community the United States was and what sort of moral community it should become. The questions were not new, but, amid the larger shifts in social thought and context, the answers were different from before.

The last quarter of the twentieth century was a renascent era for political theory. In the middle years of the century, issues of mass society and social character had dominated social thought. Sociology and social psychology had reigned ascendant; it was their categories—the production of social roles and personality and the relentless pressures of mass conformity—that seemed to hold the keys to mid-twentieth-century modernity. Even the study of fascism—that great dark political terror of the century—was subsumed within sociology's vocabulary. The rebellions and upheavals of the 1960s, however, unsettled the debate over conformity and social character and worked to bring explicitly political questions of obligation and justice to the fore. In a nation that imagined itself just and free, what requirements of mutual obedience and responsibility did each have to all? How much could the collective whole compel? How large was the circle of "we" to which the claims of justice extended? It was in answer to these questions that political theory in the 1970s and 1980s came into its own.

Of the era's attempts to rethink the nature of obligations, the most celebrated in academic circles was the work of John Rawls. For thirty years after its publication in 1971, Rawls's book *A Theory of Justice* cast its mark over social and political theory in a way that few books ever dominate a scholarly field. It generated hundreds of articles and thousands of citations. Alexander Nehamas wrote in 1997 that across the discipline of philosophy, *A Theory of Justice* was "the closest thing to a book that people are ashamed to admit that they have not read."[2]

The question with which Rawls began was explicitly a thought experiment in the justice owed by each to all. Imagine men and women coming together to form a society. Imagine that they did not already know, or guess, the place in that society that would ultimately be theirs. Imagine them to be intensely self-interested but blocked, for the moment, from knowing anything specific about their talents, their property, or their social assets. What principles of justice would they choose?

The first of the choices that Rawls reasoned his social contractors would make went back to John Stuart Mill and the traditions of nineteenth-century liberalism: each would have the most extensive realm of liberty compatible with an equally extensive liberty for all. But societies were not simply realms of toleration. They were also systems of assortment. They formed engines, Rawls argued, for the continual production of advantage and disadvantage, favoring some with wealth and status, cutting others much meaner shift. What principle of justice would society's contractors, acting "behind the veil of ignorance" of their own likely future, agree to construct to regulate the distribution of social and economic advantage?

This was Rawls's more pointed question. Society's original contractors would not choose utilitarianism, Rawls argued, for who could be sure in advance that he or she would not be among those sacrificed in the interests of maximizing some greater social good, allotted to forced labor to increase the gross national product, by chance, or scrubbed from the voting roles to make suffrage purer? By the same token, they would not choose a meritocracy, for they would be shrewd enough to guess that the systems for producing and certifying merit could all too easily be captured by those with the greatest initial assets of education and status. Choosing the principle of simple equality would be naive.

But being prudent, and knowing that once their veils were lifted they were just as likely to find themselves at the bottom as at the top of the heap of personal and social assets, they would choose a principle of justice that kept its thumb pressed on the side of the least advantaged. They would tolerate those inequalities of wealth and advantage that the economic system required to make everyone better off. But beyond that they would be consciously redistributionist, working continuously to raise the well-being of those who were the worst advantaged in society up to the point where that effort, in impinging on the productive capacity of the system as a whole, no longer brought any further gains. They would choose an "egalitarian conception of justice," by which inequalities in wealth and authority would be deemed to be just, Rawls wrote, "only if they result in compensating benefits for everyone, and in particular for the least advantaged members of society."[3]

Rawls's argument for redistributive justice proceeded through almost 600 intricately reasoned pages and no small accumulation of qualifications, but the heart of it was steeped in the analytical vocabulary of economics and rational choice. Game theory, indifference curves, and theories of economic efficiency—all the intellectual apparatus that was to contribute to the recasting of economic theory in the 1970s—were not side-excursions for readers of *A Theory of Justice*. The reasoning by which Rawls's social contractors constructed their principle of justice was precisely the reasoning of classic market actors endeavoring to maximize their advantage in a context of uncertainty. Rawls's bottom line could seem banal ("while the distribution of wealth and income need not be equal, it must be to everyone's advantage") and at other times revolutionary ("first maximize the welfare of the worst-off representative man; second, for equal welfare of the worst-off representative, maximize the welfare of the second worst-off representative man, and so on.")[4] But what was arresting about *A Theory of Justice* was Rawls's demonstration that starting with the conditions of market choice (individual, self-interested actors, in an arena of unfettered rationality), reasonable people would not choose markets as the standard of justice. In their own self-interest, they would choose something like the welfare state instead.

Rawls's theory of justice had been a long time in the making; the gist of its two principles of justice had been announced as early as 1958. But in many ways they seemed strikingly prescient of things to come. Rawls's proposition that a society would be more just if its inequalities were no greater than those which the efficiency of the economy itself demanded paralleled the convictions of many of the liberal economists who were to frame the Great Society ambitions of the mid-1960s. Those projects came as close to a program of conscious economic redistribution as the United State would undertake in the late twentieth century, driving down the incidence of poverty by half between 1960 and 1973, most importantly through Social Security expansion and the introduction of public health insurance for the elderly and the poor.[5] At the same time, the economists' concern with an inevitable trade-off between equality and efficiency—a concern that the economic turmoil of the 1970s would sharply intensify—was already Rawls's as well.[6] Rawls posed no overarching idea of the public good beyond the interests of his imagined social contractors. To the more controversial community-building and community-action projects of the Great Society's war on poverty, Rawls's theory of justice offered no philosophical support. In *A Theory of Justice*, Rawls outlined a federal department of distribution and a department of stabilization to even out fluctuations in the national economy, but he was skeptical of public works and of public goods expenditures which any significant portion of the population did not approve. He built the case for a more equal society on the most individualistic and economistic of premises. In all these ways—in the atomistic bases of its thought experiment, and in its delicate balance between social-contract Lockeanism and neo-Keynesian notions of aggregate economic efficiency—Rawls's argument seemed markedly well shaped for the turns in social thought that lay ahead.

And yet by the end of the 1980s the most important political philosophy book of its time was already marooned in public discourse. However thin Rawls's collective notion of the "we" might have been, the social imagination on which it was premised was broader and more inclusive than those that were increasingly to replace it. The imaginative act by which Rawls had asked Americans to hold open the possibility that, when the veils of ignorance were lifted, the homeless persons camped in the cities' doorways might be they themselves, became increasingly strained. Ideals of equality fled from the arena of political debate. From both left and right critics of Rawls's great social contract, forged in a sense of mutual obligation of each to all, came smaller, more intimate, but also more partial understandings of society. Rawls's vision of justice as a contract in each other's welfare that was as broad as the nation itself came to seem, in this context, more and more unreal.

Neither liberals nor conservatives abandoned the notion of a common, mutually bonded culture. For many conservatives, in particular, dreams of cultural consensus remained intensely alive. But the pressure of their own imagination ran toward disaggregation, toward a more gated image of the social, with its multiple neighborhoods of cultures and identities, its nonintersecting lines of parallel experiences, punctuated by fierce skirmishes over values. The debate over equality, redistribution, and justice into which Rawls had entered in 1971 had within a generation been almost completely reframed.

Rawls's book was hardly alone in the revival of political theory. Alternatives to Rawls's reading of the principles of justice were already issuing forth from the post-1960s shake-up of social thought and mores. Although those theories of justice were to spread far beyond Rawls's Harvard, if you stood in Harvard Square in the 1970s you could feel the buffeting of many of them without leaving campus.

Some posited much stronger collective bonds than did *A Theory of Jus-*

tice. The extreme in this regard was sociobiology, the proposition that human societies should be studied, like other social organisms, not as collections of individuals but as biological constructs of social habit, collective behavioral norms, and accumulated evolutionary advantages. Sociobiology's most prominent popularizer, the Harvard entomologist E. O. Wilson, won a Pulitzer Prize in 1979 for his book *On Human Nature,* and for an incongruous moment, cutting across the ascendant, choice-based models of human behavior, a spate of popular books pointed out the parallels between the regularities of insect behavior, the social habits of graylag geese, and the biologically driven rules of human behavior.[7]

Much more consequential was the force of liberation theology, filtering into the United States from Latin America in the late 1960s and 1970s. When the journalist-to-be E. J. Dionne arrived at Harvard as an undergraduate in the fall of 1969, he entered a campus still in turmoil over the war in Vietnam, the demands of black students for an Afro-American Studies major, the student occupation of University Hall the previous spring, and the club-wielding police the administration had brought in to clear it. Among his classes was Harvey Cox's course "Eschatology and Politics," for which the reading included liberation theology tracts hot off the mimeograph machines in Chile.[8] For the framers of liberation theology who worked within the context of Latin American poverty, politics, and Catholicism, it was senseless to think of the poor (in Rawls's terms) merely as placeholders in an abstract thought experiment about society's origins. The cry of the poor for solidarity and justice was a cry of God. "A preferential option for the poor" was not only a mandate for voluntary charity; for people of faith, it was an institutional and political imperative. Although the claims of liberation theology were moderated as they crossed into the U.S. context, scrubbed of much of the syncretic Marxism of their Latin American origins, they helped to infuse progressive Catholics in the United States with a sense of a special relationship to the peasant social movements of Catholic Latin America and to fuel one of the most sharply critical public responses to Reaganomics in the 1980s: the pastoral letter on the economy, *Economic Justice for All,* promulgated by the American Catholic bishops in 1986.[9]

The more consequential new strains in the era's debate over society, however, were marked by much weaker understandings of obligation than the thick and insistent social imperatives of sociobiology or liberation theology. The first of these to erupt onto the scene were the claims of a new libertarianism, radicalized in opposition to the Vietnam War and military conscription. Arguments that no external force could legitimately invade the sphere of liberties surrounding the self had long had their small band of adherents: Ayn Rand–inspired objectivists, converts of the Austrian School in economics, anarchists, and classical *laissez-faire* liberals. But infused by the antiauthoritarian ferment of the late 1960s, the popularity of radical antistatism mushroomed in the 1970s and early 1980s. The libertarian caucus had been expelled from the Young Americans for Freedom in 1969 after an incident in which some members had threatened to hold a draft-card burning and a march on the nearest military installation. Now, gathering up threads from the Hayek right and the countercultural left, libertarianism was to emerge as one of the most important wild cards in the era's politics.[10]

At Harvard, Dionne came upon libertarianism through the week-by-week verbal duel that the philosopher Robert Nozick and the political theorist Michael Walzer staged as the lecture course "Capitalism and Socialism" in 1971. The book that Nozick drew out of that encounter, *Anarchy, State, and Utopia,* winner of the National Book Award for philosophy in 1975, was framed not as a commentary on either capitalism or socialism, in fact, but as a head-on rebuttal to Rawls's *Theory of Justice.*[11] Nozick had had a radical phase as a young socialist graduate student before sensing himself out-argued by a libertarian classmate in the early 1960s. The problem with Rawls, Nozick now contended, was not his social prescription; it was not that Rawls gave too much (or too little) weight to equality in the scales of justice. The problem lay in the very effort to imagine the pattern of justice in advance. It made no difference whether one arrived at a vision of the just society through a thought experiment in social contract reasoning or through some made-in-advance formula like Marxism or utilitarianism. The problem was that every end-state vision of society required coercion—constant and unceasing intervention into the lives of individuals—to keep society as it actually existed from drifting away from its ideal. Little by little, individuals sold rights in themselves to the protective associations that became the modern states. They let their labor be expropriated in the form of taxes. If they did not sell themselves all the way into slavery, Nozick contended, they sold portions of themselves, found themselves stripped of more and more of their original autonomy and liberty, all in the name of some higher pattern of justice.[12]

To start from the libertarian end was not to imagine justice as an end-pattern but to think of justice as a process—to make a "historical" account of justice, as Nozick put it. If the original distribution of goods and resources was not unjust, and if the gifts and exchanges that individuals made with one another were freely consented to, then whatever result they produced could not be, in logic, anything other than just. Freely contracted actions produced just results. The syllogism could not be challenged by deploring the outcome. Justice was nothing more or less than the product of countless acts of free, private consent. Though Nozick did not put it quite this way, justice was whatever free markets made with the inputs given to them.

Although Nozick explicitly distinguished his prescriptions from anarchism, a good part of *Anarchy, State, and Utopia*'s capacity to dazzle lay in the radical thinness to which Nozick cut down ideas of obligation and society. His concluding section was a hymn to a utopian future where, free of all but the minimum state, market and commune would flourish together, where there would be a multitude of different, parallel communities, waxing and waning as individuals joined and left, where in the context of voluntarily chosen rules people would (as the countercultural rebels had put it) be genuinely "free to do their own thing." To enable this and then stand out of the way, to leave persons at liberty to realize their conceptions of themselves, helped, if they chose, by the free actions of others: "How *dare* any state or group of individuals do more," Nozick laid down the challenge. "Or less."[13]

Around propositions like these, and with Nozick's book as one of its foundational texts, a larger libertarian movement gathered force in the 1970s and 1980s. Brash in its rhetoric, restlessly imaginative in its proposals for dismantling the agencies of the state, libertarianism became a junction point where left-wing and right-wing utopianism met. At the "third-generation" gatherings of young Reagan administration activists in the mid-1980s, the debate was laced with the slogans of libertarian revolution: "smash the state," "defund government," "stamp out government wherever it occurs." The strain in conservative thought that had feared the isolated individual, consumed in his own will to power, as a source of political instability; that had insisted on the need for social stability, continuity, and respect for common customs; that had taken as its touchstone the maxim that society could not be reduced, as Locke seemed to have imagined it, merely to a convenient tool of the individuals composing it—was anathema to the new libertarians. "A nation is a mysterious organism, not a Tinkertoy to be pulled apart and reassembled willfully," the columnist George Will put the Burkean strain in traditionalist conservatism. In the flagship of conservative thought, William F. Buckley, Jr.'s, *National Review,* Ernest van den Haag read libertarianism out of the conservative movement as sociologically naive and dangerously soft on the world threat of Communism. To the young libertarians, however, Will's odes to society and statecraft, Russell Kirk's fuzzy talk about tradition, even the juggling act of big-state anti-Communism and small-state economic policy that the *National Review* called fusionism, were fusty, incoherent, and dangerous to freedom.[14]

Prone to internal fissuring and high-profile desertions, the libertarian movement was perpetually at odds with itself and with its allies in the Reagan Republican coalition. But even the movement's partial taming by its big donors and the moderating presence after 1981 of its own Washington-based policy-oriented think tank, the Cato Institute, did not stem the flow of its antistatist imagination or its infiltration of the mainstream conservative movement. The break-up of Social Security, abolition of welfare, privatization of roads, parks, schools, and prisons, drug deregulation, and massive cuts in the defense budget all moved from the fringes of political debate into the center through libertarianism's transmission systems.[15]

On one principle libertarians and conservatives agreed: that equality was a fatal ambition for a just society. "The passion for equality . . . is always dangerous to liberty because it is a passion for power: the power to impose one's ideal of justice-as-equality on other people," the neoconservative Irving Kristol hammered home the argument throughout the 1970s. Equality was the authoritarian dream of the "new class"; it was a denial of nature, which only a government-directed state could satisfy. In the conservative reviews Rawls was condemned as a modern Rousseau, the "prophet . . . for the most zealous egalitarians," apologist for the "army of government equalizers" who were already on the march. Rawls's cautious, prudential argument for equality could not be uncoupled in the minds of conservative intellectuals from their distress at the new affirmative action projects, their anger at busing for racial equalization, and their recoil from the gender-blurring prospects of the Equal Rights Amendment. The once common distinction between equality of opportunity and the (dangerous) passion for equality of results fused into a general criticism of equality-driven politics in all its forms. Freedom, merit, and excellence: these, not equality, were the aims of the good society. Michael Novak put the conservative consensus succinctly in 1990: "The rage for equality is a wicked project."[16]

For libertarians, however, the dissent from Rawls went still deeper. The notion that something so thin and spontaneous, so thoroughly a product of voluntary action and association as society could impose obligations of the sort that Rawls imagined was, in the libertarian scheme, simply a contradiction in terms. "There are only individual people, different individual people, with their own individual lives. . . . Nothing more," Nozick had written. Milton Friedman had made the same point a decade before. Society had no moral "obligations"; only individuals had these.[17] Midway into *Anarchy, State, and Utopia,* to be sure, Nozick had abruptly dropped into the argument a massive, unsettling qualification. If the original shares of social goods were not just, if they were based on fraud or conquest, then none of the subsequent transactions could wash away that original taint; the normal processes of justice could not, by themselves, set things right. Lest readers not fully grasp the gravity of the qualification, Nozick offered a footnote to the debate, then circulating intensely through black power forums, over the reparations owed to American blacks for the incalculable injuries of enslavement.[18]

For an instant, history brought logic to a stop. Down the line of analysis toward which that footnote seemed to beckon lay enough other acts of massive fraud and conquest as to leave virtually no piece of present-day property unaffected. Whether it was the wholesale appropriation of Indian lands throughout the Americas, the seizure of the monasteries, the dispossessions of the Jews, or the shattering of property rights under the boots of centuries of imperial armies, the stain of violence on property was, by any serious reckoning of history, always somewhere to be found. It would be too ironic, Nozick paused to muse, if socialism should be the punishment for those lapses from freedom.[19] But rectification posed an issue different from the one Nozick proposed to analyze, and he set it aside without an answer. Like the models of perfect markets, the libertarian vision of society was radically timeless. Its imagination, like Tom Paine's, snipped the present off neatly from its pasts. In its "historical" understanding of justice as a transmission chain of free, voluntary transactions, actual history trailed away in footnotes and silences and vanished.

If Rawls's notion of social justice was too intrusive for some, for others it was just the opposite: too slender, too tightly bound up in marketlike notions of individual calculation and choice. Down this line of thought lay the other political wild card of the era, the reimagining of society as a bundle of smaller, more intensely bound communities. To think politically, this alternative to Rawls proposed, was not to imagine oneself, even momentarily, outside of human engagements. Justice, the counterargument ran, was to be found nowhere if not in the processes of social action themselves, in the give and take of community life.

The theme morphed through many different formulations and took a multitude of names: civic republicanism, communitarianism, the new citizenship, the civil society movement, the revival of civic virtue. On this shifting terminological ground, political valences were never stable.[20] The communitarians' projects had only a fraction of the practical policy consequences of the much sharper-edged libertarian program. But if, by the end of the era, the notion of a social bargain across the great society of the nation that Rawls had taken for granted seemed illusory and archaic, the communitarians—like the libertarians, to whom they were so profoundly opposed—had no small part in it.

The idea of justice as rooted in the active work of democratic communities came, in the first instance, out of the 1960s left. It had taken shape in the direct-action political communities formed by African-American activists during the Montgomery bus boycott, the Greensboro and Nashville sit-ins, and the Mississippi voting rights crusade; in the cooperatives, caucuses, affinity groups, community organizing projects, and consciousness-raising meetings that carried the energy of new left politics. The hope of creating a new, "participational democracy" in the teeth of the bureaucratic apparatus of the state, in the face of the convoluted, rule-bound judgments of the courts and the iron triangles that gave big interests what they wanted from politics, grew out of those struggles. In the extemporized urgencies of participational democracy's organizing moment, theory making was not a high priority.

By the 1970s, however, many writers were working hard to give communitarian ideas of justice a broader political theory and a deeper history. A critically important site for both these projects was the history of the American Revolution. There historians began to discover, alongside the merchant, lawyer, and planter elites and their talk of the inviolable rights of persons and possessions, another group of revolutionaries, for whom the cause of liberty was etched not in rights but in devotion to the public good and to the cultivation of self-denying civic virtue. "Civic republicanism," this alternative was called, and its marks turned out to be stamped all across the documents of the early republic—even those that had once been thought to be merely paraphrases of Lockean individualism. Tyrannical concentrations of political power alarmed proponents of civic republicanism, but so did the specter of unbridled self-desire and the open self-interest of the marketplace. In opposition to those who imagined that one could make a great republic out of a properly calibrated mechanics of checked and balanced interests, as Madison's *Federalist* no. 10 most famously put it, they thought of publics as smaller, more intimately connected to their citizens, more demanding of their active will, and more dependent on their other-regarding civic virtue. That vision, which intensified during the armed struggle for independence only to be edged out in the ratification battles over the Constitution of 1789, remained a powerful force in nineteenth-century America, a tradition waiting to be tapped and renewed.[21]

Once the historians had named it, others moved in to elaborate the contours of civic republicanism. Law reviews in the early 1980s began to fill with articles exhuming civic republicanism and the traditions of deliberative democracy from the rights- and court-centered contests that had overwhelmed it. Others wrote in praise of strong democracy, the responsive community, and a "jurisprudence of community and context."[22] In a book that was a must-read in the mid-1980s, Robert Bellah and his collaborators traced two competing languages through the scores of Americans they interviewed: a dominant language of individual aspirations and desires but also, continuously breaking into and disrupting it, a second, barely submerged language of community-framed social obligations that they identified with civic republicanism.[23]

The most important single book to come out of the civic republican revival was, as it turned out, the work of the other charismatic teacher whose lectures Dionne had heard in 1971, Michael Walzer. Whereas his debating partner, Robert Nozick, had largely kept his distance from day-to-day policy debates, Walzer was deeply and publicly immersed in the new politics. He was a democratic socialist with active ties to the new left, an editor of *Dissent,* and leader of the anti-administration caucus on the Harvard faculty during the tumultuous spring of 1969.[24] But when *Spheres of Justice,* the book incubated in his debates with Nozick, came out in 1983, it had almost none of the traits of traditional socialism. Labor and exchange did not enter into the argument until almost halfway through the book, nor were the general tendencies of history, as Marx had understood them, addressed at all.[25]

What struck Walzer as wrong in Rawls's project of working out the principles of justice in the abstract was not (as Nozick claimed) that it violated some equally abstract notion of human autonomy, but that it imagined that justice could be formulated outside the particular community and particular relationships within which people actually lived. The assumption of philosophers had too often been that there was "one, and only one, distributive system that philosophy can rightly encompass." In contrast, the questions about which members of an actual political community cared, Walzer insisted, were much more immediate than these: "what individuals like us choose, who are situated as we are, who share a culture and are determined to go on sharing it." The principles of justice were contextual not universal, rooted in the social understandings already at work in actual lives. They "do not follow from our common humanity; they follow from shared conceptions of social goods; they are local and particular in character."[26]

The most important characteristic about justice for Walzer was its respect for boundaries: that it kept power from simultaneously swamping all the multiple spheres of social life. The key to "complex equality," as Walzer called it, was not equality across the board; it was not the work of redistribution. It was that different social goods (love, prestige, wealth, meaningful work, education, political power, and the rest) were distributed differently, by different principles and through different social mechanisms, so that birth (the great trespasser in aristocratic societies) or money (the still more aggressive trespasser in capitalist ones) could not buy them all.

That did not negate the necessity for the general welfare state. Communal provision was "as old as community itself," Walzer wrote. "Every political community tries to provide what its citizens take to be the crucial elements of their well-being. That's what political communities are for."[27] But Walzer's defense of the general welfare state was less prominent than his desire to demassify it, open it up for more active forms of associational and communal participation, to bring it closer to the ground of real, pluralistic civic life. Democracy was not a pinning down of rights and procedures and entitlements; its justice was not made in a general contract: "Democracy is the action of the rest of us, the rule of the people in their assemblies and committees, arguing over every aspect of the common life."[28] As Rawls's formulations dissolved in Walzer's new left–rooted sensibilities, in his commitment to the local, the plural, the small-scale, and the active, the idea of a single great bargain of each with all evaporated. Only by bringing the welfare state into more vital connection with the real moral communities of actual social life, Walzer would have retorted, could it create the love and loyalty it needed, under the budget exigencies and the open hostility of the Reagan coalition, to sustain it.

In this revival of the idea of civic action, conservatives did not, at first, play a conspicuous part. Traditional, organic bonds of community had often been celebrated by conservative intellectuals. In this mood, American conservatives had written admiringly of the guilds and co-fraternities of medieval Europe and praised the yeoman virtues of an imagined American South as refuges from modernity and bulwarks against the centralizing state. But deliberately constructed communities were another matter. Most conservative intellectuals were critical of "republican" readings of the Revolution that gave the radical town meetings a more central place than the constitution-writing elite. Garry Wills, who was to become one of civic republicanism's most supple articulators for a public audience, took up the theme only after he had broken, with many wounded feelings, from the *National Review* circle.[29] Since Daniel Patrick Moynihan had coined the phrase "maximum feasible misunderstanding" in 1969, it had been a staple of the conservative case against Lyndon Johnson's Great Society project that its community-action programs, filled with chaotic, localistic, participational passions, had been its most self-destructive feature. When with great fanfare the sociologist Amitai Etzioni launched a new, "communitarian" movement in 1990, with the aim of reformulating the balance between civil rights and civic responsibilities in American life, he managed to recruit a few prominent conservatives. But most of those who signed on were centrist Democrats, Robert Bellah and William Sullivan of the *Habits of the Heart* project, Stuart Eizenstat, the former director of domestic policy in the Carter White House, and the Clinton adviser and political theorist William Galston, among them.[30]

And yet if the language of participational democracy carried too much baggage for conservatives to be at first attracted to it, the pressure to identify a conservative vision of society smaller than the centralizing ambitions of the Great Society yet bigger than mere negation, bigger than tax-cutting and regulatory dismantlement, bigger than William Buckley's famous invitation to say "stop" to the juggernaut of history, induced some conservatives to try their hand at appropriation. One needed to recast the idea of virtue from a zealous regard for the public good to a code of individual right action. One needed to harness the antistatist anger of those who had felt betrayed by the social projects of the 1960s and early 1970s—court-ordered busing of their children for racial balance, state educational boards that cooperated with the secularization of the school curriculum, rising taxes and the disregard of distant bureaucrats—and translate it into the more outwardly neutral terms. One needed to reconceive of churches, clubs, private academies, and tight-knit neighborhoods not as private associations but as quintessentially social spaces: the basic ground on which public life was formed. One needed to set aside the spell of the nation. By the end of the 1970s, translation projects of this sort were under way across several fronts.

One was the mediating structures project, initiated by Peter Berger and Richard John Neuhaus at the American Enterprise Institute. Reiterating familiar conservative positions, the reports it issued in the late 1970s defended neighborhood schools and the authority of local governments to determine their own policies on religious display and pornography restriction; they urged that churches and other voluntary groups be brought more fully into the administration of social services. But as a sign of the way in which the idea of society writ small could ricochet back and forth across the divisions of politics, they also endorsed ideas of medical self-help that had once flourished in the counterculture; scattered praise on Afrocentric self-help projects and bilingual education; defended the social importance of even nontraditional families; and recycled more than a whiff of new left rhetoric in their critique of "the leviathan empire" of family and educational experts and their promise (as the clenched fist of radical posters had once broadcast it) to bring "power to the people."[31]

Another sign in the same direction was the changes that conservatives began to ring on the term "virtue." For those working within the tradition of civic republicanism, virtue's essence was the sacrifice of the self for the public weal. In much of the conservative lexicon, the word "virtue" simply became a synonym for ethical certainty, a slogan with which they set out to inject harder-edged morals into the schools than mere values clarification and to enlist families and teachers in pushing back the moral relativism of the times.[32] But for still others the term "virtue" flagged not commonweal or certainty but smaller, more piecemeal terrains of everyday practice: the common, community-embedded social practices of sympathy, duty, fairness, cooperation, and self-control that James Coleman and others had begun to call "social capital."[33]

The emergence of resistance movements in Central and Eastern Europe at the end of the 1980s, springing so wholly unexpectedly (it seemed) out of the social desert of totalitarianism, accelerated the reevaluation of everyday social practice. Later interpreters would point to the sharply disruptive arrival of satellite television in Eastern Europe with its images of Western consumer goods, or in the Polish case to the sustained organizational strengths of the Catholic Church and the labor movement. But in the first blush of Solidarity's victory in Poland and the Civic Forum's "velvet revolution" in Czechoslovakia, the power of ordinary, spontaneous civic action seemed extraordinary. Foundations on both the left and the right rushed to underwrite the study and nurture of civil society.[34] The Heritage Foundation's *Policy Review* remade itself as the organ of the civil society movement. Michael Joyce poured the resources of the conservative Bradley Foundation into a "new citizenship project" in a flurry of proposals to devolve the work of society onto the smaller associational efforts and the everyday institutions of civil society: neighborhood crime watches and neighbor-to-neighbor daycare centers, charity-funded homeless shelters and soup kitchens, private and charter schools, church social-service agencies and rehabilitation groups.[35]

"The national community idea is a dead end," William A. Schambra, the Bradley Foundation's project director, put the new line in conservative thinking most strikingly in 1994. Bill Clinton's "new covenant" and his praise for national service, John Kennedy's call for new dedication to the American promise, the national crusade against poverty, drugs, and crime, Jimmy Carter's claim that the energy crisis would "give us all a sense of unity and purpose again"—they were all spurious. Commitment to the nation could be cranked up only by the exaggerated rhetoric of war and crisis. The "national community" was nothing but a Trojan horse for the intrusion of the invasive therapeutic state. Real community, Schambra argued, was not national; it was local, small-scale, participational.[36]

In a phrase drawn from Edmund Burke that became ubiquitous in early-1990s conservative writings, the "little platoons" of society were the sites where civic life and obligations were most surely grounded. That reading was not, perhaps, one Burke himself might have recognized. "To love the little platoon we belong to in society," Burke had written in criticizing the ferocious self-interest of the third estate in Revolutionary France, "is the first principle (the germ as it were) of public affections. It is the first link in the series by which we proceed towards a love to our country and to mankind." Now, in the extracted phrase, as country and mankind were cropped out, the series of affections faltered.[37] The little became, as in Walzer's left pluralistic vision of justice, the tacit substitution for the whole.

Most conservatives, to be sure, and most liberals as well, remained powerfully moved by the symbols of nationalism: the flag, the military uniform, the somber soldier's coffin, the patriotic pride that could be so fiercely rekindled in even so small a place as Grenada. By the same token, the rights talk that writers in the communitarian vein deplored as brittle and abstract flourished, more vigorously than ever before, across the conservative as well as the liberal sectors of the political spectrum. The public-interest litigation networks that had been critically important players in the left-liberal quest for justice began to be matched by an equally powerful phalanx of public-interest litigation organizations on the right engaged in the same task of translating grievances into justiciable language to catch the ear of activist judges. The fiercest opponents of entitlements now talked rights; the opponents of affirmative action billed themselves as the new civil rights movement; school prayer advocates repositioned their case as a free speech cause. The carefully arranged worlds of political theorists dissolved in these struggles into countless untidy combinations.

Still, underneath the odd political conjunctures, the scattering of 1960s new left phrases into unexpected places, the vagueness and rhetorical abstractness of the "communitarian" manifestoes, and the utopian longings of the libertarians, an important phenomenon was visible. In both its left and right versions, the retreat from nationalism into smaller visions of association—Walzer's spheres of justice, Joyce's pluralist mosaic of subcultures and neighborhoods, the everyday practices of civil society—was a striking event. The domain of citizenship, which had expanded in the post–World War II years to bring in, for the first time, broader and broader ranges of Americans, began to shrink. Talk of a social citizenship as extensive as the nation itself was less and less often to be heard. The social contract shrank imaginatively into smaller, more partial contracts: visions of smaller communities of virtue and engagement—if not communities composed simply of one rights-holding self.

These battles of the political theory books and manifestoes did not occur in a vacuum, nor were they without tangible consequences. Their dominating background was the growing heterogeneity of American society in the last quarter of the century: its more diverse and more vocal subcultures, on the one hand, and its steadily growing economic inequalities on the other. The one touched off a cascade of arguments over schools and the common culture. The other helped ignite an intense debate over the poor and their claims on the larger society. Together they were among the most vexed and heated issues of the age. In each of those domains, the disaggregation of the social that was being played out among the public philosophers helped to frame the terms of politics.

Of all the assumptions Rawls took on board, the most erroneous, as it turned out, was that modernity would, by itself, be a great economic equalizer of human conditions. That presumption was a commonplace among post–World War II social scientists: that as productive capacity grew, it would steadily reduce, bit by bit, the enormous economic inequalities of precapitalist societies.[38] Rawls's redistributionist justice was imagined as facilitating a process that was, at some level, already in gear.

The year 1971, when *A Theory of Justice* appeared, however, was almost the last in which that assumption still held. By the mid-1970s, the engines that had worked in the United States to diminish income inequalities since 1945 had quietly slipped into reverse. Real median wages for working men stopped growing in the early 1970s and remained essentially stagnant thereafter, despite the resumption of general economic growth after 1983. Wealth generation became more and more concentrated at the top, where wealth already existed. The trends combined to widen the income gap between the richest and the poorest fifths of the population each year almost without interruption from 1971 until the mid-1990s.[39]

The "great U-turn," Bennett Harrison and Barry Bluestone called the phenomenon in 1988. Although their findings were disputed at the time, by the mid-1990s economists across the board had come to accept the point that income inequality in the United States was on the rise. The explanations were multiple and varied: one could point to the absorption of millions of new women into the paid labor force and its inevitably depressing effect on wages; one could point to the intensifying pressure from lower-wage labor markets abroad and from a migrant, transnational labor force competing for jobs in the globalizing economy; or one could point, as Bennett and Bluestone did, to the collapse of labor unions and the breakdown of the system of corporatist accommodation between big labor and big business of the 1950s and 1960s. Whatever the case, arguments about equality would now be played out against the realization that long-term economic equalization could no longer be counted on to do its historic work.[40]

Whereas the structural trend toward increased inequality was gradual and went for a long time unobserved, the crises in the lives of the urban poor were public and dramatic. The new armies of the homeless that seemed suddenly to materialize in every major city in the early 1980s, sleeping in doorways, camped under elevated highways, spreading their temporary cardboard shelters over office tower heating grates, were a startling and disturbing sight. Not since the Depression had the least-advantaged Americans been so starkly visible to the rest. The crisis of the new homeless coincided with an epidemic of crack cocaine that raced through the poorest urban neighborhoods in the mid-1980s, bringing with it sharply rising levels of violence, intensified gang warfare between rivals to the trade, and dramatic material successes for some and wreckage for many others.

In these contexts the era's great debate about the poor was more than a debate about policy. It was a debate between visions of society. In the more partial, pluralistic communities of the late twentieth century, who was inside and who was outside the imagined spheres of obligations and responsibilities? Who belonged? Whose needs required public response? Whose claims counted? In a world of deepening inequalities, who stood inside the social contract and who stood outside it altogether?

The debate began with a term that no one thought to be particularly explosive at the outset: the "underclass." It had been one of a shifting group of synonyms employed during the Johnson-era war on poverty for those families that were hardest for welfare case workers to reach: the acute poor, the hardcore poor, those most disadvantaged in skills and life chances. Liberals and social workers had used the term "underclass" to emphasize the public consequences of festering poverty. The African-American lawyer and activist Eleanor Holmes Norton warned in that vein in 1978 of the growth of "a new and angry underclass . . . a virtual pariah class." Edward Kennedy used the term in much the same way in a heralded speech to the NAACP in 1978; so did William Julius Wilson in *The Declining Significance of Race* published late the same year.[41]

What wrested the meaning of the "underclass" away from the liberal social scientists and advocates was, more than any other single incident, the aftershocks of the New York City blackout rioting and looting of 1977. The blackout riot was not, by any measure, the most destructive urban riot of the era. But it took place in the most important media hub of the nation, and to the journalists who witnessed it, it seemed maddeningly difficult to explain. Triggered by no specific incident of injustice but only by the possibilities that a vulnerable city without electricity opened up, it brought an eruption of looting and arson that seemed to many gleeful and shameless. In the absence of more explicit and tangible causes, the journalists grasped at tropes of urban despair that went back a century and more to Jacob Riis's Bowery photographs of the 1890s and William Hogarth's London etchings. In this world of "pock-marked streets, gutted tenements and broken hopes," a reporter for *Time* magazine wrote, "lives a large group of people who are more intractable, more socially alien and more hostile than almost anyone had imagined." They were the "unreachables," the heroin addicts, the homeless alcoholics, the welfare mothers, the hopeless, the drop-outs, the "strutting pimps and pushers," the pregnant teenagers. "Their bleak environment," *Time* noted, "nurtures values that are often at radical odds with those of the majority—even the majority of the poor."[42]

Passages like these were descriptions masquerading as explanation. Were those who smashed the display windows and set the shops on fire, in fact, the homeless streetcorner men? the pregnant teenage girls? the hopeless? Whatever their explanatory weakness, in the aftershocks of the blackout riot, the new terms became the peg on which editors hung their assignments and writers hung their attitudes and assumptions. Many of the urban journalists who worked over the ensuing years to make vivid the image of a new class, under and radically apart from mainstream American society, were themselves sympathetic to the poor. Ken Auletta, whose long report on the "underclass" in the *New Yorker* in 1981 was a particularly powerful example of the genre ("waves of nomadic teenagers engulf city streets—out of work, out of hope . . . These unemployed nomads are often choking with rage, which finds expression in broken windows, torched buildings, and acts of unimaginable violence") wrote essentially to celebrate the devoted labors of a Ford Foundation–supported job-training program's social workers. Nicholas Lemann's *Atlantic Monthly* piece on the underclass in 1986 (stand at the corner of 47th Street and Martin Luther King Drive in Chicago's South Side, Lemann wrote, and you were witness to a "free fall into . . . social disorganization") strove to turn the explanation for the new black underclass from the liberal cities of the North to the culture of the sharecropping South, where poverty, economic dependence on white landowners, and violence, Lemann argued, had been endemic for generations. Even *Time*'s blackout reporter had thought it clear that Jimmy Carter's plan for a big new public works program for the jobless poor would be well worth the price.[43]

But whatever the intentions of the writers, the very terms of the underclass debate cut the poor off into a country of their own. Only a minority of the poor, everyone recognized, conformed to the "underclass" image. But as homeless men and women, pushed out of mental institutions and cheap rental housing, flooded the cities in the 1980s, and as crack cocaine ratcheted up the drug economy's levels of trade and vio-lence, the image of the poor congealed into the new verbal clichés. Black, urban, crime-wracked, hypersegregated, welfare-dependent, isolated from and indifferent to mainstream American values: the underclass la-bel described a people who were, by definition, aliens in their own land.

Whereas the new portrait of an alien "underclass" was the work of many hands, the accompanying turn in poverty policy debate was largely the work of a single book and writer, Charles Murray and his work *Losing Ground* of 1984.[44] A contract policy analyst, an outsider to the debates over the sociology and economics of poverty with a gift for simple, strik-ing formulations, Murray was also, and most important, a libertarian. No-where, indeed, was the capacity of libertarian ideas to disrupt accustomed lines of social policy debate made clearer than in the explosive force of *Losing Ground.* As Murray posed the case, the antipoverty efforts launched in the mid-1960s, the hundreds of billions of dollars spent on public as-sistance programs and the cooptation of the best social science of the day, had not simply been wasted; they had, by perverse design, made poverty worse. Illegitimacy rates had shot up among poor black mothers, as Murray read the evidence; rates of workforce participation had plum-meted among poor men; dependency on public welfare had grown; crime had increased. And this was not, Murray argued, because of the high lev-els of unemployment that the economy had experienced in the 1970s, or the flight of jobs from the cities to sites of cheaper and non-unionized la-bor, or the concentration effects of race that William Julius Wilson em-phasized, or any of the other structural explanations for poverty's endur-ance in an affluent nation; rather, it was because the very incentives of support for the poor were stacked against those who tried to break out of poverty's dependency trap. In the most famous passage in *Losing Ground,* two young people in poverty, "Harold" and his pregnant friend "Phyllis," work out the costs and benefits of marrying and going to work and con-clude that it would pay better to have their baby out of wedlock and put Phyllis on welfare.

This was Murray's contention: poverty programs produced the pov-erty they paid for. The cure constructed the disease and fed on its own perverse failures. Propose any government social program, no matter how modest, the columnist Meg Greenfield wrote within a year of *Losing Ground*'s publication, and "you are likely to be 'Charles Murrayed'" by a prediction of perverse results. "When we pay for poverty, we get more of it," Benjamin Hart asserted for the new young conservatives; we now have "irrefutable and documented proof."[45] If antipoverty policies dramatically worsened poverty, Murray himself wrote in the thought experiment with which *Losing Ground* concluded, why not simply cut the knot and abolish poor support altogether?[46]

At both the macro- and the microlevels, poverty experts were quick to fault Murray's evidence. The incidence of poverty had, in fact, fallen sharply in the Great Society years that Murray had surveyed. In the most visible and controversial of the poor support programs—aid to single poor mothers with children—the numbers enrolled had shot up dramatically in the late 1960s, but thereafter, the percentage of welfare mothers in the population barely changed at all in the next two decades. The sharp increase in the percentage of all children who were born to single mothers was, to a far greater extent than the headlined numbers showed, a measure of the decline in the number of babies that *married* women were bearing. The likelihood that a poor single woman would bear a child had, in fact, not dramatically changed. The image of the dependent poor as sharply different from the rest of the population was equally an exaggeration. Although news articles on the poor were almost always accompanied (as the racial subtext all but demanded) by photographs of poor African-American urban neighborhoods, most welfare recipients did not live in inner-city ghettoes in the mid-1980s, and most were white. Even the inner-city drug economy existed in complex symbiosis with the nation at large, a point made starkly visible in the new trading marts (East Palo Alto, California, or the Williamsburg section of New York City), where drugs were handed off to the white suburbs. As for the most graphic of Murray's examples, his parable of the choices open to Harold and Phyllis, the experts quickly pointed out that Murray had gotten the incentives wrong, even for the unusually high welfare-benefit state he had suggested was typical.[47]

And yet, tendentious as Murray's data were and slipshod as were his correlations, the argument caught the experts at a vulnerable point. Whatever the details of the Harold and Phyllis story, all the experts knew that incentives were a vexed and difficult problem in welfare policy design. None of the experts had a good working explanation for the growth in the numbers of people seeking welfare assistance, or for the sharp declines in marriage rates, especially among the African-American poor, or for the relationship between either of these and fluctuations in the state of the aggregate economy. *Losing Ground* benefited substantially from the new institutions of conservative intellectual patronage. The Manhattan Institute subsidized the book's writing and spent heavily on its promotion. *The Public Interest* gave it an early preview.[48] But the force of Murray's characterization of policy's perverse and unexpected consequences, his insistence that poverty policy was rife with overreach, tapped doubts that ran far beyond the conservative counterestablishment.

At the first, *Losing Ground*'s policy arguments and the journalistic reports from the "underclass" seemed to run down non-intersecting tracks. Phyllis and Harold, Murray told his readers, were people just like themselves. Phyllis was no welfare "queen" leeching off others. She and Harold did not choose welfare dependency because they were victims of a culture of poverty. They chose it after careful calculation of its costs and benefits, for the same reason than rational market actors everywhere made the choices they did. But the two tracks in poverty writing, beginning from such different premises, quickly converged. Within a year, Murray himself had swung over to the culture of poverty theme that he had dismissed so abruptly in *Losing Ground*. The "underclass" lived in a "different world" of relations and values from society at large, Murray was telling readers of the London *Sunday Times* by the late 1980s. The poor did not calculate closely; that was why tinkering with incremental shifts in benefits—why anything short of outright abolition of welfare itself—could not produce improvements in behavior. The poor made their calculations grossly and intuitively. As long at the existence of poverty relief kept poor men and women from paying the full price of out-of-wedlock children, their sex instincts would flourish and marriage would decay. Without strong wives and fathers to curb them, young men's barbarian tendencies would run wild and unchecked. A "New Rabble" was at civilization's door, Murray sounded the "underclass" tocsin in the early 1990s, and nothing less than the survival of free institutions was at stake in the battle to hold it at bay.[49]

Other voices also joined the debate over poverty and welfare. Most striking was the Catholic bishops' pastoral letter on the economy, *Economic Justice for All,* published in 1986 after extensive public hearings and debate. This was the second of the pastoral letters on Catholic social

teaching that the newly outspoken bishops had thrust into the public debates of the 1980s, diverging sharply in both cases from the evangelical
Protestants with whom they were allied in the anti-abortion fight, as they
drew the Church's ethic of life broadly across the social spectrum. The
bishops' pastoral letter on nuclear war, formulated in the face of the
Reagan arms build-up in the early 1980s, had explicitly challenged
the morality of the nuclear deterrence policy underpinning the Cold War.
Though the bishops retreated from endorsing a "halt" (in their first draft)
to prescribing a "curb" on new nuclear weapons production, there was
no missing the boldness of their call for the world to summon "the moral
courage . . . to say 'no' to nuclear conflict; 'no' to weapons of mass destruction; 'no' to an arms race which robs the poor and the vulnerable,
and 'no' to the moral danger of a nuclear age." Now, three years later,
the bishops turned Catholic social teaching on the American economy to
call for a "commitment to eradicate poverty in our midst." Their letter's
charge that employment ("work with adequate pay for all who seek it")
was a "basic right," its suggestion that the current level of economic
inequality was morally "unacceptable," and its insistence that the ultimate moral test of economic policy was to be found not in the aggregate
growth statistics it produced but in its impact "on the poor and vulnerable" were to make *Economic Justice for All* the decade's most powerful single dissent from the new market economics. "The poor have the single
most urgent economic claim on the conscience of the nation," the letter
contended. These were not merely claims of material need or charity, the
bishops insisted; they flowed from the deeper moral claim of every person to meaningful "participation" in the nation's economic life.[50]

The Catholic hierarchy, though it had labored to bridge the tensions between its progressive and its conservative wings through both letters'
construction, did not have a united Church on its side. Led by the American Enterprise Institute scholar Michael Novak and financier and funder
of conservative causes William E. Simon, a Lay Commission on Catholic
Social Teaching and the U.S. Economy sprang into being. Novak had
played a key role in organizing a Catholic countermovement to the
bishops' letter on nuclear war. This time the Lay Commission won the
race to publication by issuing a preemptive statement in 1984, *Toward the
Future*, challenging the bishops' competence to speak on either economic
or foreign policy. "Wealth creation," not distribution and certainly not

any preferential option for the poor, was the ethical test of a moral economy, Novak's group insisted. And yet, although the Lay Commission invited testimony from Charles Murray, and although it was heavily stocked with social conservatives, it ultimately concluded that the divergence in the experts' testimony it had heard was too great for it to recommend any substantial change in existing welfare policy.[51]

Both conservative and liberal thinking on welfare policy was, indeed, far from settled in the 1980s. George Will, speaking for an older conservative tradition, defended a "wholesome ethic of common provision" as a means of fostering social stability and cohesion. William F. Buckley, Jr., who came closer to acting as keeper of conservative intellectual orthodoxy than any other figure of the day, had written in the early 1970s that state-administered welfare provision for the poor was "a question of fine moral, political, and economic tuning" which could not be answered dogmatically in the abstract. Martin Anderson, Ronald Reagan's first chief domestic policy adviser, thought all radical suggestions for welfare reform were unworkable and that it was better to focus on weeding welfare frauds out from the ranks of the genuinely needy. The Heritage Foundation's chief domestic policy expert in the mid-1980s heralded a program of empowering the poor. Look closely at the neighborhoods of the "underclass," Stuart Butler argued, and you found not hopelessness and social disorganization but neighborhoods alive with self-help and sweat-equity ventures, waiting for tax relief, encouragement, and capital.[52] Reagan's budget director, David Stockman, declared, "'Welfare' as we know it should be abolished for all but the nonworking—the aged, blind, and disabled." But the Reagan administration itself, fearful that dramatic changes in welfare policies would cost it popularity, was content to keep existing programs in place and let the real value of welfare benefits erode. On the liberal side, some urged expansion of the program initiated by Gerald Ford of extending tax credits to the working poor, so that work in the low-wage economy could be made to pay.[53]

But as the debate spiraled down on the morals and behavior of the underclass, the argument that the welfare-dependent poor lived not within the circle of social obligations but in another moral country altogether found more and more traction. Welfare support was "the umbilical cord though which the mainstream society sustains the isolated ghetto society," Mickey Kaus wrote in a left-wing version of the new line.

It had created "this new thing, which we have called 'behavioral dependency,'" the American Enterprise Institute's blue-ribbon working group on poverty concluded: not a deficit of material resources but a deficit of values and culture.[54] Constructing and sustaining its own inner aliens, public support did not weave the fabric of society more tightly and securely, it was said. Rather, it made its own outsiders.

In these shifting contexts, those who moved into the welfare debate increasingly carried harsher prescriptions. One was Lawrence Mead, a policy outsider like Murray, a political scientist with an interest in political theory whose research on poverty issues had until then been confined to a small-scale study of the expectations of welfare case workers. The Achilles' heel of welfare policy, Mead argued in a series of widely circulated books and articles in the late 1980s and early 1990s, was not its incentives but its failure to be "authoritative" enough. It had not demanded enough from recipients of public assistance; it had not been sufficiently "tutelary" and "paternalistic." Mead's prescription was much stricter work rules for the poor. In dropping out of work, Mead argued, the underclass had broken its bond of obligation to the rest of society. To become genuine Americans again, to gain the acceptance and support of mainstream society, the poor must shoulder the common obligation of labor. "They must be made *less* free in certain senses rather than more," Mead wrote.[55]

Whereas Mead saw the problem of authority and discipline as a problem of labor, others bore down on the issue of marriage and sexuality. The Welfare Crisis group, organized under the Heritage Foundation's auspices in the early 1990s, with William Bennett and Charles Murray as its most public spokesmen, insisted that to shrink the underclass the most pressing need was not to institute work requirements but to cut the lifeline that sustained single-parent households in the first place. Whereas Mead, knowing that nonworking poor men could not be touched by a welfare program whose primary recipients were mothers with children, was eager to see welfare expanded to bring many more men under its discipline, the Bennett-Murray group preferred to think in terms of deterrents. By cutting off all public support for single mothers who bore additional children, it looked toward welfare's shrinkage and longed for a restoration of the society's natural incentives toward chastity and marriage. "The social science evidence is in," Bennett wrote. "Illegitimacy is the sure road to economic poverty and social decay."[56] If single-parentage precipitated people into poverty, then to cut off public support for single-parentage was to empower. To deny was to liberate: to increase poor women's life chances.

Either way, down Murray's line of reasoning or Mead's, the turn in debate over poverty and welfare by the early 1990s was striking. The critical issue was not one of human capital investments, as mainstream economists in the 1960s had had it. It was not about principles of distributional justice. The larger trends toward greater aggregate inequality were irrelevant. The bishops' defense of the moral claims of the poor was almost completely sidelined. The sociological studies of the inner worlds of poor urban families, their networks of mutual help and kin relations, their struggle with minimum wage and high-turnover jobs, their participation in the same culture of consumer gratifications and sex- and violence-hyped entertainment as other Americans, figured only weakly in the debates. The poor were outsiders. By the compelling power of authority, or the discipline of marriage, or the shock treatment of exposure to the market, they were to be forced back into the social contract—or simply let go.

Historians of the welfare reform act of 1996 have found many ways to tell the story of the process by which a Democratic president was maneuvered into helping abolish the welfare system that Ronald Reagan had not dared to touch. The triumph of a speechwriter's phrases ("end welfare as we know it," "two years and you're off") over policy substance and presidential indifference to detail played a part, as Jason DeParle has shown. So did the political calculation that it was in liberals' interest to get off the Democratic party's back a program that had been coded in the public debate as both African-American and ineffectual. So did the changing work patterns that made welfare-supported poor mothers an increasing anomaly in an economy where most mothers now worked outside the home for pay. But so, also, did the shifting debates over society and social obligation.[57]

The act that eventually came out of the compromise between Clinton and the congressional conservative majority, ending the centerpiece of poor support as it had existed since the 1950s, was a hybrid of all these ambitions. Caught between the Bennett project of encouraging marriage and the fears of other conservatives that abolition of child support for poor single women would simply encourage more abortions, Congress left policies concerning out-of-wedlock births to the states to decide. The act incorporated, Mead style, a regime of far stricter work requirements, but these were offset by time limits (five years of welfare support over the course of one's lifetime) that ensured that no one would stay on the welfare rolls long in the first place and by incentives encouraging the states to shed welfare rolls as quickly as possible. Shrinkage was, indeed, the major result. Within five years, the numbers receiving public poor assistance had dropped almost by half, far faster than any of the experts had predicted.[58]

The upshot of the era's debate over the application of distributory justice to the poor was, in short, not to renegotiate the question of social obligation as much as it was, as Murray had desired, to precipitate the welfare poor into the market to do its work: incorporating, disciplining, assorting, punishing, and rewarding. Private charitable aid would keep the poor from outright starvation, conservatives reassured themselves; some of Clinton's key welfare advisers looked to tighter child support requirements on dead-beat fathers. But for the rest, civil society would move into the breach with its networks of neighbors and churches, its webs of kin relations, its little platoons of voluntary assistance. To add Rawls-like social obligations onto that was, the consensus now held, only to bring back welfare's tangle of unintended consequences. The formal question of what each might owe to all was set aside. In the fabric of unequal and weakly intersecting social worlds that increasingly characterized late-twentieth-century U.S. society, it was hoped that the poor would be made Americans once more.

The "underclass" was only one of the terms that sprang into currency as vessels for the doubts and anxieties running below the era's rhetoric of resurgent confidence. A parallel part was played by "multiculturalism." It was an oddly bland term to carry the controversial freight that it was made to bear. A nation that had begun as a fragile composite of its diverse regional cultures, whose racial and immigrant histories were etched deeply into its social fabric, and which kept its sectional political antagonisms intensely alive, had been, by sober fact, multicultural from the beginning. By the late 1980s, however, a backlash against the sprawling, loosely jointed, often antagonistic array of subcultures that was America was under way once more. In the era's flag extravaganzas, its arguments over the school curriculum and the literary canon, and its battles over English-only rules and immigration policy, a rising volume of voices began to be heard lamenting the weakening of a common American culture.

The controversy focused most sharply on the schools and colleges—the institutions where, if anywhere, as the broad media audiences of the post–World War II years were split into targeted market shares, a common culture was to be forged. Allan Bloom's *Closing of the American Mind* in 1987 had included a plea for a common Great Books curriculum in the colleges as a breakwater against the rising tide of cultural relativism. That same year, the University of Virginia English professor E. D. Hirsch, Jr., tapped many of the same readers with an argument that basic literacy required not only grammatical skills but also recognition of a nation's core cultural vocabulary. From Goldilocks and Confucius through Tom Paine, Ralph Nader, Buffalo Bill, and J. P. Morgan, his *Cultural Literacy* appended a list of the common words that all Americans should know. Hirsch, a Democrat, resisted the pairing of his project with Bloom's classics-focused elitism, but together their emphasis on the contents of a common education helped intensify the spotlight on curricular politics.[59] When in 1988 the Stanford University faculty, one of the few to require a common introductory college course of any sort, voted to modify its existing "Western Culture" options to accommodate more texts by women and persons of color, the war over the "canon" suddenly went national. Secretary of Education William Bennett appeared on campus to defend a common European-centered core; Jesse Jackson joined the Black Student Union's rallies seeking to abolish the course altogether.[60]

An even more protracted argument erupted in 1991 out of New York State's effort to rewrite its guidelines for American history and social studies teaching in the schools. The ethnic consultants to the special state commission pushed hard for celebration of the achievements of non-white Americans and for much sharper recognition of their unjust treatment in the American past. To their critics their project seemed radically divisive: an exercise in myth-making and the exaggerated claims of victimhood. Like the Stanford debate, the New York State controversy quickly went national, promoted by Arthur Schlesinger's alarmist book *The Disuniting of America* and echoed in the vigorous work of the op-ed columnists.[61] The term "multiculturalism" swept all this up in a phrase. A borrowing from Canadian debates over educational and cultural policy, rarely used in a U.S. context before 1990, it now became polemical and ubiquitous.

The curricular battles between the forces of pro- and antimulticulturalism were simultaneously contests of peoples and politics. The return of immigration rates to their late-nineteenth-century levels, as the 1965 immigration reform act took hold and global labor markets expanded, set off (as immigration had before in the American past) fierce countermovements of cultural defense. The ongoing battles over bilingual instruction in the schools, the heated conflicts over English Only legislation in Miami, Monterey Park, California, Lowell, Massachusetts, and elsewhere, and the intensified debates over legal and illegal immigration as the ethnic pieces in the nation's shifting mosaic scraped sharply against one another, all marked the age. On the campuses, much more diverse than they had been in earlier eras, different groups clashed with more political charge than before. Liberals accused the conservative foundations of trying to buy off the curriculum with politically targeted grants. Conservative students, angry at having their opinions about gender, race, or culture dismissed in some classrooms, mounted a vigorous counterattack in the early 1990s on the "political correctness" police.[62]

As in all such battles, nuggets of misinformation raced through the system, sharpening the polemics on every side. An English professor's casual guess that Alice Walker's book *The Color Purple* might be more often assigned in English classes than Shakespeare, as Gerald Graff later observed, was picked up within days in a *Wall Street Journal* piece; from there it moved into William Bennett's speeches, the National Endowment for the Humanities report, and Dinesh D'Souza's widely read attack on the left-wing culture of the campuses, *Illiberal Education,* without anyone stopping to note that it was patently wrong. The core curriculum that conservatives lamented had, in fact, vanished from most universities fifty years earlier as a much more democratically recruited student body fled the humanities for the practical and professional educational tracks where there was rarely a Great Book of any sort to be read.[63]

But amid the exaggerations, the false nostalgia, the racial and ethnic mythmaking, the concern for a common culture was genuine and palpable. It came from no single part of the political spectrum. William Bennett's plea for a "common education," Arthur Schlesinger's alarm at the erosion of a common history, and the curricular modernizers' desire that every student (not just black students) learn something about the achievements of African civilizations and that every student (not just Women's Studies concentrators) hear the voices of women writers, all drew from the same well of desire for common, national ideals and knowledge. But for those conservative intellectuals who had not taken the libertarian turn, who still imagined society in organic terms, as braided through with shared traditions, values, and customs, the concerns were particularly intense. Sociologists in the early 1970s had still been writing of the existence of a strong common consensus, a "civil religion" running even beneath the civil disruptions of the late 1960s.[64] Now in the late 1980s, lament at the erosion of common cultural threads was much the stronger theme. If America was ultimately a set of ideas, a fragile but vital agreement on certain common propositions, where but in the schools and universities—the culture's intellectual commons—would the conversation begin?

Imagining the institutional structure of a common culture would not prove an easy task, however, where the very words for talking about society were shifting so rapidly. A striking example was the quickness with which the speech-code project foundered on the university campuses. Speech rules (against blasphemy, radical politics, and other forms of defiance of the colleges' cultural authority) had been a normal part of higher education in nineteenth-century America. Most small, church-affiliated colleges, including Falwell's, still had them in the 1970s and 1980s. As minority students' numbers grew on university campuses after 1970 and incidents of harassment quickly mounted, there was a widespread call for new codes of civility and equal respect. Women's Studies seminars in the 1970s had often experimented with rules of speech and turn-taking to keep the quieter voices from being quashed by the louder, more strident ones. In the late 1980s, starting with Stanford and the University of Michigan, university faculty and administrators began to craft hate-speech codes to try to put some forms of expression beyond the pale. The University of Michigan discussion began when a pile of handbills announcing an "open hunting season" on blacks was found in a dormitory lounge and someone hung a Ku Klux Klan costume in a dormitory window overlooking the rally that minority students had mounted in protest. In other cases, the movement was triggered by student quarrels that erupted into epithets and name calling. At their height in the early 1990s, before the courts began to strike them down, codes of civil speech, designed to preserve an open commons of ideas from those who shouted and intimidated, had spread to several hundred American campuses.[65]

But on neither side of the battles over the universities did the speech-code projects find many defenders. For liberals committed to strong First Amendment readings, speech codes, even when intended to promote more democratic speech, were hard to accept, as the long and often agonized law review articles made clear.[66] Conservatives, by contrast, had historically been sympathetic to codes of decency. They were eager to curb displays of sex and violence in the media. They were deeply concerned by the law cases, moving through the courts at just that moment, that sought to protect burning of the American flag as a free speech right. For decades they had used their deep opposition to the American Civil Liberties Union as a fund-raising device. But they rallied almost immediately in opposition to the campus speech codes. The National Association of Scholars, the new organ of academic conservatism, opposed speech-code writing across the board; the conservative congressman Henry Hyde introduced legislation to encourage legal challenges to them; the conservative columnists excoriated them as the tools of a new McCarthyism.[67]

There were reasons to be critical of speech codes. Though they were common in other democracies, where the notion of speech as an open market of competing intellectual goods was less deeply instantiated than in the United States, speech codes could freeze open discussion as quickly as could an epithet. They could be clumsily enforced. In practice, Henry Louis Gates and others worried, it was not the vulnerable who most often sought their protection but, rather, the already privileged.[68] To the extent that conservative readers of Dinesh D'Souza and Roger Kimball imagined that university faculties had fallen into the hands of their ideological enemies, self-interest might have told against conservatives' cooptation into the speech-code project. As it was, however, the argument that trumped all the others, among the codes' conservative opponents as well their liberal ones, was the libertarian argument that could have been taken straight from the Free Speech Movement of 1960s Berkeley. Radical and explosive in 1964–1965, it was now the common sense of the matter. Universities were arenas of open speech, crossroads at which differently minded individuals met. To each, his or her own rights of expression, however much they might wound the sensitivities of another.[69]

Conservative rights talk collided on the speech-code terrain with conservative longings for a common educational culture. They bent each other in strange, distorted combinations. But they could not generate a vision of a university as a more tightly woven community than the open, multiperspectival marketplace that conservatives simultaneously applauded and feared.

An even more striking sign of the unsettled image of society in conservative thought was to be found in the debates over vouchers and public schooling. In earlier periods of panic at the incursions of immigrants and outsiders, reformers had turned to public schools as the engine of social and cultural assimilation. Horace Mann's project for a system of free, tax-supported, "common" schools in which rich and poor, Irish and Yankee, would be brought up in a common civic culture was rooted in a vision of the public schools as little republics, miniatures of the great Republic itself. The same assimilative assumptions infused the big public school systems of turn-of-the-century American cities, with their standardized curricula, their civics lessons, their thousands of immigrant students drilled in rote learning and the language of Americanism. No other nation made heavier investments in public, tax-supported education than the immigrant magnet that was the United States in the early twentieth century. Yet by the end of the century cultural conservatives were working hard to supplant public schools with markets and choice.

The idea of replacing public, tax-supported schools with tax-supported grants to parents to spend at whichever schools they might choose for their children had a mixed heritage. Libertarians like Milton Friedman had never been sympathetic to the idea of publicly administered schooling. Catholic families had long pressed for relief from the double burden of public school taxes and parochial school fees, though payments to parents (as opposed to payments directly to schools) had not been the method most Catholic educators preferred. More directly formative for the school voucher idea were the proposals of white segregationists, launched in the backlash against *Brown v. Board of Education,* to abandon public education and transfer tax-collected school moneys to parents in payments that they could redeem at whites-only academies, if they chose. As school integration orders moved to the North in the 1960s, the voucher idea found support in parents angry at busing for racial balance.

The first practical school voucher projects, however, came not from libertarians or segregationists but from liberals worried about equality. The Office of Economic Opportunity, umbrella agency for the Johnson administration's war on poverty, commissioned a study of voucher systems in the late 1960s as a way of equalizing the educational chances of poor children who were locked in inferior schools while the middle class fled to the suburbs.[70] Law professors John Coons and Stephen Sugarman floated a voucher scheme in 1970 in the course of a proposal to reduce the radical disparities between the per pupil expenses of rich and poor public school districts.[71] Left-wing critics of the schools in the early 1970s wrote searingly of the unresponsiveness of public school bureaucracies, the classroom's hidden curriculum of social discipline and control, and the class-reinforcing character of school finance and curricular tracking. "Imperial institutions," the education historian Michael Katz called Horace Mann's legacy in 1971: "tax-supported, free, compulsory, bureaucratic, racist, and class-based."[72] Like schemes for local control of urban schools and bureaucratic devolution, vouchers appealed as a way of redistributing power and resources from elites to those whose voices were weakest.

The markets outlined in the early voucher proposals were highly controlled. Many of the early proposals envisioned a sliding scale of contributions so that poor families making efforts to educate their children that were proportionally equivalent to those of wealthier families would gain the same educational credits. They would have prohibited schools that participated in the voucher program from charging fees beyond the vouchers' values, so that they could simply carry on as elite institutions shored up with new public subsidies. Some of the proposals would have given older children a choice in their school applications, independent of their parents. Equality of educational access was the point. "By moving away from the distribution of compulsory packaged education, government can begin to redistribute the means of self-determination in the formation of will and intellect," Coons and Sugarman wrote in favor of their "family power equalizing plan" in 1978.[73]

In these debates, neither the redistributionist thread in the early school voucher proposals nor their complex institutional design endeared the voucher idea to conservatives. In his compendium of new right ambitions and projects in 1982, the Heritage Foundation's Burton Yale Pines moved quickly past vouchers to place his emphasis heavily on basic, common education: more emphasis on reading and mathematics, more homework and testing, more discipline and classroom order, more dress codes and flag salutes. The Reagan administration's most important educational statement, *A Nation at Risk,* stressed excellence and the New Basics, not choice. In the Free Congress Foundation's manifesto on educational reform in 1984, a handful of voices endorsed vouchers. But others worried that tax-financed vouchers would only insinuate government regulators all the more deeply into existing private schools, as the IRS threat to revoke the tax-exempt status of disproportionately white private academies in the South in the late 1970s had already underscored. Linda Chavez, writing in the same collection, urged that the overriding issue was not school choice; it was the schools' inculcation of real, deeply absorbed patriotism.[74]

Yet by the late 1980s, just as conservative positions on welfare policy and decency codes were turning, policy positions on vouchers were also shifting rapidly. Contributing to that movement and symptomatic of it was John Chubb and Terry Moe's work on markets and schooling, published between 1988 and 1990 with research support from both the liberal Brookings Institution and the conservative Bradley and Smith Richardson foundations. What accounted for high private school achievement, Chubb and Moe proposed, in an argument that merged the radical school critique of the 1960s with the market fundamentalism of the 1980s, was not the private schools' codes of discipline; nor was it their exceptionally committed parents. It was private schools' exemption from the top-down, bureaucratic control that public institutions inevitably promoted. Whereas public control inevitably ossified, markets "naturally function to promote and nurture the kinds of effective schools that reformers have wanted all along." Out of the "natural dynamics of competition and choice" came accountability, responsiveness, effectiveness, teacher teamwork, and bottom-up control. Tinkering with the public school curriculum or teachers' standards was a wasted effort. "Good theories are simple," they wrote: "choice *is* a panacea." Changing the political framework of the schools from democratic control to market competition "has the capacity *all by itself* to bring about the kind of transformation that reformers have been seeking to engineer for years in myriad other ways."[75]

The rallying of conservatives to the new educational libertarianism in the late 1980s was swift and vocal. In Wisconsin, Michael Joyce injected the Bradley Foundation into an effort to expand dramatically the scope of a small voucher program for poor Milwaukee families, initiated by the Republican governor Tommy Thompson and the former Jesse Jackson state campaign manager Annette Williams in 1989. When that endeavor came up against political limits, the foundation raised private money for a private voucher system that quickly overshadowed in scale the public one.[76] "Every student that moves from the public schools into private schools creates one less parent who is willing to vote for those bond referendums to raise money for government-run schools," the conservative political strategist Grover Norquist had advised in the mid-1980s. "If we could pass a voucher or tuition credit initiative, I think we would see a hemorrhaging from the public schools." Jerry Falwell, speaking for the evangelical Protestant church- and home-schooling movements, was already predicting the eventual extinction of public schools.[77] When a school voucher proposal was put on the California ballot in 1993, William Bennett, tribune of the "common education" campaign, spoke at its rallies. In the responses of some three dozen conservative leaders to the *Policy Review*'s invitation to outline their cultural agenda for the 1990s, the item that dominated the lists was school vouchers.[78]

The public was not so ready to agree. Fueled in part by fears that an open market in educational vouchers would accelerate the multicultural trends already under way, nurturing more Afrocentric schools, Spanish-language schools, Muslim schools, fundamentalist Protestant schools, and certainly more Catholic schools, voters rejected most of the voucher initiatives. But from a radical idea in the late 1960s, the voucher idea had gone mainstream, gathering into its shifting rationale the ascendant metaphors of the age. Vouchers would not privatize schools, Chubb and Moe insisted. Rather, vouchers offered a means of democratic control that was quicker and surer than the cumbersome rigmarole of school board meetings and local school elections.

As equality drifted out of the school voucher debate, democracy and choice moved into its center. Local public school governance had long been one of the most distinguishing features of the American polity.

Since Alexis de Tocqueville's day, local governance of town and school affairs had seemed to foreign observers to exemplify the spirit of a democratic culture. But in the new turn in conservative writing on education, public schooling had become synonymous not with democracy but with a new authoritarianism. The public education establishment was "education's evil empire," the Heritage Foundation's *Policy Review* wrote: a system of fear and intimidation. Like Soviet socialism, the *Wall Street Journal*'s editors insisted, public schooling could not be fixed by half-way measures.[79] In the terms of the economist Albert Hirschman, public school boards were an arena for the people's "voice"—for democratic deliberation, compromise, argument, tax referenda, and election. But "voice" in the arguments of the new voucher proponents was not the essence of democracy. What mattered was "exit."[80] Give unsatisfied education consumers the power to walk away, to invest their resources elsewhere. This was not school privatization, they contended: the "choice system" was the truly public and democratic system.

The terms combined and recombined in strange configurations. Markets were more democratic than elective systems. Private schools were more public than government ones. Voting with their vouchers freed parents from the burdens of trying to make majoritarian decision making work. Alliances took on strange forms as well. Cultural conservatives yearning for renewal of a common culture found themselves allied with Afrocentrist schooling advocates. The radical "free school" language of Ivan Illich became mundane. The notion of the schools as a public commons where children of highly diverse backgrounds might learn the habits of civil society strained against a countervision of schooling as a good which each citizen purchased privately. In its divided visions of a good society, Coons and Sugarman argued, the nation was "a virtual menagerie."[81] Amid this fundamentally fragmented pluralism, who but the family should decide on the American values in which its children should be schooled?

Almost no one noticed the caution voiced by James S. Coleman, one of the earliest school voucher advocates and the pioneer of modern sociological studies of the factors of school achievement, that the educational success of Catholic schools and their ability to draw forth unusual commitment from both students and parents came from their enmeshment within larger functional communities of kin and neighborhood. Schools created simply by parental choice, by the thin bonds of value communities, did more poorly, Coleman concluded, than public schools. The success of school choice might not rest in choice, after all, but in the deeper, organic power of community.[82]

The strange alliance of arguments and interests in the school voucher movement was partly the product of policy entrepreneurialism at work, the normal pasting together of constituents and rationales in search of a winning combination. But intellectually the significance ran deeper. Eager for cultural conformity, dismayed by the real and growing pluralism of a multicultural nation, by the multiplying demands of its constituents for a history of their own, and fearful of what seemed a rising tide of relativism and the unmooring of moral values, conservative intellectuals by the end of the 1980s still yearned for a common culture. They could half-remember and half-invent in their mind's eye a more consensual age, when terms like "civil religion" and the "American creed" had been sociological commonplaces. They could desire a common culture. But their ideas of society had been infiltrated by the new market metaphors, the notion of communities of choice, the narrowing of the language of obligation, and the appeal of the idea of natural, spontaneous civil society. They could desire a common culture. But only in fragmented ways could they envision the institutions that might create it.

"There is no such thing as society," Margaret Thatcher remarked in an aside in 1987 that quickly made the rounds among her critics as the essence of the new conservatism. "And who is society? There is no such thing! There are individual men and women and there are families." In fact, Thatcher talked a great deal about society during the years in which she occupied the new conservatism's bully pulpit in Britain. "Man is a social creature, born into family, clan, community, nation, brought up in mutual dependence," she had declared in her MacLeod Lecture in 1977. "We do not achieve happiness or salvation in isolation from each other but as members of society," she elaborated the point the next year. She believed, she said in 1986, in "a Britain which takes care of the weak in their time of need."[83] The claim that conservative intellectuals lost the language for society, dissolved it into nothing but isolated atoms of market-seeking desires, distorts and simplifies.

At the end of the age as at its beginning, talk of society was still current.

The early 1990s saw an explosion of debates over the concept of "social capital." A dense array of social networks, sustained by widespread norms of reciprocity and trustworthiness, a chorus of sociologists began to argue, was an essential capital accumulation in a successful society. Like human resource capital or physical capital, social capital was a collective resource; it made individual action more efficient and made cooperative action possible across the play of divergent desires. Drawn from the work of James Coleman and others, the term was quickly taken up in the sociology and policy study seminars. There was a flurry of interest in counting aggregate membership in voluntary associations across the American past as a measure of social capital, both as a test of Robert Putnam's contention about social capital's contemporary decline and as a means of predicting its future. Critics of the "social capital" concept pointed out that the very term, even as it qualified the dominant market language of the age, absorbed and reinforced many of its premises.[84] The mid-twentieth-century sociologists' search for organic "community" had silently morphed into a hunt for a new species of capital; trust became a possession, a measurable asset. Still, Rawls's theory of justice had rested a case for egalitarian justice on even more explicitly individualistic foundations. Like the new concern with "mediating institutions" or the now-ubiquitous talk of "civil society," the social capital debate kept an idea of the social alive.

In the end, Robert Putnam's fear of a society in which individuals turned back on themselves and their kin in distrust of all others, in the each-for-one's-self vortex that he thought he had observed in parts of southern Italy, was not in the offing. Society had not disappeared from the general stock of concepts and desires. But like other concepts of the age it had grown thinner and more fragmented as older meanings fell out of it. Rawls's assumption that to think about justice was to begin by imagining what each owed to all across the moral community of the nation had the air of an antique piece. The idea of equality had lost its urgency. What society conjured up now was something smaller, more voluntaristic, fractured, easier to exit, and more guarded from others. Like the flags, the older, stronger terms endured, but they waved now over a differently imagined landscape than before.

Wrinkles in Time

What we may be witnessing is not just the end of the Cold War, or the passing of a particular period of postwar history, but the end of history as such.

Francis Fukuyama, "The End of History?"

"Nostalgia was everywhere," David Lowenthal writes of the last quarter of the twentieth century.[1] One saw it across the fractured terrains of civil society in the growing interest in local history museums and heritage sites. One saw it in the new platoons of adult men, garbed in quaint clothing and bearing period arms, devoting their off-work hours to reenactments of Revolutionary and Civil War battles. One saw it in the rage for family histories and growing lines at the genealogical libraries. Where globalizing markets had shortened time expectations, where careers and jobs and neighborhoods were increasingly in flux, where permanence was "dead," as Alvin Toffler had put it, dreams of possessing a piece of the past flourished in compensation. As the very language for society threatened to break into fragments, the past became a sphere onto which desires for community and cohesion could be projected. A truly changeless society would have no need to dwell on its history. In contrast, a sense of living within fragmenting and accelerating time made history a point of acute importance.

Although there was nostalgia on both sides of the "culture wars," a sense of the compensatory powers of heritage was particularly intense among those most uneasy with the fracturing tendencies of the times. In E. D. Hirsch's *Cultural Literacy*, published in the year of Allan Bloom's *Closing of the American Mind*, references to the past ran like a healing thread. Through the maze of things that Americans in contemporary, pluralistic times should be expected to know, the names and facts mined from history seemed to give Hirsch's idea of a common cultural vocabulary its ballast. To be part of the national conversation in 1987, Hirsch contended, Americans needed to know the meaning of boat people and brainwashing, mañana and meltdown, the prodigal son and the proletariat; they needed to understand what was meant by the Holocaust, the guillotine, and Maoism, by silicon chip and software. But they also needed to recognize the proper nouns of U.S. history: Plymouth Rock and Valley Forge, George Washington and Susan B. Anthony, the Declaration of Independence and the Gettysburg Address, the "melting pot" and the Confederacy, the Underground Railroad and the "separate but equal" doctrine. Amid the onrushing force of markets, fads, and technologies that had crowded out more classical references in Americans' minds, amid the "shopping mall high schools" and their "cafeteria education," Hirsch and others seemed to suggest, a deeper sense of history might hold the national conversation together.[2]

History was a "river," Reagan's speechwriters reiterated the claim: a stream whose long, winding course bound together the generations of the past. It was a "ribbon," a connecting "thread." To evoke its scenes, to reel through the celluloid film of American history, as Michael Paul Rogin put it, became a set-piece of Reagan speech writing.[3] Its episodes cohered not only sequentially but also thematically and providentially. "Call it mysticism if you will," Reagan said at the rededication of the Statue of Liberty in 1986, but through the American past ran a single story: a "common thread that binds us to those Quakers on the tiny deck of the *Arbella*, to the beleaguered farmers and landowners signing the Declaration in Philadelphia in that hot Philadelphia hall, to Lincoln on a train ready to guide his people through the conflagration, to all the millions crowded in the steerage who passed this lady and wept at the sight of her."[4]

History was an unbroken line of reassurance up and down which the imagination could freely run. To dip into the past through a pilgrimage to a local heritage site or through the reconstruction of a family tree was to be reminded of history as a force that undergirded, propelled, and vouchsafed the present. In that sense the mid-twentieth-century sensitivity to the powers of history, to the slow, glacial processes of patterned social change, was sustained in the last decades of the century.

And yet another strain in Reagan's speechwriters' invocations of history ran in a very different direction. Here history did not unfold step by step, organizing the chaotic patterns of causation and change, explaining the past's continuous, irreversible pressure on the present. In this alternative vein, the boundary between past and present virtually dissolved. History's massive social processes disappeared. One traveled between past, present, and future in the momentary blink of the imagination, through a wrinkle in time.

The most striking feature of the historical vignettes scattered through Reagan's speeches, in this regard, was their visual immediacy. On a day "very much like this one today," Reagan told the crowd assembled to observe the two hundredth anniversary of the battle of Yorktown with cinematic vividness, "the trees were turning brilliant with the hues of red and gold and brown." When the moment came for the British to surrender, "the pageantry was spectacular." The French lined the road "in their spotless white uniforms." The British soldiers marched to surrender to the muffled beat of drums covered with black handkerchiefs, tears streaming down many of their faces. The "ragged Continentals . . . brown and dreary," a "grab-bag army" of men "with bandaged feet and muskets that couldn't be counted on to fire," stood erect and intensely proud as the British band played "The World Turned Upside Down."[5] In set-pieces like these the past was propelled into the present—made as immediately accessible as an old movie, as the anitromic figures, springing to life, who spoke their parts in the Presidents' Hall at Disney World.

In one of the influential books of the era, the political scientist Benedict Anderson described the formation of modern nationalism as the process of bringing together events scattered across space into a sense of simultaneous time. To be able to think of a tornado strike in Greeley, Kansas, a championship spelling bee in Orlando, Florida, and a racial altercation in Boston, Massachusetts, not as coincidental news fragments but as part of an organically connected national story was to make the imaginative leap that separated national consciousness from those other forms of political community that asked to be imagined as descending in time through tradition or lineages. The nation was an "imagined community," Anderson wrote, organized by folding geographically dispersed events together, like the national news columns of the newspapers which, he suggested, had been instrumental in bringing modern nationalism into being.[6]

But even as they folded space, Reagan's speeches went still further.

The work of their historical vignettes was to fold the very processes of time back upon themselves. It was to make the nation's past and present part of each other: equally and immediately present. In these endeavors the particulars sometimes slipped. The band on the crowded deck of the *Arbella* were not Quakers, as Reagan had misidentified them, but Puritans. When Quakers had shown up in the Massachusetts Bay colony in the late seventeenth century, the Puritan authorities had banished them and, in fury and terror, hanged those who were stubborn enough to return. The authors of Reagan's Farewell Address identified the *Arbella* band as Pilgrims, which was closer but still not right. (The Pilgrims had been settled at Plymouth for a decade before the first Puritans took sail.) Still, whatever liberties the speechwriters took with history's details, whatever the shortcomings of their compression, their intuitive understanding of the way that consciousness of time had begun, in some quarters, to be folded in upon itself captured something important to the age.

Already in his best-selling book *Future Shock* in 1970, Alvin Toffler had raised time's radical compression as a central experience of contemporary life. By Toffler's *Third Wave* in 1980, history's processes crashed into one another in a perfect storm of simultaneity.[7] The rebellions of the 1960s, with their immediacy-laced demands for Freedom Now, had already challenged many of the assumptions of gradual, linear historical motion that had undergirded Cold War social science. Now moving from the streets to the law courts and the foreign affairs forums, metaphors of folded, instantaneously accessible time burst into once-settled debates. Time became penetrable. Legal conservatives, who had once defended continuity and tradition, began to argue that the courts should vault over history in one jump, back to the original meaning of the Constitution. As the Soviet sphere of influence disintegrated after 1989, experts and managers of the major international economic institutions urged that the transition from centrally planned economies to market economics could not be made gradually, *within* historic time, but only through a heroic, all-at-once socioeconomic leap into a post-Communist future.

It was no accident that assumptions of radically foreshortened, instantly accessible time were mainstays of the era's economic model making. In the new classical economic models that Robert Lucas's work had inspired, the frictions at the explanatory core of Keynes's business-cycle theory virtually disappeared. The imaginations of rational economic actors raced instantly to anticipate the future. Where institutions, society, and power all seemed to be in recession, where change appeared to accelerate, nostalgia and anticipation became equally and immediately graspable. The microeconomic idea of time was brought out of perfect market theory and thrust into the world at large.

The deepest hope of those who urged a greater focus on American history had not been to obliterate time; their ambition was integrative, to use a firmer knowledge of the past to hold the little platoons of society more firmly together. Alarm at the condition of historical consciousness, exacerbated by studies of schoolchildren's inability to remember the facts of American history, could be found across the spectrum of politics, but it was a source of particular concern for those who, pushing back against the force of "multiculturalism," championed the cause of a common culture.[8] Against progressive educators' case for social studies in the school curriculum, with its focus on the social problems of the present, conservatives stressed the need for history lessons in deeper time and in the national and Western traditions. History teaching, the National Endowment for the Humanities' chair Lynne Cheney urged, was not to be understood only as a recital of fact. It was the nation's site for the preservation of "cultural memory," the transmission point of experience from one generation to another, its encounter with the "wisdom of the ages."[9]

American history teaching had always been understood, in this sense, as an engine of patriotism: an integrative and acculturating force in a pluralist, immigrant nation. But precisely because its stakes were so high, history teaching in the United States had never been seamlessly integrative. Whose history was to prevail when there so many versions of the past and so many rival morals to be drawn from them? Ethnic and regional tensions had long been particularly sensitive points. Since the mid–nineteenth century, Protestant schoolbook writers and Catholic immigrants had sparred over rival historical narratives. In the Catholic parochial schools, U.S. history texts lingered on Columbus, the Church, and the Jesuit and Franciscan missionaries; the public schools taught a radically different Anglo-Protestant story that essentially began with the Pilgrims and the Roanoke band. In the wake of the Civil War, Northern and Southern educators carried on the fight over the war's meaning in the classrooms. Don't reject a Northern-published textbook simply because it fails to give your grandfather his due, the historian-general of the Daughters of the Confederacy advised public school textbook selection committees throughout the South in the 1910s, but "reject a book that speaks of the Constitution other than [as] a Compact between Sovereign States . . . that says the South fought to hold her slaves . . . that speaks of the slave-holder of the South as cruel and unjust to his slaves . . . that glorifies Abraham Lincoln and vilifies Jefferson Davis." In the 1920s, the Hearst newspapers railed against the pro-British bias their editors discerned in the decade's leading history textbook. Conservatives in the 1930s denounced Harold Rugg's widely adopted American history textbook as a stalking horse for Communism.[10]

These history battles eased in the 1950s and early 1960s, as textbook publishers began to acquire a more sophisticated sense of their multiple markets and as the sources of new Americans seeking a place in the pages of the American story shrank with the closing of most new immigration. In intellectual circles, readings of the consensual strain in American society gained a traction never before equaled in the American past. The major historians of the mid-twentieth century stressed the power and endurance of cultural consensus. In sociology, Robert Bellah's notion of a unifying "civil religion" to which not only the nation's centrists but also its radical moral prophets like Martin Luther King, Jr., paid homage, put into currency in 1967, still carried weight a decade later. Even the cultural upheavals of the 1960s did not immediately shatter that sense of a common (even if contested) past and a dominant culture. In an account in 1981 of the highly disruptive politics of the late 1960s, the political scientist Samuel P. Huntington argued that what made those conflicts so intense was that radicals and conservatives did not begin from different premises but, rather, were locked into an intrafamily feud in which both sides agreed on the same American creed. A "single, all-pervasive 'ought'" prevailed, Huntington wrote, disruptive in that it "rampages wildly beyond the control of the 'is.'"[11]

When the approach of the Bicentennial of American independence in 1976 put notions of a common historical consciousness to a public test, nervousness abounded. At the epicenter of the Bicentennial celebration, Philadelphia's mayor Frank Rizzo called for 15,000 federal troops to repel the radical elements that he thought were poised to converge on the city. But the FBI refused Rizzo's request, and across the nation huge crowds turned out for a national birthday party of fireworks, steamboat races, parades, and picnics. Gathering together the Bicentennial thoughts of some four dozen disparate Americans, *Newsweek*'s editors found dissenting voices. "I'll be glad when the Fourth of July gets here and gone," a black welfare recipient told the magazine's reporter. The Bicentennial should be "a year of atonement" and change, a radical priest lamented. *U.S. News and World Report* chose to emphasize the problems the next century would bring: slower economic growth, increasing natural resource scarcity, and new bureaucratic rigidities in American governance. But the overwhelming mood the reporters thought they found on Bicentennial day was confidence and "oneness." "Something wonderful happened," President Ford exclaimed. "A spirit of unity and togetherness deep within the American soul sprang to the surface in a way we had almost forgotten."[12]

By 1992, however, the Columbus Quincentenary was altogether different. Not unity but dissent and cacophony reigned. Almost from the outset the Columbus celebration fell apart in arguments over the course and meaning of history. Native-American activists took the lead in protesting what they read as the legacy of invasion, dispossession, and genocide that began with Columbus. The National Council of Churches issued a call to repentance and reflection on the historical consequences of Columbus's voyage. The moral balance sheet of the Columbian exchange was hotly debated in the intellectual reviews. In response, some Hispanic-American and conservative Catholic spokespersons retorted that condemnation of Columbus's legacy amounted to a racist depreciation of their people, their faith, and the "whole of Western Civilization." Nervous at venturing into this nest of disputes, corporate sponsors of the Quincentenary pulled back their support. Even the plans of city officials in Columbus, Ohio, to artfully sidestep these controversies through a display of the continent's biotic zones, floral gardens with topiary Disney characters, and a multiscreen "I Love This Land" film, could not bring a consensual reading of the past into being.[13]

By the summer of the Columbus Quincentenary, a general history war was already going full blast over textbooks and curricula. The public hearings in 1991 over the California State Board of Education's new history textbook series designed to "accurately portray the cultural and racial diversity of our society" had been flashpoints of controversy. Critics quarreled over claims of firsts (was John Wesley Powell the first person to travel the length of the Grand Canyon or merely the first Anglo to follow a well-known track?); they upbraided passages of cultural insensitivity (was making paper figures to illustrate a Native-American sun dance any less irreligious than making popsicle-stick crucifixes?); they questioned proportions and omissions.[14] A George H. W. Bush administration initiative to create a common, culturally unifying set of U.S. history standards reignited the conflict at the national level in 1994–1995. Rush Limbaugh, Oliver North, Pat Buchanan, the American Federation of Teachers, and elite university historians all waded into the debate. National Endowment for the Humanities chair Lynne Cheney, who had commissioned the history standards project, ultimately repudiated its work. The U.S. Senate cast a vote of censure.[15]

Some of the antagonists in the battle over the shape of American history teaching wanted a return to a simpler, single-line story. "From the arrival of English-speaking colonists in 1607 until 1965 . . . from the Jamestown colony and the Pilgrims, through de Tocqueville's *Democracy in America,* up to Norman Rockwell's paintings of the 1940s and 1950s . . . there was one continuous civilization built around a set of commonly accepted legal and cultural principles," the one-time history teacher and Republican Speaker of the House Newt Gingrich contended.[16] Others accepted much greater levels of complexity and diversity. The American Federation of Teachers' spokesman on the issue, the historian Paul Gagnon, wanted more emphasis on the Western tradition not as a story of triumph but as a means of teaching students to "distrust the simple answer and dismissive explanation," to discover "that most questions worth asking have no final answers and that no themes worth examining have endings," to understand that "the struggle for liberty, equality, and human dignity is a way of living, not a settled destination." The University of California at Los Angeles historian Gary Nash, the most important figure of the new history curriculum movement, wanted much more attention to the lives of ordinary, anonymous persons: more "pain," more "diversity, contingency, competing points of view, and compromise."[17]

However one tried it by the end of the 1980s, bringing the historical past into the present meant ending up in a nest of controversies. Whose stories counted? Whose heroic figures demanded mention? Whose pictures were to be included, whose experiences told? Who were history's victims, and how large a place in the history books did their tragedy deserve? What did it take to get students in an increasingly diverse America, whose families had lived elsewhere for generations or had lived in America as slaves or second-class citizens, to see the deeper pasts of American history as theirs?

Notwithstanding the anguished pleas for more emphasis on common threads, common narratives, and connected histories, the more marked trend, in the face of these disputes, was a disaggregation of history into histories. To answer the demand for less secular readings of the American past, evangelical Protestant publishing houses were already circulating countertextbooks, highlighting the guiding hand of God in American history and, as they saw it, the deep religious orthodoxy of the nation's founding generation.[18] The American Social History Project produced *Who Built America?*, a bottom-up story from the left, which put rank-and-file workers at the center of the American story. The former new left intellectual Paul Johnson produced a coffee table alternative for conservatives ("The Sinister Legacy of Myrdal" and "Family Collapse and Religious Persecution" headlined two parts of his post-1960 chapter) which put "greatness" at its thematic center.[19] Mainstream publishers learned to navigate through this fractured audience with sidebars and inserts for different readerships.

"Every group its own historian," was the historian Peter Novick's observation of the trend.[20] By the early 1990s, Bellah's concept of civil religion, with its Durkheimian premises of symbolic unity, no longer had any prominent adherents among sociologists. Even the quest for nostalgia quickly fractured. Neo-Confederates flocked to the Civil War reenactments to reclaim the moral cause of secession. A public attempt to memorialize the end of the Pacific War in 1945 all but shattered on the irreconcilable desires of the war veterans' associations and nuclear arms opponents. Ethnic museums proliferated. The private historical project of genealogy boomed as never before. The terrain of history had disaggregated. The mystic ribbons of time could not hold it together.

And yet, if the hope of forging a common historical narrative out of the diverse, tangled, and often colliding stories of the past proved much harder than Reagan's speechwriters imagined, their implicit notion of drilling through the messiness of history through a wrinkle in time was more than a speechwriters' quirk. In an era of more quickly acting markets and more quickly acting models of human nature, notions of compressed time were to be played out across registers on both the right and the left of culture and politics.

One site of foreshortened time was the aesthetics of postmodernity. Avant-garde architects, artists, and critics abandoned the modernist movement's call for forms that would herald the modern age's emancipation from the past and turned back on history as big, open warehouse of reusable styles. The most famous of the postmodern icons was Philip Johnson's AT&T building constructed in midtown Manhattan in 1984, where Johnson capped a modern steel-frame office skyscraper with a mechanical storage loft shaped as a huge "Chippendale" pediment, openly plagiarized from eighteenth-century furniture-book design. Pastiche and juxtapositions formed the postmodern style: motifs extracted from the past and jammed up against each other. The postmodern aesthetic "is indifferent to consistency and continuity," Todd Gitlin wrote in 1988; "it self-consciously splices genres, attitudes, styles . . . it fancies copies, repetition, and the recombination of hand-me-down scraps." "Postmodernism swims, even wallows, in the fragmentary and the chaotic currents of change," one of the phenomenon's leading critical theorists, David Harvey, wrote in the same vein. Hostile to structures, to metanarratives, to claims of depth (as opposed to the exuberant play of surfaces), postmodernist artists and critics reveled in the possibilities of extracted and recombined time. "History was . . . scattered," the critic Terry Eagleton wrote of the 1980s avant-garde; "adjacency eclipsed sequentiality." History was not a process to be advanced or resisted. History was a great consignment shop of reusable fashions.[21]

Everything fractured in postmodern aesthetics, as its critics were quick to point out. Fact pressed unsettlingly into fiction in E. L. Doctorow's *Ragtime* and fiction into fact in Simon Schama's *Dead Certainties*.[22] Genres blurred and ruptured. Totalities were accounted the new aesthetic enemy. The play of time—time wrenched from history's strata, sliced and recombined, twisted and tumbled all over itself—was only a part of the larger avant-garde movement. Fredric Jameson's and David Harvey's efforts to see in the postmodern sensibility the logic of late-capitalist transformations of space and time, with its instant information portals and its power to bring even the most widely flung goods into juxtaposition, downplayed the sheer contagion of styles, metaphors, and innovations in the postmodern arts. But at the cutting edge of the arts there was no missing the experiments in folded time: the exuberance of a kind of transgressive time travel.

On the cultural right there was no sympathy for the postmodern avant-garde. In the Bible-quoting churches, the bright line between truth and fiction was a cardinal principle of faith. History in these settings was directional, irreversible, and providential. There was no playfulness in its chronologies. And yet the new Bible churches became a powerful site, in their own key and language, for notions of short-circuiting time: for making not only the past but the future immediately accessible to the present.

To be able to see the end of historical time while still enveloped in its midst by matching signs to prophecies had long been an enduring hope in many Christian traditions. In the early nineteenth century when new movements of prophetic Protestantism of all sorts flourished in Europe and the Americas, the Anglo-Irish evangelist John Nelson Darby had worked out an elaborate timeline of sacred history from the age of innocence to the millennium, imagined as a series of successive Dispensations, each pinned to its Biblical texts. Nurtured and elaborated in fundamentalist Protestantism's Bible colleges in the nineteenth and early twentieth centuries, Dispensationalism's late ages came to be mapped onto the events of the Cold War in the 1950s. But it was the Israeli conquest of the historic old city of Jerusalem in the Six-Day War of 1967 that reshaped and regalvanized End Times prophecy. "Israel," which had long been read as metaphor for the Christian church, became the nation of Israel. The forces of anti-Christ, long associated with Catholicism in Protestant fundamentalist circles, were re-identified as the forces of world government fronted by the European Union, the United Nations, and the ecumenical churches. The Battle of Armageddon would now play itself out in a nuclear holocaust, sparked by a disastrous Russian invasion of the Holy Land, over the hills of Israel. The faithful, raptured out of harm's way, would not have to witness the terrible tribulations of history's end, but they could know it in detail, map it unerringly onto the trends of the present, and prefigure it precisely in their mind's eye.[23]

Spread with the growth of the new Bible churches, End Times prophecy swept through evangelical Protestant culture by the 1970s and 1980s. Megasellers like Hal Lindsey's *Late Great Planet Earth* (1970) and Tim

LaHaye's *Left Behind* series (1995–) helped give it a consuming urgency. "We have more scriptural evidence for believing Christ could come in our lifetime than any generation of Christians since our Lord ascended into heaven," LaHaye wrote. "The decade of the 1980s," Lindsey urged, "could very well be the last decade of history as we know it." Pat Robertson, the televangelist contender for the Republican presidential nomination in 1988, played heavily on "new world order" prophecy and its mandates for U.S. foreign policy. The ribbon of history could be fast-forwarded, foreshortened in the mind, and, with faith, escaped. This was not postmodernism's jumbled time but the present and the future projected into one another: folded prophetically together.[24]

By the time the argument over "originalist" interpretations of the Constitution erupted in the mid-1980s, then, there were already in some conservative circles ways of thinking that leaped, with textually rooted and extremely confident prevision, across vast reaches of time. Constitutional originalism was a nostalgia of a very different sort from the hunger for history's completion embedded in End Times prophecy. Originalism looked backward to the eighteenth-century Constitution rather than forward, through the Bible's prophetic chapters, to the end of the world. Originalism's arguments rattled through the elite law reviews, not the churches that had once been on the cultural margins. But the idea of short-circuiting time by reimagining what the Constitution must have originally meant and projecting that past into the present cut almost as broad a swath through conservative legal circles as Dispensationalism had through conservative Protestantism.

Among legal conservatives, distress with the current state of Constitutional interpretation had been a litmus test ever since the Warren Court's reforms of the 1950s and 1960s. That Court's banishing of prayers and Bible reading from public school routines, its attack on racial segregation in the schools, its solicitousness for the procedural rights of the criminally accused, its augmentation of the rights of privacy and free speech, and its understanding of itself as adapting the fundamental principles of the Bill of Rights to circumstances of the present, even at the cost of serious social dislocation—all this had been a point of political opposition and intellectual anguish among conservatives since the 1960s. Critics of the Supreme Court's judicial "activism" had pleaded for "strict construction" of the text of the Constitution, for more stringent policing of court appointments, for restrictions on the courts' jurisdiction, and, above all, for more deference to existing customs and popularly elected legislatures. They had urged a rollback of the most controversial court decisions and a new deference to established legal tradition and social custom. Caution and continuity were the true marks of judicial conservatism, it was said; the Warren Court's great failure was its zeal to override custom and continuity in quest of abstract justice.

None of these considerations, however, pushed conservative legal theorists back toward deep historical time. When the Federalist Society, the new pressure group of conservative law students and law teachers funded by the conservative foundations, devoted its second annual meeting to "judicial activism" in 1983, the discussion turned almost entirely on the power of Congress to restrict the range of cases that the federal courts could decide, not on the original meaning of the Constitution.[25] The route through history seemed much more problematic than the route through limitation of the courts' powers. From time to time, figures on the Supreme Court had appealed to the Constitution as its writers must have intended it to be read: "construed now as it was understood at the time of its adoption," as Chief Justice Roger Taney had written in his notorious *Dred Scott* decision in 1857, through which the Court had dismissed the idea that more liberal public opinion vis-à-vis slavery and blacks could alter by a jot the meaning of the Constitution. Subsequent evocations of original understanding had come from no consistent corner of the political map. Justice Sutherland, one of Franklin D. Roosevelt's most consistent opponents on the 1930s Supreme Court, had appealed to the need of the Constitution's interpreters to "give effect to the intent of its framers and the people who adopted it." In the late 1940s, in the series of cases in which Justice Hugo Black had persuaded the Court to apply the federal Bill of Rights to the states (to "incorporate" the first eight amendments of the Constitution into fundamental state law, as the law schools taught it, and in the process radically expand their force in day-to-day American life), Black had insisted that he was fulfilling nothing more than a plain reading of the "original purpose" of the Fourteenth Amendment's enactors.[26]

Out of these contradictory thrusts and counterthrusts a more systematic, historically rooted jurisprudence did not take shape. In the landmark case of *Brown v. Board of Education,* the Supreme Court had been presented with extensive historical evidence by both defenders and opponents of public school segregation. But that evidence was simply too "inconclusive" to determine "with any degree of certainty" what the Fourteenth Amendment's framers intended for future courts to decide about the justice of racially segregated schools, the Court ultimately advised. Dissatisfied with this dismissive answer, the most thoughtful of the 1950s legal conservatives, Alexander Bickel, had pored over the historical record only to concur that the writers of the Fourteenth Amendment had used terms so "open," general, and unspecific, a "language [so] capable of growth," that they must have intended not to pin down precisely that amendment's guarantees but to leave them open "to be decided another day."[27]

Robert Bork, who was to emerge as one of the most forceful advocates of original-intention jurisprudence in the mid-1980s, published a sweeping attack on the Warren Court in 1971—on its extemporized judgments, its eagerness to declare new fundamental rights, its refusal to defer to democratic majorities, and its cavalier departures from "text and history." But the lessons of history, in Bork's mind in 1971, were not, in fact, of much help. "The Court cannot conceivably know how these long-dead men would have resolved these issues" at the time of the Fourteenth Amendment's adoption, had they been posed to them, Bork wrote. As for the First Amendment, "like the rest of the Bill of Rights, [it] appears to have been a hastily drafted document upon which little thought was expended," and the subsequent writings of the framers "do not tell us what the men who adopted the first amendment meant." The urgent need of the Court, Bork argued, was to return not to the deep past but to a set of clear, neutral principles. "We cannot solve our problems simply by reference to the text or to its history."[28]

It was not in the center of the law's discourse, then, that the idea of going back to the original minds and intentions of the Constitution writers gathered traction but on its less professionalized margins. A particularly important case was the work of Raoul Berger, a law professor, self-trained historian, and maverick political liberal who, in a series of books in the 1970s on judicial review, the impeachment clause, and executive privilege, set out to prove exactly what the Constitution's framers must have meant, generally along lines compatible with a liberal Democrat's expectations. His bombshell of a book, however, was his history of the Fourteenth Amendment, published as *Government by Judiciary* in 1977. This time Berger emerged from his historical research convinced that there was not a shred of historical evidence to support Justice Black's contention that the Fourteenth Amendment's framers had imagined that their work would touch the rights that had been traditionally adjudicated by the states. The "incorporation" decisions bringing state law under the authority of the federal Bill of Rights were entirely wrong. *Brown,* decided on a reading of the Fourteenth Amendment that was historically distorted, was invalid. Where "the intention of the framers is unmistakably expressed," Berger wrote, where "that intention is as good as written into the text," to ignore it as inconclusive was "a naked usurpation of power."[29]

Berger's rejection of *Brown* made his work something of a hot rail not only in liberal circles but also in those conservative circles where a sense of the need for historical continuity carried weight. But among more radical conservatives, Berger's arguments gathered a receptive audience. A particularly active figure in those circles was James McClellan, an ardent, Southern, states-rights conservative, onetime member of Senator Jesse Helms's staff, whose Center for Judicial Studies, established with conservative foundation money in 1983, was to become one of the hothouses for the production of Constitutional arguments to the right of the Reagan administration.[30] In Mobile, Alabama, in 1982, where twenty years after public school prayers had been declared unconstitutional by the Supreme Court public school classrooms were still saturated with them, a parent had filed suit. The Alabama legislature had passed a bill the previous year affirming the right of teachers to lead willing children in any prayer or meditation they chose. When the case reached the district court, the expected line of decision would have been simply to apply the two decades of Supreme Court precedents to the case. Instead, in an extremely long opinion, prefaced by a quotation from Raoul Berger and written under the inspiration of the "vision" that James McClellan had provided (some in Alabama said that McClellan had written most of the opinion himself), Judge Brevard Hand set out to show that history proved the Supreme Court wrong.[31]

At the time of its adoption, the First Amendment had not been imagined as touching the states, Hand wrote. When the Fourteenth Amendment was adopted, only a minority of its framers had suggested that the "privileges and immunities" that it had guaranteed explicitly included the protections of the First Amendment. The incorporation doctrine was, as Raoul Berger had contended, fundamentally wrong. Two sharply different modes of Constitutional interpretation had come before the court, Hand wrote. Either the court could attempt "to ascertain the intent of the adopters . . . and apply the Constitution as the adopters intended it to be applied," or it could treat the Constitution as "a living document, chameleon-like in its complexion, which changes to suit the needs of the times and whims of the interpreters." The latter path was "unconstitutional and illegal"; it was the path of Hitler, not that of the Founders, Hand warned. Properly understood in the light of history, the First Amendment did not bind the states. That being the case, Hand declared, the state of Alabama was free to establish whatever religion and publicly endorsed religious practices it might choose.[32]

Jaffree was an extraordinary opinion, perhaps no more than a voice "blowing in the hurricane," as Hand himself admitted. When it was overturned, Hand reopened the trial, brought in a new group of expert witnesses, as he had threatened to do in his first opinion, and with their help concluded that the textbooks used in the Mobile public schools were so saturated with opinions hostile to religion that secular humanism was effectively being taught as a state religion. His decision banned the use of six home economics textbooks that the witnesses held gave too much weight to the autonomy of human beings in making value choices and nine U.S. history textbooks that underplayed the central role of religion in U.S. history.[33]

Like Hand's first opinion, his secular humanism ruling was swiftly overturned. But Hand's and McClellan's quixotic venture into Constitutional "intention" brought a tangle of threads to the surface: the vulnerability of the Warren Court's ventures into new realms of rights declaration; the multiple, rival American histories in circulation; the yearnings of Americans on the conservative side of the "culture wars" for permanence and certainty; the countermobilization of expertise which the conservative foundations were now able to bring to bear against the legal and educational establishments; and the sectional rivalries running so strongly through politics. (When states lost the right to decide for themselves who their voters should be and what rights their citizens held after the Civil War, McClellan argued, the heart was cut out of the Constitution.)[34] Quickly dismissed and impotent in the law, the *Jaffree* and *Smith* decisions nonetheless set things in motion. When Hand's first ruling was overturned by the Supreme Court, Justice Rehnquist's dissenting opinion did not endorse the McClellan-Berger argument that the religious-establishment clause did not touch the states. But on the basis of a very long historical argument, Rehnquist insisted that the "wall of separation" metaphor that had grounded the Court's church and state decisions since the 1940s, taken from a Jefferson letter written years after the Bill of Rights' adoption, had no standing as a genuinely historical foundation for the framers' real intentions.[35]

This was the context into which the new attorney general, Edwin Meese, strode a month later to announce that the Reagan administration would pursue, henceforth, a systematic "jurisprudence of original intention." In a speech pointed in its praise for Rehnquist's *Wallace v. Jaffree* dissent, Meese declared that the incorporation doctrine was "a politically violent and constitutionally suspect blow" to the original meaning of the Constitution. The courts were not to make ad hoc policy decisions, he stated in this and a flurry of subsequent speeches. They were not to weigh cases by their impact on "the well-being of our society" or "the living development of constitutional justice." They must not drift back "toward the radical egalitarianism and expansive civil libertarianism" of the Warren Court. The task of jurisprudence was to "resurrect the original meaning" of Constitutional provisions and statutes: "the plain words as originally understood."[36]

Over the next decade debate over a jurisprudence of "original intention" was to draw a vast amount of intellectual energy into its vortex. Nominated to the Supreme Court in 1987, Robert Bork, whom Antonin Scalia had skewered three years earlier for being altogether too ready to admit the need for "continuing evolution of doctrine," dropped his earlier doubts about the clarity of the historical record and declared himself an originalist. On the other side, Justice Brennan had already entered the fray, three months after Meese, with a sharp attack on the arrogance of those who thought they could know with certainty the intentions of the Constitution's framers. The Constitution's drafters had disagreed and had "hid their differences in cloaks of generality" that they passed on for new times and circumstances, Brennan contended. "The genius of the Constitution rests not in any static meaning it might have had in a world that is dead and gone, but in the adaptability of its great principles to cope with current problems and current needs."[37]

As justices and law professors lined up on either side of the "original-intentions" debate, their argument was partly about change: the conservatives were eager to pull the courts permanently back from the sort of extrapolations and rights inventions that they associated with the Warren Court. "Not even a scintilla of evidence supports the argument that the framers and the ratifiers of the various amendments intended the judiciary to develop new individual rights," Bork had insisted.[38] It was partly an argument about authority and the courts' deference to the democratic institutions of governance. The "plain words" of the Constitution were in safer hands when entrusted to the common people in their legislatures, the originalists maintained, than when commandeered by law school professors or power-aggrandizing judges. It was partly an argument between the forward-looking and backward-looking obligations of the law. From the side of a frankly "pragmatic" jurisprudence, the law and economics movement's Richard Posner insisted that what judges weighed were not timeless or original principles but social effects: "consequences in the world of fact." Law was functional, future-oriented, and policy-saturated, Posner wrote. Justice Benjamin Cardozo had been right: "Not the origin, but the goal, is the main thing."[39]

But what the original-intentions debate brought most sharply into relief was a different question of time: how clearly one could penetrate through the incomplete and muddied historical record to its original, undistorted core. The illusion of original-intentions' advocates, the Constitution's leading historian Jack Rakove wrote, was that "a particular set of pristine meanings, uncorrupted by interpretation, was somehow locked into the text of the Constitution at the moment of its adoption." But could one know with any useful certainty what lay behind the words the Constitution's drafters had used, when there were so many points of view in the convention, so many verbal compromises to accomplish, when they kept their own deliberations secret and barred the records from publication, when they themselves in the political arguments of the 1790s explicitly rejected the idea that statements of intention should resolve the

Constitution's meaning?[40] How could one reenact with any confidence an event whose script was lost?

With Scalia in the lead, originalism's defenders shifted from Meese's case for a jurisprudence of original intention to a jurisprudence of original meaning, by which they meant not the secret intentional mind of the text's writers but how the words they used must have been read by those at the time.[41] But whose readings gave the Constitution force? The majority at the constitutional convention or the vastly larger, often starkly divided delegates at the state ratifying conventions, who, Madison among others insisted, were the ones who had truly brought the Constitution into being? Precisely the same could be said about the Fourteenth Amendment, as the law review articles, which quickly complicated Berger's simple picture, made clear. Was there only one moment of Constitution jurisgenesis, supplemented by later realizations of its original design? Or, as Yale Law School's Bruce Ackerman argued in his widely read book *We the People* in 1991, was there a series of historical moments when the Constitution was essentially remade and given a new popular base: the ratification moment of 1788–1789; the years of Reconstruction, when its compromises with slavery were wrung out of it; and the New Deal years, when courts, Congress, and the people essentially recast it once more?[42]

The generalized vocabulary of the Constitution compounded the interpretational difficulties—the "inescapable open-endedness" of many of its most important provisions, as the legal philosopher John Hart Ely put it. At what level of abstraction were the "privileges and immunities" of citizens or the "equal protection of the laws" to be read, or the altogether unnamed rights reserved to the people in the Ninth Amendment? Justice Clarence Thomas insisted that a "plain reading" of the Constitution would show that the spirit of the Declaration of Independence had been fully absorbed in every phrase of its text, though it was a line of argument with only the shakiest of actual historical foundations. Gary McDowell, who was said to have drafted Meese's original speech, argued that what was determinative was not the particular historical circumstances of the founding period but the Constitution's overall "design and objects." Justice Rehnquist had said the same thing prior to *Wallace:* that justice was done not by jurisprudential "literalism" but by taking seriously the "logic of the constitutional scheme" and the "tacit postulates . . . engrained in the fabric of the document."[43]

In readings like these, reasoning from logic and principle jostled against the sovereignty of text and word. Virtually every one of originalism's defenders thought it prudent to find a way to include *Brown* in the Constitution's original design rather than to see it as the result of wiser, experience-tested judgment. In repudiating the *Plessy* era's racially separate school systems, Meese claimed, the Court "was not giving a new life to old words, or adapting a 'living,' 'flexible' Constitution to new reality. It was restoring the original principle of the Constitution to constitutional law." Bork's admission that a sound Constitutional jurisprudence required a "principle," a "core value," a "major premise" fairly discoverable in text would have gotten no dissent from the very activists on the Warren Court whom Bork now strongly opposed. The task, Bork wrote, was to choose "no level of generality higher than that which interpretation of the words, structure, and history of the Constitution fairly support[s]."[44] This drift from literalism to interpretation was the conceptual fuzz around originalism that led Posner to charge that it was almost "completely plastic . . . a rhetoric that can be used to support any result the judge wants to reach." Ronald Dworkin charged that Bork "has no theory at all," and Ackerman that he demonstrated no serious engagement with history.[45]

For the dwindling number of conservatives whose sense of history had been shaped in the traditions of Edmund Burke, questions of modesty, continuity, and precedent all cautioned against the path of Meese and Hand. Originalism was a project for breaking the law's continuity, Thomas W. Merrill objected at the Federalist Society's gathering on the tenth anniversary of Meese's opening salvo; it was but another face of radicalism. "Read Burke's account of the French Revolution."[46] Least of all is it clear that even conservative Americans would have wanted to bring back to life the words and practices of the Constitution's origins. The early republic whose day-to-day practices Antonin Scalia was beginning to press into the Court record with a density they had never had before was a world in which slavery and servitude were an omnipresent fact in society and economy, in which married women were virtually nonpersons in the law, in which religious dissidents were taxed to pay for other Americans' standing clergy. It hardly resembled the early 1950s that the Warren Court's critics actually yearned to restore.[47]

Like all forms of nostalgia, that on the conservative side of the legal-cultural controversies was selective and sentimental. The originalist argument tapped not a desire to go back to any actual past but a desire to escape altogether from time's slipperiness—to locate a trap door through which one could reach beyond history and find a simpler place outside of it. Originalism's appeal to the past was, like the economists' modelings of time, profoundly ahistorical. Indeed, to legal critics worried about subjective judgments in the law, worried that the law's ruling principles carried too abundantly the marks of change and adaptation upon it, originalism's ahistoricism was precisely what gave it such power and attraction.

In the end, after consuming so much political-intellectual energy in the late 1980s, the arguments over original meaning began to slacken in the 1990s. The incorporation doctrine that originalism's first proponents had hoped to reverse endured. But open defense of the "living Constitution" such as Brennan had made—expanding, adapting, adjusting to the new circumstances and mores of the day—sharply diminished as well. There was more historical argument in Constitutional law briefs now than before, most observers agreed. But defenders of Meese's project of a systematic original-intentions jurisprudence struggled to overcome that project's internal contradictions. On the Supreme Court even Scalia, though he sustained originalism's rhetoric, strayed far from history, as whim would take him, into the sort of psychological and social arguments for which he and others had once pilloried the Warren Court. The law reviews offered an "originalism for nonoriginalists," which, compared with the doctrine's first moment in the mid-1980s, was hardly originalism at all.[48]

Still, for well over a decade, the idea of penetrating time, folding history over upon itself so that one could slip out of its complexities, had been a powerful intellectual project. Against conservative fears of legal subjectivism run wild, originalism's prospect of slipping instantly across time, propelled by the words of a text, was tangible and real. Continuity had traditionally been conservatism's cardinal principle. But the notion of the long course of history, with its institutions and power, its precedents and inertia, its relapses and its progress, had been replaced by other metaphors. Originalism was Constitutional conservatism's flirtation with timelessness.

The authentic, original Constitution was the object of desire and imagination; by contrast, the sudden collapse of Soviet Communism and the Cold War was an imaginative fantasy that became, virtually overnight, a sober fact. For forty years, the Cold War had touched every phase of intellectual life. The very character of twentieth-century American society had been defended and defined within the polar antitheses that the Soviet Union had provided. Now suddenly that great intellectual and geopolitical rivalry, as the slang phrase went, was history. Capitalism's great antagonist was dead and voiceless. Between Mikhail Gorbachev's ascent to the party's reins in 1985 and 1992, when the Soviet Union ceased to exist, a dominant fixture of the century's landscape, powerful and seemingly permanent, disintegrated.

Every phase of that process generated argument, in which history, economy, and society were all at stake. Economists, Russian experts, and political commentators tangled over each turn of events and what it held in store. To comprehend the historical processes under way, to imagine the possibilities for reform within the structures of totalitarian society, and finally to seize on and accelerate the forces of transition so that the centralized, command economies of Communism could be transformed, in a single eye-blink of historic time, into market societies: these were issues in which questions of time and history came inevitably to the fore. Once again, ambition to short-circuit time, to imagine being propelled across the tortured processes of history in a single bound, played a powerful role. This time both intellectuals on the right and their centrist and liberal rivals would be susceptible to it.

As the events in the Soviet Union and Eastern Europe unfolded in the 1980s, comprehension of them in the West built on layers of preexisting historical assumptions. One of these was the extremely limited capacity of Communist society for meaningful change. The very definition of "totalitarianism," forged in 1940s and 1950s social science, implied a society frozen in time, in which the totalizing control of party, ideology, and the state snuffed out every meaningful trace of social spontaneity. The aging of the Soviet Union's leadership, the hardening of its ideological arteries, and its isolation from the emerging patterns of global commerce and communication all reinforced the sense of a regime suspended in time. When Jeane Kirkpatrick added to her widely circulated attack on Jimmy Carter's human rights policy a stark distinction between "authoritarian" regimes, which had a capacity to evolve into democracies under the right circumstances, and "totalitarian" regimes, which did not, these assumptions about time and change were central to them.[49]

Some experts on the Soviet Union, to be sure, had begun to suggest greater capacity for change. From the 1960s on there grew an active discussion of the possibilities for internal reform and scenarios of a "post-totalitarian" future. Within the Soviet economic bloc itself, there was active talk of mitigating the worst of its economic rigidities with marketlike incentives. The radical swings through which Chinese domestic policy moved after 1958, from the Great Leap Forward, with its vision of an industrial revolution literally springing up from millions of rural peasant plots, to the Cultural Revolution's frenzied assault on the nation's technical elite, to the post-Mao experiments with market Communism, showed anything but stasis.[50]

Still, it is fair to say that the more conservative one's political orientation, the less likely one was to think of Communism as capable of adapting to the forces of history. Moderate and liberal Sovietologists could imagine scenarios of reform from within, by which Communist states might slowly converge toward Western models of industrial society. Conservative predictions of Communism's future, by contrast, were apocalyptic. Ultimately Communism would be swept away; that was the point of Reagan's reference to Communism as a "bizarre chapter in human history whose last pages even now are being written." It was axiomatic to American conservatives that in the end Communism could not ultimately prevail. It was unnatural; the costs of its inefficiency were a massive economic and social drain; it violated the natural aspirations of men and women for autonomy and freedom. But the usual scenario looked first to ossification and then to convulsive and protracted crisis. Jean-François Revel's claim that the "transition to totalitarian rule is by definition irrevocable except in the case of some cataclysm like a world war," was no longer the dominant line by the early 1980s. "Nothing in nature is permanent and immutable," the most influential of the conservative Soviet experts, Richard Pipes, wrote in 1984, a year before Gorbachev came to power. Still, the end of Communism, as conservatives imagined it, was bound to be bloody and drawn out, as a system slipping into systemic "general crisis" summoned its last energies to destroy its agents of change. Gradual reform adaptation was not in the cards. "For most of the cold war," the *National Interest*'s Owen Harries wrote in retrospect of his fellow conservative intellectuals, almost all of them "accepted—more or less uncritically—a theory of totalitarianism that attributed to it implacable power and a virtually immutable nature."[51]

None of this changed when Reagan assumed office, except for the hardening of the sense of imminent danger, triggered by the Soviet invasion of Afghanistan in 1979 and Soviet muscle flexing in Africa. Later, after the fact, it was said that the new administration had set out to precipitate the collapse of Communism by outspending it on military expenditures. There is not a shred of evidence, however, that the Soviet Union's actual demise was on anyone's agenda. The Reagan administration's proximate goal was to contain and roll back the Soviet Union's expanded military presence in the world, to regain nuclear war–fighting superiority, and to push the Soviet leadership toward more accommodationist policies. The National Security Strategy, adopted in May 1982, hoped to "discourage Soviet adventurism, and weaken the Soviet alliance system by forcing the USSR to bear the brunt of its economic shortcoming, and to encourage long-term liberalizing and nationalist tendencies within the Soviet Union and allied countries." But nothing implied that this would happen soon. The national security directive on US-USSR relations adopted the next year set as its goal "to promote, within the narrow limits available to us, the process of change in the Soviet Union toward a more pluralistic political and economic system in which the power of the privileged ruling elite is gradually reduced." This was a policy "for the long haul." The best it could say about the coming five to ten years was that they "will be a period of considerable uncertainty." Reagan's secretary of state wrote in a memo to the president in early 1983: "To be sure the Soviet system is beset by serious weaknesses. But it would be a mistake to assume that the Soviet capacity for competition with us will diminish at any time during your presidency." Jeane Kirkpatrick, Reagan's outspokenly anti-Communist United Nations ambassador, when asked that same year if U.S. policy might bring the Soviet Union to the brink of collapse, responded that she did not think that "collapse" was likely.[52]

A sense of the exceptional resilience of the Soviet Union, to the contrary, dominated conservative Cold War thought through the end of the decade and beyond. As Gorbachev, coming to power in 1985, began to spin off a bewildering variety of reforms—*perestroika, glasnost,* decentralization of the command economy, military withdrawal from Afghanistan, the first serious nuclear arms reduction initiatives, and a warming personal relationship with Reagan—the reaction of Soviet observers to the right of the administration was to warn against assuming that any significant change had occurred. George Will wrote that "*glasnost* can never be more than a carefully controlled Kremlin tactic to confuse the West and motivate Soviet masses with a tantalizing mirage of freedom just over a forever receding horizon." Alain Besançon, a regular writer for *Commentary,* where this line of argument was most strenuously pursued, was certain *glasnost* was an elaborate bluff designed to weaken the vigilance of the West. Even Richard Pipes as late as 1990 warned that the release of the Eastern European satellite regimes from the Soviet Union's control was a ploy to offload their economic liabilities onto the capitalist nations. The danger that haunted conservative commentators was the possibility that, fooled by ruse and illusions of change, the West would ease the pressure on the Soviet system, grasp the false threads of *détente,* and in the process postpone the long death throes of internal collapse. The "fallacy of misplaced malleability," Jeane Kirkpatrick had named this illusion in another context.[53]

It was in the midst of this strenuous concern that anti-Communists not relax the long, ongoing international struggle that the conservative foreign policy journal the *National Interest* published a piece by a young foreign policy consultant, Francis Fukuyama, announcing that the Cold War was over. Fukuyama's "End of History?" appeared in the summer of 1989, a season of mixed signals. That was the summer in which Solidarity, legalized that spring, won a sweeping victory in parliamentary elections in Poland; it was also the summer in which protesters gathered by the thousands in Beijing's Tiananmen Square only to be routed by government tanks and arrested by government agents. The precipitous collapse of the Communist governments in Hungary, East Germany, Czechoslovakia, and Bulgaria, like a line of teetering dominoes, took place between October and November. The Berlin Wall fell in November. But here in July, before any of this was clear, Fukuyama had announced that Communism was already essentially vanquished. The West had triumphed. And with the exhaustion of one pole of the twentieth century's great political dialectic, history itself had come to an end. What the West was witnessing was not only the end of the Cold War, Fukuyama wrote. "What we may be witnessing is . . . the end of history as such: that is, the end point of mankind's ideological evolution and the universalization of Western liberal democracy as the final form of human government."[54]

The quick and extraordinary media hyping of "The End of History?" stemmed partly from the fact that it followed close on the heels of the historian Paul Kennedy's much more pessimistic work *The Rise and Fall of the Great Powers* (1987). In a sweeping history of imperial overstretch, Kennedy had warned that contemporary U.S. global military hegemony, with its massive burden of military expenditures, could not last forever. Kennedy's "declinism" and Fukuyama's "endism" feuded as paired antagonists in the reviews. Whereas Kennedy grounded his predictions in comparative history, Fukuyama fitted his out with what many called amateur philosophy, much of it inspired by his undergraduate teacher Allan Bloom. That blubber of philosophizing grew thicker as Fukuyama transformed his *National Interest* article into a book. Plato, Nietzsche, Leo Strauss, Alexander Koyève, the obscure dissident Marxist who was Strauss's favored interpreter of Hegel, and, above all, Hegel himself were all injected into Fukuyama's pages to demonstrate the sudden exhaustion of historical time.[55]

Hegel's presence was part of what infuriated many conservative reviewers of "The End of History?" They saw its dialectical spin as a mark of Fukuyama's absorption of Marxist notions of history. "Marxist ideology is alive and well in Fukuyama's arguments to refute it," Samuel Huntington put the frequent charge. It would be wiser to recognize history as unpredictable, as a "succession of contingencies, catastrophes, and occasional lapses into peace and civilization," as the *National Review*'s critic put it: a terrain of continual vigilance and continual struggle. Fukuyama's "endism" struck others as naive. On the terrain of real geopolitics, the Russians had never been stronger, Richard Pipes rushed to reassert the consensus of conservative foreign policy experts.[56]

In the course of these heated disputes, it was not always clear exactly what Fukuyama thought had come to an end. World conflicts, he insisted, were not likely to disappear. In the parts of the world where the

"posthistorical" turn had not yet taken place, nationalist and ethnic violence would remain high, he suggested; terror and wars of national liberation would persist. What was new about the present moment,
Fukuyama seemed to argue, was the turn in philosophical consciousness
that had occurred. Ideologically, Communism was played out, and with
Communism's intellectual demise liberalism's only rival claimant to universal history had evaporated. To imagine that there was no end goal
to history was to slip into the pit of relativism and nihilism, Fukuyama
worried in the tones of Strauss and Bloom. The "total exhaustion of viable systematic alternatives to Western liberalism" meant that history had
finally realized itself.[57]

An end-times prediction by an obscure and unknown writer, wrapped
in Hegel's philosophical trappings, "The End of History?" was an outward
anomaly: overwhelmed but not defeated by its rebuttals from both left
and right. Its timing was lucky and prescient. But it also tapped with extraordinary force the notions of folded and short-circuited time that ran
through late-twentieth-century social thought. It promised a great leap
forward across institutions and inertia into a "universal homogeneous
state" of markets, property, science, personal liberties, and democracy.
Ronald Reagan's favorite line from Tom Paine, that we have it in our
power "to begin the world over again," moved in the Fukuyama craze
from self-actualization rhetoric into the vexed and power-filled world of
international affairs.

The work of folding the future into the present was to be the task of centrist and liberal economists. As the old regimes suddenly unraveled in
1989–1992, as the dismantlers pushed out the system-committed reformers like Gorbachev, while conservative columnists wrung their hands
over the illusion that outside forces could alter the long-term legacies of
totalitarianism, an army of U.S. and Western European experts poured
into post-Communist Eastern Europe to make the conversion to capitalism real. The retinue included legal and constitutional experts, parlia-
mentarians, academic consultants, human rights lawyers, Ford and Soros
foundation staffers, European Union officials, business consultants, and
investors looking for a deal. But the economists, coming first, set the pa-
rameters and the tone. Jeffrey Sachs, the young Harvard economist who
was to become the most visible face of "transition" economics, had begun

consulting for Solidarity in the summer of 1989; when the Balcerowicz plan for an end to Poland's Soviet-style economy was announced in January 1990, Sachs was already in place as a consultant and publicist. Months before the final collapse of Gorbachev's schemes of market socialism in late 1991, Boris Yeltsin and his economics minister, Yegor Gaidar, had determined to take the Russian economy down a similar course of sweeping decontrols and privatization, pushed and shaped in part by International Monetary Fund and Western advisers, Sachs among them.[58]

The challenge, as reformers inside and outside the former Communist system understood it, was to transform its economic institutions into market economies as rapidly as possible. Within three years after Poland's first experiment with "shock therapy," transition to capitalism—abolition of price controls and central planning agencies, privatization of state enterprises, and dismantling of barriers to trade and investment—had become official policy throughout virtually all the spheres of the former USSR.[59]

At another historical moment that task might have been imagined institutionally: as a matter of mapping comparably functional institutions in capitalist and Soviet societies upon each other, translating social processes from one system to another, and harnessing existing traditions to new tasks. Many people at the time, not the least Gorbachev himself, imagined that what might emerge was some middle ground, a viable "third way" between the market individualism of the United States and the promises of Soviet socialism, combining, perhaps, much stronger price incentives for economic managers with some version of the basic housing, income, health, and transportation guarantees that (whatever the shortages and however costly in time the queues might be) had sustained the system's social legitimacy. John Kenneth Galbraith, at the twilight of his career now in 1990, said as much.[60] But what might have been a debate about institutions and a multitude of potential destinations quickly became a debate about time.

"Shock therapy" was the popular name for the immediatist program. The term had been coined by Sachs in an article with a consciously Leninist title, "What Is to Be Done?" published in the *Economist* in January 1990—though Sachs was only the most conspicuous of shock therapy's multiple devisers in both the West and the East. Everything, shock therapy's advocates advised, must be pursued simultaneously: liberalization of prices, privatization and extensive deregulation of state industries, free international trade and currency exchange, the collapse and restructuring of inefficient firms, and reduced public spending to achieve strictly balanced budgets. The leap into the market economy had to be done boldly and precipitously: in one "big bang" or not at all. Sachs's timeframe for Poland's transition to a market economy was one year.[61]

The economics establishment's insistence on the need for radically compressed time stemmed in part from a quick analogy between the conditions of "transition" economics and the conditions of hyperinflation in 1980s Latin America, where Sachs, among others, had been a prominent traveling consultant. Only a radical deflation of wages and prices, produced at once and held to with adamant resolve, could (as Robert Lucas had insisted years before) change the expectations of economic actors in a condition of hyperinflation. The massive gap between pent-up consumer demand and atrophied production put post-Communist societies in a condition of real or latent hyperinflation almost by definition. The solution for one economic disease became the cure for the other, not the least because it was one that the doctors imagined they knew how to manage.[62] To this was added, particularly among the Eastern European economists who enlisted in the shock-therapy project, a widespread and not inaccurate conviction that five years of piecemeal Gorbachev-led gradualist reforms had been an economic disaster. In an economy structurally organized to respond to central production orders, the reformers' introduction of economic incentives for firm managers had set off a cascade of coordination problems. Production declined; goods vanished from the stores.[63]

To the appeal of shocking the economic system, all at once, into capitalism were added political considerations. Gradualism, it was argued, only gave those with vested interests in the status quo time to blunt the effects of change and frustrate the hopes of the reformers. It allowed the painful short-term effects of transition to fester into widespread, "populist" political opposition, powerful enough to force the economic reformers into retreat before their initiatives had a chance to work. The project of transition was as much about destruction as it was about change. "An entire world must be discarded," the economist Richard Ericson advised in 1991. The only reform capable of sustaining itself must be "trenchantly negative . . . disruptive on an historically unprecedented scale." That was what the group of Russian economic reformers around Yegor Gaidar meant in specifying to their Western consultants that they wanted "real" reform of the sort that Sachs had advocated in Poland; they had no interest in conversations with Western specialists in Russian history or Soviet institutions.[64]

Framing all these issues of power, analogy, and experience, finally, were the new economic models of instantly adjusting time. The economic institutions, habits, and expectations that had developed in post-1917 Russia and the nations of post-1945 Eastern Europe were massive social investments. But shock therapy's promise was that in returning the economy to its "natural" state, the processes of history could be made to pivot in a virtual instant. "To make a switch to market prices in one motion is a severe, forced, but necessary measure," Boris Yeltsin announced in October 1991; but by the fall of 1992 "the economy will have stabilized and people's lives will gradually get better." A recovery should be under way "within two years or so," the IMF experts had advised in 1990.[65]

The economic theorists of transition did not, for the most part, come from the conservative wing of the profession. The MIT and Harvard economics departments were much more prominently engaged in consultancies to the post-Communist regimes than were the University of Chicago group. Most of the consultants were neither economic libertarians nor historical naifs. Sachs's program had entailed both an extensive safety net of health and unemployment benefits and massive Western aid to finance it. From the beginning, Sachs had acknowledged that "the transition is fraught with danger." Later, frustrated by the failure of his hoped-for tens of billions of dollars in aid to materialize, he was to insist: "I never thought the markets would do it by themselves—never."[66] But for all the distance between transition macroeconomists and the University of Chicago stance in the macrowars, shock therapy's advocates had fully absorbed the new models of rapid market-clearing action and instantly acting time. Belief in market time's virtually frictionless action was the escape hatch through which they imagined circumventing the power and institution-strewn terrain of history.

In the feverishly active conferences on transition economics, a minority of economists held out for alternatives to the do-everything-at-once program. Some emphasized the importance of sequencing. Slowing down plans for the immediate privatization of the large state enterprises through a general distribution of voucher shares, with their particularly uncertain outcomes, guided almost wholly by exercises in theory, was a common suggestion. Others pointed to the need to take existing institutional structures seriously. The Columbia University economist Peter Murrell was a particularly articulate advocate of letting a new market economy gradually take root alongside the state-managed economy, slowly to subsume it.[67] The China road of gradual economic liberalization was floated as shock therapy's alternative. "Crossing the river by feeling the stones underfoot," its advocates called the dual-economy course, in contrast to the dominant transition mantra: that a chasm could never be crossed piecemeal, in a series of timid hops. The conflict of social theory was also a battle of metaphors. "The chasm between socialism and capitalism is not a crack in the ground" to be vaulted over, the historian Jerry Hough was to write much later. "It is the Grand Canyon . . . it must be crossed by tortuous and indirect mule trails."[68]

But these were the voices of a small minority in the wake of the upheavals of 1989, the influx of experts, and the heavy institutional pressure of the international financial agencies. Notions of monoeconomics and monopolitics, good for all times and places, transportable through the conduits of internationally mobile experts and pressure groups, were at their height in the late 1980s. The campaign for universal human rights, reignited by the Carter administration over the strenuous objections of many conservative foreign policy experts, had become mainstream by the mid-1980s. Conservatives' fears that aggressive human rights advocacy might undermine the stability of friendly regimes, that it would distract public attention from the particularly oppressive crimes of Communism, and that it would play into socialist demands for economic and collective rights, retreated as conservatives learned how to mobilize human rights rhetoric for their own politically compatible ends. The particular abuses that moved, quickly and fitfully, in and out of the spotlights of the human rights crusade were constructions of politics; but like the new economics, human rights politics carried a new, overt universalism. Individual liberties, market economics, and democracies—once stacked in time as the products of modernization—slipped out of history to become universal, global, immediate goals.[69]

In this context, it was taken for granted that there could be only one viable, natural destination for the post-Soviet economies. Either the transition to Western-style capitalism was leaped successfully or it grounded out on some ledge in the abyss. There was no "third way," Sachs argued. The advocates of workers' control who joined the bands of advice dispensers in Eastern Europe, urging that the state industries be turned over to labor cooperatives, were, in the minds of most of the transition economists, a dangerous nuisance. Set the incentives right, let the forces of structural adjustment proceed as rapidly as possible to their new equilibrium, counting on universal human nature to do the rest, and time could be, if not annihilated, as the Lucas model had had it, radically foreshortened.[70] Much later, the economist Joseph Stiglitz, among the many players in the transition economics conferences, was to charge that shock therapy was the work of "market Bolsheviks" who had deluded themselves into thinking that their textbook simplifications were a working model of reality.[71] In fact, it was precisely the power of economic theory, as it had passed through the intellectual wringer of the 1970s, that made the confidence of 1989–1991 so massive—that made transition's prophets think that, if they seized the moment, they could fold the long-term future into immediate realization.

In the end, short-circuiting time turned out to be far from easy. Persuading the former Communist elites to throw in their lot with the new economic order did not prove a major stumbling block. In Russia, as David Kotz, Fred Weir, and others argue, the state enterprise managers and party-state elite quickly decided their interests lay with the market reformers rather than with *perestroika*'s hybridism, and converted themselves overnight to quasi-capitalists. The more dramatic problem was not the resistance of the elites but that the expected economic adjustment to price liberalization did not materialize nearly as quickly or as surely as the models of foreshortened time had had it. By 1992 there was already considerable worry in the economic symposia that the process would be much more drawn out than had been imagined. Even Sachs began to admit that the "valley of tears" in Poland between the old society and the new was likely to be "several years" in width.[72] By 1994, almost everyone but Sachs was admitting that Eastern Europe had plunged into an economic depression of virtually unprecedented length and dimensions.

The scale of the crisis differed from economy to economy. In Poland, where the market sector under Communism was unusually extensive and Western aid particularly forthcoming, the gross domestic product had fallen 14 percent from its 1989 level by the time the post-transition depression bottomed out in 1991. In the Russian case it was catastrophic: a decline of 47 percent that reached bottom only in 1998. In the Ukraine, where the contraction was even larger, the economy was still sliding downward in 1999. The Sachs group, deprecating the meaning of the early signs, argued that the statistics grossly overestimated the production of the Soviet economies and failed to measure the increases in available consumer goods. "Wildly exaggerated" was how Sachs's chief collaborator, the Swedish economist Anders Åslund, described the reported decline in the Russian standard of living in 1995.[73] But even as books heralding the coming Russian boom crowded into the bookstores, capital investment collapsed. A new oligarchy snapped up ownership of the rapidly privatized state enterprises. At the other end of the newly pronounced wealth gap, the number of people in poverty shot up dramatically: ten- to twentyfold, by some estimates. Kotz and Weir sum up the Russian result of transition economics as "the longest and deepest economic depression ever experienced by any major country in peacetime."[74]

Nor, in the end, did "transition"—with its assumption that there was only one natural goal for economies released from central direction—turn out to be the right name. Some of the economic consultants tried to model the phenomenon as a prolonged, inertia-plagued U-curve. Others suggested that the process had a wide number of stable variations, from the ultimately successful marketization in the Polish, Czech, Hungarian, and Baltic republic cases to the emergence of a new, oil-revenue-fueled, self-serving oligarchy in Russia. Questions of culture that had seemed irrelevant in the euphoria of 1989–1991 came back to the fore. Whereas it had once seemed self-evident that proper incentives would bring out the behavioral responses of universal economic man, Sachs by the late 1990s was consumed with frustration at the capacities of Russian culture to frustrate economic change.[75]

As a new, more sober recognition of the power of habits and institutions took hold, the dream of vaulting the post-Soviet economies into capitalism diminished. The exhaustion of Marxism was an accomplished fact, but the Great Leap Forward to a market society proved vastly more difficult than many had let themselves imagine. The prolonged and violent general crisis that conservative Sovietologists had foreseen proved a misreading of the times, but the new "universal homogenous state" that Francis Fukuyama had predicted was no less illusory. History worked sometimes with glacial slowness, at other times with revolutionary and unpredictable swiftness. But it was not an empty chasm that could be leaped. It could not be folded up upon itself or short-circuited. In thinking so, however, shock therapy's prescribers had tapped a contagious intellectual metaphor of the age. For a moment, time itself had seemed almost infinitely thin and pliable.

The rosy scenarios advanced for the post-Soviet future were not the first instance in modern times in which social scientists had mispredicted the course of events. The advocates of original-intentions jurisprudence were not the first to imagine restoring Constitutional law to an earlier, purer state. Francis Fukuyama's vision of a liberal end to history had its precedents. And yet, the sense of the time that flowed through them all brought to the surface some of the key intellectual shifts of the age.

The new models of time and change reflected a widespread sense of the naturalness of markets—not merely their utility, or their astonishing capacity for productivity and innovation, but their very congruence with human nature itself. They drew on a new confidence in the economics profession in the wake of its 1970s intellectual crisis: its assumption of global monoeconomics, the portability and generalizability of its models through the institutional regimes for their internationalization. The era's sense of foreshortened time mirrored the new image of the global markets' instant capacities for adjustment, the new managerial rhetoric of quick response and flexible production. Confidence that one might engage the ratifiers of the Constitution and its amendments in a direct conversation unmediated by time mirrored the eagerness of postmodernist architects to pluck symbols and motifs out of the past into a pastiche for the present. Institutions, inertia, and power all retreated in these discussions from the analytical center. Even history disaggregated into histories, intensely possessed but held on terms more private than before. In all their late-twentieth-century forms, the new variations on ideas of time brushed past the force of society and custom, the counterdrag of traditions and solidarities, the dynamics of power and resistance.

Like the battles over heritage and history, all these were contested claims with articulate critics. But they dominated, nonetheless, the new models of time and change. In the middle of the twentieth century, history's massive, inescapable, larger-than-life presence had weighed down on social discourse. To talk seriously was to talk of the long, large-scale movements of time. Modernization theory and Marxism, theories of long-term economic development and cultural lag, the inexorabilities of the business cycle and the historians' *longue durée*, the structures of culture and endurance of archetypes in the psyche: these framed the language of social thought and debate. But now time had wrinkled. One might reach nostalgically for a fragment of the past, but the time that dominated late-twentieth-century social thought was now.

Epilogue 9/11

Another world began that day.

Andrew Sullivan, *"This Is What a Day Means"*

The crisis that had launched the age was a breakdown in economic predictability and performance, drawn out over a decade. The crisis that seemed to mark its end, though it had been brewing for a long time, came in an instant. A world that many had imagined to be converging on human rights and global markets seemed suddenly to turn dangerous and, for Americans, murderously close at hand. There had been missteps before on the road to convergence: the unpredicted debacle of the Russian economy, the breakup of Yugoslavia into ethnic fragments and civil war. But now, with suicide bombers turning airplanes, the most mundane vehicles of the global economy, into massively destructive weapons, with preemptive war suddenly normalized and U.S. forces soon propelled into military action on a scale not seen since the Vietnam War, with new regimes forcing their way into the once-closed club of nuclear powers, with new cultures of fear and violence spreading across the world, the geopolitical setting for Americans' ideas and action broke into new patterns. War on a global scale—more diffuse than the Cold War but just as urgent—seemed suddenly to have returned.

In the effort to comprehend the new contexts of danger and interdependence, strains of thought that had been muted in the age of fracture would rise to the fore. Writers found themselves reaching back into older public languages, reverting to the mid-twentieth-century rhetoric of the high Cold War. Talk of choice gave way, for a moment, to talk of collective will, obligations, and connections. A new and strenuous nationalism sprang into being. The demands of the whole suddenly became imaginatively and insistently real. Crisis events rattle, even if only momentarily, an intellectual culture's certainties. They bring into focus some of the alternatives running below the surface. They hold suspended in the air, for a moment, some of that intellectual culture's multiple possibilities.

All this flowed out of the crises at the twentieth century's end. And yet, even amid the newly articulated talk of public duties and the common good, even within the emergency cultures of collective anger and grief, much of the distinctive intellectual character of the age of fracture would endure. Its dominant ways of imagining self and society would be pressed into new service, stretched hard over the new realities. Everything changed with the current global circumstances, observers said, and yet everything didn't.

For many of those who witnessed it, September 11, 2001, seemed to be a day when history broke apart. In the films that played in endless loops across the television screens, time literally stood still: the planes coming suddenly into sight, flying far too low over Manhattan's skyline, the terrifying fireballs that leapt out of their collision with the World Trade Center towers, the bodies falling from broken windows hundreds of feet above the ground, the crumbling of the great skyscrapers as their steel skeletons buckled in the superheated flames, crushing thousands of people trapped inside them and enveloping the lower city in a vast gray cloud of smoke and debris. It was a day, it was almost instantly said, that altered all the old realities: a day in which a new era had begun. Repeating within a week what had already become a cliché in the media, David Ansen wrote in *Newsweek* that since 9/11 "the entire culture had shifted under . . . our feet."[1]

Finding words for the culture the disaster had produced was far from easy. Shock, confusion, fear, and numbness dominated many of the first reactions to the 9/11 attacks. Cries of rage and revenge welled up instantly.[2] But out of the welter of responses, a powerful theme quickly emerged: the attacks had brought Americans together. The disaggregating tendencies of the age seemed to many observers to have been jammed into reverse. Talk of the common good revived. Themes of interdependence, of society as a mass of collectively intertwined fates, came back to prominent voice. What counted now, it was said, was not the private satisfaction of individual desires but the suddenly pressing claims of the whole. Unity and responsibility were the new catchwords. Calmness and deliberation were important, former senator Sam Nunn advised on television, but "most of all solidarity." The attacks had joined Americans in a "kinship of grief," President George W. Bush stated three days later. They woke us up to the fact that "we are part of a national community," the journalist George Packer wrote of the new patriotism. The assaults had trigged "an outbreak of civic-mindedness so extreme that it seemed American character had changed overnight."[3]

The most striking expression of the new collective imperative was an outpouring of nationalist signs and sentiments. Even more than the candlelight vigils that sprang out of the need to share one's feelings with those of others, the spontaneous eruption of flags defined the weeks after 9/11. Not even at the height of the Bicentennial celebrations had they been so numerous. Virtually overnight they were fixed on apartment windows, swung over city streets, stenciled on overpasses, painted on barns and city walls, decaled onto bumpers and rear windows. Walmart alone sold almost half a million flags in the three days after 9/11. Flags sprouted from houses along suburban streets; aerial flags on car windows turned highways into streams of red, white, and blue. The flag was a "brilliant dreamcoat [that] warms and protects us," Jonathan Alter wrote. "At least for now."[4]

A reaggregation of the social imagination seemed to go on not only in the flag purchases but at every level. Blood donations spiked after 9/11. The institutions of government came in for celebration. The Postal Service issued a new stamp with the slogan of the moment, "United We Stand," imprinted against a muscularly rippling flag. The heroic actions of the World Trade Center rescue teams, the firefighters who had lost their lives in the collapsing buildings, were not the work of small communities of identity, it was pointed out. They were the work of public servants who put everything at risk for the common good, for people they didn't know.

Identity talk shifted. Voices judged unpatriotic came in for angry censoring, as some Americans found themselves suddenly thrust outside the new culture of unity. Others wrote of self-transformation. A young musician who had identified herself before 9/11 as an artist, a woman, a lesbian, a Jew, and something of a political radical, wrote that she had put an American flag on her backpack. Her sense of self, which had multiplied out in choices and possibilities, had been reconcentrated overnight. Now, "I am calling myself a patriot."[5]

Solidarity was the lesson of the day: a shift in the field of the social imagination from small to large, from individual choice to patriotic duty, from the little platoons of civil society to the nation imagined as one. "What I dread now is a return to normality," to the "hedonisms" of the past," George Packer wrote: "instead of public memorials, private consumption; instead of lines to give blood, restaurant lines." As George W. Bush put the ascendant theme in his State of the Union Address that winter: "We have glimpsed what a new culture of responsibility could look like. We want to be a nation that serves goals larger than self. . . . We were reminded that we are citizens with obligations to each other, to our country, and to history."[6]

If praise of a culture of obligation was one sign of the crisis's mobilization of ideas and sentiments, a second was a rebirth of stronger conceptions of power. In the journals of politics and foreign affairs, there was a rush to rebut the illusion that history had played itself out to a benign end: that power and institutions no longer had a dominant part to play on the global scene. Francis Fukuyama's "end of history" thesis, the object of much of the new polemics, had already been a target for critics before the 9/11 attacks. At the forefront of the Fukuyama bashing in the 1990s, the political scientist Samuel Huntington had argued that with the collapse of Communism the world was not converging toward liberal democratic sameness but, rather, splintering into sharply antagonistic civilizations: Sinic, Hindu, Russian Orthodox, Western, and Islamic cultural blocs, each organized around a distinctly different system of values, ambitions, and social organization. Wherever they grated up against each other like geological plates, in "fault line wars" in the Balkans, the Near East, Chechnya, and elsewhere, Huntington warned, the system would be at its most fragile and explosive. After 9/11, pessimistic readings of global history, though not always pitched in Huntington's terms, crowded into the debate. Notions of world convergence on democracy, which had flourished in the early and mid-1990s when shock therapy for Russia and the "Washington consensus" for the developing world were at their heights, drew sharper questioning. In international affairs, culture, social institutions, and history were increasingly said to matter.[7]

The rush toward thicker, denser notions of power and society had its ugly sides as well. Anger erupted quickly out of the rubble and the carnage. Anti-Muslim rage surged through parts of talk radio. Students who could be singled out by a Muslim-sounding name reported receiving batches of hate e-mails in the weeks after 9/11. The creation of a newly insistent and imperious "we" simultaneously constructed others as outsiders. It triggered a sense of being besieged by enemies abroad and infiltrated by aliens at home. Alarmed at the inroads into civil liberties that the antiterrorist campaign had set in motion—the racial and ethnic profiling of suspects, the orange- and red-coded terror alerts, and the nerve-rattling cautions to keep a coldly vigilant eye out for any suspicious behavior on the part of one's workmates and neighbors—the former president of the American Historical Association, Joyce Appleby, was reminded of the 1950s: "It looks as though we're moving right back into that cold-war mindset."[8]

Not everything changed, of course, nor could it have. "This is . . . the end of the triumph of economics," Fareed Zakaria had been certain.[9] The unpaid volunteers, the firefighters, police officers, and emergency workers who labored, exhausted, through the crisis made notions that markets could do everything best seem silly. But the habits and ideas of a market society came quickly back. Lobbyists converged on Washington, D.C., looking for tax relief to get Americans back onto airplanes and into restaurants. ("Restaurants are part of who we are as Americans," the National Restaurant Association sloganized.)[10] Corporations picked up patriotic ad themes. Commerce and consumerism shifted effortlessly to the new market opportunities. Stores drenched their display windows in flags. Street vendors hawked flag pins and flag regalia in hundreds of different designs. At the beginning of the era, in 1968, the yippie radical Abbie Hoffman had been hauled into court and fined for flag desecration after showing up at an antigovernment rally in an American flag shirt. Now, in the aftermath of 9/11, the flag was wearable in any consumer form and taste: as a T-shirt, a swimsuit, gym gear, a blanket, a Santa Claus suit, even baby diapers.[11]

Polemics from the culture wars, amplified in the more polarized media outlets of the late 1990s, spilled into the crisis, pushing back against the new talk of unity. Depictions of gender roles snapped back to more traditional forms, Susan Faludi has argued.[12] Among cultural conservatives there was a rush to blame the vulnerability of the United States on the moral relativism that postmodernism was said to have unleashed. Jerry Falwell worried aloud that an angry God, impatient with a nation tainted by abortion, paganism, feminism, and homosexuality, had withdrawn his veil of protection over the United States. The radio and television scourge of liberalism, Sean Hannity, blamed a declining belief in "absolute moral standards" for weakening the nation's defenses. It was a commonplace to describe the murderous attacks as the work of "nihilism"—of an unmitigated "evil" beyond understanding or explanation.[13] Stanley Fish, in postmodernism's defense, responded that to imagine that the suicide attackers did not have their reasons and their own sense of right and universal justice, to imagine that they were pure "moral anarchists," was not only foolish; it cut the ground out from any serious attempt to comprehend what they might do next or to imagine any serious counterstrategies. There was more than enough in Americans' democratic ideals and practices, Fish wrote, to condemn the acts of 9/11 without fantasizing the existence of pure "evil" or "grasping for the empty rhetoric of universal absolutes" which all the world defined differently. The "values" crusader William Bennett responded by comparing Fish to the 1960s infamous mass murderer and cultist Charles Manson.[14]

It was in the nature of the crisis to throw up into the air all the culture's voices and intellectual fragments, old and new. Antagonisms and sentiments forged in the culture wars, preexisting ideas and identities, premade global strategies manufactured after the first Gulf War, newfound commercial ambitions, rage, and crisis-made yearnings for unity and solidarism all swirled together. But after three decades in which the very language for society had grown thinner, in which the "little platoons" of freely choosing selves commanded more and more of the social imagination, in which block identities seemed to have grown more fractured and fluid, in which power and history seemed to have become more pliable and diminished, what was most striking was the suddenly resurgent talk of solidarity, unity, and the public good. Amalgams of ideas have their countermotifs as well as their dominant strains, their points of hesitation and resistance. In the wake of 9/11, a powerful recessive strain assumed new power and urgency. It looked, Appleby mused, like the mindset of the Cold War all over again.

Even more than on most occasions, the task of finding public words adequate to the crisis fell on the chief executive. Verbal gestures, everyone knew, were an immediate imperative—not only to defuse the voices of panic but also to reflect, amplify, and shape the furious thinking in the air. A notion of society had to be articulated; words with traction in the public mind needed to be offered. Presidential rhetoric was, as always, an imperfect window into the culture at large, but it was a potentially revealing window nonetheless.

The new president, George W. Bush, was not a natural for the role. The first president in over a hundred years to enter office with fewer popular votes than his opponent, he had come within a hair's breadth—and a vote-recount dispute that had been carried all the way to the Supreme Court—of not reaching the White House at all. Of all the presidents during the age of fracture he was the one most uncomfortable with words. And yet, it was one of the many contingencies of the moment that he had in his employ one of the era's most talented and morally ambitious speechwriters. Amid the strong and diverse figures in the George W. Bush speech writing office, the one most adept at the phrases that "reached for the marble," as the saying went, was its head, Michael Gerson. He was a figure out of the same evangelical Protestant milieu in which George W. Bush had reinvented himself in middle age. Gerson had started out as a speechwriter for Charles Colson's evangelical prison ministry, but somewhere along the way he had absorbed a large slice of Catholic social theory: a fervent faith in the subsidiary institutions of society (families, religious congregations, labor unions, civic associations, "the whole complex web of community") and in an ethic of solidarity with the weak and poor, which saw in them the "guises of God." He kept not only Harriet Beecher Stowe and Martin Luther King, Jr., in his pantheon of heroes, but also William Lloyd Garrison (who had once burned the Constitution to denounce the way it propped up slavery), the labor radical and mine workers' organizer Mother Jones, and the Catholic Workers' founder Dorothy Day. He thought the religious right's embroilment in battles over sexuality and traditional family values had been far too narrow and divisive. The real issues on which evangelical Protestant moral energy should be focused, he was to write, were hunger, poverty, the global AIDS crisis, and genocide. To the language of the men's Bible study group that he shared effortlessly with Bush, Gerson fused a deliberately antilibertarian "Catholic-influenced conservatism-of-the-common-good."[15]

This distinctive combination of president and speechwriter had already been evident in Bush's First Inaugural. No twentieth-century president before him had described America not as a nation born into liberty but as a "slave-holding society" by origin, whose "flawed and fallible people" had nonetheless found their way to become servants of freedom. Not since Lyndon Johnson had a president suggested that "in the quiet of the American conscience, we know that deep, persistent poverty is unworthy of our nation's promise." The poor did not inhabit another moral country, as they had been depicted in the welfare debates only a few years before. "Americans in need are not strangers, they are citizens, not problems, but priorities," Bush promised. The dreaming motifs in Reagan's speeches were gone. The antigovernment jibes of the past were explicitly discarded: "Government has great responsibilities for public safety and public health, for civil rights and common schools." The sermon form was restored, more explicit in its theology than ever. Tom Paine was routed from the pantheon. In place of the "freedom" motif that had dominated presidential speech making for decades, responsibility, sacrifice, commitments, community, compassion, and "service to one another" were the resonant words in Bush's Inaugural. Choice was not their equivalent. "We find the fullness of life not only in options, but in commitments," Bush declared: "the commitments that set us free." Writing in the *New Yorker,* Hendrik Hertzberg was struck that it might have been an expression of the sentiments of his defeated opponent, Al Gore, as easily as Bush's. Hertzberg was sure it was "by far the best Inaugural Address in forty years."[16]

It took time for Bush and his speechwriters to bring a coherent voice to bear on the crisis of 9/11. Bush's repeated line, straight out of a Western movie script, that he wanted Osama bin Laden "dead or alive" seemed to critics only to pile anger onto an already enraged and fearful public. Pulling back momentarily in his Joint Congressional Session speech on September 20, Bush simultaneously proclaimed a state of war, where the very survival of civilization was at stake, and urged a return to emotional normalcy. To the question, "What is expected of us?" Bush's answers were disconcertingly minimalist. To "live your lives and hug your children," to pray, to respect the faiths of others, to keep up your confidence in the economy.[17]

But by the State of the Union message in January Bush had found not only his foreign policy cause: pursuit of a global war on terror wherever that might lead, including preemptive invasion and attack, and relentless pressure on regimes in the "axis of evil" and elsewhere that harbored or might abet it. He had also found his domestic rhetoric. A new civic culture was emerging: "In the sacrifice of soldiers, the fierce brotherhood of firefighters, and the bravery and generosity of ordinary citizens, we have glimpsed what a new culture of responsibility could look like." Recycling an idea that Republicans had ridiculed when Clinton had advanced it, Bush called for thousands of new recruits to the federal service corps, for a new influx of teachers and mentors into the inner cities and Peace Corps workers overseas. For all those for whom this was not possible, he challenged them to pledge no less than two years of their lives to voluntary service for neighbors and nation.[18]

This is "a moment we must seize to change our culture," Bush caught the theme of the op-ed writers. In this "time of testing," our enemies had believed that "we would splinter in fear and selfishness." But they were wrong. "We are one country, mourning together and facing danger together." Through "millions of acts of service and decency and kindness, I know we can overcome evil with greater good." It was a theme he was to repeat in hurricane-devastated New Orleans when the next crisis hit: "We're tied together in this life, in this Nation, and . . . the despair of any touches us all."[19] The words might have been taken as an epitaph for the social metaphors of the age just past.

At every level, the 9/11 responses brought to the surface the complexity of thought and desire in the late twentieth century: the crosscurrents that ran hard beneath its ascendant themes. But a culture and an administration steeped in market models of human action did not throw them off quickly. Visions of society as a spontaneous, naturally acting array of choices and affinities had been the most striking intellectual production of the age of fracture. Now for all the presidential talk of a new common culture, the revival of Cold War rhetoric of duty and peril, and the anniversary observances of "The Day America Changed," those market-imbued visions pervaded the crisis moment.

Within the Bush administration, the disconnect between social aspirations was particularly striking. After two decades of Republican party assertion that private citizens knew how to spend their money better than did tax-extracting government officials, there was to be no back-tracking on tax cutting. The war on terror was, from its very inception, designed as global, relentless, and tax-free. To finance the administration's massive increases in military spending through tax increases, Bush warned, would only weaken the nation's effort. "It is victory or holocaust," Bush speechwriter David Frum echoed the administration's moral urgencies, as he worked to drum up support for invasion of Iraq in early 2003; but the new front of the war could be paid for by holding the line on domestic spending and borrowing the rest.[20] As the Laffer curve returned to public policy and the fiscal costs of the war were shifted anywhere except to taxpayers, the word "sacrifice" skidded toward the third person. What the war of terror meant for Americans, the repeated presidential line now went, was that "we" should show our gratitude for "their sacrifice."

At the operational level, the new business models of a flexible core and outsourced services defined the practical conduct of war. Never had a major military venture relied so heavily on private commercial bidders as the war on terror was to do. From the use of Afghan rebel troops to rout the Taliban to the employment of hired military contractors for the front lines of security, subcontracting pervaded the war. Chafing at the stinginess of his co-Republicans when it came to public expenses, Gerson struggled to resist the antigovernment, antispending, "leave us alone" coalition in the administration and the Congress. But his hopes for a massive AIDS relief campaign in Africa, for massive new foreign aid grants tied to improvements in health and education, and (perhaps most quixotically) for establishment of a tax-subsidized savings account for each American child born into poverty were blocked or radically whittled down.[21] For all the talk of a new nationalism and a new citizenship, markets and politics had by now become radically intertwined. Governance operated more and more through acts of contract: marketizing, outsourcing, and incentivizing the supply of public goods.

Even the Bush/Gerson message of a new culture of responsibility and commitment was intertwined with visions of spontaneous social order. Already in his First Inaugural Bush's praise of the work of "government" shifted almost imperceptibly to an emphasis on the work of the "nation"—the myriad individual acts of decency and compassion that, in return, made people feel fulfilled, the "small things [done] with great love." The two great moral stories of our time were the civil rights movement and the War on Poverty, Gerson told a reporter.[22] But his own vision for poverty's alleviation was, like Bush's, deeply personalistic. Opening the way for more churches to provide public social services, tapping more deeply the powers of faith and charity, was central to the administration's domestic agenda. "I ask you to be citizens," Bush had urged: "citizens, not spectators: citizens, not subjects; responsible citizens, building communities of service and a nation of character." But citizenship resolved quickly into small acts of neighborliness. "Find somebody in need and give them a hand," Bush advised. "Look after a neighbor and surround the lost with love," he urged at the outset of his second term. In the age of fracture, the structural dimensions of poverty, sickness, and inequality had receded almost into invisibility.[23]

By the Second Bush Inaugural in 2005 even this privatized appeal to a culture of obligations had been reduced to a remnant. Now, in a vein that was both audacious and familiar, Bush's theme was freedom. "Ending tyranny" wherever it was found would henceforth be the great objective of the nation: "We have lit a fire . . . in the minds of men . . . and one day this untamed fire of freedom will reach the darkest corner of our world." Reaching back to one of Reagan's keywords, Bush told Congress two weeks later that this was the "dream" that would inspire the age: not simply freedom's vigilant defense (as the Cold War rhetorical formulas had it) but an extension of freedom to every people in the world.[24]

The dress rehearsal for an age of global liberation was the war to liberate Iraq, launched in early 2003. It had been an invasion predicated not only on what turned out to be faulty and faultily interpreted evidence but, in an extension of the microeconomic models that had gained traction in the policy schools, on a radical foreshortening of time. In virtually an instant, a flexible, highly mobile military force would reach Baghdad and "decapitate" the governing regime. Seven days, the deputy secretary of defense, Paul Wolfowitz, predicted it would take.[25] In fact, it took only three weeks. But beyond the toppling of the government, there had been little sense among the administration's policy makers and intellectuals of the need for more extensive planning. "Nation building," the secretary of defense, Donald Rumsfeld, had stated a month before the invasion began, was not to be a part of the war on terror. Long-term presence on foreign soil created "dependency"; it "distorted" the local economy; it was "unnatural." The point was not to remake Iraq but to release it from constraints: to "liberate the Iraqi people from oppression."[26]

Some administration officials imagined that a wave of democratization might follow regime change in Iraq and spread, contagiously, over all the Middle East. But the more dominant view was that shock therapy, military style, would by itself bring Iraq back into the fold of the West. The counterpart to a flexible fighting force was the assumption of a culture capable of springing back to its natural order from the artificial distortions that tyranny had imposed on it. Through an instantaneous wrinkle in time, transition to democracy would be achieved. "We're going to stand up an interim Iraqi government, hand power over to them, and get out of there in three to four months," Rumsfeld's man on the ground declared as the invasion began. "We don't owe the people of Iraq anything," he added, fending off questions about postwar reconstruction. "We're giving them their freedom. That's enough."[27]

The project of regime change in Iraq was premised on compressed and foldable time, on a view of Iraqi history as thin and its institutions as pliable, on the ability of universal human incentives to kick in surely and quickly. "It was free-market thinking applied to geopolitics," the historian of foreign relations John Lewis Gaddis would write. "Just as the removal of economic constraints allows the pursuit of self-interest automatically to advance a collective interest, so the breaking up of an old international order would encourage a new one to emerge, more or less spontaneously, based on a universal desire for security, prosperity and liberty."[28] Despite the harder, more pessimistic notions of power running through the foreign policy journals, metaphors drawn from models of self-acting markets had pervaded the war from the beginning.

By 2005, when Bush took the promise of liberation global with the goal "of ending tyranny in our world," the war in Iraq had already begun to go badly. The resistance that had melted away in the spring of 2003 had returned by summer in a spate of bomb attacks, not only on U.S. and U.N. personnel but on thousands of Iraqi civilians, as rival factions armed, fiercely held group loyalties reasserted themselves with a vengeance, and the country drifted toward civil war. Bush's popularity at home, which had stood at near record highs in the weeks after 9/11, and briefly shot up again with the Iraq invasion, had resumed its long-term decline. The "liberate and leave" policy bogged down in a dangerous and politically divisive military occupation.

Bush's Second Inaugural pledge that "we are ready for the greatest achievements in the history of freedom" was less an acknowledgment of these circumstances than an effort to transcend them. Iraq was nowhere mentioned. Peggy Noonan, who had done her own reaching for the marble in Reagan's speech writing office, thought Bush's Second Inaugural a "dreamy" speech, unconnected with the realities of human imperfection and the humanly possible. "The speech did not deal with specifics—9/11, terrorism, particular alliances, Iraq," she wrote. "It was, instead, assertively abstract." In both the liberal and the conservative reviews, doubts and dissent poured forth. Critics of the "end of history" illusion turned their criticism on the new utopianism of the president.[29]

But in the very abstractions of Bush's declaration for the liberation of the world, projected against a placeless and undifferentiated tyranny, some of the most powerful of the pre-9/11 ways of thinking were appropriated, amplified, and pressed into new service. The age's impatience with history and institutions, its difficulty in imagining power and solidarities, were reflected there. The "drumbeat" of the young conservatives in the Reagan White House, Noonan had written, was "freedom." It was a traveling, universal metaphor, which could be plugged into any policy specific:

> we'll free up more of your money,
> we'll free up more of the world,
> freedom freedom freedom—[30]

In the face of a war that was going badly, a rationale for invasion that turned out to have been illusory, a vision of transcending time that had bogged down in time's realities, an impatient and divided electorate, Bush and his speechwriters reached for placeless and timeless freedom.

Later in the fall of 2005 two books shot onto the best-seller lists. Thomas Friedman's work *The World Is Flat* stayed on the nonfiction best-seller list for 103 weeks, Steven Levitt and Stephen Dubner's *Freakonomics* for 101 weeks.[31] Iraq and the war on terror were only marginally visible in either of them, though Friedman had written a good deal about Middle East matters in his newspaper columns. The authors did not write as partisans of the Bush administration's dream of the liberation of the world. They wrote, rather, of a world which, as they explained it, was already liberated.

Friedman's subject was the spread of global outsourcing, which, in barely half a decade, had already transformed the world's economy. Call centers in Bangalore, research centers in Beijing, Walmart clones in To-kyo, he reported, were now joined by a web of moving goods and in-stantly moving electronic information that had been all but unimaginable even at the height of 1980s and 1990s economic globalization. Orders flashed across the continents to be responded to overnight. While you eased up to a McDonald's window in Missouri, your Big Mac requests sped out to Colorado Springs and back. It was a world, Friedman wrote, in which space had been virtually annihilated, time made instantaneous, and power diffused to small businesses owners around the world: "The small shall act big . . . and the big shall act small." Hierarchies of re-gion and scale were being dramatically upended in the networked global economy: pyramids of power were being made flat.

Levitt and Dubner offered not an epic but a compendium of detec-tive stories: tales of the ways in which even the most puzzling human behaviors could be explained by microeconomic analysis, imaginatively and rigorously applied. Why had crime rates fallen, they asked? Because women in poor and crime-ridden neighborhoods, recognizing the realis-tic life chances their children might have, had chosen to bear fewer ba-bies. In consequence, fewer children grew up to be criminals. Why did imposing fines on parents who picked their children up late from daycare produce more tardiness rather than less? Because the internalized cost of shame had been greater than the new, modest, shame-absolving fines. *"Incentives are the cornerstone of modern life,"* they wrote. "And understand-ing them . . . is the key to solving just about any riddle, from violent crime to sports cheating and online dating."[32]

For all the publishers' hype surrounding both megasellers, their appeal lay in their skillful repackaging of the old and the familiar. Friedman echoed the cosmic optimism of Alvin Toffler. Steven Levitt, despite his co-author's catchy book title, was, analytically speaking, a thoroughly con-ventional microeconomist: the decade's new Gary Becker. Power was diminishing, time was foreshortening, structures could be remade in a virtual instant, people were a legible bundle of desires and preferences, choice was on the march. Markets were in ascendance, and the world that had seemed to shatter on 9/11, had—in the best-seller lists, at any rate, and for a moment—been restored.

In other parts of the culture, desires for thicker, deeper notions of society endured. Rick Warren's and Jim Wallis's efforts to forge more generous, even radical frames for evangelical Protestant social thought were on or about to hit the best-seller lists, where their voices would complicate the gladiatorial polarities of Bill O'Reilly, Ann Coulter, Stephen Colbert, and Al Franken. The much more consequential newcomer to the best-seller lists, Barack Obama, was to arrive there in late 2006.[33] The immense crowds that Obama would gather on his way to the presidency in 2008 with his talk of the "common good" and an end to the politics of fracture, the social movement rhetoric ("yes, we can!") that inspired his partisans and the mood of high expectation that unified them, spoke volumes to the hunger for connections that the crisis had helped bring to the surface. So, for that matter, did the anti-Obama protesters who, in a much more frightened and anti-elitist version of populist politics, were to mobilize in angry masses against the big-business bailouts through which the Bush and Obama administrations tried to stem the catastrophic economic crash of 2008–2009. Both were, in their way, reactions against the market metaphors that had dominated the age.

If there was to be a lasting reaggregation of social thought, however, it would not be a simple return to the assumptions of the Cold War. Since the middle years of the twentieth century, much had broken up and much had been liberated. Block understandings of power and structure had fractured. Identities were more openly imagined now: more fluid and multiple, less tightly packaged by gender and social-role theory, less quickly read as the expression of social norms and structures. Despite the backlash of the culture wars, a broader range of being human was tolerated than before. Racism had hardly disappeared, but race was less confining a conceptual cage than it had been three decades before. The subtle powers of culture were more closely analyzed than they had been in the middle years of the century. History seemed less relentless in its course, less determinative, less antagonistic to human agency. The mass society that had so deeply worried mid-twentieth-century social scientists had broken up; its conduits of communication had been multiplied; its plural, loosely intersecting pieces were much more sharply seen. The era's emphasis on choice, the most contagious of the age's metaphors, was not merely a simplification of ideas of human nature under the influence of the economic model makers. There *were* more choices than before—not just more consumer goods but more worlds of ideas and selves and aspirations from which to choose.

But in the course of those shifts of ideas and imagination, the webs of dependence and connection that joined the disaggregated selves had become far harder to articulate. There were fewer intellectual resources now for understanding the ways in which the past pressed its legacies on the present, whether it be across the political landscapes of Iraq and Afghanistan, haunted by memories, or the still troubled landscape of race relations in the United States. Even as the structures underlying the stock markets' race to limitless wealth collapsed in the economic crisis of 2008–2009 and the institutional giants of finance imploded, the constraining power of structures and institutions was harder now to hold in focus. Interdependence was an insistent fact of the new age. Even the "tea party" movement's antitax and antibailout partisans felt it, their rage against Bush-Obama "socialism" and their populist-libertarian rhetoric notwithstanding. But beyond talk of markets and exchange, the words for society were thinner than before. Older solidaristic terms like "race" and "sisterhood" had partially unraveled; others, like "class," had virtually fallen out of use. Equality had come and gone as a social idea with traction, even among liberal intellectuals. Debates over taxes and social services—from privately managed social security accounts to health insurance provisions—were pitched in more personalistic terms than before. The hunger for connections and responsibilities, even in a world of strangers, that the terror attacks had momentarily released groped for correspondingly powerful words.

"Historians will surely say, 'This was the week that America changed,'" the *Newsweek* columnist Fareed Zakaria wrote in September 2001. "In the midst of the jagged emotions of the moment—horror, rage, grief—we can all sense that the country has crossed a watershed. But we don't quite know what that means."[34] Pieces of old and new social paradigms filled the air, full of promise and full of danger. They formed the fragments out of which the new century's debates would be constructed. The disaggregation of the block categories of mid-century had run its course. The age of fracture had permanently altered the play of argument and ideas. The pieces would have to be reassembled on different frames, the tensions between self and society resolved anew. But how that would be done, amid the anger and the confusion, the liberations and the anxieties, still hung in the balance.

Notes

Prologue

1. Peggy Noonan, *What I Saw at the Revolution: A Political Life in the Reagan Era* (New York: Random House, 1990), 100, 99.
2. Paul Weyrich is quoted in Richard A. Viguerie, *The New Right: We're Ready to Lead* (Falls Church, Va.: Viguerie Press, 1981), 55; Amy Wilentz, "On the Intellectual Ramparts," *Time,* September 1, 1986, 22; John L. Kelley, *Bringing the Market Back In: The Political Revitalization of Market Liberalism* (Basingstoke, UK: Macmillan, 1997), 180.
3. William J. Clinton, Remarks at Georgetown University, July 6, 1995, in John Woolley and Gerhard Peters, *The American Presidency Project* (online). Santa Barbara: University of California (hosted). http://www.presidency.ucsb.edu.ws.
4. Irving Kristol, "On Conservatism and Capitalism," *Wall Street Journal,* September 11, 1975, quoted in Christopher DeMuth and William Kristol, eds., *The Neoconservative Imagination: Essays in Honor of Irving Kristol* (Washington, D.C.: AEI Press, 1995), 179.
5. Stuart Hall, "Cultural Studies: Two Paradigms," in *Media, Culture, and Society: A Critical Reader,* ed. Richard Collins et al. (Beverly Hills, Calif.: SAGE Publications, 1986), 33.
6. Theodore Rosenof, *Realignment: The Theory That Changed the Way We Think about American Politics* (Lanham, Md.: Rowman and Littlefield, 2003); Byron E. Shafer, ed., *The End of Realignment?: Interpreting American Electoral Eras* (Madison: University of Wisconsin Press, 1991); Stefano Lucani, "The End of Realignment and the Deadlock of American Democracy," in *Towards a New American Nation: Redefinitions and Reconstruction,* ed. Anna Maria Martellone (Keele, UK: Ryburn, 1995). A more partisan version of the argument was made at the time by Thomas Ferguson and Joel Rogers, "The Myth of American's Turn to the Right," *Atlantic Monthly,* May 1986, 43–53.
7. Joseph Epstein is quoted in Angela D. Dillard, *Guess Who's Coming to Dinner*

Now? Multicultural Conservatism in America (New York: New York University Press, 2001), 76. On the long shadow the 1960s cast over the next decade, see the essays by Stephen Tuck, Simon Hall, and others on "the long 1960s" in *Journal of Contemporary History* 43 (2008): 617–688.

8. C. Wright Mills, *White Collar: The American Middle Classes* (New York: Oxford University Press, 1951); Hannah Arendt, *The Origins of Totalitarianism* (New York: Harcourt, Brace, 1951); David Riesman, *The Lonely Crowd: A Study of the Changing American Character* (New Haven: Yale University Press, 1950).

9. Robert D. Putnam, "Bowling Alone: America's Declining Social Capital," *Journal of Democracy* 6 (January 1995): 65–78; Everett Carll Ladd, *The Ladd Report* (New York: Free Press, 1999); Theda Skocpol and Morris P. Fiorina, eds., *Civic Engagement in American Democracy* (New York: Russell Sage Foundation, 1999).

10. Tom Wolfe, "The Me Decade and the Third Great Awakening," in Wolfe, *Mauve Gloves & Madmen, Clutter & Vine, and Other Stories, Sketches, and Essays* (New York: Farrar, Straus and Giroux, 1976); Ivan Boesky is quoted in Michael Schaller, *Right Turn: American Life in the Reagan-Bush Era, 1980–1992* (New York: Oxford University Press, 2007), 115.

11. For an attempt to aggregate public opinion poll responses into readings of popular "mood": James A. Stimson, *Public Opinion in America: Moods, Cycles, and Swings,* 2nd ed. (Boulder, Colo.: Westview Press, 1999). But see also the skeptical methodological counterstatement by John Zaller and Stanley Feldman: "A Simple Theory of the Survey Response: Answering Questions versus Revealing Preferences," *American Journal of Political Science* 36 (1992): 579–616.

12. William E. Simon, *A Time for Truth* (New York: McGraw-Hill, 1978), 238, 230.

13. The literature here is enormous. For a start: Richard Cockett, *Thinking the Unthinkable: Think-Tanks and the Economic Counter-Revolution, 1931–1983,* rev. ed. (London: HarperCollins, 1995); Alice O'Connor, "Financing the Counterrevolution," in *Rightward Bound: Making America Conservative in the 1970s,* ed. Bruce J. Schulman and Julian E. Zelizer (Cambridge, Mass.: Harvard University Press, 2008); Burton Yale Pines, *Back to Basics: The Traditionalist Movement That Is Sweeping Grass-Roots America* (New York: Morrow, 1982); Sidney Blumenthal, *The Rise of the Counter-Establishment: From Conservative Ideology to Political Power* (New York: Times Books, 1986); James Fallows, "The New Celebrities of Washington," *New York Review of Books,* June 12, 1986, 41–49; Gregg Easterbrook, "Ideas Move Nations," *Atlantic Monthly,* January 1986, 66–80; Eric Alterman, "The 'Right' Books and Big Ideas," *Nation,* November 22, 1999, 16–21; Eric Alterman, *Sound and Fury: The Making of the Punditocracy* (Ithaca: Cornell University Press, 1999).

14. The most aggressive conservative foundation, the John M. Olin Foundation, was one-fiftieth the size of the Ford Foundation in the early 1980s; Ford could have endowed a foundation of Olin's size with one year of its regular

grant allotments. *Foundation Center Source Book Profiles,* 1984 (New York: Foundation Center, 1984). On the think tanks: R. Kent Weaver, "The Changing World of Think Tanks," *PS: Political Science and Politics* 22 (1989): 563–578; Diane Stone, *Capturing the Political Imagination: Think Tanks and the Policy Process* (London: Frank Cass, 1996); James Allen Smith, *Brookings at Seventy-Five* (Washington, D.C.: Brookings Institution, 1991); Patrick Ford, "American Enterprise Institute for Public Policy Research," in *Organizations for Policy Analysis: Helping Government Think,* ed. Carol H. Weiss (Newbury Park, Calif.: Sage, 1991).

15. Fredric Jameson, *Postmodernism, or, The Cultural Logic of Late Capitalism* (Durham: Duke University Press, 1991); David Harvey, *The Condition of Postmodernity: An Enquiry into the Origins of Cultural Change* (Oxford: Blackwell, 1990).

16. Niall Ferguson et al., eds., *The Shock of the Global: The 1970s in Perspective* (Cambridge, Mass.: Harvard University Press, 2010).

1. Losing the Words of the Cold War

Epigraph: Kenneth Khachigian, notes of a conversation with Ronald Reagan, January 12, 1981, SP100, WHORM: Subject File, Ronald Reagan Presidential Library.

1. Jeffrey K. Tulis, *The Rhetorical Presidency* (Princeton: Princeton University Press, 1987), 63, 81, and passim. The comprehensive electronic archive of presidential speeches is John Woolley and Gerhard Peters, *The American Presidency Project* (online). Santa Barbara: University of California (hosted). http://www.presidency.ucsb.edu.ws. This is the source for all subsequent references to presidential speeches.

2. John F. Kennedy, State of the Union Address, January 11, 1962; Barry Goldwater, Acceptance Speech at the Republican National Convention in 1964, as quoted in E. J. Dionne, Jr., *Why Americans Hate Politics* (New York: Simon and Schuster, 1991), 178.

3. Harry S Truman, Inaugural Address, January 20, 1949 ("new hope"); Lyndon B. Johnson, Inaugural Address, January 20, 1965 ("new purpose"); Richard M. Nixon, Inaugural Address, January 20, 1973 ("new era"). For the "new beginning" phrase: Richard M. Nixon, Remarks Announcing Intention to Nominate Gerald R. Ford to be Vice President, October 12, 1973; Jimmy Carter, Inaugural Address, January 20, 1977; Ronald Reagan, Inaugural Address, January 20, 1981.

4. Peggy Noonan, *What I Saw at the Revolution: A Political Life in the Reagan Era* (New York: Random House, 1990), 52. On genres and forms: Karlyn Kohrs Campbell and Kathleen Hall Jamieson, *Deeds Done in Words: Presidential Rhetoric and the Genres of Governance* (Chicago: University of Chicago Press, 1990).

5. Dwight D. Eisenhower, Inaugural Address, January 21, 1957; Dwight D. Eisenhower, State of the Union Address, January 10, 1957; John F. Kennedy, Inaugural Address, January 20, 1961; Lyndon B. Johnson, State of the Union Address, January 10, 1967.

6. Dwight D. Eisenhower, State of the Union Address, January 6, 1955.

7. John F. Kennedy, State of the Union Address, January 11, 1962; Lyndon B. Johnson, State of the Union Address, January 10, 1967.

8. John F. Kennedy, Inaugural Address, January 20, 1961; Lyndon B. Johnson, State of the Union Address, January 10, 1967; Richard M. Nixon, Inaugural Address, January 20, 1973.

9. Dwight D. Eisenhower, Inaugural Address, January 21, 1957; Dwight D. Eisenhower, State of the Union Address, January 7, 1960; Dwight D. Eisenhower, State of the Union Address, January 9, 1959.

10. Dwight D. Eisenhower, Inaugural Address, January 21, 1957; John F. Kennedy, Inaugural Address, January 20, 1961.

11. Richard M. Nixon, Inaugural Address, January 20, 1969.

12. Jimmy Carter, Inaugural Address, January 20, 1977; Jimmy Carter, State of the Union Address, January 19, 1978.

13. Jimmy Carter, Inaugural Address, January 20, 1977; Jimmy Carter, State of the Union Address, January 19, 1978. On Carter's rhetoric see Dan F. Hahn, "The Rhetoric of Jimmy Carter, 1976–1980," *Presidential Studies Quarterly* 14 (1984): 265–288; and the much more critical assessment by James Fallows, "The Passionless Presidency," *Atlantic Monthly,* May 1979, 33–48, and June 1979, 75–81.

14. Jimmy Carter, Inaugural Address, January 20, 1977; Jimmy Carter, State of the Union Address, January 23, 1979; Jimmy Carter, Address to the Nation on Energy and National Goals, July 15, 1979.

15. Jimmy Carter, Address to the Nation on Energy and National Goals, July 15, 1979; Craig Allen Smith and Kathy B. Smith, *The White House Speaks: Presidential Leadership as Persuasion* (Westport, Conn.: Praeger, 1994), 157.

16. Ronald Reagan, "A Time for Choosing" (1964) and "Encroaching Control" (1961), in Ronald Reagan, *A Time for Choosing: The Speeches of Ronald Reagan, 1961–1982* (Chicago: Regnery Gateway, 1983), 56, 38, 55, 24–25.

17. John F. Kennedy, State of the Union Address, January 14, 1963; Jimmy Carter, State of the Union Address, January 19, 1978. Reagan recycled and vernacularized the Carter line in his standard stump speech in 1984: "America's best days are yet to come. And I know it galls my opponents, but you ain't seen nothin' yet." Ronald Reagan, Remarks at a Reagan-Bush Rally at Portland, Oregon, October 23, 1984.

18. Water Mondale in Democratic National Committee, *The Official Proceedings of the Democratic National Convention, New York City, July 1976* (1976), 400; Ronald Reagan, State of the Union Address, January 25, 1984.

19. Ronald Reagan, "A Time for Choosing" (1964) and "A Moment of Truth: Our Rendezvous with Destiny" (1965), both in *A Time for Choosing.*

20. Ronald Reagan, Inaugural Address, January 20, 1981.

21. Ronald Reagan, Address before a Joint Session of Congress on the Program for Economic Recovery, April 28, 1981; Ronald Reagan, State of the Union Address, February 6, 1985; Lyndon B. Johnson, Inaugural Address, January 20, 1965; Jimmy Carter, Address to the Nation on Energy and National Goals, July 15, 1979; Ronald Reagan, Address at Eureka College, February 6, 1984; Ronald Reagan, State of the Union Address, January 25, 1984; Ronald Reagan, Acceptance Speech at the Republican National Convention, August 23, 1984.

22. Ronald Reagan, "A Time for Choosing" ("anti-heap of totalitarianism"); Ronald Reagan, Address to the California Senate and Assembly, January 7, 1969 ("anarchy and insurrection"), California Legislature, Senate Journal, January 7, 1969, p. 49.

23. Ronald Reagan, State of the Union Address, January 27, 1987; Ronald Reagan, "A Time for Choosing," 41; Ronald Reagan, State of the Union Address, January 25, 1984.

24. Lyndon B. Johnson, State of the Union Address, January 10, 1967; Lyndon B. Johnson, Inaugual Address, January 20, 1965; Ronald Reagan, State of the Union Address, January 27, 1987.

25. Eric Foner, *Tom Paine and Revolutionary America* (New York: Oxford University Press, 2005), 270; George Will, *The New Season: A Spectator's Guide to the 1988 Election* (New York: Simon and Schuster, 1987), 81; Ronald Reagan, Address to the Republican National Convention, July 17, 1980; Ronald Reagan, Remarks to the Republican National Convention, August 15, 1988; Ronald Reagan, Address to the National Association of Evangelicals, March 8, 1983.

26. Ronald Reagan, Address to the Nation on United States Assistance for the Nicaraguan Democratic Resistance, June 24, 1986; Ronald Reagan, Address to the Nation on Events in Lebanon and Grenada, October 27, 1983; Ronald Reagan, Remarks to Members of the Royal Institute of International Affairs (London), June 3, 1988.

27. Martin J. Medhurst, "Writing Speeches for Ronald Reagan: An Interview with Tony Dolan," *Rhetoric and Public Affairs* 1 (1998): 250; William K. Muir, Jr., "Ronald Reagan: The Primacy of Rhetoric," in *Leadership in the Modern Presidency*, ed. Fred I. Greenstein (Cambridge, Mass.: Harvard University Press, 1988), 276.

28. Kenneth Khachigian, Notes of a conversation with Ronald Reagan, January 12, 1981, SP100, WHORM: Subject File, Ronald Reagan Presidential Library. Reagan's radio addresses of 1975–1980, the great majority of which he wrote without a speechwriter's assistance, are collected in *Reagan in His Own Hand*, ed. Kiron K. Skinner, Annelise Anderson, and Martin Anderson (New York:

Free Press, 2001). His major speeches as president all began as drafts composed by his speechwriting staff.

29. Ronald Reagan, Address to the National Association of Evangelicals, March 8, 1983; Dwight D. Eisenhower, State of the Union Address, January 6, 1955; Dwight D. Eisenhower, State of the Union Address, January 9, 1958; Ronald Reagan, "Address to the American Conservative Union," February 6, 1977, in *A Time for Choosing.*

30. Anthony Dolan, Second Inaugural Draft, December 26, 1984, and Ronald Reagan, Handwritten revision of the Second Inaugural, January 8, 1985, both in SP100–286397, WHORM: Subject File, Ronald Reagan Presidential Library.

31. Noonan, *What I Saw at the Revolution,* 72. For specific examples, see Morton Kondrake, "Speech, Speech! Author, Author!" *New Republic,* July 5, 1982, 21ff, and the anguished correspondence within the speechwriting office over Reagan's 1987 State of the Union Address, in which the Iran-Contra issue had to be openly confronted.

32. Reagan, State of the Union Address, January 26, 1982; Reagan, Remarks at the Republican National Convention, August 15, 1988.

33. Noonan, *What I Saw at the Revolution,* 283–284; Frank I. Luntz, *Candidates, Consultants, and Campaigns: The Style and Substance of American Electioneering* (Oxford: Blackwell, 1988), 208.

34. Haig Bosmajian, "Reaganspeak as a Case Study in the Use of Godterms, Adwords, Euphemisms, and Faulty Metaphors," *Et cetera* 42 (1985): 101–108. This was essentially the same list that Newt Gingrich was to circulate to his Republican congressional colleagues in 1990 and afterward. "Accentuate the Negative," *Harper's Magazine,* November 1990, 17–18.

35. *The Collected Speeches of Margaret Thatcher,* ed. Robin Harris (London: HarperCollins, 1997), 134, 76–77, 131, 120.

36. Reagan, Program for Economic Recovery, April 28, 1981. Cf. Richard E. Crable and Steven L. Vibbert, "Argumentative Stance and Political Faith Healing: 'The Dream Will Come True,'" *Quarterly Journal of Speech* 69 (1983): 290–301.

37. *A National Agenda for the Eighties: Report of the President's Commission for a National Agenda for the Eighties* (Englewood Cliffs, N.J.: Prentice-Hall, 1980); Reagan, State of the Union Address, February 4, 1986.

38. Reagan, State of the Union Address, February 6, 1985.

39. Medhurst, "Writing Speeches for Ronald Reagan," 253.

40. Meg Greenfield as quoted in James W. Caesar, "The Theory of Governance in the Reagan Administration," in *The Reagan Presidency and the Governing of America,* ed. Lester M. Salamon and Michael S. Lund (Washington, D.C.: Urban Institute Press, 1984), 66.

41. Ronald Reagan, Inaugural Address, January 20, 1981; Ron Rosenbaum,

"Who Puts the Words in the President's Mouth?" *Esquire,* December 1985, 251.

42. Ronald Reagan, Inaugural Address, January 20, 1985; Ronald Reagan, Re-marks Accepting the Presidential Nomination at the 1984 Republican National Convention, August 23, 1984. On "rubbish" and "schmaltz": Aram Bakshian, exit interview, August 9, 1983, audio tape, Ronald Reagan Presidential Library.

43. Jimmy Carter, Address to the Nation on Energy and National Goals, July 15, 1979; Kathleen Hall Jamieson, *Eloquence in an Electronic Age: The Transformation of Political Speechmaking* (New York: Oxford University Press, 1988), 160. See also William F. Lewis, "Telling America's Story: Narrative Form and the Reagan Presidency," *Quarterly Journal of Speech* 73 (1987): 280–302.

44. Measured as the percentage of their months in office in which they received approval ratings in the Gallup Poll of less than 50 percent, the post-1952 presidents ranked as follows: Kennedy (0), Eisenhower (1 percent), George H. W. Bush (25 percent), Clinton (27 percent), Reagan (39 percent), Nixon (41 percent), Johnson (55 percent), Carter (63 percent), Ford (71 percent). In some months no poll was taken. The data can be found at John Woolley and Gerhard Peters, *The American Presidency Project* (online). Santa Barbara: University of California (hosted). http://www.presidency.ucsb.edu.ws.

45. Richard Darman, as quoted in Paul D. Erickson, *Reagan Speaks: The Making of an American Myth* (New York: New York University Press, 1985), 100.

46. Ronald Reagan, State of the Union Address, January 27, 1987.

47. Fred Barnes, "Speechless," *New Republic,* February 16, 1987, 10; Ronald Reagan, "Address to the California Legislature," January 5, 1967, California Legislature, Senate Journal, January 5, 1967, 68; Ronald Reagan, State of the Union Address, January 27, 1987.

48. Ronald Reagan, "A Time for Choosing," 43.

49. Jimmy Carter, State of the Union Address, January 19, 1978; Jimmy Carter, Address to the Nation on Energy and National Goals, July 15, 1979.

50. Eric Alterman, *Sound and Fury: The Making of the Punditocracy* (Ithaca: Cornell University Press, 1999); James Fallows, "The New Celebrities of Washington," *New York Review of Books,* June 12, 1986, 41–49.

51. Ronald Reagan, Program for Economic Recovery, April 28, 1981; Benjamin R. Barber, "Celluloid Vistas: What the President's Dreams Are Made Of," *Harper's Magazine,* July 1985, 74.

52. Ronald Reagan, Remarks Accepting the Presidential Nomination at the Republican National Convention, August 23, 1984.

53. For introductions to the extended debate over Reagan's foreign policy: John Lewis Gaddis, "The Unexpected Ronald Reagan," in Gaddis, *The United States and the End of the Cold War: Implications, Reconsiderations, Provocations* (New York: Oxford University Press, 1992); Melvyn P. Leffler, *For the Soul of Man-*

kind: The United States, the Soviet Union, and the Cold War (New York: Hill and Wang, 2007); Peter Schweizer, *Victory: The Reagan Administration's Secret Strategy That Hastened the Collapse of the Soviet Union* (New York: Atlantic Monthly Press, 1994); Coral Bell, *The Reagan Paradox: American Foreign Policy in the 1980s* (New Brunswick, N.J.: Rutgers University Press, 1989). For the alarm of conservative intellectuals: Norman Podhoretz, "The Neo-Conservative Anguish over Reagan's Foreign Policy," *New York Times Magazine,* May 2, 1982, SM30ff; George F. Will, *The Morning After: American Successes and Excesses, 1981–1986* (New York: Free Press, 1986); George F. Will, *Suddenly: The American Idea Abroad and at Home, 1986–1990* (New York: Free Press, 1990).

54. Democratic National Committee, *Official Proceedings of the 1992 Democratic National Convention, New York, NY, July 13–16, 1992* (Washington, D.C.: Democratic National Committee, 1992); Democratic National Committee, *Official Report of the Proceedings of the Democratic National Convention, New York City, NY, August 11–14, 1980* (Washington, D.C.: Democratic National Committee, 1980), 588.

2. The Rediscovery of the Market

Epigraphs: James Tobin, "Are New Classical Models Plausible Enough to Guide Policy?" *Journal of Money, Credit, and Banking* 12 (1980): 796; and Robert E. Lucas, Jr., *Models of Business Cycles* (Oxford: Basil Blackwell, 1987), 107.

1. Ronald Reagan, Radio Address to the Nation on Taxes, Tuition Tax Credit, and Interest Rates, April 24, 1982, at John Woolley and Gerhard Peters, *The American Presidency Project* (online), Santa Barbara: University of California (hosted). http://www.presidency.ucsb.edu.ws.
2. William J. Baumol and Alan S. Blinder, *Economics: Principles and Policy,* 5th ed. (San Diego: Harcourt Brace Jovanovich, 1991), 5.
3. Elizabeth Fones-Wolf, *Selling Free Enterprise: The Business Assault on Labor and Liberalism, 1945–1960* (Urbana: University of Illinois Press, 1994); Wendy L. Wall, *Inventing the "American Way": The Politics of Consensus from the New Deal to the Civil Rights Movement* (New York: Oxford University Press, 2008).
4. Charles Schultze as quoted in Stephen Breyer, "Analyzing Regulatory Failure: Mismatches, Less Restrictive Alternatives, and Reform," *Harvard Law Review* 92 (1979): 553.
5. Three fine general accounts of economic experience, policy, and ideas in the period, organized around quite different interpretive paradigms, are: Mark Blyth, *Great Transformations: Economic Ideas and Institutional Change in the Twentieth Century* (Cambridge: Cambridge University Press, 2002), chaps. 5–6; Robert M. Collins, *More: The Politics of Economic Growth in Postwar America* (New York: Oxford University Press, 2000); and Paul Krugman, *Peddling Prosperity: Economic Sense and Nonsense in the Age of Diminished Expectations* (New

York: W. W. Norton, 1994). For monthly unemployment rates: U.S. Department of Labor, Bureau of Labor Statistics, (Seas) Unemployment Rate at www.bls.gov. For the misery index averages: www.miseryindex.us. For comparable European, Japanese, and Canadian data: Brian Snowdon et al., *A Modern Guide to Macroeconomics: An Introduction to Competing Schools of Thought* (Aldershot, UK; Edward Elgar, 1994), tables 1.2, 1.3, 1.4. The "great expansion" phrase is from Robert M. Collins, *Transforming America: Politics and Culture in the Reagan Years* (New York: Columbia University Press, 2007), 88.

6. Adam Smith, *An Inquiry into the Nature and Causes of the Wealth of Nations* (1776; Harmondsworth, UK: Penguin, 1970); David Ricardo, *On the Principles of Political Economy and Taxation* (London: John Murray, 1817), iii. More generally, Roger Friedland and A. F. Robertson, "Beyond the Marketplace," in *Beyond the Marketplace: Rethinking Economy and Society,* ed. Friedland and Robertson (New York: Aldine de Gruyter, 1990).

7. Alfred Marshall, *Principles of Economics,* 8th ed. (London: Macmillan, 1920), bk. 5, chap. 1.

8. Robert M. Solow, "How Did Economics Get That Way and What Way Did It Get?" *Daedalus* 126 (Winter 1997): 41. In the same vein: William J. Barber, "Reconfigurations in American Academic Economics: A General Practitioner's Perspective," *Daedalus* 126 (Winter 1997): 87–103.

9. Mary S. Morgan and Malcolm Rutherford, "American Economics: The Character of the Transformation," in *From Interwar Pluralism to Postwar Neoclassicism,* ed. Morgan and Rutherford, Annual Supplement to *History of Political Economy* 30 (Durham: Duke University Press, 1998); Michael A. Bernstein, "American Economics and the American Economy in the American Century: Doctrinal Legacies and Contemporary Policy Problems," in *Understanding American Economic Decline,* ed. Michael A. Bernstein and David E. Adler (New York: Cambridge University Press, 1994); Michael A. Bernstein, *A Perilous Progress: Economists and Public Purpose in Twentieth-Century America* (Princeton: Princeton University Press, 2001).

10. Joseph E. Stiglitz, "On the Market Principles of Economics Textbooks: Innovation and Product Differentiation," *Journal of Economic Education* 19 (1988): 173; Paul A. Samuelson, *Economics,* 9th ed. (New York: McGraw-Hill, 1973).

11. Paul A. Samuelson, *Economics: An Introductory Analysis,* 2nd ed. (New York: McGraw-Hill, 1951), 9–10; Paul A. Samuelson, *Economics,* 10th ed. (New York: McGraw-Hill, 1976), 632. The most important exception to the macro-first rule was Armen A. Alchian and William R. Allen, *University Economics,* 2nd ed. (Belmont, Calif.: Wadsworth, 1967). But its equally conservative rivals, James D. Gwartney, *Economics: Private and Public Choice* (New York: Academic Press, 1976), and Roger LeRoy Miller, *Economics Today* (San Francisco: Canfield Press, 1973), followed the Samuelson convention in putting macroeconomics first.

12. Arthur Okun is quoted in Bernstein, *Perilous Progress,* 138. For a statement of

macroeconomics at its most confident: James Tobin, *The New Economics, One Decade Older* (Princeton: Princeton Univesity Press, 1974).

13. Donald N. McCloskey, *The Rhetoric of Economics* (Madison: University of Wisconsin Press, 1985), xvii.

14. Paul A. Samuelson and Robert M. Solow, "Problem of Achieving and Maintaining a Stable Price Level: Analytical Aspects of Anti-Inflationary Policy," *American Economic Review* 50 (1960): 177–194; Robert M. Solow, "Down the Phillips Curve with Gun and Camera," in *Inflation, Trade, and Taxes,* ed. David A. Belsley et al. (Columbus: Ohio State University Press, 1976).

15. A clear graphical representation of the Phillips curve experience through 1979 may be found in John L. Scadding, "Inflation: A Perspective," in *The Economy in the 1980s: A Program for Growth and Stability,* ed. Michael J. Boskin (San Francisco: Institute for Contemporary Studies, 1980), 63.

16. Allen J. Matusow, *Nixon's Economy: Booms, Busts, Dollars, and Votes* (Lawrence: University Press of Kansas, 1998); *The Conference on Inflation, Held at the Request of President Gerald R. Ford and the Congress of the United States, Sept. 27–28, 1974* (Washington, D.C.: Government Printing Office, 1974), 293; W. Carl Biven, *Jimmy Carter's Economy: Policy in an Age of Limits* (Chapel Hill: University of North Carolina Press, 2002); Anthony S. Campagna, *Economic Policy in the Carter Administration* (Westport, Conn.: Greenwood Press, 1995); John T. Woolley, "Exorcising Inflation-Mindedness: The Transformation of Economic Management in the 1970s," in *Loss of Confidence: Politics and Policy in the 1970s,* ed. David Brian Robertson (University Park: Pennsylvania State University Press, 1998); Bruce J. Schulman, "Slouching Toward the Supply Side: Jimmy Carter and the New American Political Economy," in *The Carter Presidency: Policy Choices in the Post–New Deal Era,* ed. Gary M. Fink and Hugh Davis Graham (Lawrence: University Press of Kansas, 1998); Herbert Stein, *Presidential Economics: The Making of Economic Policy from Roosevelt to Reagan and Beyond,* rev. ed. (New York: Simon & Schuster, 1985). On public opinion and wage controls: Woolley, "Exorcising Inflation-Mindedness," 138; Leonard Silk, *Economics in the Real World: How Political Decisions Affect the Economy* (New York: Simon and Schuster, 1984), 156.

17. The Council of Economic Advisers is quoted in Robert Heilbroner and William Milberg, *The Crisis of Vision in Modern Economic Thought* (Cambridge: Cambridge University Press, 1995), 57; Robert E. Lucas, Jr., "Remarks at the 27th Annual Management Conference in Chicago, April 26, 1979," in *Viewpoints on Supply-Side Economics,* ed. Thomas J. Hailstones (Reston, Va.: Reston Publishing, 1982), 5; Daniel Bell as quoted in Bernard D. Nossiter, "The Cupboard of Ideas is Bare," *Washington Post,* May 20, 1979, B5; Paul A. Samuelson, "How Economics Has Changed," *Journal of Economic Education* 18 (1987): 109.

18. Melvin W. Reder, "Chicago Economics: Permanence and Change," *Journal of Economic Literature* 20 (1982): 1–38.

19. Milton Friedman and Anna Jacobson Schwartz, *A Monetary History of the United States, 1867–1960* (Princeton: Princeton University Press, 1963); Milton Friedman, "The Methodology of Positive Economics," in Friedman, *Essays in Positive Economics* (Chicago: University of Chicago Press, 1953); Milton Friedman, *Inflation: Causes and Consequences* (Bombay: Council for Economic Education, 1963).

20. Harry G. Johnson, "The Keynesian Revolution and the Monetarist Counter-Revolution," *American Economic Review* 61 (1971): 1–14; Milton Friedman, *Capitalism and Freedom* (Chicago: University of Chicago Press, 1962). For the charge that Friedman's economics was pure macro: Alfred L. Malabre, *Lost Prophets: An Insider's View of the Modern Economists* (Boston: Harvard Business School Press, 1994), 244 (citing Hayek); Peter Drucker, "Toward the Next Economics," in *The Crisis in Economic Theory,* ed. Daniel Bell and Irving Kristol (New York: Basic Books, 1981), 9n.

21. Milton Friedman, *Bright Promises, Dismal Performance: An Economist's Protest* (San Diego: Harcourt Brace Jovanovich, 1983), 196.

22. Milton Friedman, "The Role of Monetary Policy," *American Economic Review* 58 (1968): 3–17.

23. Juan Gabriel Valdés, *Pinochet's Economists: The Chicago School in Chile* (Cambridge: Cambridge University Press, 1995).

24. Richard Cockett, *Thinking the Unthinkable: Think-Tanks and the Economic Counter-Revolution, 1931–1983* (New York: HarperCollins, 1994); Peter A. Hall, "The Movement from Keynesianism to Monetarism: Institutional Analysis and British Economic Policy in the 1970s," in *Structuring Politics: Historical Institutionalism in Comparative Analysis,* ed. Sven Steinmo et al. (Cambridge: Cambridge University Press, 1992).

25. An additional 25 percent agreed to the proposition "with provisions"; 61 percent disagreed altogether. J. R. Kearl et al., "A Confusion of Economists?" *American Economic Review* 69 (1979): 30.

26. Martin Feldstein, ed., *American Economic Policy in the 1980s* (Chicago: University of Chicago Press, 1994), chap. 2; William A. Niskanen, *Reaganomics: An Insider's Account of the Policies and the People* (New York: Oxford University Press, 1988), chap. 5; John W. Sloan, *The Reagan Effect: Economics and Presidential Leadership* (Lawrence: University Press of Kansas, 1999); William Keegan, *Mrs. Thatcher's Economic Experiment* (London: Allen Lane, 1984).

27. Thus Friedman's claim, "No monetarist experiment was carried out in the period 1979–82," quoted in Snowdon et al., *Modern Guide to Macroeconomics,* 177. The mainstream conclusion is reflected in Thomas Mayer, "What Remains of the Monetarist Counter-Revolution?" in *Reflections on the Development of Modern Macroeconomics,* ed. Brian Snowdon and Howard R. Vane (Cheltenham, UK: Edward Elgar, 1997); Stein, *Presidential Economics,* 404–405; the exchange between Benjamin M. Friedman and William Poole in *Journal of Economic Perspectives* 29 (Summer 1988): 51–100; and J. Bradford

DeLong, "The Triumph of Monetarism?" *Journal of Economic Perspectives* 14 (Winter 2000): 83–94.

28. Peter Bernstein, "The Man Who Brought You Milton Friedman," *Fortune,* February 1980, 108–112. The book that resulted from the television series, Milton Friedman and Rose Friedman, *Free to Choose: A Personal Statement* (New York: Harcourt Brace Jovanovich, 1980), stayed on the best-seller lists for a year.

29. Arjo Klamer and David Colander, *The Making of an Economist* (Boulder: Westview Press, 1990), 162.

30. Marc Allen Eisner, *Antitrust and the Triumph of Economics: Institutions, Expertise, and Policy Change* (Chapel Hill: University of North Carolina Press, 1991); Edmund W. Kitch, "The Fire of Truth: A Remembrance of Law and Economics at Chicago, 1932–1970," *Journal of Law and Economics* 26 (1983): 163–234.

31. R. H. Coase, "The Problem of Social Cost," *Journal of Law and Economics* 3 (1960): 1–44.

32. R. H. Coase, *The Firm, the Market, and the Law* (Chicago: University of Chicago Press, 1988); R. H. Coase, *Essays on Economics and Economists* (Chicago: University of Chicago Press, 1994). See also Steven G. Medema, *Ronald H. Coase* (Basingstoke, UK: Macmillan, 1994); Richard A. Posner, "Ronald Coase and Methodology," in Posner, *Overcoming Law* (Cambridge, Mass.: Harvard University Press, 1995).

33. Richard A. Posner, *Economic Analysis of Law* (Boston: Little, Brown, 1972), 395.

34. Arthur Allen Leff, "Economic Analysis of Law: Some Realism about Nominalism," *Virginia Law Review* 60 (1974): 451–482; Ronald M. Dworkin, "Is Wealth a Value?" *Journal of Legal Studies* 9 (1980): 191–226; Cass R. Sunstein, *Free Markets and Social Justice* (New York: Oxford University Press, 1997); Guido Calabresi, "The New Economic Analysis of Law: Scholarship, Sophistry, or Self-Indulgence?" *Proceedings of the British Academy* 68 (1982): 90. Calabresi had launched a more supple and eclectic form of law and economic analysis at the Yale Law School almost simultaneously with Coase; but the bulk of the citations and foundation support went to the Chicago version. See Guido Calabresi, "Some Thoughts on Risk Distribution and the Law of Torts," *Yale Law Journal* 70 (March 1961): 499–553; Guido Calabresi, "The Pointlessness of Pareto: Carrying Coase Further," *Yale Law Journal* 100 (March 1991): 1211–1237.

35. *American Lawyer* 21 (December 1999), 107; "Interpreting Legal Citations," a special issue of *The Journal of Legal Studies* 29, no. 1, pt. 2 (2000).

36. Jon Wiener, "Dollars for Neocon Scholars: The Olin Money Tree," in Wiener, *Professors, Politics, and Pop* (London: Verso, 1991); Steven M. Teles, *The Rise of the Conservative Legal Movement: The Battle for Control of the Law* (Princeton: Princeton University Press, 2008); Henry G. Manne, "How Law and Economics Was Marketed in a Hostile World: A Very Personal History," in *The Origins*

of Law and Economics: Essays by the Founding Fathers, ed. Francesco Parisi and Charles K. Rowley (Cheltenham, UK: Edward Elgar, 2005); Gregory C. Staple, "Free-Market Cram Course for Judges," *Nation,* January 26, 1980, 78–81; special issue on Manne's work, *Antitrust Law and Economics Review,* 14 no. 2 (1982).

37. William L. Prosser, *Handbook of the Law of Torts,* 4th ed. (St. Paul, Minn.: West Publishing, 1971), 2–3.

38. Stephen Breyer is quoted in Eisner, *Antitrust and the Triumph of Economics,* 113.

39. Gabriel Kolko, *The Triumph of Conservatism: A Reinterpretation of American History 1900–1916* (Glencoe, Ill.: Free Press, 1963); Grant McConnell, *Private Power and American Democracy* (New York: Knopf, 1966).

40. Alfred E. Kahn, "Applications of Economics to an Imperfect World," *American Economic Review* 69 (1979): 1–13; Thomas K. McCraw, *Prophets of Regulation: Charles Francis Adams, Louis D. Brandeis, James M. Landis, Alfred E. Kahn* (Cambridge, Mass.: Harvard University Press, 1984), chap. 7. The quotation is from p. 274.

41. Murray L. Weidenbaum and Robert DeFina, *The Cost of Federal Regulation of Economic Activity* (Washington, D.C.: American Enterprise Institute, 1978); George C. Eads and Michael Fix, *Relief or Reform? Reagan's Regulatory Dilemma* (Washington, D.C.: Urban Institute Press, 1984), chap. 2.

42. *Conference on Inflation,* 481–486; The Economists' Conference on Inflation, *Report* (Washington, D.C.: Government Printing Office, 1974), vol. 1, 11–13, 141–164.

43. Breyer, "Analyzing Regulatory Failure." In the same vein was Charles L. Schultze, *The Public Use of Private Interest* (Washington, D.C.: Brookings Institution, 1977), an early version of which helped persuade Jimmy Carter to appoint Schultze as his Council of Economic Advisers chair.

44. Martha Derthick and Paul J. Quirk, *The Politics of Deregulation* (Washington, D.C.: Brookings Institution, 1985), 53 and passim; Thomas H. Hammond and Jack H. Knott, "The Deregulatory Snowball: Explaining Deregulation in the Financial Industry," *Journal of Politics* 50 (1988): 3–30.

45. Robert C. Ellickson, "Bringing Culture and Human Frailty to Rational Actors: A Critique of Classical Law and Economics," *Chicago-Kent Law Review* 65 (1989): 23–55.

46. Gary S. Becker, *The Economic Approach to Human Behavior* (Chicago: University of Chicago Press, 1976), 5 and passim; Richard Swedberg, *Economics and Sociology: Redefining Their Boundaries. Conversations with Economists and Sociologists* (Princeton: Princeton University Press, 1990), chap. 1.

47. Robert E. Lucas, Jr., "Expectations and the Neutrality of Money," *Journal of Economic Theory* 4 (April 1972): 103–124; Stanley Fischer, ed., *Rational Expectations and Economic Policy* (Chicago: University of Chicago Press, 1980). The original rational expectations proposition was advanced by John Muth in

1961, but as McCloskey has shown, Muth's paper remained virtually unnoticed until the changed circumstances of the mid-1970s. McCloskey, *Rhetoric of Economics*, 87.

48. Mark H. Willes, "'Rational Expectations' as a Counterrevolution," in *Crisis in Economic Theory*, ed. Bell and Kristol, 85; Robert E. Lucas, Jr., "Unemployment Policy," *American Economic Review* 68 (May 1978): 356; Lucas, "Remarks at the 27th Annual Management Conference," 3; Robert E. Lucas and Thomas J. Sargent, "After Keynesian Macroeconomics," in *After the Phillips Curve: Persistence of High Inflation and High Unemployment*, Federal Reserve Bank of Boston conference series, no. 19, June 1978; Robert Barro, "New Classicals and Keynesians, or the Good Guys and the Bad Guys," *Schweizerische Zeitschrift für Volkswirtschaft und Statistik* 125 (1989): 263–273. More generally, Arjo Klamer, ed., *Conversations with Economists: New Classical Economists and Opponents Speak Out on the Current Controversy in Macroeconomics* (Totowa, N.J.: Rowman and Allanheld, 1983); Krugman, *Peddling Prosperity*.

49. Robert J. Gordon, "Fresh Water, Salt Water, and Other Macroeconomic Elixirs," *Economic Record* 65 (1989): 178; Lucas, *Models of Business Cycles*, 107; Klamer and Colander, *Making of an Economist*, 136.

50. David Colander, "Evolution of Keynesian Economics: From Keynesian to New Classical to New Keynesian," in *Keynes and Public Policy after Fifty Years*, ed. Omar F. Hamouda and John N. Smithin, vol. 1: *Economics and Policy* (Aldershot, UK: Edward Elgar, 1988); John B. Taylor, "The Evolution of Ideas in Macroeconomics," *Economic Record* 65 (1989): 185–189; N. Gregory Mankiw, "A Quick Refresher Course in Macroeconomics," *Journal of Economic Literature* 28 (1990): 1645–1660; Bennett T. McCallum, "Macroeconomics after Two Decades of Rational Expectations," *Journal of Economic Education* 25 (1994): 219–234; Alan S. Blinder et al., "Is There a Core of Practical Macroeconomics That We Should All Believe?" *American Economic Review* 87 (1997): 233–246; Brian Snowdon and Howard R. Vane, eds., *Conversations with Leading Economists: Interpreting Modern Macroeconomics* (Cheltenham, UK: Edward Elgar, 1999).

51. David M. Kreps, "Economics—The Current Position," *Daedalus* 126 (Winter 1997): 59–86; John Conlisk, "Why Bounded Rationality?" *Journal of Economic Literature* 34 (1996): 669–700; Esther-Mirjam Sent, "Behavioral Economics: How Psychology Made Its (Limited) Way Back into Economics," *History of Political Economy* 36 (2004): 735–760; Richard H. Thaler, *Quasi Rational Economics* (New York: Russell Sage Foundation, 1991); Oliver E. Williamson, *The Economic Institutions of Capitalism: Firms, Markets, Relational Contracting* (New York: Free Press, 1985). More generally: Diane Coyle, *The Soulful Science: What Economists Really Do and Why It Matters* (Princeton: Princeton University Press, 2007).

52. George A. Akerlof and Janet L. Yellen, "Can Small Deviations from Rational-

ity Make Significant Differences to Economic Equilibria?" *American Economic Review* 75 (1985): 708–720; Robert J. Gordon, "What Is New Keynesian Economics?" *Journal of Economic Literature* 28 (1990): 1115–1171; N. Gregory Mankiw, "The Reincarnation of Keynesian Economics," *European Economic Review* 36 (1992): 559–565; Bruce Greenwald and Joseph Stiglitz, "New and Old Keynesians," *Journal of Economic Perspectives* 7 (Winter 1993): 23–44; N. Gregory Mankiw and David Romer, eds., *New Keynesian Economics* (Cambridge, Mass.: MIT Press, 1991).

53. James Tobin, "Price Flexibility and Output Stability: An Old Keynesian View," *Journal of Economic Perspectives* 7 (Winter 1993): 47.

54. Robert L. Bartley, *The Seven Fat Years and How to Do It Again* (New York: Free Press, 1992), chap. 3; Krugman, *Peddling Prosperity,* chap. 3; Malabre, *Lost Prophets,* chap. 6; Milton Friedman, "The Kemp-Roth Free Lunch" (1978), in Friedman, *Bright Promises.* Robert Lucas is quoted in *Viewpoints on Supply-Side Economics,* ed. Hailstones, 5.

55. Lester C. Thurow, *The Zero-Sum Society: Distribution and the Possibilities for Economic Change* (New York: Basic Books, 1980).

56. Bruce Bartlett and Timothy P. Roth, eds., *The Supply-Side Solution* (Chatham, N.J.: Chatham House, 1983).

57. David Vogel, *Fluctuating Fortunes: The Political Power of Business in America* (New York: Basic Books, 1989), chaps. 7–8.

58. Robert Kuttner, *The Revolt of the Haves: Tax Rebellions and Hard Times* (New York: Simon and Schuster, 1980); Frank Levy, "On Understanding Proposition 13," *Public Interest* 56 (1979): 66–89; Arthur B. Laffer and Jan P. Seymour, eds., *The Economics of the Tax Revolt: A Reader* (New York: Harcourt Brace Jovanovich, 1979).

59. U.S. Congress, House Committee on Ways and Means, *Tax Reductions: Economists' Comments on H.R. 8333 and S. 1860,* 95th Cong., 2nd sess., 1978, pp. 46, 101, and passim.

60. Jack Kemp, *An American Renaissance: A Strategy for the 1980s* (New York: Harper and Row, 1979); David Warsh, "'Yellow Rain' and 'Supply-Side Economics': Some Rhetoric That Failed," in *The Consequences of Economic Rhetoric,* ed. Arjo Klamer, Donald McCloskey, and Robert M. Solow (Cambridge, UK: Cambridge University Press, 1988), 258.

61. Jude Wanniski, *The Way the World Works: How Economies Fail—And Succeed* (New York: Basic Books, 1978).

62. George Gilder, *Wealth and Poverty* (New York: Basic Books, 1981), 10, 31, 259.

63. Jude Wanniski, "Taxes, Revenues, and the 'Laffer Curve,'" *Public Interest* 50 (1978): 3–16; Eric Alterman, "The 'Right' Books and Big Ideas," *Nation,* November 22, 1999, 16–21; Vogel, *Fluctuating Fortunes,* 227; David A. Stockman, *The Triumph of Politics: How the Reagan Revolution Failed* (New York: Harper and Row, 1986); Paul Craig Roberts, *The Supply-Side Revolution: An Insider's Account*

of Policymaking in Washington (Cambridge, Mass.: Harvard University Press, 1984). On the drafting of *A Program for Economic Recovery:* Niskanen, *Reaganomics,* 6.

64. Martin Feldstein, "Supply Side Economics: Old Truths and New Claims," *American Economic Review* 76 (1986): 26–30; Stein, *Presidential Economics,* 377–396; Krugman, *Peddling Prosperity,* 74, 126; Sloan, *Reagan Effect,* chap. 9. Also proved wrong were the Keynesians' predictions that the tax cuts would produce a "tidal wave" of inflation. For example, Walter Heller, "The Kemp-Roth-Laffer Free Lunch" (1978), reprinted in *Economics of the Tax Revolt,* ed. Laffer and Seymour, 49.

65. Otis L. Graham, Jr., *Losing Time: The Industrial Policy Debate* (Cambridge, Mass.: Harvard University Press, 1992).

66. Paul Mosley, Jane Harrigan, and John Toye, *Aid and Power: The World Bank and Policy-Based Lending* (London: Routledge, 1990).

67. Albert O. Hirschman, "The Rise and Decline of Development Economics," in Hirschman, *Essays in Trespassing: Economics to Politics and Beyond* (New York: Cambridge University Press, 1981); John Williamson, "What Washington Means by Policy Reform," in *Latin American Adjustment: How Much Has Happened?* ed. John Williamson (Washington, D.C.: Institute for International Economics, 1990); Marion Fourcade-Gourinchas and Sarah L. Babb, "The Rebirth of the Liberal Creed: Paths to Neoliberalism in Four Countries," *American Journal of Sociology* 108 (2002): 533–579; John G. Ikenberry, "The International Spread of Privatization Policies: Inducements, Learning, and Policy Bandwagoning," in *The Political Economy of Public Sector Reform and Privatization,* ed. Ezra N. Suleiman and John Waterbury (Boulder: Westview Press, 1990); John Markoff and Verónica Montecinos, "The Ubiquitous Rise of Economics," *Journal of Public Policy* 13 (1993): 37–68.

68. Daniel Bell, *The Cultural Contradictions of Capitalism* (New York: Basic Books, 1976); Irving Kristol, *Two Cheers for Capitalism* (New York: Basic Books, 1978); Friedrich von Hayek is quoted in David Marquand, "The Paradoxes of Thatcherism," in *Thatcherism,* ed. Robert Skidelsky (London: Chatto and Windus, 1988), 168.

69. Walter Wriston and Thomas Friedman are quoted in Thomas Frank, *One Market, Under God: Extreme Capitalism, Market Populism, and the End of Economic Democracy* (New York: Doubleday, 2000), 55, 93.

70. Karl Case, "Observations on the Use of Textbooks in the Teaching of Principles of Economics," *Journal of Economic Education* 19 (1988): 165; Kevin D. Hoover, "Teaching Macroeconomics While Taking Complexity Seriously," in *The Complexity Vision and the Teaching of Economics,* ed. David C. Colander (Northampton, Mass.: Edward Elgar, 2000), 178–179.

71. Paul A. Samuelson and William D. Nordhaus, *Economics,* 14th ed. (New York: McGraw-Hill, 1992), xvi.

3. The Search for Power

Epigraphs: Michel Foucault, *The History of Sexuality,* vol. I: *An Introduction* (French edition, 1976; New York: Pantheon, 1978), 93; and Joseph Stiglitz, "Post Walrasian and Post Marxian Economics," *Journal of Economic Perspectives* 7 (Winter 1993): 111.

1. John Kenneth Galbraith, "Power and the Useful Economist," *American Economic Review* 63 (1973): 2, 6.
2. Oliver Williamson and Joseph Stiglitz, exchange over Samuel Bowles and Herbert Gintis, "The Revenge of Homo Economicus: Contested Exchange and the Revival of Political Economy," *Journal of Economic Perspectives* 7 (Winter 1993): 107, 111; Paul Krugman, *Peddling Prosperity: Economic Sense and Nonsense in the Age of Diminished Expectations* (New York: Norton, 1994), 13–14.
3. Donella H. Meadows et al., *The Limits to Growth: A Report for the Club of Rome's Project on the Predicament of Mankind* (New York: Universe Books, 1972). On the hype surrounding the book: Robert Gillette, "The Limits to Growth: Hard Sell for a Computer View of Doomsday," *Science,* March 10, 1972, 1088–1092.
4. Robert L. Heilbroner, *An Inquiry into the Human Prospect* (New York: Norton, 1974).
5. Michael C. Jensen, "The Eclipse of the Public Corporation," *Harvard Business Review,* Sept.–Oct. 1989, 61–74; Bengt Holmstrom and Steven N. Kaplan, "Corporate Governance and Merger Activity in the United States: Making Sense of the 1980s and 1990s," *Journal of Economic Perspectives* 15 (Spring 2001): 121–144; George P. Baker and George David Smith, *The New Finance Capitalists: Kohlberg Kravis Roberts and the Creation of Corporate Value* (Cambridge: Cambridge University Press, 1998); Pascal Petit, "Managerial Capitalism by Any Other Name," *Challenge* 48 (September 2005): 62–78.
6. Robert A. Dahl, *Who Governs? Democracy and Power in an American City* (New Haven: Yale University Press, 1961).
7. Ivan Szelenyi, "The Three Waves of New Class Theories," *Theory and Society* 17 (1988): 645–667; Christopher Lasch, *The Culture of Narcissism: American Life in an Age of Diminishing Expectations* (New York: Norton, 1979); Christopher Lasch, *Haven in a Heartless World: The Family Besieged* (New York: Basic Books, 1977). Lasch himself rejected "new class" terminology: Christopher Lasch, "Same Old New Class," *New York Review of Books,* September 28, 1967.
8. Irving Kristol, "Business and the 'New Class,'" *Wall Street Journal,* May 19, 1975, reprinted in Kristol, *Two Cheers for Capitalism* (New York: Basic Books, 1978); Robert H. Bork, *The Tempting of America: The Political Seduction of the Law* (New York: Free Press, 1990), 8; Edwin Meese III, "Address to the Jo-

seph Story Awards Banquet," in *Major Policy Statements of the Attorney General: Edwin Meese III, 1985–1988* (Washington, D.C.: Government Printing Office, n.d.); James Q. Wilson, *American Government: Institutions and Policies* (Lexington, Mass.: D.C. Heath, 1980), 116–121; Peter L. Berger, "Ethics and the Present Class Struggle," *Worldview,* April 1978, 6.

9. Kristol, "Business and the 'New Class,'" 28.

10. Kristol, "Business and the 'New Class,'" 29; Jeane Kirkpatrick as quoted in William F. Buckley, Jr., "St. Jeane of the UN-II," *National Review,* January 27, 1984, 62; William A. Rusher, "A New Party Eventually: Why Not Now?" *National Review,* May 23, 1975, 550–551. See also B. Bruce-Biggs, ed., *The New Class?* (New Brunswick, N.J.: Transaction Books, 1979); Peter L. Berger, *The Capitalist Revolution: Fifty Propositions about Prosperity, Equality, and Liberty* (New York: Basic Books, 1986), 66–70.

11. Daniel Bell, "The New Class: A Muddled Concept," in *The New Class?* ed. Bruce-Biggs, 169; James Burnham, "What New Class?" *National Review,* January 20, 1978, 99.

12. On the sociology of the new class: Nathan Glazer, "Lawyers and the New Class," in *The New Class?* ed. Bruce-Biggs; Daniel Bell, *The Coming of Post-Industrial Society: A Venture in Social Forecasting* (New York: Basic Books, 1973); Peter L. Berger, "Foreword" to *Hidden Technocrats: The New Class and New Capitalism,* ed. Hansfried Kellner and Frank W. Heuberger (New Brunswick, N.J.: Transaction Publishers, 1992).

13. William H. Riker, *The Theory of Political Coalitions* (New Haven: Yale University Press, 1962); James M. Buchanan and Gordon Tullock, *The Calculus of Consent: Logical Foundations of Constitutional Democracy* (Ann Arbor: University of Michigan Press, 1962); Mancur Olson, Jr., *The Logic of Collective Action: Public Goods and the Theory of Groups* (Cambridge, Mass.: Harvard University Press, 1965); William C. Mitchell, "Virginia, Rochester, and Bloomington: Twenty-five Years of Public Choice and Political Science," *Public Choice* 56 (1988): 101–119.

14. The quotation is from William H. Riker and Barry R. Weingast, "Constitutional Regulation of Legislative Choice: The Political Consequences of Judicial Deference to Legislatures," *Virginia Law Review* 74 (1988), 374. On public choice theory more generally: William H. Riker, *Liberalism against Populism: A Confrontation between the Theory of Democracy and the Theory of Social Choice* (San Francisco: W. H. Freeman, 1982); James M. Buchanan, "A Contractarian Paradigm for Applying Economic Theory," *American Economic Review* 65 (1975): 225–236; James M. Buchanan, "Politics without Romance: A Sketch of Positive Public Choice Theory and Its Normative Implications" (1979), reprinted in *Contemporary Political Theory,* ed. Philip Pettit (New York: Macmillan, 1991); James M. Buchanan, "The Economic Theory of Politics Reborn," *Challenge* 31 (March-April 1988): 4–10; James M. Buchanan, "Pub-

lic Choice: The Origins and Development of a Research Program," www.
publicchoice.soc.org/about_pc.html (accessed September 13, 2007); Anne O.
Krueger, "The Political Economy of the Rent-Seeking Society," *American Economic Review* 64 (1974): 291–303; James M. Buchanan, Robert D. Tollison,
and Gordon Tullock, eds., *Toward a Theory of the Rent-Seeking Society* (College
Station: Texas A & M Press, 1980); and the essays in *Virginia Law Review*, special issue on "Public Choice," 74, no. 2 (1988). The moral that Kenneth Arrow drew from his work was quite different: Kenneth J. Arrow, "Two Cheers
for Government Regulation," *Harper's*, March 1981, 18–22.

15. Riker and Weingast, "Constitutional Regulation of Legislative Choice," 380;
Buchanan and Tullock, *Calculus of Consent*, 5; Buchanan, "Politics without Ro-
mance," 218; Mancur Olson, Jr., "Ideology and Economic Growth," in *The
Legacy of Reaganomics: Prospects for Long-Term Growth*, ed. Charles R. Hutten
and Isabel V. Sawhill (Washington: Urban Institute Press, 1984); Mancur
Olson, Jr., "The Case for Liberalizing Markets," *Challenge* 40 (September-
October 1997): 59–76.

16. Rogers M. Smith, "Still Blowing in the Wind: The American Quest for a
Democratic, Scientific Political Science," *Daedalus* 126 (Winter 1997), 282;
Donald P. Green and Ian Shapiro, *Pathologies of Rational Choice Theory: A Critique of Applications in Political Science* (New Haven: Yale University Press,
1994), 3; James Q. Wilson, "Interests and Deliberation in the American Republic, or, Why James Madison Would Never Have Received the James Madison Award," *PS: Political Science and Politics* 23 (1990), 561; David Apter,
"Structure, Contingency, and Choice: A Comparison of Trends and Tendencies in Political Science," in *Schools of Thought: Twenty-Five Years of Interpretive Social Science*, ed. Joan W. Scott and Debra Keates (Princeton: Princeton
University Press, 2001).

17. Jon Elster, *Making Sense of Marx* (New York: Cambridge University Press,
1985); Jane J. Mansbridge, ed., *Beyond Self-Interest* (Chicago: University of
Chicago Press, 1990); Jeffrey Friedman, ed., *The Rational Choice Controversy:
Economic Models of Politics Reconsidered* (New Haven: Yale University Press,
1996).

18. See, for example, the general descriptions of American politics by one prominent rational choice scholar, Morris P. Fiorina. For two examples among
many: Morris P. Fiorina, "The Decline of Collective Responsibility in American Politics," *Daedalus* 109 (Summer 1980): 25–45; Morris P. Fiorina, "Coalition Governments, Divided Governments, and Electoral Theory," *Governance*
4 (1991): 236–249.

19. Peter B. Evans, Dietrich Rueschemeyer, and Theda Skocpol, eds., *Bringing the
State Back In* (Cambridge: Cambridge University Press, 1985). An early text-
book reflection of the turn to rational choice was Samuel Kernell and Gary
C. Jacobson, *The Logic of American Politics* (Washington, D.C.: CQ Press, 2003).

But see also Jay Dow and Michael Munger, "Public Choice in Political Science: We Don't Teach It, But We Publish It," *PS: Political Science and Politics* 23 (1990): 604–609.

20. James N. Baron and Michael T. Hannan, "The Impact of Economics on Contemporary Sociology," *Journal of Economic Literature* 32 (1994): 1111–1146; Mark Granovetter, "Economic Action and Social Structure: The Problem of Embeddedness," *American Journal of Sociology* 91 (1985): 481–510.

21. Richard Swedberg, *Economics and Sociology: Redefining Their Boundaries. Conversations with Economists and Sociologists* (Princeton: Princeton University Press, 1990), 49; James S. Coleman et al., *Equality of Educational Opportunity* (Washington, D.C.: U.S. Department of Health, Education, and Welfare, 1966); James S. Coleman, *Power and the Structure of Society* (New York: Norton, 1974); James S. Coleman, *Foundations of Social Theory* (Cambridge, Mass.: Harvard University Press, 1990), 3; James S. Coleman, "Editor's Introduction," *Rationality and Society* 1 (1989): 5–6. When Coleman was asked to suggest a political scientist for a symposium on *Foundations of Social Theory,* his suggestion was someone from James Buchanan's public choice center at George Mason University. Jon Clark, ed., *James S. Coleman* (Bristol, Penn.: Falmer, 1996), 6.

22. Anthony Giddens, *The Constitution of Society: Outline of the Theory of Structuration* (Berkeley: University of California Press, 1984); Pierre Bourdieu, *The Logic of Practice,* trans. Richard Nice (Stanford: Stanford University Press, 1990).

23. Swedberg, *Economics and Sociology,* 56; Coleman, *Foundations of Social Theory,* 133–134; William H. Riker and Peter C. Ordeshook, *An Introduction to Positive Political Theory* (Englewood Cliffs, N.J.: Prentice-Hall, 1973), 163.

24. Harold D. Lasswell, *Politics: Who Gets What, When, How* (New York: McGraw-Hill, 1936).

25. Geoff Eley, *A Crooked Line: From Cultural History to the History of Society* (Ann Arbor: University of Michigan Press, 2005), chap. 2.

26. E. P. Thompson, *The Making of the English Working Class* (1963; New York: Vintage Books, 1966), 11 and passim. Asked to list the books that had influenced them most in a *Journal of American History* poll in the early 1990s, respondents ranked Thompson fourth, behind the Bible, Richard Hofstadter, and Karl Marx, and slightly ahead of Shakespeare and Tocqueville: "The Practice of History: A Special Issue," *Journal of American History* 81, no. 3 (1994): 1203–1205.

27. Thompson, *Making,* 9.

28. William H. Sewell, Jr., "How Classes Are Made: Critical Reflections on E. P. Thompson's Theory of Working-class Formation," in *E. P. Thompson: Critical Perspectives,* ed. Harvey J. Kaye and Keith McClelland (Cambridge: Polity Press, 1990), 50–51.

29. Herbert G. Gutman, *Work, Culture, and Society in Industrializing America: Essays in American Working-Class and Social History* (New York: Knopf, 1976); Herbert

G. Gutman, *Power and Culture: Essays on the American Working Class* (New York: Pantheon, 1987); Michael H. Frisch and Daniel J. Walkowitz, eds., *Working-Class America: Essays on Labor, Community, and American Society* (Urbana: University of Illinois Press, 1983); Sean Wilentz, "Against Exceptionalism: Class Consciousness and the American Labor Movement, 1790–1920," *International Labor and Working-Class History* 26 (1984): 1–24; Leon Fink, *In Search of the Working Class: Essays in American Labor History and Political Culture* (Urbana: University of Illinois Press, 1994).

30. David R. Roediger, *The Wages of Whiteness: Race and the Making of the American Working Class* (London: Verso, 1991); Mari Jo Buhle, *Women and American Socialism, 1870–1920* (Urbana: University of Illinois Press, 1981).

31. Alice Kessler-Harris, "A New Agenda for American Labor History," in *Perspectives on American Labor History: The Problems of Synthesis,* ed. J. Carroll Moody and Alice Kessler-Harris (DeKalb: Northern Illinois University Press, 1989), 219. For other responses to the DeKalb conference: David Brody, "The Old Labor History and the New: In Search of an American Working Class," *Labor History* 20 (1979): 111–126; Michael Frisch, "Sixty Characters in Search of Authority," *International Labour and Working-Class History* 27 (1985): 100–103; Mari Jo Buhle, "The Future of American Labor History: Toward a Synthesis?" *Radical Historians Newsletter* 44 (1984): 1–2; Barbara Fields, "Correspondence," *Radical Historians Newsletter* 45 (1985): 1 ff.

32. Thompson, *Making,* 194. See also E. P. Thompson, "The Moral Economy of the English Crowd in the Eighteenth Century," *Past and Present* 50 (1971), 76–136; E. P. Thompson, "Time, Work-Discipline, and Industrial Capitalism," *Past and Present* 38 (1967): 56–97.

33. The debates are summarized in Kaye and McClelland, *E. P. Thompson;* Paul Buhle, "E. P. Thompson and His Critics," *Telos* 49 (1981): 127–137.

34. John W. Blassingame, *The Slave Community: Plantation Life in the Antebellum South* (New York: Oxford University Press, 1972); Lawrence W. Levine, *Black Culture and Black Consciousness: Afro-American Folk Thought from Slavery to Freedom* (New York: Oxford University Press, 1977).

35. Peter Bachrach and Morton S. Baratz, "Two Faces of Power," *American Political Science Review* 56 (1962): 947–952; Steven Lukes, *Power: A Radical View* (London: Macmillan, 1974); Murray Edelman, *Politics as Symbolic Action: Mass Arousal and Quiescence* (Chicago: Markham, 1971); John Gaventa, *Power and Powerlessness: Quiescence and Rebellion in an Appalachian Valley* (Urbana: University of Illinois Press, 1980).

36. Antonio Gramsci, *Selections from the Prison Notebooks,* ed. and trans. Quintin Hoare and Geoffrey Nowell Smith (New York: International Publishers, 1971).

37. Gwynn A. Williams, "The Concept of 'Egemonia' in the Thought of Antonio Gramsci: Some Notes on Interpretation," *Journal of the History of Ideas* 21 (1960): 587. See also Walter L. Adamson, *Hegemony and Revolution: A Study of*

Antonio Gramsci's Political and Cultural Theory (Berkeley: University of California Press, 1980); Perry Anderson, "The Antinomies of Antonio Gramsci," *New Left Review* 100 (1976–1977): 5–78; Chantal Mouffe, ed., *Gramsci and Marxist Theory* (London: Routledge and Kegan Paul, 1979).

38. Eugene D. Genovese, *Roll, Jordan, Roll: The World the Slaves Made* (New York: Pantheon, 1974); Eugene D. Genovese, "On Antonio Gramsci," in Genovese, *In Red and Black: Marxian Explorations in Southern and Afro-American History* (New York: Pantheon, 1968).

39. Genovese, *Roll, Jordan, Roll,* 597, 594; Elizabeth Fox-Genovese and Eugene D. Genovese, "The Political Crisis of Social History: A Marxian Perspective," *Journal of Social History* 10 (1976): 205–220.

40. Gutman, *Power and Culture,* 353.

41. Leon Fink, "The New Labor History and the Powers of Historical Pessimism: Consensus, Hegemony, and the Case of the Knights of Labor," *Journal of American History* 75 (1988): 115–136, with responses by John Patrick Diggins, Jackson Lears, George Lipsitz, and Mari Jo and Paul Buhle. The quotation is from George Lipsitz, "The Struggle for Hegemony," ibid., 147. Two other important exchanges on hegemony were: T. J. Jackson Lears, "The Concept of Cultural Hegemony: Problems and Possibilities," *American Historical Review* 90 (1985): 567–593; and John Patrick Diggins, "Comrades and Citizens: New Mythologies in American Historiography," *American Historical Review* 90 (1985): 614–638; Thomas L. Haskell, "Capitalism and the Origins of the Humanitarian Sensibility," *American Historical Review* 90 (1985): 339–361 and 547–566; David Brion Davis, "Reflections on Abolitionism and Ideological Hegemony," *American Historical Review* 92 (1987): 797–812; Thomas L. Haskell, "Convention and Hegemonic Interest in the Debate over Antislavery: A Reply to Davis and Ashworth," *American Historical Review* 92: (1987): 829–878.

42. E. P. Thompson, "Patrician Society, Plebeian Culture," *Journal of Social History* 7 (1974): 387.

43. Stuart Hall, "The Toad in the Garden: Thatcher Among the Theorists," in *Marxism and the Interpretation of Culture,* ed. Cary Nelson and Lawrence Grossberg (Urbana: University of Illinois Press, 1988), 42.

44. J. G. A. Pocock, *The Machiavellian Moment: Florentine Political Thought and the Atlantic Republican Tradition* (Princeton: Princeton University Press, 1975); J. G. A. Pocock, *Politics, Language and Time: Essays on Political Thought and History* (New York: Atheneum, 1971); Daniel T. Rodgers, "Republicanism: The Career of a Concept," *Journal of American History* 79 (1992): 11–38; "Editorial: Language and History," *History Workshop* 10 (1980): 1; Gareth Stedman Jones, *Languages of Class: Studies in English Working-Class History, 1832–1982* (Cambridge: Cambridge University Press, 1983).

45. Clifford Geertz, *Peddlers and Princes: Social Change and Economic Modernization in Two Indonesian Towns* (Chicago: University of Chicago Press, 1963). Geertz

came to read his intellectual career more linearly than his own writings suggest: Clifford Geertz, "Commentary," in *Clifford Geertz by His Colleagues,* ed. Richard A. Schweder and Byron Good (Chicago: University of Chicago Press, 2005), 122; Clifford Geertz, *A Life of Learning* (ACLS Occasional Paper, New York, 1999).

46. Clifford Geertz, *The Interpretation of Cultures: Selected Essays* (New York: Basic Books, 1973), 10.

47. Geertz, *Interpretation of Cultures,* 29, 28. The term "foundational critique" is from Clifford Geertz, *After the Fact: Two Countries, Four Decades, and One Anthropologist* (Cambridge, Mass.: Harvard University Press, 1995), 114.

48. Paul Shankman, "The Thick and the Thin: On the Interpretive Program of Clifford Geertz," *Current Anthropology* 25 (1984): 261–279, and responses; Sherry B. Ortner, "Theory in Anthropology since the Sixties," *Comparative Studies in Society and History* 26 (1984): 126–166.

49. Robert Darnton, *The Great Cat Massacre and Other Episodes in French Cultural History* (New York: Basic Books, 1984), 3; Ronald G. Walters, "Signs of the Times: Clifford Geertz and Historians," *Social Research* 47 (1980): 537–556; William H. Sewell, Jr., *Logics of History: Social Theory and Social Transformation* (Chicago: University of Chicago Press, 2005), chap. 1.

50. "The New History: The 1980s and Beyond," *Journal of Interdisciplinary History* 12, nos. 1–2 (1981); William H. Sewell, Jr., "Whatever Happened to the 'Social' in Social History?" in *Schools of Thought,* ed. Scott and Keates, 215; Joan Wallach Scott, "A Statistical Representation of Work: *La Statistique de l'industrie à Paris, 1847–1848*" (1986), in Scott, *Gender and the Politics of History* (New York: Columbia University Press, 1988). For the record of a particularly poignant collision between the old social history and the new: Charles Tilly et al., "Problems in Social History: A Symposium," *Theory and Society* 9 (1980): 667–681.

51. Clifford Geertz, *Negara: The Theatre State in Nineteenth-Century Bali* (Princeton: Princeton University Press, 1980), 135.

52. Geertz, *Negara,* 136, 63, 13.

53. Roger M. Keesing, "Anthropology as Interpretive Quest," *Current Anthropology* 28 (1987): 161–169, with responses.

54. The literature on Foucault is vast. Among the particularly useful introductions: Alan Ryan, "Foucault's Life and Hard Times," *New York Review of Books,* April 8, 1993; Hubert L. Dreyfus and Paul Rabinow, *Michel Foucault: Beyond Structuralism and Hermeneutics* (Chicago: University of Chicago Press, 1982); Mark Poster, "Foucault and History," *Social Research* 49 (1982): 116–142; Edward W. Said, "Michel Foucault, 1926–1984," *Raritan* 4 (Fall 1984), reprinted in *After Foucault: Humanistic Knowledge, Postmodern Challenges,* ed. Jonathan Arac (New Brunswick, N.J.: Rutgers University Press, 1988).

55. Michel Foucault, *Madness and Civilization: A History of Insanity in the Age of Reason,* trans. Richard Howard (1961; New York: Pantheon, 1965), 3.

56. Michel Foucault, *The Order of Things: An Archaeology of the Human Sciences* (1966; New York: Pantheon, 1970); Michel Foucault, "Orders of Discourse" (1970), published as an appendix of Michel Foucault, *The Archaeology of Knowledge*, trans. A. M. Sheridan Smith (New York: Pantheon, 1972).

57. Michel Foucault, *Discipline and Punish: The Birth of the Prison*, trans. Alan Sheridan (1975: New York: Pantheon, 1977).

58. Foucault, *Discipline and Punish*, 209; Michel Foucault, *Power/Knowledge: Selected Interviews and Other Writings, 1972–1977*, ed. Colin Gordon (Brighton, UK: Harvester Press, 1980), 98. On these themes: Peter Digeser, "The Fourth Face of Power," *Journal of Politics* 54 (1992): 977–1007; Mark Filp, "Foucault on Power: A Problem in Radical Translation?" *Political Theory* 11 (1983): 29–52.

59. Foucault, *Power/Knowledge*, 39; Michel Foucault, *The History of Sexuality*, vol. I: *Introduction*, trans. Robert Hurley (1976; New York: Pantheon, 1978), 93, 94, 95.

60. Clifford Geertz, "Stir Crazy," *New York Review of Books*, January 26, 1978; Noam Chomsky and Michel Foucault, "Human Nature: Justice versus Power," in *Reflexive Water: The Basic Concerns of Mankind*, ed. Fons Elders (London: Souvenir Press, 1974).

61. Nancy Fraser, *Unruly Practices: Power, Discourse, and Gender in Contemporary Social Theory* (Minneapolis: University of Minnesota Press, 1989), 32; Edward W. Said, *Orientalism* (New York: Pantheon, 1978); Edward W. Said, "Michel Foucault as an Intellectual Imagination," *Boundary 2* 1, (1972): 1–36; Edward W. Said, "Traveling Theory," in Said, *The World, the Text, and the Critic* (Cambridge, Mass.: Harvard University Press, 1983), 245, 246. See also Michael Walzer, "The Politics of Michel Foucault," *Dissent* (Fall 1983): 481–490; David Couzens Hoy, ed., *Foucault: A Critical Reader* (New York: Pantheon, 1986).

62. "Ten Most Influential Books of the Past 25 Years," *Contemporary Sociology* 25 (May 1996): ix, 293–324.

63. Herman Kahn and Anthony J. Wiener, *The Year 2000: A Framework for Speculation on the Next Thirty-Three Years* (New York: Macmillan, 1967), chap. 8.

64. Alvin Toffler, *Future Shock* (New York: Random House, 1970), 223, 430.

65. Alvin Toffler, *The Third Wave* (New York: William Morrow, 1980). Repackaged as *Creating a New Civilization: The Politics of the Third Wave* (Atlanta: Turner Publishing, 1994), this was among the books that Newt Gingrich set as required reading for the new Republican congressional majority in 1994. For a more complicated reading of Toffler's work: John B. Judis, "Newt's Not-So-Weird Gurus," *New Republic*, October 9, 1995, 16–25; and Toffler's long interview with the editors of the South End Press in Alvin Toffler, *Previews and Premises* (New York: William Morrow, 1983). Toffler titled the third book in his trilogy *Powershift: Knowledge, Wealth, and Violence in the Twenty-first Century* (New York:

Bantam Books, 1990), but he used the term simply to reiterate the theme of a shift to an information-based society.

66. John Naisbitt, *Megatrends: Ten New Directions Transforming Our Lives* (New York: Warner Books, 1982), 251, 175, 2; John Naisbitt and Patricia Aburdene, *Megatrends 2000: Ten New Directions for the 1990's* (New York: William Morrow, 1990), 298.

4. Race and Social Memory

Epigraph: Stuart Hall, "Minimal Selves," in *Identity,* ed. Lisa Appignanesi (London: Institute of Contemporary Arts, 1987), 45.

1. For overviews: George M. Fredrickson, *Racism: A Short History* (Princeton: Princeton University Press, 2002); Thomas C. Holt, *The Problem of Race in the Twenty-first Century* (Cambridge, Mass.: Harvard University Press, 2000).
2. David A. Hollinger, *Postethnic America: Beyond Multiculturalism* (New York: Basic Books, 1995).
3. James Baldwin, "White Man's Guilt" (1965), in Baldwin, *Price of the Ticket: Collected Nonfiction, 1948–1985* (New York: St. Martin's Press, 1985), 410.
4. Robert C. Smith, *We Have No Leaders: African Americans in the Post–Civil Rights Era* (Albany: State University of New York Press, 1996); Charles T. Clotfelter, *After Brown: The Rise and Retreat of School Desegregation* (Princeton: Princeton University Press, 2004).
5. On Atlanta: Adolph Reed, Jr., "A Critique of Neo-Progressivism in Theorizing about Local Development Policy: A Case from Atlanta," in *The Politics of Urban Development,* ed. Clarence N. Stone and Heywood T. Sanders (Lawrence: University Press of Kansas, 1987). On Richmond: W. Avon Drake and Robert D. Holsworth, *Affirmative Action and the Stalled Quest for Black Progress* (Urbana: University of Illinois Press, 1996).
6. Jesse Jackson, *Straight from the Heart,* ed. Roger D. Hatch and Frank E. Watkins (Philadelphia: Fortress Press, 1987), 5, 36, 18.
7. Jackson, *Straight from the Heart,* 300–301; Jesse Jackson, *A Conversation with the Reverend Jesse Jackson: The Quest for Economic and Educational Parity* (Washington, D.C.: American Enterprise Institute, 1978); Marshall Frady, *Jesse: The Life and Pilgrimage of Jesse Jackson* (New York: Random House, 1996).
8. Toni Morrison, "Rediscovering Black History," *New York Times Magazine,* August 11, 1974, 14ff; Middleton Harris, ed., *The Black Book* (New York: Random House, 1974).
9. Michael Bérubé, "Public Academy," *New Yorker,* January 9, 1995, 73–80; Robert S. Boynton, "The New Intellectuals," *Atlantic Monthly,* March 1995, 53–70.
10. Houston A. Baker, Jr., *Black Studies, Rap, and the Academy* (Chicago: University

of Chicago Press, 1993), chap. 1; Molefi Kete Asante, "A Note on Nathan Huggins' Report to the Ford Foundation on African-American Studies," *Journal of Black Studies* 17 (1986): 255–262; Molefi Kete Asante, *The Afrocentric Idea* (Philadelphia: Temple University Press, 1987).

11. Martin Bernal, *Black Athena: The Afroasiatic Roots of Classical Civilization* (London: Free Association Books, 1987); Mary R. Lefkowitz and Guy MacLean Rogers, eds., *Black Athena Revisited* (Chapel Hill: University of North Carolina Press, 1996); Robert S. Boynton, "The Bernaliad," *Lingua Franca*, November 1996, 43–50.

12. For a partial guide to this terrain: Nelson George, *Post-Soul Nation: The Explosive, Contradictory, Triumphant, and Tragic 1980s as Experienced by African Americans (Previously Known as Blacks and before That Negroes)* (N.Y.: Viking, 2004).

13. Reed, "A Critique of Neo-Progressivism in Theorizing about Local Development Policy"; Adolph Reed, Jr., "The Black Urban Regime: Structural Origins and Constraints," in Reed, *Stirrings in the Jug: Black Politics in the Post-Segregation Era* (Minneapolis: University of Minnesota Press, 1999).

14. For an especially critical account of the phenomenon: Adolph Reed, Jr., "'What Are the Drums Saying, Booker?' The Curious Role of the Black Public Intellectual," in Reed, *Class Notes: Posing as Politics and Other Thoughts on the American Scene* (New York: New Press, 2000). See also Adolph L. Reed, Jr., *The Jesse Jackson Phenomenon: The Crisis of Purpose in Afro-American Politics* (New Haven: Yale University Press, 1986).

15. bell hooks and Cornel West, *Breaking Bread: Insurgent Black Intellectual Life* (Boston: South End Press, 1991), 134.

16. Alex Haley, *Roots* (Garden City, N.Y.: Doubleday, 1976).

17. James Baldwin, review of *Roots* in *New York Times*, September 26, 1976, reprinted in Baldwin, *Price of the Ticket*, 556; Nancy L. Arnez, "From His Story to Our Story: A Review of 'Roots,'" *Journal of Negro Education* 46 (1977): 367; Harold Beaver, review of *Roots*, *Yearbook of English Studies* 8 (American Literature Special Number, 1978), 304.

18. Smith, *We Have No Leaders*, table 2.1.

19. "Black Americans Speak Out: A Self Portrait," *Black Enterprise*, August 1980, 98; Smith, *We Have No Leaders*, table 2.1; Michael C. Dawson, *Black Visions: The Roots of Contemporary African-American Political Ideologies* (Chicago: University of Chicago Press, 2001), table A1.1.

20. Howard Schuman, Charlotte Steeh, and Lawrence Bobo, *Racial Attitudes in America: Trends and Interpretations* (Cambridge, Mass.: Harvard University Press, 1997), chap. 5; Smith, *We Have No Leaders*, table 2.1; Dawson, *Black Visions*, table A1.1. On the Jesse Jackson vote: E. J. Dionne, Jr., "Jackson Share of Votes by Whites Triples in '88," *New York Times*, June 13, 1988, B7. See also the interviews in John Langston Gwaltney, *Drylongso: A Self Portrait of Black America* (New York: Random House, 1980).

21. "Black Americans Speak Out," 102; Schuman, *Racial Attitudes*, 257; Dawson,

Black Visions, table A1.1. See also Ellis Cose, *The Rage of a Privileged Class* (New York: HarperCollins, 1993).

22. Robert Gooding-Williams, ed., *Reading Rodney King: Reading Urban Uprising* (New York: Routledge, 1993).

23. Jackson, *Straight from the Heart,* 62; Bernard Weinraub, "At Alma Mater, Jackson Looks Back and Ahead," *New York Times,* May 9, 1988, A17.

24. On the Nation of Islam: Joseph D. Eure and Richard M. Jerome, eds., *Back Where We Belong: Selected Speeches by Minister Louis Farrakhan* (Philadelphia: P. C. International Press, 1989); Adolph Reed, Jr., "The Rise of Louis Farrakhan," in Reed, *Class Notes;* Robin D. G. Kelley, *Yo' Mama's Disfunktional! Fighting the Culture Wars in Urban America* (Boston: Beacon Press, 1997), chap. 3. On the theme of moral regeneration: Shelby Steele, *The Content of Our Character: A New Vision of Race in America* (New York: St. Martin's Press, 1990); Glenn C. Loury, *One By One from the Inside Out: Essays and Reviews on Race and Responsibility in America* (New York: Free Press, 1995); Stephen L. Carter, *Reflections of an Affirmative Action Baby* (New York: Basic Books, 1991); Eleanor Holmes Norton, "Restoring the Black Family," *New York Times Magazine,* June 2, 1985, SM 43ff.; Cornel West, "Nihilism in Black America," *Dissent,* Spring 1991, 221–226.

25. Robert Chrisman and Robert L. Allen, eds., *Court of Appeal: The Black Community Speaks Out on the Racial and Sexual Politics of Clarence Thomas vs. Anita Hill* (New York: Ballantine Books, 1992); Toni Morrison, ed., *Race-ing Justice, En-Gendering Power: Essays on Anita Hill, Clarence Thomas, and the Construction of Social Reality* (New York: Pantheon, 1992). Joseph Lowery is quoted in Chrisman, *Court of Appeal,* 285.

26. Maya Angelou, "I Dare to Hope," *New York Times,* August 25, 1991, A15; Stephen L. Carter, "The Black Table, the Empty Seat, and the Tie," in *Lure and Loathing: Essays on Race, Identity, and the Ambivalence of Assimilation,* ed. Gerald Early (New York: Penguin, 1993), 79.

27. William Julius Wilson, *The Declining Significance of Race: Blacks and Changing American Institutions* (Chicago: University of Chicago Press, 1978). The quotation is from William Julius Wilson, "Poor Blacks' Future," *New York Times,* February 28, 1978, 33.

28. Aldon Morris, "What's Race Got to Do with It?" *Contemporary Sociology* 25 (1996): 309–313; Kenneth B. Clark, "No, No. Race, Not Class, Is Still at the Wheel," *New York Times,* March 22, 1978, A25; Charles Vert Willie, ed., *The Caste and Class Controversy* (Bayside, N.Y.: General Hall, 1979), 177–178.

29. "Black Americans Speak Out," 97.

30. William Julius Wilson, *The Truly Disadvantaged: The Inner City, the Underclass, and Public Policy* (Chicago: University of Chicago Press, 1987).

31. Joseph R. Washington, Jr., ed., *The Declining Significance of Race? A Dialogue among Black and White Social Scientists* (Philadelphia: University of Pennsylvania, 1979), 36.

32. Loïc J. D. Waquant and William Julius Wilson, "The Cost of Racial and Class Exclusion in the Inner City," *Annals of the American Academy of Political and Social Science* 501 (1989): 8–25; William Julius Wilson, "The Underclass: Issues, Perspectives, and Public Policy," *Annals of the American Academy of Political and Social Science* 501 (1989): 182–192. For the "tangle of pathology" phrase: Wilson, *The Truly Disadvantaged,* 21.

33. William Julius Wilson, *When Work Disappears: The World of the New Urban Poor* (New York: Alfred A. Knopf, 1996), chap. 5; Wilson, *Declining Significance of Race,* 144.

34. W. E. B. Du Bois, *The Souls of Black Folk* (Chicago: A. C. McClurg, 1903); St. Clair Drake and Horace R. Cayton, *Black Metropolis: A Study of Negro Life in a Northern City* (New York: Harcourt, Brace, 1945).

35. Ronald P. Formisano, *Boston Against Busing: Race, Class, and Ethnicity in the 1960s and 1970s* (Chapel Hill: University of North Carolina Press, 1991); Dan T. Carter, *From George Wallace to Newt Gingrich: Race in the Conservative Counterrevolution, 1963–1994* (Baton Rouge: Louisiana State University Press, 1996); Thomas Byrne Edsall with Mary D. Edsall, *Chain Reaction: The Impact of Race, Rights, and Taxes on American Politics* (New York: W. W. Norton, 1991); Matthew Frye Jacobson, *Roots Too: White Ethnic Revival in Post–Civil Rights America* (Cambridge, Mass.: Harvard University Press, 2006).

36. Michael Novak, *The Rise of the Unmeltable Ethnics: Politics and Culture in the Seventies* (New York: Macmillan, 1972). On Novak's political odyssey: Patrick Allitt, *Catholic Intellectuals and Conservative Politics in America, 1950–1985* (Ithaca: Cornell University Press, 1993), chap. 7. On the white ethnic movement: Thomas J. Sugrue and John D. Skrentny, "The White Ethnic Strategy," in *Rightward Bound: Making America Conservative in the 1970s,* ed. Bruce J. Schulman and Julian E. Zelizer (Cambridge, Mass.: Harvard University Press, 2008).

37. Michael Novak, *The Guns of Lattimer: The True Story of a Massacre and a Trial, August 1897–March 1898* (New York: Basic Books, 1978); Michael Novak, *Further Reflections on Ethnicity* (Middletown, Penn.: Jednota Press, 1977).

38. Amy Elizabeth Ansell, *New Right, New Racism: Race and Reaction in the United States and Britain* (Basingstoke, UK: Macmillan, 1997); Etienne Balibar, "Is There a Neo-Racism?" in *Race, Nation, Class: Ambiguous Identities,* ed. Etienne Balibar and Immanuel Wallerstein (London: Verso, 1991).

39. Dinesh D'Souza, *The End of Racism: Principles for a Multiracial Society* (New York: Free Press, 1995).

40. Richard J. Herrnstein and Charles A. Murray, *The Bell Curve: Intelligence and Class Structure in American Life* (New York: Free Press, 1994).

41. Heritage Foundation, *Mandate for Leadership II: Continuing the Conservative Revolution* (1984), quoted in Angela D. Dillard, *Guess Who's Coming to Dinner Now? Multicultural Conservatism in America* (New York: New York University Press, 2001), 87. Robert Bork is quoted in Terry H. Anderson, *The Pursuit of Fairness:*

A History of Affirmative Action (New York: Oxford University Press, 2004), 197. See also Stanley Fish, "How the Right Hijacked the Magic Words," *New York Times*, August 13, 1995, A15.

42. Clayborne Carson, "Celebrate King's Achievements by Lifting the Shroud of Myth," *Atlanta Constitution*, January 19, 1987, A11; Gary Daynes, *Making Villains, Making Heroes: Joseph R. McCarthy, Martin Luther King, Jr., and the Politics of American Memory* (New York: Garland, 1997).

43. Martin Luther King, Jr., *I Have a Dream: Writings and Speeches That Changed the World*, ed. James Melvin Washington (New York: Harper Collins, 1992), 102–106.

44. Andrew Kull, *The Color-Blind Constitution* (Cambridge, Mass.: Harvard University Press, 1992), 146.

45. *Board of Education v. Swann*, 402 US 43 (1971) at 46.

46. Clarence Pendleton is quoted in Michael Omi and Harold Winant, *Racial Formation in the United States: From the 1960s to the 1980s* (New York: Routledge and Kegan Paul, 1986), 1; Ronald Reagan, Press Conference, February 11, 1986, accessed at John Woolley and Gerhard Peters, *The American Presidency Project* (online). Santa Barbara: University of California (hosted). http://www.presidency.ucsb.edu.ws. On Reynolds: Nancy MacLean, *Freedom Is Not Enough: The Opening of the American Workplace* (Cambridge, Mass.: Harvard University Press, 2006), 303 and passim; William Bradford Reynolds, "Individualism vs. Group Rights: The Legacy of *Brown*," *Yale Law Journal* 93 (1984): 995–1005; William Bradford Reynolds, "Our Nation's Goal: A Color-Blind Society," *Lincoln Review* 4 (Winter 1984): 31–40; Raymond Wolters, *Right Turn: William Bradford Reynolds, the Reagan Administration, and Black Civil Rights* (New Brunswick, N.J.: Transaction, 1996). See also Edwin Meese's address at Dickinson College in *Major Policy Statements of the Attorney General: Edwin Meese III, 1985–1988* (Washington, D.C.: U.S. Department of Justice, 1989).

47. MacLean, *Freedom Is Not Enough;* John David Skrentny, *The Ironies of Affirmative Action: Politics, Culture, and Justice in America* (Chicago: University of Chicago Press, 1996); Hugh Davis Graham, "Since 1964: The Paradox of American Civil Rights Regulation," in *Taking Stock: American Government in the Twentieth Century*, ed. Morton Keller and R. Shep Milnick (Cambridge: Cambridge University Press, 1999).

48. For a sample of this very large field of debate: Owen Fiss et al., *Affirmative Action: The Answer to Discrimination? An AEI Round Table* (Washington, D.C.: American Enterprise Institute, 1976); Marshall Cohen, Thomas Nagel, and Thomas Scanlon, eds., *Equality and Preferential Treatment* (Princeton: Princeton University Press, 1977); Nathan Glazer, *Affirmative Discrimination: Ethnic Inequality and Public Policy* (New York: Basic Books, 1975); Terry Eastland and William J. Bennett, *Counting by Race: Equality from the Founding Fathers to Bakke and Weber* (New York: Basic Books, 1979); Nicolaus Mills, ed., *Debating*

Affirmative Action: Race, Gender, Ethnicity, and the Politics of Inclusion (New York: Delta, 1994); Steven M. Cahn, ed., *The Affirmative Action Debate* (New York: Routledge, 1995); George E. Curry, ed., *The Affirmative Action Debate* (Reading, Mass.: Addison-Wesley, 1996); Charles R. Lawrence III and Mari J. Matsuda, *We Won't Go Back: Making the Case for Affirmative Action* (New York: Basic Books, 1996); Anthony Appiah and Amy Gutman, *Color Conscious: The Political Morality of Race* (Princeton: Princeton University Press, 1997); Nathan Glazer, "In Defense of Preference," *New Republic,* April 6, 1998, 18–21, 24–25; Nathan Glazer, "The Case for Racial Preferences," *Public Interest,* Spring 1999, 45–63; Dennis A. Deslippe, "'Do Whites Have Rights?' White Detroit Policemen and 'Reverse Discrimination' Protests in the 1970s," *Journal of American History* 91 (2004): 932–960. On incommensurable paradigms: Bob Blauner, "Talking Past Each Other: Black and White Languages of Race," *American Prospect* 10 (Spring 1992): 55–64; Jennifer L. Hochschild, "Affirmative Action as Culture War," in *The Cultural Territories of Race: Black and White Boundaries,* ed. Michèle Lamont (Chicago: University of Chicago Press, 1999); Jennifer L. Hochschild, "The Strange Career of Affirmative Action," *Ohio State Law Journal* 59 (1998): 997–1037; Lawrence Blum, *"I'm Not a Racist, But . . .": The Moral Quandary of Race* (Ithaca: Cornell University Press, 2002).

49. Hochschild, "Affirmative Action as Culture War."

50. George Gilder, "The Myths of Racial and Sexual Discrimination," *National Review,* November 14, 1980, 1381; Walter E. Williams, "A Tragic Vision of Black Problems," *American Quarterly* 47 (1995): 409.

51. Cose, *Rage of a Privileged Class,* 4. Also Patricia J. Williams, *Seeing a Color-Blind Future: The Paradox of Race* (London: Virago Press, 1997).

52. Jackson, *Straight from the Heart,* 275. Clarence Pendleton is quoted in Ansell, *New Right, New Racism,* 132.

53. Burke Marshall, "A Comment on the Nondiscrimination Principle in a 'Nation of Minorities,'" *Yale Law Journal* 93 (1984): 1010; Jackson, *A Conversation with the Reverend Jesse Jackson,* 24, 14.

54. Antonin Scalia, "The Disease as Cure: 'In Order to Get Beyond Racism, We Must First Take Account of Race,'" *Washington University Law Quarterly* (1979): 147–157; Clarence Thomas in *Adarand v. Pena,* 515 U.S. 200 (1995) at 240–241.

55. *Fullilove v. Klutznick,* 448 U.S. 448 (1980).

56. *City of Richmond v. J. A. Croson Co.,* 488 U.S. 469 (1989).

57. *Regents of University of California v. Bakke* 438 U.S. 265 (1978); *Metro Broadcasting Inc. v. Federal Communications Commission* 497 U.S. 547 (1990).

58. *International Brotherhood of Teamsters v. U.S.* 431 U.S. 324 (1977).

59. *Wards Cove Packing Co. v. Antonio* 490 U.S. 642 (1989).

60. *Bakke,* p. 400.

61. *Wygant v. Jackson Board of Education,* 476 U.S. 267 (1986) at 296; *Richmond v. Croson,* p. 558.

62. *Wards Cove Packing*, p. 662.

63. *Richmond v. Croson*, p. 561.

64. John David Skrentny, "Republican Efforts to End Affirmative Action: Walking a Fine Line," in *Seeking the Center: Politics and Policymaking in the New Century*, ed. Martin A. Levin, Mark K. Landy, and Martin Shapiro (Washington, D.C.: Georgetown University Press, 2001); Hugh Davis Graham, "The Politics of Clientele Capture: Civil Rights Policy and the Reagan Administration," in *Redefining Equality*, ed. Neal Devins and Davison M. Douglas (New York: Oxford University Press, 1998); Charles C. Moskos and John Sibley Butler, *All That We Can Be: Black Leadership and Racial Integration the Army Way* (New York: Basic Books, 1996).

65. Omi and Winant, *Racial Formation*, 133.

66. On the state referenda: Lydia Chávez, *The Color Bind: California's Battle to End Affirmative Action* (Berkeley: University of California Press, 1998).

67. Henry Louis Gates, Jr., ed., *"Race," Writing, and Difference* (Chicago: University of Chicago Press, 1986), first published in *Critical Inquiry* 12 (1985) and 13 (1986).

68. Gunnar Myrdal, *An American Dilemma: The Negro Problem and Modern Democracy* (New York: Harper and Brothers, 1944), 115; Omi and Winant, *Racial Formation*, 68.

69. Barbara J. Fields, "Ideology and Race in American History," in *Region, Race, and Reconstruction*, ed. J. Morgan Kousser and James M. McPherson (New York: Oxford University Press, 1982). Also Barbara J. Fields, "Whiteness, Racism, and Identity," *International Labor and Working-Class History* 60 (2001): 48–56.

70. Gates, *"Race," Writing, and Difference*, 4, 403; Joyce A. Joyce, "The Black Canon: Reconstructing Black American Literary Criticism," *New Literary History* 18 (1987): 335–344; Henry Louis Gates, Jr., "'What's Love Got to Do with It?' Critical Theory, Integrity, and the Black Idiom," *New Literary History* 18 (1987): 345–362; Houston A. Baker, Jr., "In Dubious Battle," *New Literary History* 18 (1987): 363–369; Joyce A. Joyce, "'Who the Cap Fit': Unconsciousness and Unconscionableness in the Criticism of Houston A. Baker, Jr., and Henry Louis Gates, Jr.," *New Literary History* 18 (1987): 371–383. Also Norman Harris, "'Who's Zoomin' Who?' The New Black Formalism," *Journal of the Midwest Modern Language Association* 20 (1987): 37–45; Barbara Christian, "The Race for Theory," *Feminist Studies* 14 (1988): 67–79.

71. Henry Louis Gates, Jr., *Figures in Black: Words, Signs, and the "Racial" Self* (New York: Oxford University Press, 1987); Gates, ed., *"Race," Writing, and Difference;* Kwame Anthony Appiah and Henry Louis Gates, Jr., eds., *Identities* (Chicago: University of Chicago Press, 1995).

72. Stuart Hall, "New Ethnicities," in *Black Film/British Cinema*, ed. Kobena Mercer, ICA Document 7 (London: Institute of Contemporary Arts, 1988), 28.

73. Stuart Hall, "The Question of Cultural Identity," in *Modernity and Its Futures*,

ed. Stuart Hall, David Held, and Tony McGrew (Cambridge, UK: Polity Press, 1992), 275, 277; Stuart Hall, "What Is This 'Black' in Black Popular Culture?" in *Black Popular Culture,* ed. Gina Dent (Seattle: Bay Press, 1992); Paul Gilroy, *The Black Atlantic: Modernity and Double Consciousness* (London: Verso, 1993), xi, 28. Another important voice in this vein was: Kwame Anthony Appiah, *In My Father's House: Africa in the Philosophy of Culture* (London: Methuen, 1992); Kwame Anthony Appiah, "The Conservation of 'Race,'" *Black American Literature Forum* 23 (1989): 37–70.

74. Gloria T. Hull, Patricia Bell Scott, and Barbara Smith, eds., *All the Women Are White, All the Blacks Are Men, But Some of Us Are Brave: Black Women's Studies* (Old Westbury, N.Y.: Feminist Press, 1982), 16; Kimberlé Crenshaw, "Mapping the Margins: Intersectionality, Identity Politics, and Violence against Women of Color" (1989), reprinted in *Critical Race Theory: The Key Writings That Formed the Movement,* ed. Kimberlé Crenshaw, Neil Gotanda, Gary Peller, and Kendall Thomas (New York: New Press, 1995). See also bell hooks, *Ain't I a Woman: Black Women and Feminism* (Boston: South End Press, 1981); Patricia Hill Collins, *Black Feminist Thought: Knowledge, Consciousness, and the Politics of Empowerment* (Boston: Unwin Hyman, 1990).

75. "Readers' Forum on Black Male/Female Relationships," *Black Scholar* (special issue) 10, nos. 8–9 (1979).

76. Lisa Kennedy, "The Body in Question," in *Black Popular Culture,* ed. Dent, 109; Angela P. Harris, "Race and Essentialism in Feminist Legal Theory," *Stanford Law Review* 42 (1990): 584.

77. Molefi Kete Asante, "Racism, Consciousness, and Afrocentricity," in *Lure and Loathing,* ed. Early, 136; Houston A. Baker, Jr., "'You Cain't Trus' It': Experts Witnessing in the Case of Rap," in *Black Popular Culture,* ed. Dent, 133; Reed, *Class Notes,* 140.

78. Linda Chavez, "Promoting Racial Harmony," in *Affirmative Action Debate,* ed. Curry, 316; bell hooks, "Postmodern Blackness," in hooks, *Yearning: Race, Gender and Cultural Politics* (Boston: South End Press, 1991).

79. Sharon M. Lee, "Racial Classifications in the U.S. Census, 1890–1990," *Ethnic and Racial Studies* 16 (1993): 75–94; Yen Le Espiritu, *Asian American Panethnicity: Bridging Institutions and Identities* (Philadelphia: Temple University Press, 1992); Graham, *Collision Course;* Maria P. P. Root, ed., *The Multiracial Experience: Racial Borders as the New Frontier* (Thousand Oaks, Calif.: Sage Publications, 1996), 7.

80. Lisa Lowe, "Heterogeneity, Hybridity, Multiplicity: Asian American Differences," *Diaspora* 1 (Spring 1991): 24–44; Kendall Thomas, "'Ain't Nothin' Like the Real Thing': Black Masculinity, Gay Sexuality, and the Jargon of Authenticity," in *The House That Race Built,* ed. Wahneema Lubiano (New York: Pantheon, 1997), 132. In the same vein: Ian F. Haney López, "The Social Construction of Race: Some Observations on Illusion, Fabrication, and Choice," *Harvard Civil Rights and Civil Liberties Law Review* 29 (1994): 1–62.

81. Henry Louis Gates, Jr., *The Signifying Monkey: A Theory of Afro-American Literary Criticism* (New York: Oxford University Press, 1988), 6; Henry Louis Gates, Jr., "2 Live Crew, Decoded," *New York Times,* June 19, 1990, A23; Henry Louis Gates, Jr., "Talking Black: Critical Signs of the Times," in Gates, *Loose Canons: Notes on the Culture Wars* (New York: Oxford University Press, 1992), 79; Henry Louis Gates, Jr., "Critical Remarks," in *Anatomy of Racism,* ed. David Theo Goldberg (Minneapolis: University of Minnesota Press, 1990), 324. Also Henry Louis Gates, Jr., "Canon Formation, Literary History, and the Afro-American Tradition: From the Seen to the Told," in *Afro-American Literary Study in the 1990s,* ed. Houston A. Baker, Jr., and Patricia Redmond (Chicago: University of Chicago Press, 1989).

82. Cornel West is quoted in John Rajchman, ed., *The Identity in Question* (New York: Routledge, 1995), 15; Reginald McKnight, "Confessions of a Wannabe Negro," in *Lure and Loathing,* ed. Early, 112. See also Cornel West, "The New Cultural Politics of Difference," *October* 53 (1990): 93–109; Angela P. Harris, "The Jurisprudence of Reconstruction," *California Law Review* 82 (1994): 741–786; Michael Dyson, "Contesting Racial Amnesia: From Identity Politics to Post-Multiculturalism," in *Higher Education under Fire: Politics, Economics, and the Crisis of the Humanities,* ed. Michael Bérubé and Cary Nelson (New York: Routledge, 1995); Howard Winant, "Racial Dualism at the Century's End," in *House that Race Built,* ed. Lubiano.

83. D'Souza, *End of Racism,* 398; Trey Ellis, "The New Black Aesthetic," *Callaloo* 38 (1989): 233–243.

84. Michael Eric Dyson, *Reflecting Black: African-American Cultural Criticism* (Minneapolis: University of Minnesota Press, 1993), xv.

85. Stuart Hall as quoted in Henry Louis Gates, Jr., *Thirteen Ways of Looking at a Black Man* (New York: Random House, 1997), xiv.

5. Gender and Certainty

Epigraphs: Judith Butler, *Gender Trouble: Feminism and the Subversion of Identity* (New York: Routledge, 1990), ix; and Michael Novak, *Awakening from Nihilism: Why Truth Matters* (London: Institute of Economic Affairs, 1995), 19.

1. Cornel West quoted in Jervis Anderson, "The Public Intellectual," *New Yorker,* January 17, 1994, 48.

2. James Davison Hunter, *The Culture Wars: The Struggle to Define America* (New York: Basic Books: 1991).

3. Patrick J. Buchanan, Address to the 1992 Republican National Convention, at www.buchanan.org.

4. Sara M. Evans, *Tidal Wave: How Women Changed America at the Century's End* (New York: Free Press, 2003); Suzanne Levine and Harriet Lyons, eds., *The Decade of Women: A Ms. History of the Seventies in Words and Pictures* (New York:

Putnam, 1980); Betty Friedan, *The Feminine Mystique* (New York: Norton, 1963). The underlying data may be found in Cynthia Taeuber, ed., *Statistical Handbook on Women in America* (Phoenix: Oryx Press, 1991), 111, 261.

5. Kate Millett, *Sexual Politics* (Garden City, N.Y.: Doubleday, 1970); Gayle Rubin, "The Traffic in Women: Notes on the 'Political Economy' of Sex," in *Toward an Anthropology of Women*, ed. Rayna R. Reiter (New York: Monthly Review Press, 1975); Catharine A. MacKinnon, *Toward a Feminist Theory of the State* (Cambridge, Mass.: Harvard University Press, 1989); Gerda Lerner, *The Creation of Patriarchy* (New York: Oxford University Press, 1986).

6. Kathy Ferguson as quoted in Lucinda M. Finley, "Choice and Freedom: Elusive Issues in the Search for Gender Justice," *Yale Law Journal* 96 (1987): 933.

7. Ruth Rosen, *The World Split Open: How the Modern Women's Movement Changed America* (New York: Viking, 2000).

8. Elaine Showalter, "Feminist Criticism in the Wilderness," *Critical Inquiry* 8 (1981): 184; Elaine Showalter, ed., *The New Feminist Criticism: Essays on Women, Literature, and Theory* (New York: Pantheon, 1985); Adrienne Rich, *On Lies, Secrets, and Silence: Selected Prose, 1966–1978* (New York: Norton, 1979), 13.

9. Carol Gilligan, *In a Different Voice: Psychological Theory and Women's Development* (Cambridge, Mass.: Harvard University Press, 1982). For a spectrum of feminist responses: Linda K. Kerber et al., "*In a Different Voice:* An Interdisciplinary Forum," *Signs* 11 (1985): 304–333.

10. "The Fourth World Manifesto" (1971), quoted in Evans, *Tidal Wave,* 146.

11. Adrienne Rich "Compulsory Heterosexuality and Lesbian Existence" (1980), in Adrienne Rich, *Blood, Bread, and Poetry: Selected Prose, 1979–1985* (New York: Norton, 1986), 51.

12. Linda Gordon, "On Difference," *Genders* 10 (1991): 91–107.

13. Gilligan, *In a Different Voice;* Mary Daly, *Beyond God the Father: Toward a Philosophy of Women's Liberation* (Boston: Beacon Press, 1973); Adrienne Rich, *Of Woman Born: Motherhood as Experience and Institution* (New York: Norton, 1976).

14. Ann Snitow, "A Gender Diary," in *Conflicts in Feminism,* ed. Marianne Hirsch and Evelyn Fox Keller (New York: Routledge, 1990), 4.

15. Donald T. Critchlow, *Phyllis Schlafly and Grassroots Conservatism: A Woman's Crusade* (Princeton: Princeton University Press, 2005); Jane J. Mansbridge, *Why We Lost the ERA* (Chicago: University of Chicago Press, 1986); David W. Brady and Kent L. Tedin, "Ladies in Pink: Religion and Political Ideology in the Anti-ERA Movement," *Social Science Quarterly* 56 (1976): 564–575.

16. U.S. National Commission on the Observance of International Women's Year, *The Spirit of Houston: The First National Women's Conference. An Official Report to the President, the Congress, and the People of the United States* (Washington, D.C., 1978).

17. Marjorie J. Spruill, "Gender and America's Right Turn," in *Rightward Bound: Making America Conservative in the 1970s,* ed. Bruce J. Schulman and Julian Zelizer (Cambridge, Mass.: Harvard University Press, 2008); Beverly LaHaye, *Who But a Woman? Concerned Women Can Make a Difference* (Nashville: Thomas Nelson, 1984); *Spirit of Houston,* 146.

18. Susan Bolotin, "Voices from the Post-Feminist Generation," *New York Times Magazine,* October 17, 1982, SM 28ff; Eloise Salholz, "Feminism's Identity Crisis," *Newsweek,* March 31, 1986, 58–59; "Women Face the '90s," *Time Magazine,* December 4, 1989; Ann Snitow, "Feminism and Motherhood: An American Reading," *Feminist Review* 40 (1992): 40.

19. Audre Lorde, *Sister Outsider: Essays and Speeches* (Trumansburg, N.Y.: Crossing Press, 1984); bell hooks, *Ain't I a Woman: Black Women and Feminism* (Boston: South End Press, 1981); Alice Walker, *In Search of Our Mothers' Gardens: Womanist Prose* (San Diego: Harcourt Brace Jovanovich, 1983); Barbara Smith, ed., *Home Girls: A Black Feminist Anthology* (New York: Kitchen Table, Women of Color Press, 1983); Cherrie Moraga and Gloria Anzaldúa, eds., *This Bridge Called My Back: Writings by Radical Women of Color,* 2nd ed. (New York: Kitchen Table, Women of Color Press, 1983); Winifred Breines, *The Trouble Between Us: An Uneasy History of White and Black Women in the Feminist Movement* (New York: Oxford University Press, 2006). Bernice Reagon is quoted in Evans, *Tidal Wave,* 153.

20. Andrea Dworkin, *Letters from a War Zone: Writings 1976–1987* (New York: Dutton, 1989); MacKinnon, *Toward a Feminist Theory of the State;* Wendy Brown, "Consciousness Razing," *Nation,* January 8/15, 1990, 61–64.

21. Carole S. Vance, ed., *Pleasure and Danger: Exploring Female Sexuality* (Boston: Routledge, 1984).

22. Mary Louise Adams, "There's No Place Like Home: On the Place of Identity in Feminist Politics," *Feminist Review* 31 (1989): 22–33; Brown, "Consciousness Razing," 64; Meaghan Morris, "The Pirate's Fiancée: Feminists and Philosophers, or Maybe Tonight It'll Happen" (1979), in *Feminism and Foucault: Reflections on Resistance,* ed. Irene Diamond and Lee Quinby (Boston: Northeastern University Press, 1988), 24; Adrienne Rich, "Notes Towards a Politics of Location" (1984), in Rich, *Blood, Bread, and Poetry,* 210, 217.

23. Deborah Tannen, *That's Not What I Meant! How Conversational Style Makes or Breaks Relationships* (New York: Ballantine, 1987); John Gray, *Men Are from Mars, Women Are from Venus: A Practical Guide for Improving Communication and Getting What You Want in Your Relationships* (New York: HarperCollins, 1992).

24. Donna Haraway quoted in Judith Butler, "Contingent Foundations: Feminism and the Question of 'Postmodernism'" (1991), in *Feminists Theorize the Political,* ed. Judith Butler and Joan W. Scott (New York: Routledge, 1992), 131; Leslie Heywood and Jennifer Drake, eds., *The Third Wave Agenda: Being Feminist, Doing Feminism* (Minneapolis: University of Minnesota Press, 1997), 61.

25. Sheila Rowbotham, "The Trouble with 'Patriarchy,'" in Raphael Samuel, ed., *People's History and Social Theory* (London: Routledge and Kegan Paul, 1981).

26. Simone de Beauvoir, *The Second Sex* (New York: Knopf, 1953), xvi–xvii.

27. Robert W. Gordon, "New Developments in Legal Theory," in *The Politics of Law: A Progressive Critique,* ed. David Kairys (New York: Pantheon, 1982), 289; Mark G. Kelman, "Trashing," *Stanford Law Review* 36 (1984): 293–348. A rare attempt to put the deconstruction movements in the law and in literature in conversation was J. M. Balkin, "Deconstructive Practice and Legal Theory," *Yale Law Journal* 96 (1987): 743–786.

28. Joan W. Scott, "The Tip of the Volcano," *Comparative Studies in Society and History* 35 (April 1993): 440. For introductions to poststructuralism and its transit to the United States: Terry Eagleton, *Literary Theory: An Introduction* (Oxford: Blackwell, 1983); Christopher Norris, *Deconstruction: Theory and Practice* (London: Methuen, 1982); Francois Cusset, *French Theory: Foucault, Derrida, Deleuze & Cie et les mutations de la vie intellectuelle aux États-Unis* (Paris: La Découverte, 2003); Jonathan Culler, "Literary Criticism and the American University," in Culler, *Framing the Sign: Criticism and Its Institutions* (Oxford: Basil Blackwell, 1988); Michèle Lamont, "How to Become a Dominant French Philosopher: The Case of Jacques Derrida," *American Journal of Sociology* 93 (1987): 584–622. On postmodernity: Fredric Jameson, *Postmodernism, or, The Cultural Logic of Late Capitalism* (Durham: Duke University Press, 1991); David Harvey, *The Condition of Postmodernity: An Enquiry into the Origins of Cultural Change* (Oxford: Basil Blackwell, 1989); Michael Rosenthal, "What Was Post-Modernism?" *Socialist Review* 22 (July-September 1992): 83–105.

29. Colin Campbell, "The Tyranny of the Yale Critics," *New York Times Magazine,* February 9, 1986, 20ff.

30. Jane Gallop, *Around 1981: Academic Feminist Literary Theory* (London: Routledge, 1992); Jacques Derrida, *Of Grammatology,* trans. Gayatri Chakravorty Spivak (Baltimore: Johns Hopkins University Press, 1976); Elaine Marks and Isabelle de Courtivron, eds., *New French Feminisms: An Anthology* (Amherst: University of Massachusetts Press, 1980); Mari Jo Buhle, "Gender and Labor History," in *Perspectives on American Labor History,* ed. J. Carroll Moody and Alice Kessler-Harris (DeKalb: Northern Illinois University Press, 1989), 72. Also Mari Jo Buhle and Paul Buhle, "The New Labor History at the Cultural Crossroads," *Journal of American History* 75 (1988): 151–157.

31. Among the early contributions to the debate: Jane Flax, "Postmodernism and Gender Relations in Feminist Theory," *Signs: Journal of Women in Culture and Society* 12 (1987): 621–643; Linda Alcoff, "Cultural Feminism versus Poststructuralism: The Identity Crisis in Feminist Theory," *Signs* 13 (1988): 405–436; Catharine R. Stimpson, "Nancy Reagan Wears a Hat: Feminism and Its Cultural Consensus," *Critical Inquiry* 14 (1988): 223–243; "Feminism and

Deconstruction," special issue of *Feminist Studies* 14, no. 1 (1988); "The Essential Difference: Another Look at Essentialism," special issue of *Differences: A Journal of Feminist Cultural Studies* 1, no. 2 (1989). The quotation is from Wendy Brown, "Feminist Hesitations, Postmodern Exposures," *Differences* 3 (Spring 1991): 72.

32. Louise A. Tilly and Joan W. Scott, *Women, Work, and Family* (New York: Holt, Rinehart and Winston, 1978); Elaine Abelson, David Abraham, and Marjorie Murphy, "Interview with Joan Scott," *Radical History Review* 45 (1989): 41–59.

33. Joan W. Scott, "Gender: A Useful Category of Historical Analysis," *American Historical Review* 91 (1986): 1053–1075; Joan W. Scott, "The Sears Case," in Scott, *Gender and the Politics of History* (New York: Columbia University Press, 1988), first published as "Deconstructing Equality-versus-Difference; or, The Uses of Post-Structuralist Theory for Feminism," *Feminist Studies* 14 (1988): 33–50.

34. Joan W. Scott, "Multiculturalism and the Politics of Identity," in *The Identity in Question*, ed. John Rajchman (New York: Routledge, 1995), 11. For her deconstruction of "experience": Joan W. Scott, "The Evidence of Experience," *Critical Inquiry* 17 (1991): 773–797.

35. In addition to the sources cited in note 31, these debates can be followed in Hester Eisenstein and Alice Jardine, eds., *The Future of Difference* (Boston: G. K. Hall, 1980); Mary Russo, "Female Grotesques: Carnival and Theory," in *Feminist Studies, Critical Studies*, ed. Teresa de Lauretis (Bloomington: Indiana University Press, 1986); Linda J. Nicholson, ed., *Feminism/Postmodernism* (New York: Routledge, 1989); Judith Butler and Joan W. Scott, eds., *Feminists Theorize the Political* (New York: Routledge, 1992). See also Linda Gordon's and Joan W. Scott's critical back-to-back reviews of each other's work published in *Signs* 15 (1990): 848–860.

36. Leslie Wahl Rabine, "A Feminist Politics of Non-Identity," *Feminist Studies* 24 (1988): 11.

37. Laura Lee Downs, "If 'Woman' Is Just an Empty Category, Then Why Am I Afraid to Walk Alone at Night? Identity Politics Meets the Postmodern Subject," *Comparative Studies in Society and History* 35 (1993): 414–437; Sharon Marcus, "Fighting Bodies, Fighting Words: A Theory and Politics of Rape Prevention," in *Feminists Theorize the Political*, ed. Butler and Scott, 339.

38. Steven Seidman, ed., *Queer Theory/Sociology* (Cambridge, Mass.: Blackwell, 1996); Arlene Stein, "Sisters and Queers: The Decentering of Lesbian Feminism," *Socialist Review* 22 (January-March 1992): 33–55; Ed Cohen, "Who Are 'We'?" Gay 'Identity' as Political (E)motion (A Theoretical Rumination)," in *Inside/Out: Lesbian Theories, Gay Theories*, ed. Diana Fuss (New York: Routledge, 1991).

39. Judith Butler, *Gender Trouble: Feminism and the Subversion of Identity* (New

York: Routledge, 1990), 142; Judith Butler, "Contingent Foundations: Feminism and the Question of 'Postmodernism,'" in *Feminists Theorize the Political,* ed. Butler and Scott, 9.

40. Judith Butler, "For a Careful Reading," in *Feminist Contentions: A Philosophical Exchange,* ed. Seyla Benhabib, Judith Butler, Drucilla Cornell, and Nancy Fraser (New York: Routledge, 1995), 136, 135. Also Judith Butler, "Imitation and Gender Insubordination," in *Inside/Out,* ed. Fuss.

41. Teresa de Lauretis, ed., "Feminist Studies/Critical Studies: Issues, Terms, and Contexts," in *Feminist Studies, Critical Studies,* ed. de Lauretis, 9; Stimpson, "Nancy Reagan Wears a Hat," 236; Denise Riley, *"Am I That Name?" Feminism and the Category of "Women" in History* (Basingstoke, UK: Macmillan, 1988), 114; Jane Flax, "The End of Innocence," in *Feminists Theorize the Political,* ed. Butler and Scott, 445; Martha C. Nussbaum, "The Professor of Parody," *New Republic,* February 22, 1999, 37–45.

42. Heywood and Drake, eds., *Third Wave Agenda.*

43. Mansbridge, *Why We Lost the ERA;* Jane Sherron DeHart, "Gender on the Right: Meanings behind the Existential Scream," *Gender and History* 3 (1991): 246–267; Phyllis Schlafly, *The Power of the Positive Woman* (New Rochelle: Arlington House, 1977).

44. Anita Bryant and Bob Green, *Raising God's Children* (Old Tappan, N.J.: Revell, 1977); White House Conference on Families, *Listening to America's Families: The Report* (Washington, D.C., 1980); Rosemary Thomson, *Withstanding Humanism's Challenge to Families: Anatomy of a White House Conference* (Morton, Ill.: Traditional Publications, 1981); Diane Ravitch, "In the Family's Way," *New Republic,* June 28, 1980, 18ff.

45. John T. McGreevy, *Catholicism and American Freedom: A History* (New York: Norton, 2003), chaps. 9–10; Timothy A. Byrnes and Mary C. Segers, eds., *The Catholic Church and the Politics of Abortion* (Boulder, Colo.: Westview Press, 1992); Michael W. Cuneo, "Life Battles: The Rise of Catholic Militancy within the American Pro-Life Movements," in *Being Right: Conservative Catholics in America,* ed. Mary Jo Weaver and R. Scott Appleby (Bloomington: Indiana University Press, 1995); David J. Garrow, *Liberty and Sexuality: The Right to Privacy and the Making of Roe v. Wade* (New York: Macmillan, 1994).

46. Reagan devoted only one of his over 1,000 radio broadcasts between 1975 and 1979 to the issue of abortion. *Reagan, In His Own Hand,* ed. Kiron K. Skinner, Annelise Anderson, Martin Anderson (New York: Free Press, 2001), 380–385. On Jerry Falwell and the abortion issue: Susan Friend Harding, *The Book of Jerry Falwell: Fundamentalist Language and Politics* (Princeton: Princeton University Press, 2000), 303.

47. Kristin Luker, *Abortion and the Politics of Motherhood* (Berkeley: University of California Press, 1984); Scott Flipse, "Below-the-Belt Politics: Protestant Evangelicals, Abortion, and the Foundation of the New Religious Right, 1960–1975," in *The Conservative Sixties,* ed. David Farber and Jeff Roche (New

York: Peter Lang, 2003); Andrew H. Merton, *Enemies of Choice: The Right-to-Life Movement and Its Threat to Abortion* (Boston: Beacon Press, 1981); Michele McKeegan, *Abortion Politics: Mutiny in the Ranks of the Right* (New York: Free Press, 1992). "The Pro-Family Statement of Principles" was reprinted in Thomson, *Withstanding Humanism's Challenge,* 40–41.

48. McGreevy, *Catholicism and American Freedom;* Patrick Allitt, *Catholic Intellectuals and Conservative Politics in America, 1950–1985* (Ithaca: Cornell University Press, 1993); Garry Wills, *Bare Ruined Choirs: Doubt, Prophecy, and Radical Religion* (Garden City, N.Y.: Doubleday, 1972); John Tracy Ellis, "American Catholics and the Intellectual Life," *Thought* 30 (1955): 351–388.

49. Timothy A. Byrnes, *Catholic Bishops in American Politics* (Princeton: Princeton University Press, 1991); Jim Castelli, *The Bishops and the Bomb: Waging Peace in a Nuclear Age* (Garden City, N.Y.: Doubleday, 1983); George Gallup, Jr., and Jim Castelli, *The American Catholic People: Their Beliefs, Practices, and Values* (Garden City, N.Y.: Doubleday, 1987).

50. Christian Smith, *American Evangelicalism: Embattled and Thriving* (Chicago: University of Chicago Press, 1998); Nancy T. Ammerman, "North American Protestant Fundamentalism," in *Fundamentalisms Observed,* ed. Martin E. Marty and R. Scott Appleby (Chicago: University of Chicago Press, 1991); Susan Rose, "Christian Fundamentalism and Education in the United States," in *Fundamentalisms and Society: Redeeming the Sciences, the Family, and Education,* ed. Martin E. Marty and R. Scott Appleby (Chicago: University of Chicago Press, 1993).

51. Robert Wuthnow, *The Restructuring of American Religion: Society and Faith since World War II* (Princeton: Princeton University Press, 1988); Tim LaHaye, *The Battle for the Mind* (Old Tappan, N.J.: Fleming H. Revell, 1980), 179. On the origins of the Moral Majority: Frances Fitzgerald, *Cities on a Hill: A Journey through Contemporary American Cultures* (New York: Simon and Schuster, 1986), chap. 2; David Snowball, *Continuity and Change in the Rhetoric of the Moral Majority* (New York: Praeger, 1991).

52. Jerry Falwell, *Strength for the Journey: An Autobiography* (New York: Simon and Schuster, 1987), 443; Randall A. Terry, *Operation Rescue* (Springdale, Penn.: Whittier House, 1988), 216; Beverly LaHaye, *Who But a Woman?* 137.

53. Katharine T. Bartlett, "Some Factual Correctness about Political Correctness," *Wall Street Journal,* June 6, 1991, A19. Bartlett credited the idea to Daphne Patai, "Minority Status and the Stigma of 'Surplus Visibility,'" *Chronicle of Higher Education,* October 30, 1991, A52.

54. Luker, *Abortion and the Politics of Motherhood.*

55. Edward E. Hindson, *The Total Family* (Wheaton, Ill.: Tyndale House, 1980); Michael Lienesch, *Redeeming America: Piety and Politics in the New Christian Right* (Chapel Hill: University of North Carolina Press, 1993), chap. 2.

56. The quotations are from Faye Ginsburg, "The 'Word-made' Flesh: The Disembodiment of Gender in the Abortion Debate," in *Uncertain Terms: Negoti-*

ating Gender in American Culture, ed. Faye Ginsburg and Anna Lowenhaupt Tsing (Boston: Beacon Press, 1990), 71; Pamela Johnston Conover and Virginia Gray, *Feminism and the New Right: Conflict over the American Family* (New York: Praeger, 1983), 71.

57. Thomson, *Withstanding Humanism's Challenge to Families,* 94–95; Brenda E. Brasher, *Godly Women: Fundamentalism and Female Power* (New Brunswick, N.J.: Rutgers University Press, 1998), 155–156.

58. Judith Stacey, *Brave New Families: Stories of Domestic Upheaveal in Late-Twentieth-Century America* (New York: Basic Books, 1990); Clyde Wilcox, "Premillennialists at the Millennium: Some Reflections on the Christian Right in the Twenty-First Century," *Sociology of Religion* 55 (1994): 243–261; Justin Watson, *The Christian Coalition: Dreams of Restoration, Demands for Recognition* (New York: St. Martin's Press, 1997).

59. "A Diversity of Opinion Regarding Abortion Exists among Committed Catholics," *New York Times,* October 7, 1984, E7; Kenneth A. Briggs, "Women and the Church," *New York Times Magazine,* November 6, 1983, 120ff.; Pamela D. H. Cochran, *Evangelical Feminism: A History* (New York: New York University Press, 2005); Julie Ingersoll, *Evangelical Christian Women: War Stories in the Gender Battles* (New York: New York University Press, 2003); Letha Scanzoni and Nancy Hardesty, *All We're Meant to Be: A Biblical Approach to Women's Liberation* (Waco, Tex.: Word Books, 1975).

60. Paul DiMaggio, John Evans, and Bethany Bryson, "Have Americans' Social Attitudes Become More Polarized?" *American Journal of Sociology* 102 (1996): 690–755; Christian Smith, *A Christian America?: What Evangelicals Really Want* (Berkeley: University of California Press, 2000). Also Alan Wolfe, *One Nation After All: What Middle-Class Americans Really Think about God, Country, Family, Racism, Welfare, Immigration, Homosexuality, Work, the Right, the Left, and Each Other* (New York: Penguin Books, 1998).

61. National Conference of Catholic Bishops, *Partners in the Mystery of Redemption: A Pastoral Response to Women's Concerns for Church and Society. First Draft, March 23, 1988* (Washington, D.C.: National Conference of Catholic Bishops, 1988).

62. Edward E. Hindson, *The Total Family* (Wheaton, Ill.: Tyndale House, 1980); James C. Dobson, *The New Dare to Discipline* (Wheaton: Ill.: Tyndale House, 1992); Beverly LaHaye, *I Am a Woman By God's Design* (Old Tappan, N.J.: Fleming H. Revell, 1980). The quotation is from Bryant and Green, *Raising God's Children,* 57.

63. Council on Biblical Manhood and Womanhood, "The Danvers Statement," published as an advertisement in *Christianity Today,* January 13, 1989; John Piper and Wayne A. Grudem, eds., *Recovering Biblical Manhood and Womanhood: A Response to Evangelical Feminism* (Wheaton, Ill.: Crossway Books, 1991), 55, 33.

64. Brenda E. Brasher, *Godly Women: Fundamentalism and Female Power* (New Brunswick, N.J.: Rutgers University Press, 1998); Christel J. Manning, *God*

Gave Us the Right: Conservative Catholic, Evangelical Protestant, and Orthodox Jewish Women Grapple with Feminism (New Brunswick, N.J.: Rutgers University Press, 1999); Judith Stacey and Susan Elizabeth Gerard, "We Are Not Doormats: The Influence of Feminism on Contemporary Evangelicals in the United States," in *Uncertain Terms,* ed. Ginsburg and Tsing; Susan D. Rose, "Women Warriors: The Negotiation of Gender in a Charismatic Community," *Sociological Analysis* 48 (1987): 245–258; Stephen Prothero, *American Jesus: How the Son of God Became a National Icon* (New York: Farrar, Straus and Giroux, 2003), chap. 4; Heather Hendershot, *Shaking the World for Jesus: Media and Conservative Evangelical Culture* (Chicago: University of Chicago Press, 2004).

65. Harding, *Book of Jerry Falwell,* 275.

66. Stanley Fish, *There's No Such Thing as Free Speech, and It's a Good Thing, Too* (New York: Oxford University Press, 1994), 4.

67. Allan Bloom, *The Closing of the American Mind: How Higher Education Has Failed Democracy and Impoverished the Souls of Today's Students* (New York: Simon and Schuster, 1987); Allan Bloom, "The Crisis in Liberal Education" (1967), in Bloom, *Giants and Dwarfs: Essays 1960–1990* (New York: Simon and Schuster, 1990).

68. Bloom, *Closing of the American Mind,* 25, 132, 100. Among the reviewers to point out how little Bloom seemed to know about the American culture he criticized: Jean Bethke Elshtain, "Allan in Wonderland," *Cross Currents* 37 (1987–1988): 476–479.

69. Saul Bellow, *Ravelstein* (New York: Viking, 2000); D. T. Max, "With Friends Like Saul Bellow," *New York Times Magazine,* April 16, 2000, SM 70ff.

70. William J. Bennett, *The De-Valuing of America: The Fight for Our Culture and Our Children* (New York: Summit Books, 1992); Gertrude Himmelfarb, *The De-Moralization of Society: From Victorian Virtues to Modern Values* (New York: Knopf, 1995); Lynne V. Cheney, *Telling the Truth: Why Our Culture and Our Country Have Stopped Making Sense—and What We Can Do about It* (New York: Simon and Schuster, 1995); Michael Novak, *Awakening from Nihilism: Why Truth Matters* (London: Institute of Economic Affairs, 1995); Roger Kimball, *Tenured Radicals: How Politics Has Corrupted Our Higher Education* (New York: Harper and Row, 1990); Dinesh D'Souza, *Illiberal Education: The Politics of Race and Sex on Campus* (New York: Free Press, 1991); William J. Bennett and Edwin J. Delattre, "Moral Education in the Schools," *Public Interest* 50 (1978): 81–98; William J. Bennett, ed., *The Book of Virtues: A Treasury of Great Moral Stories* (New York: Simon and Schuster, 1993).

71. Novak, *Awakening from Nihilism,* 19; Charles Colson and Richard John Neuhaus, eds., *Evangelicals and Catholics Together: Toward a Common Mission* (Dallas: World, 1995), 4, 6; Paul Johnson, *Modern Times: The World from the Twenties to the Eighties* (New York: Harper and Row, 1983), 48. An important, earlier statement of the theme by another ex-liberal was Richard John

Neuhaus, *The Naked Public Square: Religion and Democracy in America* (Grand Rapids, Mich.: William B. Eerdmans, 1984).

72. Richard Rorty, *The Consequences of Pragmatism (Essays: 1972–1980)* (Minneapolis: University of Minnesota Press, 1982), 167. Rorty pointed his criticism directly at Bloom in Richard Rorty, "That Old-Time Philosophy," *New Republic,* April 4, 1988, 28–32.

73. Richard Rorty, *Contingency, Irony, and Solidarity* (Cambridge: Cambridge University Press, 1989), 4, 40; Rorty, *Consequences of Pragmatism,* xliv.

74. Casey Nelson Blake, "Private Life and Public Commitment: From Walter Rauschenbusch to Richard Rorty," in *A Pragmatist's Progress?: Richard Rorty and American Intellectual History,* ed. John Pettegrew (Lanham, Md.: Rowman and Littlefield, 2000); Sheldon S. Wolin, "Democracy in the Discourse of Postmodernism," *Social Research* 57 (1990): 5–30; Norman Geras, "Language, Truth, and Justice," *New Left Review* 209 (1995): 110–135. Also Jean Bethke Elshtain, "Don't Be Cruel: Reflections on Rortyian Liberalism," in *The Politics of Irony: Essays in Self-Betrayal,* ed. Daniel W. Conway and John E. Seery (New York: St. Martin's Press, 1992).

75. Rorty, *Contingency,* 94; Fish, *There's No Such Thing,* 4, 10, 41.

76. Jodi Dean, *Solidarity of Strangers: Feminism after Identity Politics* (Berkeley: University of California Press, 1996), 1.

6. The Little Platoons of Society

Epigraph: Robert N. Bellah et al., *Habits of the Heart: Individualism and Commitment in American Life* (Berkeley: University of California Press, 1985), 271.

1. Marc Leepson, *Flag: An American Biography* (New York: St. Martin's Press, 2005); "'Clean Up America' Rally at Capitol," *Washington Post,* April 28, 1979, C1; Megan Rosenfeld, "The Evangelist and His Empire," *Washington Post,* April 28, 1979, B1; "The State House: Forum for the One and the Many," *New York Times,* December 21, 1980, NJ 30.

2. John Rawls, *A Theory of Justice* (Cambridge, Mass.: Harvard University Press, 1971); Alexander Nehamas, "Trends in Recent American Philosophy," in *American Academic Culture in Transformation: Fifty Years, Four Disciplines,* ed. Thomas Bender and Carl E. Schorske (Princeton: Princeton University Press, 1997), 240.

3. Rawls, *Theory of Justice,* 100, 14–15.

4. Rawls, *Theory of Justice,* 61, 83.

5. Sheldon H. Danziger and Daniel H. Weinberg, "The Historical Record: Trends in Family Income, Inequality, and Poverty," in *Confronting Poverty: Prescriptions for Change,* ed. Sheldon H. Danziger et al. (Cambridge, Mass.: Harvard University Press, 1994), table 2.2.

6. Arthur M. Okun, *Equality and Efficiency: The Big Tradeoff* (Washington, D.C.: Brookings Institution, 1975).

7. Edward O. Wilson, *Sociobiology: The New Synthesis* (Cambridge, Mass.: Harvard University Press, 1975). Edward O. Wilson, *On Human Nature* (Cambridge, Mass.: Harvard University Press, 1978).

8. "Ideas Matter in Politics: Conversation with E. J. Dionne," conducted by Harry Kreisler, March 8, 2001, Institute of International Studies, University of California, Berkeley. http://globetrotter.berkeley.edu/people/Dionne/dionne-con0.html.

9. National Conference of Catholic Bishops, *Economic Justice for All: Pastoral Letter on Catholic Social Teaching and the U.S. Economy* (Washington, D.C.: U.S. Catholic Conference, 1986).

10. Brian Doherty, *Radicals for Capitalism: A Freewheeling History of the Modern American Libertarian Movement* (New York: Public Affairs, 2007); John L. Kelley, *Bringing the Market Back In: The Political Revitalization of Market Liberalism* (Basingstoke, UK: Macmillan, 1997); Justin Raimondo, *An Enemy of the State: The Life of Murray N. Rothbard* (Amherst, N.Y.: Prometheus Books, 2000).

11. More than ten years later, Randall Rothenberg redescribed the clash to general readers as the key political philosophy battle of the generation: Randall Rothenberg, "Philosopher Robert Nozick vs. Philosopher John Rawls," *Esquire*, March 1983, 201–209.

12. Robert Nozick, *Anarchy, State, and Utopia* (New York: Basic Books, 1974).

13. Nozick, *Anarchy, State and Utopia*, 334.

14. John Judis, "Libertarianism: Where the Left Meets the Right," *Progressive*, September 1980, 36–38; Benjamin Hart, ed., *The Third Generation: Young Conservative Leaders Look to the Future* (Washington, D.C.: Regnery Books, 1987), 71, 166, 126; George F. Will, *The Morning After: American Successes and Excesses, 1981–1986* (New York: Free Press, 1986), 367; Ernest van den Haag, "Libertarians and Conservatives," *National Review* 31 (June 8, 1979): 725–739; Lawrence V. Cott, "Cato Institute and the Invisible Finger," *National Review* 31 (June 8, 1979): 740–742.

    On Nozick's libertarian ties: Jonathan Lieberson, "Harvard's Nozick: Philosopher of the New Right," *New York Times Magazine*, December 17, 1978, SM 19ff; Stan Lehr and Louis Rossetto Jr., "The New Right Credo—Libertarianism," *New York Times Magazine*, January 10, 1971, 24ff. Nozick had joined Walzer and other Harvard faculty members in signing an open letter criticizing the war in Vietnam in 1971. The *Harvard Crimson* cited Nozick as the faculty adviser to the Sons of Liberty in 1975 and to the Students for a Libertarian Society in 1979. He spoke that year at a rally against the military draft in Boston. M. David Landau, "Only 68 Professors Sign Open Letter to Kissinger," *Harvard Crimson*, March 31, 1971; Anne Strassner, "Libertarian Group Says Ec 10 Slights Conservative View," *Harvard Crimson*, November 25, 1975; "Libertarians Protest Draft," *Harvard Crimson*, March 15, 1979; Robert O. Boorstin, "Boston Protesters Rally Against Draft," *Harvard Crimson*, May 2, 1979. www.thecrimson.com.

15. David Boaz and Edward H. Crane, eds., *Beyond the Status Quo: Policy Proposals for America* (Washington, D.C.: Cato Institute, 1985); Edward H. Crane and David Boaz, eds., *An American Vision: Policies for the '90s* (Washington, D.C.: Cato Institute, 1989).

16. Irving Kristol, "Thoughts on Equality and Egalitarianism," in *Income Redistribution,* ed. Colin D. Campbell (Washington, D.C.: American Enterprise Institute, 1977), 42; George E. Jones, "Equality: American Dream—Or Nightmare?" *U.S. News and World Report,* August 4, 1975, 26. Michael Novak is quoted in Gary Dorrien, *The Neoconservative Mind: Politics, Culture, and the War of Ideology* (Philadelphia: Temple University Press, 1993), 261. See also Irving Kristol, "About Equality," *Commentary* 54 (November 1972): 41–47; Robert Nisbet, "The Pursuit of Equality," *Public Interest* 35 (1974): 103–120; John Cobbs, "Egalitarianism: Threat to a Free Market," *Business Week,* December 1, 1975, 62–65.

17. Nozick, *Anarchy, State, and Utopia,* 33; Milton Friedman, "The Social Responsibility of Business Is to Increase Its Profits," *New York Times Magazine,* September 13, 1970, SM 17ff.

18. Nozick, *Anarchy, State, and Utopia,* 152–153.

19. Ibid., 231.

20. Amy Gutmann, "Communitarian Critics of Liberalism," *Philosophy and Public Affairs* 14 (1985): 308–322; Clarke E. Cochran, "The Thin Theory of Community: The Communitarians and Their Critics," *Political Studies* 37 (1989): 422–435; Robert Booth Fowler, *The Dance with Community: The Contemporary Debate in American Political Thought* (Lawrence: University Press of Kansas, 1991).

21. These debates are summarized in Daniel T. Rodgers, "Republicanism: The Career of a Concept," *Journal of American History* 79 (1992): 11–38.

22. Those were the key phrases of Benjamin Barber, Amitai Etzioni, and Suzanna Sherry respectively. Benjamin R. Barber, *Strong Democracy: Participatory Politics for a New Age* (Berkeley: University of California Press, 1984); Amitai Etzioni, ed., *The Responsive Community: Rights and Responsibilities* (Washington, D.C.: Center for Policy Research, 1991–2004); Suzanna Sherry, "Civic Virtue and the Feminine Voice in Constitutional Adjudication," *Virginia Law Review* 72 (1986): 543–616. See also Michael J. Sandel's much-discussed critique of Rawls: *Liberalism and the Limits of Justice* (New York: Cambridge University Press, 1982).

23. Bellah et al., *Habits of the Heart.*

24. Michael Walzer, *Radical Principles: Reflections of an Unreconstructed Democrat* (New York: Basic Books, 1980). Walzer's campus activities can be followed in the online archives of the *Harvard Crimson.*

25. Michael Walzer, *Spheres of Justice: A Defense of Pluralism and Equality* (New York: Basic Books, 1983).

26. Ibid., 5, xv.

27. Michael Walzer, "The Community," *New Republic,* March 31, 1982, 11; Mi-

chael Walzer, "Dissatisfaction in the Welfare State," in Walzer, *Radical Principles.*

28. Walzer, *Radical Principles,* 17.

29. Garry Wills, *Inventing America: Jefferson's Declaration of Independence* (Garden City, N.Y.: Doubleday, 1978); Garry Wills, *Explaining America: The Federalist* (Garden City, N.Y.: Doubleday, 1981).

30. Daniel P. Moynihan, *Maximum Feasible Misunderstanding: Community Action in the War on Poverty* (New York: Free Press, 1969); Amitai Etzioni, *The Spirit of Community: Rights, Responsibilities, and the Communitarian Agenda* (New York: Crown, 1993). Francis Fukuyama and Mary Ann Glendon, whose *Rights Talk: The Impoverishment of Political Discourse* (New York: Free Press, 1991) came out the next year, were also signers, and in Glendon's case, an important collaborator.

31. Peter L. Berger and Richard John Neuhaus, *To Empower People: The Role of Mediating Structures in Public Policy* (Washington, D.C.: American Enterprise Institute, 1977); Brigitte Berger and Sidney Callahan, eds., *Child Care and Mediating Structures* (Washington, D.C.: American Enterprise Institute, 1979); Lowell S. Levin and Ellen L. Idler, *The Hidden Health Care System: Mediating Structures and Medicine* (Cambridge, Mass.: Ballinger, 1981); Robert L. Woodson, *A Summons to Life: Mediating Structures and the Prevention of Youth Crime* (Cambridge, Mass.: Ballinger, 1981). In much the same vein: William A. Schambra, "From Self-Interest to Social Obligation: Local Communities v. the National Community," in *Meeting Human Needs: Toward a New Public Philosophy,* ed. Jack A. Meyer (Washington, D.C.: American Enterprise Institute, 1982).

32. William J. Bennett and Edwin J. Delattre, "Moral Education in the Schools," *Public Interest* 50 (1978): 81–98; William J. Bennett, *Our Children and Our Country: Improving America's Schools and Affirming the Common Culture* (New York: Simon and Schuster, 1988); William J. Bennett, *The De-Valuing of America: The Fight for Our Culture and Our Children* (New York: Summit Books, 1992); William J. Bennett, ed., *The Book of Virtues: A Treasury of Great Moral Stories* (New York: Simon and Schuster, 1993).

33. James S. Coleman, "Social Capital in the Creation of Human Capital," *American Journal of Sociology* 94 suppl. (1988): S95-S120. Also James Q. Wilson, "The Rediscovery of Character: Private Virtue and Public Policy," *Public Interest* 81 (1985): 3–16; Howard Fineman, "The Virtuecrats," *Newsweek,* June 13, 1994, 30; Nina J. Easton, "Merchants of Virtue," *Los Angeles Times Magazine,* August 21, 1994, 16ff.

34. For an important critical dissent: David Rieff, "The False Dawn of Civil Society," *Nation,* February 22, 1999, 11–16.

35. Adam Meyerson, "A Letter to Our Readers," *Policy Review,* January–February 1996, 5–6; David M. Shribman, "Conservatives Pin Hopes on a New Kind of Citizenship," *Boston Globe,* December 31, 1995, 79; John P. Walters, "The

New Citizenship: A People's Manifesto," *Washington Times,* November 11, 1994, A25; Mary Ann Glendon and David Blankenhorn, eds., *Seedbeds of Virtue: Sources of Competence, Character, and Citizenship in American Society* (Lanham, Md.: Madison Books, 1995).

36. William A. Schambra, "By the People: The Old Values of the New Citizenship," *Policy Review* 69 (1994): 32–38.

37. Edmund Burke, *Reflections on the Revolution in France,* 2nd ed. (London: J. Dodsley, 1790), 68–69.

38. For example, Herbert J. Gans, *More Equality* (New York: Pantheon, 1973).

39. U.S. Bureau of the Census, Selected Measures of Household Income Dispersion: 1967–2008, Table A-3, www.census.gov/hhes/www/income/histinc/IE-1.

40. Bennett Harrison and Barry Bluestone, *The Great U-Turn: Corporate Restructuring and the Polarizing of America* (New York: Basic Books, 1988); Sheldon Danziger and Peter Gottshalk, *America Unequal* (New York: Russell Sage Foundation, 1995); Frank Levy and Richard J. Murnane, "U.S. Earnings Levels and Earnings Inequality: A Review of Recent Trends and Proposed Explanations," *Journal of Economic Literature* 30 (1992): 1333–1381.

41. James Lardner, "UDC Graduates Warned about a New Minority," *New York Times,* May 15, 1978, C3; Myra McPherson, "Senator Kennedy Alone with the Legacy," *Washington Post,* June 4, 1978, M1; William Julius Wilson, *The Declining Significance of Race: Blacks and Changing American Institutions* (Chicago: University of Chicago Press, 1978).

42. "The American Underclass," *Time,* August 29, 1977, 14, 17.

43. Ken Auletta, *The Underclass* (New York: Random House, 1982), 236; Nicholas Lemann, "The Origins of the Underclass," *Atlantic Monthly,* June 1986, 35.

44. Charles Murray, *Losing Ground: American Social Policy, 1950–1980* (New York: Basic Books, 1984). On Murray's intellectual formulation: Charles Murray, *What It Means to Be a Libertarian: A Personal Interpretation* (New York: Broadway Books, 1997).

45. Meg Greenfield, "Mirage-Words That We Live By," *Washington Post,* February 6, 1985, A19; Hart, ed., *Third Generation,* 22.

46. Murray, *Losing Ground,* 227–233; Charles Murray and Jesse Jackson, "What Does the Government Owe the Poor?" *Harper's,* April 1986, 35–47. For a brilliant comparison between Charles Murray and Thomas Malthus: Margaret R. Somers and Fred Block, "From Poverty to Perversity: Ideas, Markets, and Institutions over 200 Years of Welfare Debate," *American Sociological Review* 70 (2005): 260–287.

47. David T. Ellwood and Lawrence H. Summers, "Is Welfare Really the Problem?" *Public Interest* 83 (1986): 57–78; Robert Greenstein, "Losing Faith in 'Losing Ground,'" *New Republic,* March 25, 1985, 12–17; Christopher Jencks, "How Poor Are the Poor?" *New York Review of Books,* May 9, 1985; Isabel V. Sawhill, "Poverty in the U.S.: Why Is It So Persistent?" *Journal of Economic Literature* 26 (1988): 1073–1119; Christopher Jencks and Paul E. Peterson,

eds., *The Urban Underclass* (Washington, D.C.: Brookings Institution, 1991); Rebecca M. Blank, *It Takes a Nation: A New Agenda for Fighting Poverty* (Princeton: Princeton University Press, 1996). On the evolution of poverty theory: Alice O'Connor, *Poverty Knowledge: Social Science, Social Policy, and the Poor in Twentieth-Century U.S. History* (Princeton: Princeton University Press, 2001); Michael B. Katz, ed., *The "Underclass" Debate: Views from History* (Princeton: Princeton University Press, 1993).

48. Greenstein, "Losing Faith in 'Losing Ground.'"

49. Charles Murray, "No Welfare Isn't Really the Problem," *Public Interest* 84 (1986): 3–11; Charles Murray et al., *Charles Murray and the Underclass: The Developing Debate* (London: IEA Health and Welfare Unit, 1996).

50. National Conference of Catholic Bishops, *The Challenge of Peace: God's Promise and Our Response* (Washington, D.C.: United States Catholic Conference, 1983), 101; National Conference of Catholic Bishops, *Economic Justice for All: Pastoral Letter on Catholic Social Teaching and the U.S. Economy* (Washington, D.C.: U.S. Catholic Conference, 1986), 95, 37, 69, 92, 158, 44.

51. Lay Commission on Catholic Social Teaching and the U.S. Economy, *Toward the Future: Catholic Social Thought and the U.S. Economy* (New York: Lay Commission on Catholic Social Teaching and the U.S. Economy, 1984).

52. George Will, "In Defense of the Welfare State," *New Republic,* May 9, 1983, 20–25; William F. Buckley, Jr., *Four Reforms: A Guide for the Seventies* (New York: G. P. Putnam's Sons, 1973), 25; Martin Anderson, *Welfare: The Political Economy of Welfare Reform in the United States* (Stanford, Calif.: Hoover Institution Press, 1978); Martin Anderson, "Welfare Reform on 'the Same Old Rocks,'" *New York Times,* November 27, 1978, A19; Stuart Butler and Anna Kondratas, *Out of the Poverty Trap: A Conservative Strategy for Welfare Reform* (New York: Free Press, 1987).

53. Gareth Davies, "The Welfare State," in *The Reagan Presidency: Pragmatic Conservatism and Its Legacies,* ed. W. Elliot Brownlee and Hugh Davis Graham (Lawrence: University Press of Kansas, 2003); David T. Ellwood, *Poor Support: Poverty in the American Family* (New York: Basic Books, 1988). Stockman is quoted in Tom Bethell, "Treating Poverty," *Harper's,* February 1980, 24.

54. Mickey Kaus, "The Work Ethic State," *New Republic,* July 7, 1986, 22–33; Mickey Kaus, *The End of Equality* (New York: Basic Books, 1992); Michael Novak et al., *The New Consensus on Family and Welfare* (Washington, D.C.: American Enterprise Institute, 1987), 5.

55. Lawrence M. Mead, *Beyond Entitlement: The Social Obligations of Citizenship* (New York: Free Press, 1986), x, 4; U.S. Congress, Joint Economic Committee, *The Underclass: Hearing before the Joint Economic Committee,* May 25, 1989, 101 Cong., 1st sess. (1989), 25. Mead first broached these themes in Lawrence M. Mead, "Social Programs and Social Obligations," *Public Interest* 69 (1982): 17–32.

56. William J. Bennett and Peter Wehner, "Shifting Targets in the Welfare Trenches," *Washington Times,* January 25, 1994, A14.

57. Jason DeParle, *The American Dream: Three Women, Ten Kids, and a Nation's Drive to End Welfare* (New York: Viking, 2004); R. Kent Weaver, *Ending Welfare as We Know It* (Washington, D.C.: Brookings Institution Press, 2001); Peter Edelman, "The Worst Thing Bill Clinton Has Done," *Atlantic Monthly,* March 1997, 43–50; David T. Ellwood, "Welfare Reform as I Knew It: When Bad Things Happen to Good Policies," *American Prospect,* May–June 1996, 22–29; Gwendolyn Mink, *Welfare's End* (Ithaca: Cornell University Press, 1998).

58. Rebecca M. Blank, "Evaluating Welfare Reform in the United States," *Journal of Economic Literature* 40 (2002): 1105–1166.

59. Allan Bloom, *The Closing of the American Mind* (New York: Simon and Schuster, 1987); E. D. Hirsch, Jr., *Cultural Literacy: What Every American Needs to Know* (Boston: Houghton Mifflin, 1987). On his resistance to being paired with Bloom: E. D. Hirsch, Jr., *The Schools We Need and Why We Don't Have Them* (New York: Doubleday, 1996), 12.

60. Raoul V. Mowatt, "Stanford's Revolution That Wasn't Quite" (1991), reprinted in *Beyond PC: Toward a Politics of Understanding,* ed. Patricia Aufderheide (St. Paul, Minn.: Graywolf Press, 1992); John Searle, "The Storm over the University," *New York Review of Books,* December 6, 1990, 34–42; Russell Jacoby, *Dogmatic Wisdom: How the Culture Wars Divert Education and Distract America* (New York: Doubleday, 1994).

61. Arthur M. Schlesinger, Jr., *The Disuniting of America: Reflections on a Multicultural Society* (New York: Norton, 1992); "Mr. Sobol's Planet," *New Republic,* July 15 and 22, 1991, 5–6; John Fonte, "We the Peoples: The Multiculturalist Agenda Is Shattering the American Identity," *National Review,* March 25, 1996, 47–49. Schlesinger's book was an expanded version of his "A Dissent on Multicultural Education," *Partisan Review* 58 (1991). For more moderate responses: Nathan Glazer, "In Defense of Multiculturalism," *New Republic,* September 2, 1991, 18–22; Nathan Glazer, *We Are All Multiculturalists Now* (Cambridge, Mass.: Harvard University Press, 1997); Diane Ravitch, "Multiculturalism: E Pluribus Plures," *American Scholar* 59 (1990): 337–354.

62. Dinesh D'Souza, *Illiberal Education: The Politics of Race and Sex on Campus* (New York: Free Press, 1991); Roger Kimball, *Tenured Radicals: How Politics Has Corrupted Our Higher Education* (New York: Harper and Row, 1990); Joan Wallach Scott, "The Campaign against Political Correctness: What's Really at Stake?" *Change* 23 (November-December 1991): 30–43; Paul Berman, ed., *Debating P.C.: The Controversy over Political Correctness on College Campuses* (New York: Dell, 1992); Aufderheide, ed., *Beyond PC.*

63. Gerald Graff, *Beyond the Culture Wars: How Teaching the Conflicts Can Revitalize Education* (New York: Norton, 1992), 16–25. See also Jacoby, *Dogmatic Wisdom;* Lawrence W. Levine, *The Opening of the American Mind: Canons, Culture, and History* (Boston: Beacon Press, 1996), chap. 3; David Bromwich, *Politics By Other Means: Higher Education and Group Thinking* (New Haven: Yale University Press, 1992).

64. Robert N. Bellah, "Civil Religion in America," *Daedalus* 96 (Winter 1967): 1–21; Russell E. Richey and Donald G. Jones, eds., *American Civil Religion* (New York: Harper and Row, 1974).

65. Timothy C. Shiell, *Campus Hate Speech on Trial* (Lawrence: University Press of Kansas, 1998). The trigger incident at Stanford was an argument over whether Beethoven was part black, which escalated into cartoons and defaced posters. For the defense of speech codes: Mari J. Matsuda et al., *Words That Wound: Critical Race Theory, Assaultive Speech, and the First Amendment* (Boulder, Colo.: Westview Press, 1993).

66. For example: Richard Delgado, "Campus Antiracism Rules: Constitutional Narratives in Collision," *Northwestern University Law Review* 85 (1991): 343–387; Robert Post, "The Constitutional Concept of Public Discourse: Outrageous Opinion, Democratic Deliberation, and *Hustler Magazine v. Falwell,*" *Harvard Law Review* 103 (1990), 601–686; Thomas Grey, "Civil Rights vs. Civil Liberties: The Case of Discriminatory Verbal Harassment," *Social Philosophy and Policy* 8 (1991): 81–107.

67. National Association of Scholars, "The Wrong Way to Reduce Campus Tensions" (1991), at www.nas.org/polStatements; Thomas J. Jipping, "What Washington Can Do to Protect Campus Free Speech," *Heritage Foundation Reports,* June 12, 1991; George F. Will, "Catharine MacKinnon's Angry Serenity," in Will, *The Leveling Wind: Politics, the Culture, and Other News, 1990–1994* (New York: Viking, 1994), 29.

68. Henry Louis Gates, Jr., "War of Words: Critical Race Theory and the First Amendment," in Henry Louis Gates, Jr., et al., *Speaking of Race, Speaking of Sex: Hate Speech, Civil Rights, and Civil Liberties* (New York: New York University Press, 1994). See also Glenn C. Loury, "Self-Censorship and Public Discourse: A Theory of Political Correctness and Related Phenomena," in Loury, *One By One from the Inside Out: Essays and Reviews on Race and Responsibility in America* (New York: Free Press, 1995).

69. Carol Innerst, "Anti-PC College Students Form an SDS of the Right," *Washington Times,* April 5, 1994, A1; Dave Gentry, "Full Circle for the Berkeley Free Speech Movement," *Washington Times,* December 2, 1994, A23.

70. Christopher Jencks et al., *Education Vouchers: A Report on Financing Elementary Education by Grants to Parents* (Cambridge, Mass.: Center for the Study of Public Policy, 1970). See also Christopher Jencks, "Is the Public School Obsolete?" *Public Interest* 2 (1966): 18–27.

71. John E. Coons and Stephen D. Sugarman, *Education by Choice: The Case for Family Control* (Berkeley: University of California Press, 1978). Walzer had been more skeptical. Michael Walzer, "Democratic Schools" in his *Radical Principles.*

72. Michael B. Katz, *Class, Bureaucracy and Schools: The Illusion of Educational Change in America* (New York: Praeger, 1971), xvii, xx.

73. Coons and Sugarman, *Education by Choice,* 2.

74. Burton Yale Pines, *Back to Basics: The Traditionalist Movement That Is Sweeping Grass-Roots America* (New York: Morrow, 1982); National Commission on Excellence in Education, *A Nation at Risk: The Imperative for Educational Reform* (Washington, D.C.: U.S. Government Printing Office, 1983); Connaught Marshner, ed., *A Blueprint for Education Reform* (Chicago: Regnery/Gateway, 1984). The *National Review* kept up a consistent, low-level interest in school voucher plans, articulated most clearly by Russell Kirk, "Free Choice: A Voucher Plan," *National Review,* June 17, 1969, 598, but the issue did not acquire prominence until the late 1980s.

75. John E. Chubb and Terry M. Moe, "America's Public Schools: Choice *Is* a Panacea," *Brookings Review,* Summer 1990, 4–12 (the quoted passages are from pp. 5, 7, and 8); John E. Chubb, "A Blueprint for Education," *Wall Street Journal,* June 6, 1990, A16; John E. Chubb and Terry M. Moe, *Politics, Markets, and America's Schools* (Washington, D.C.: Brookings Institution, 1990). For critiques: Jack Tweedie et al., "Should Market Forces Control Educational Decision Making?" *American Political Science Review* 84 (1990): 549–567; John F. Witte and Mark E. Rigdon, "Education Choice Reforms: Will They Change America's Schools?" *Publius* 23 (Summer 1993): 95–114.

76. John F. Witte, *The Market Approach to Education: An Analysis of America's First Voucher Program* (Princeton: Princeton University Press, 2000); Adam Meyerson, "A Model of Cultural Leadership: The Achievements of Privately-Funded Vouchers," *Policy Review* 93 (1999): 20–24.

77. Grover Norquist in Hart, ed., *Third Generation,* 165; Jerry Falwell, *America Can Be Saved* (1979), as quoted in Eugene F. Provenzo, Jr., *Religious Fundamentalism and American Education: The Battle for the Public Schools* (Albany: State University of New York Press, 1990), xvii.

78. Alan Bonsteel and Carlos A. Bonilla, *A Choice for Our Children: Curing the Crisis in America's Schools* (San Francisco: ICS Press, 1997); "The Vision Thing: Conservatives Take Aim at the '90s," *Policy Review* 52 (1990), 4–37. For a more cautious response: Diane Ravitch, "The Schools and Uncle Sam," *New Republic,* December 3, 1984, 38–41.

79. Adam Meyerson, "Education's Evil Empire," *Policy Review* 93 (1999): 4; "Teachers vs. Kids," *Wall Street Journal,* June 6, 1990, A16. In the same vein: Chester E. Finn, Jr., *We Must Take Charge: Our Schools and Our Future* (New York: Free Press, 1991).

80. Albert O. Hirschmann, *Exit, Voice, and Loyalty: Responses to Decline in Firms, Organizations, and States* (Cambridge, Mass.: Harvard University Press, 1970); Mickey Kaus, "Paradigm's Loss," *New Republic,* July 27, 1992, 16–22.

81. Coons and Sugarman, *Education by Choice,* 1. See also Alan Wolfe, ed., *School Choice: The Moral Debate* (Princeton: Princeton University Press, 2003).

82. James S. Coleman and Thomas Hoffer, *Public and Private High Schools: The Impact of Communities* (New York: Basic Books, 1987). In the same vein, An-

thony S. Bryk, Valerie E. Lee, and Peter B. Holland, *Catholic Schools and the Common Good* (Cambridge, Mass.: Harvard University Press, 1993).

83. Margaret Thatcher, *The Collected Speeches of Margaret Thatcher*, ed. Robin Harris (London: HarperCollins, 1997), 576, 62, 76, 267.

84. Coleman, "Social Capital"; Robert D. Putnam, *Making Democracy Work: Civic Traditions in Modern Italy* (Princeton: Princeton University Press, 1993); Robert D. Putnam, "Bowling Alone: America's Declining Social Capital," *Journal of Democracy* 6 (January 1995): 65–78; Stephen Samuel Smith and Jessica Kulynych, "It May Be Social, But Why Is It Capital: The Social Construction of Social Capital and the Politics of Language," *Politics and Society* 30 (2002): 149–186.

7. Wrinkles in Time

Epigraph: Francis Fukuyama, "The End of History?" *National Interest,* Summer 1989, 4.

1. David Lowenthal, *Possessed by the Past: The Heritage Crusade and the Spoils of History* (New York: Free Press, 1996), 4.

2. E. D. Hirsch, Jr., *Cultural Literacy: What Every American Needs to Know* (Boston: Houghton Mifflin, 1987).

3. Ronald Reagan, Remarks at Fudan University in Shanghai, China, April 30, 1984 ("river); Ronald Reagan, Inaugural Address, January 21, 1985 ("ribbon"); Ronald Reagan, Remarks at the Opening Ceremonies of the Statue of Liberty Centennial Celebration, July 3, 1986 ("thread"); accessed at John Woolley and Gerhard Peters, *The American Presidency Project* (online). Santa Barbara: University of California (hosted). http://www.presidency.ucsb.edu.ws. Michael Rogin, *"Ronald Reagan," the Movie, and Other Episodes in Political Demonology* (Berkeley: University of California Press, 1987).

4. Reagan, Remarks at the Opening Ceremonies of the Statue of Liberty Centennial Celebration, July 3, 1986.

5. Ronald Reagan, Remarks at the Bicentennial Observance of the Battle of Yorktown, October 19, 1981, accessed at Woolley and Peters, *The American Presidency Project.*

6. Benedict Anderson, *Imagined Communities: Reflections on the Origin and Spread of Nationalism* (London: Verso, 1983).

7. Alvin Toffler, *Future Shock* (New York: Random House, 1970); Alvin Toffler, *The Third Wave* (New York: Morrow, 1980).

8. Diane Ravitch and Chester E. Finn, Jr., *What Do Our 17-Year-Olds Know? A Report on the First National Assessment of History and Literature* (New York: Harper and Row, 1987).

9. Lynne V. Cheney, *American Memory: A Report on the Humanities in the Nation's*

Public Schools (Washington D.C.: National Endowment for the Humanities, 1987), 5, 27.

10. Gary B. Nash, Charlotte Crabtree, and Ross E. Dunn, *History on Trial: Culture Wars and the Teaching of the Past* (New York: Knopf, 1997), chap. 2; Frances FitzGerald, *America Revised: History School Books in the Twentieth Century* (Boston: Little, Brown, 1979). The quoted passage is from Jonathan Zimmerman, *Whose America? Culture Wars in the Public Schools* (Cambridge, Mass.: Harvard University Press, 2002), 37.

11. Robert N. Bellah, "Civil Religion in America" (1967), reprinted in *American Civil Religion,* ed. Russell E. Richey and Donald G. Jones (New York: Harper and Row, 1974); Samuel P. Huntington, *American Politics: The Promise of Disharmony* (Cambridge, Mass.: Harvard University Press, 1981), 60.

12. "The Big Birthday," *U.S. News and World Report,* July 5, 1976, 31; "Our America: A Self-Portrait at 200," *Newsweek,* July 4, 1976, 67, 74; "The Best Birthday," *Newsweek,* July 19, 1976, 48. *Time* magazine's editors wrote that "The nation may be in better shape, this July 4, than it has been since at least Nov. 22, 1963," that is, since John F. Kennedy's assassination. *Time,* July 4, 1976, 6.

13. Charles Krauthammer, "Hail Columbus, Dead White Male," *Time,* May 27, 1991, 74; James Muldoon, "The Columbus Quincentennial: Should Christians Celebrate It?" *America,* October 27, 1990, 300–303; National Council of Churches in the U.S.A., "A Faithful Response to the 500th Anniversary of the Arrival of Christopher Columbus," in *Confronting Columbus: An Anthology,* ed. John Yewell et al. (Jefferson, N.C.: McFarland, 1992); Garry Wills, "Goodbye Columbus," *New York Review of Books,* November 22, 1990; Arthur M. Schlesinger, Jr., "Was America a Mistake?" *Atlantic Monthly,* September 1992, 16–30; Wilcomb E. Washburn, "Columbus: On and off the Reservation," *National Review,* October 5, 1992, 55–58; Barbara Vobejda, "Columbus, Which Legacy? Explorer's Image Changes with the Times," *Washington Post,* October 11, 1992, A1 ff. On the celebration: Garry Wills, "Columbus, Go Home," *Playboy,* January 1, 1992; Ruth Heimbuecher, "Say Hello to Columbus," *St. Petersburg Times,* March 22, 1992, 2E; "History Towed into Baltimore: Re-creation of Columbus' Voyage Ends in Doldrums," *Washington Post,* May 30, 1992, D1 ff. On Columbus's earlier reputation in the U.S.: Thomas J. Schlereth, "Columbia, Columbus, and Columbianism," *Journal of American History* 79 (1992): 937–968.

14. Robert Reinhold, "Class Struggle," *New York Times Magazine,* September 29, 1991, 26ff.

15. On the National History Standards debate: Nash, *History on Trial;* Lynne Cheney, "The End of History," *Wall Street Journal,* October 20, 1994, A22; Lynne Cheney, "New History Standards Still Attack Our Heritage," *Wall Street Journal,* May 2, 1996, A14; Charles Krauthammer, "History Hijacked," *Washington Post,* November 4, 1994, A25; John Leo, "The Hijacking of American

History," *U.S. News and World Report,* November 14, 1994, 36; John Leo, "History Standards Are Bunk," *U.S. News and World Report,* February 6, 1995, 23; Diane Ravitch and Arthur M. Schlesinger, Jr., "The New, Improved History Standards," *Wall Street Journal,* April 3, 1996, A14. The text of the final standards was published in the Organization of American Historians, *Magazine of History* 9 (Spring 1995): 7–35.

16. Newt Gingrich, *To Renew America* (New York: HarperCollins, 1995), 7. On Gingrich as historian: Garry Wills, "The Visionary," *New York Review of Books,* March 23, 1995.

17. Paul Gagnon, "Why Study History?" *Atlantic Monthly,* November 1988, 44–45; Gary B. Nash, "History for a Democratic Society: The Work of All the People," in *Historical Literacy: The Case for History in American Education,* ed. Paul Gagnon and the Bradley Commission on History in Schools (New York: Macmillan, 1989), 248.

18. Peter Marshall and David Manuel, *The Light and the Glory* (Old Tappan, N.J.: Revell, 1977); Peter Marshall and David Manuel, *From Sea to Shining Sea* (Old Tappan, N.J.: Revell, 1986); Pat Robertson, *America's Dates with Destiny* (Nashville: Thomas Nelson, 1986).

19. Bruce Levine et al., *Who Built America? Working People and the Nation's Economy, Politics, Culture, and Society* (New York: Pantheon, 1989); Paul Johnson, *A History of the American People* (New York: HarperCollins, 1997), chap. 8.

20. Peter Novick, *That Noble Dream: The "Objectivity Question" and the American Historical Profession* (New York: Cambridge University Press, 1988).

21. Todd Gitlin, "Hip-Deep in Post-modernism," *New York Times Book Review,* November 6, 1988, 35; David Harvey, *The Condition of Postmodernity: An Enquiry into the Origins of Cultural Change* (Oxford: Blackwell, 1990), 44; Terry Eagleton, "Capitalism, Marxism, and Postmodernism" (1984), in Eagleton, *Against the Grain: Essays, 1975–1985* (London: Verso, 1986), 91. Also Michael Rosenthal, "What Was Postmodernism?" *Socialist Review* 22 (July-September 1992): 83–105; Fredric Jameson, *Postmodernism, or the Cultural Logic of Late Capitalism* (Durham: Duke University Press, 1991).

22. E. L. Doctorow, *Ragtime* (New York: Random House, 1975); Simon Schama, *Dead Certainties: Unwarranted Speculations* (New York: Knopf, 1991).

23. Michael Lienesch, *Redeeming America: Piety and Politics in the New Christian Right* (Chapel Hill: University of North Carolina Press, 1993), chap. 5; Richard Kyle, *The Last Days Are Here Again: A History of the End Times* (Grand Rapids: Baker Books, 1998); George M. Marsden, *Fundamentalism and American Culture: The Shaping of Twentieth-Century Evangelicalism, 1870–1925* (New York: Oxford University Press, 1980).

24. Hal Lindsey, *The Late Great Planet Earth* (Bantam edition; New York: Bantam Books, 1973); Tim LaHaye and Jerry B. Jenkins, *Left Behind: A Novel of the Earth's Last Days* (Wheaton, Ill.: Tyndale House, 1995); Garry Wills, *Under God: Religion and American Politics* (New York: Simon and Schuster, 1990);

Nicholas Guyatt, *Have a Nice Doomsday: Why Millions of Americans Are Looking Forward to the End of the World* (New York: HarperCollins, 2007). The quotations are from Tim LaHaye, *The Beginning of the End* (Wheaton, Ill.: Tyndale House, 1971), x; Hal Lindsey, *The 1980s: Countdown to Armageddon* (New York: Bantam, 1981), 8.

25. "Judicial Activism: Problems and Responses," *Harvard Journal of Law and Public Policy* 7 (1984), 1–176.

26. Jonathan O'Neill, *Originalism in American Law and Politics: A Constitutional History* (Baltimore: Johns Hopkins University Press, 2005). Taney and Sutherland are cited in Alexander M. Bickel, "The Original Understanding and the Segregation Decision," *Harvard Law Review* 69 (1955): 1–65. Justice Black's phrase is from his dissent in *Adamson v. California,* 332 U.S. 46 (1947) at 89.

27. *Brown v. Board of Education,* 347 U.S. 483 (1954) at 489; Bickel, "Original Understanding and the Segregation Decision," 63.

28. Robert Bork, "Neutral Principles and Some First Amendment Problems," *Indiana Law Journal* 47 (1971): 16, 14, 22.

29. Raoul Berger, *Government by Judiciary: The Transformation of the Fourteenth Amendment* (Cambridge, Mass.: Harvard University Press, 1977), 7.

30. The activities of the Center for Judicial Studies can be followed in its *Benchmark,* 1983–1993.

31. Art Harris, "Defiant Town Starts School with Prayers," *Washington Post,* February 5, 1983, A4; *Jaffree v. Board of School Commissioners of Mobile County,* 554 F. Supp. 1104 (S.D. Ala. 1983). For the suggestion of McClellan's authorship: Lincoln Caplan, *The Tenth Justice: The Solicitor General and the Rule of Law* (New York: Knopf, 1987), 99. Cf. James McClellan, "The Making and the Unmaking of the Establishment Clause," in *A Blueprint for Judicial Reform,* ed. Patrick B. McGuignan and Randall R. Roder (Washington, D.C.: Free Congress Research and Education Foundation, 1981).

32. *Jaffree,* 1126, 1129, and passim.

33. *Smith v. Board of Commissioners of Mobile County,* 655 F. Supp 939 (S.D. Ala. 1987). When the *Washington Post*'s reporter canvassed legal authorities for their reaction to the secular humanism decision, the only voice they found in its favor was McClellan's. Barbara Vobejda, "Legal Experts Astonished by Textbook Ban," *Washington Post,* March 6, 1987, A3.

34. James McClellan, "The Constitution from a Conservative Perspective," speech at the Heritage Foundation, Washington, D.C., March 10, 1988, read online at the Heritage Foundation website: www.heritage.org.

35. *Wallace v. Jaffree,* 472 U.S. 38 (1985).

36. Edwin Meese III, "The Attorney General's View of the Supreme Court: Toward a Jurisprudence of Original Intention," *Public Administration Review* 45 (1985): 701–704; Edwin Meese III, "Toward a Jurisprudence of Original Intent," *Harvard Journal of Law and Public Policy* 11 (1988): 5–12.

37. Robert H. Bork, "The Constitution, Original Intent, and Economic Rights,"

San Diego Law Review 23 (1986): 823–832; William J. Brennan, Jr., "The Constitution of the United States: Contemporary Ratification" (1985), reprinted in *Interpreting the Constitution: The Debate over Original Intent,* ed. Jack N. Rakove (Boston: Northeastern University Press, 1990), 25, 27. Scalia and Bork had sparred in *Ollman v. Evans,* 750 F. 2d. 970 (D.C. Cir. 1984).

38. Robert H. Bork, "The Impossibility of Finding Welfare Rights in the Constitution," *Washington University Law Quarterly* (1979): 697.

39. Richard A. Posner, *The Problems of Jurisprudence* (Cambridge, Mass.: Harvard University Press, 1990), 467; Richard A. Posner, "Bork and Beethoven," *Stanford Law Review* 42 (1990): 1380.

40. Jack N. Rakove, "Fidelity through History (or to It)," *Fordham Law Review* 65 (1997): 1591. On the historical defects of originalism: Paul Brest, "The Misconceived Quest for the Original Understanding," *Boston University Law Review* 60 (1980): 204–238; H. Jefferson Powell, "Rules for Originalists," *Virginia Law Review* 73 (1987): 659–699; James H. Hutson, "Riddles of the Federal Constitution," *William and Mary Quarterly* 44 (1987): 412–423; Leonard W. Levy, *Original Intent and the Framers' Constitution* (New York: Macmillan, 1988); Charles A. Lofgren, "The Original Understanding of Original Intent?" *Constitutional Commentary* 5 (1988): 77–113.

41. Antonin Scalia, "Originalism: The Lesser Evil," *University of Cincinnati Law Review* 57 (1989): 849–865; Ralph A. Rossum, "Text and Tradition: The Originalist Jurisprudence of Antonin Scalia," in *Rehnquist Justice: Understanding the Court Dynamic,* ed. Earl M. Maltz (Lawrence: University Press of Kansas, 2003); Ralph A. Rossum, *Antonin Scalia's Jurisprudence: Text and Tradition* (Lawrence: University Press of Kansas, 2006); Frank Easterbrook, "The Role of Original Intent in Statutory Construction," *Harvard Journal of Law and Public Policy* 11 (1988): 59–66.

42. Bruce Ackerman, *We the People* (Cambridge, Mass.: Harvard University Press, 1991). On the context of Ackerman's search for a liberal, historically-rooted jurisprudence: Laura Kalman, *The Strange Career of Legal Liberalism* (New Haven: Yale University Press, 1996).

43. John Hart Ely, "Constitutional Interpretivism: Its Allure and Impossibility," *Indiana Law Journal* 53 (1978): 436; Clarence Thomas, "Toward a 'Plain Reading' of the Constitution: The Declaration of Independence in Constitutional Interpretation," *Howard Law Journal* 30 (1987): 983–996; Harry V. Jaffe, "Judge Bork's Mistake," *National Review,* March 4, 1988, 38–40; Gary McDowell as quoted in Stephen Macedo, ed., *The New Right v. the Constitution* (Washington, D.C.: Cato Institute, 1987), 108; William H. Rehnquist dissent in *Nevada v. Hall,* 440 U.S. 410 (1979) at 439, 433.

44. Edwin Meese III, "Address before the D.C. Chapter of the Federalist Society Lawyers Division" (1986), reprinted in *Interpreting the Constitution,* ed. Rakove; Bork, "Constitution, Original Intent, and Economic Rights," 826, 828.

45. Posner, "Bork and Beethoven"; Ronald Dworkin, "The Bork Nomination," *New York Review of Books,* August 13, 1987; Bruce Ackerman, "Robert Bork's Grand Inquisition," *Yale Law Journal* 99 (1990): 1419–1439.

46. Thomas W. Merrill, "Bork v. Burke," *Harvard Journal of Law and Public Policy* 19 (1996): 523. In the same vein: Henry Paul Monaghan, "Our Perfect Constitution," *New York University Law Review* 56 (1981): 353–396; Henry Paul Monaghan, "*Stare Decisis* and Constitutional Adjudication," *Columbia Law Review* 88 (1988): 723–773.

47. On the move from eighteenth-century texts to eighteenth-century practice: Erwin Chermerinsky, "The Constitutional Jurisprudence of the Rehnquist Court," in *The Rehnquist Court: A Retrospective,* ed. Martin H. Belsky (New York: Oxford University Press, 2002); Rossum, *Antonin Scalia's Jurisprudence.*

48. Randy E. Barnett, "An Originalism for Nonoriginalists," *Loyola Law Review* 45 (1999): 611–654; Cass R. Sunstein, "Five Theses on Originalism," *Harvard Journal of Law and Public Policy* 19 (1996): 311–315; Sanford Levinson, "The Limited Relevance of Originalism in the Actual Performance of Legal Roles," *Harvard Journal of Law and Public Policy* 19 (1996): 495–508. For an example of Scalia's readiness to leap into psychological theory-making with all the confidence of the Warren Court's justices: *Lee v. Weisman* 505 U.S. 577 (1992) at 637–639.

49. Jeane Kirkpatrick, "Dictatorships and Double Standards" (1979), in Kirkpatrick, *Dictatorships and Double Standards: Rationalism and Reason in Politics* (New York: Simon and Schuster, 1982).

50. Juan J. Linz, "Totalitarian and Authoritarian Regimes," in *Handbook of Political Science,* vol. 3, ed. Fred I. Greenstein and Nelson W. Polsby (Reading, Mass.: Addison Wesley, 1975); Terry McNeill, "Images of the Soviet Future: The Western Scholarly Debate," in *The Soviet Union and the Challenge of the Future,* vol. 1, ed. Alexander Shtromas and Morton A. Kaplan (New York: Paragon House, 1988); Zbigniew Brzezinski, ed., *Dilemmas of Change in Soviet Politics* (New York: Columbia University Press, 1969); Zbigniew Brzezinski, "The Soviet Past and Future," *Encounter* 34 (March 1970): 3–16. More generally, David C. Engerman, *Know Your Enemy: The Rise and Fall of America's Soviet Experts* (New York: Oxford University Press, 2009).

51. Ronald Reagan, Remarks at the Annual Convention of the National Association of Evangelicals, March 8, 1983, accessed at Woolley and Peters, *The American Presidency Project;* Jean-François Revel as quoted in Garry Dorrien, *The Neoconservative Mind: Politics, Culture, and the War of Ideology* (Philadelphia: Temple University Press, 1993), 371; Richard Pipes, "Can the Soviet Union Reform?" *Foreign Affairs* 63 (1984): 48; Owen Harries, "The Cold War and the Intellectuals," *Commentary,* October 1991, 20.

52. "U.S. National Security Strategy," NSDD 32 (May 20, 1982): 2; "U.S. Relations with the USSR," NSDD 75 (January 17, 1983): 1, 8, 6, at www.fas.org/irp/offdocs/; Secretary of State George Schultz as quoted in Beth A. Fischer,

"Reagan and the Soviets: Winning the Cold War?" in *The Reagan Presidency: Pragmatic Conservatism and Its Legacies,* ed. W. Elliot Brownlee and Hugh Davis Graham (Lawrence: University Press of Kansas, 2003), 122; Jeane Kirkpatrick, "American Foreign Policy in a Cold Climate: A Long Conversation," *Encounter* 61 (November 1983): 24. On the debate over prediction of the Soviet Union's collapse: Francis Fukuyama et al., "The Strange Death of Communism: An Autopsy," *National Interest,* special issue, Spring 1993, especially Peter Rutland, "Sovietology: Notes for a Post-Mortem," 120–122; Peter Schweizer, *Victory: The Reagan Administration's Secret Strategy That Hastened the Collapse of the Soviet Union* (New York: Atlantic Monthly Press, 1994).

53. George Will is quoted in John Judis, "Conservatism and the Price of Success," in *The Reagan Legacy,* ed. Sidney Blumenthal and Thomas Byrne Edsall (New York: Pantheon, 1988), 166; Alain Besançon, "Gorbachev without Illusion," *Commentary,* April 1988, 47–57; Richard Pipes, "Gorbachev's Russia: Breakdown or Crackdown?" *Commentary,* March 1990, 13–25; Kirkpatrick, *Dictatorships and Double Standards,* 7. See also: Walter Laquer, "Is There Now, or Has There Ever Been, Such a Thing as Totalitarianism?" *Commentary,* October 1985, 29–35; Jean-François Revel, "Is Communism Reversible?" *Commentary,* January 1989, 17–24; and more generally John Ehrman, *The Rise of Neoconservatism: Intellectuals and Foreign Affairs, 1945–1994* (New Haven: Yale University Press, 1995); Eric Alterman, *Sound and Fury: The Washington Punditocracy and the Collapse of American Politics* (New York: HarperCollins, 1992), chap. 10.

54. Francis Fukuyama, "The End of History?" *National Interest,* Summer 1989, 3–18. The quoted line is from p. 4. On the extraordinary attention given to the article: Jonathan Alter, "The Intellectual Hula Hoop," *Newsweek,* October 9, 1989, 39; James Atlas, "What Is Fukuyama Saying? And To Whom Is He Saying It?" *New York Times Magazine,* October 22, 1989, 38–42.

55. Paul Kennedy, *The Rise and Fall of the Great Powers: Economic Change and Military Conflict from 1500 to 2000* (New York: Random House, 1987); Paul Kennedy, "The (Relative) Decline of America," *Atlantic Monthly,* August 1987, 29–38; Francis Fukuyama, *The End of History and the Last Man* (New York: Free Press, 1992).

56. Samuel P. Huntington, "No Exit: The Errors of Endism," *National Interest,* Fall 1989, 10; John Gray, "The End of History—or of Liberalism?" *National Review,* October 27, 1989, 35; Richard Pipes, "The Russians Are Still Coming," *New York Times,* October 9, 1989, A17. For other critical readings of Fukuyama's use of Hegel: Alan Ryan, "Professor Hegel Goes to Washington," *New York Review of Books,* March 26, 1992; Leon Wieseltier, "Spoilers at the Party," *National Interest,* Fall 1989, 12–16.

57. Fukuyama, "End of History?" 3; Francis Fukuyama, "A Reply to My Critics," *National Interest,* Winter 1989–1990, 21–28.

58. Janine R. Wedel, *Collision and Collusion: The Strange Case of Western Aid to East-*

ern Europe, 1989–1998 (New York: St. Martin's Press, 1998); Jacques deLisle, "Lex Americana? United States Legal Assistance, American Legal Models, and Legal Change in the Post-Communist World and Beyond," *University of Pennsylvania Journal of International Economic Law* 20 (1999): 179–308. On Sachs: Janine R. Wedel, "The Economist Heard Round the World, Part II," *World Monitor,* October 1990, 33–42; Peter Passell, "Dr. Jeffrey Sachs, Shock Therapist," *New York Times Magazine,* June 27, 1993, SM 20ff.; James Surowiecki, "Dr. Shock," *Lingua Franca,* June/July 1997, 61–73.

59. T. Ivan Berend, *Central and Eastern Europe, 1944–1993: Detour from the Periphery to the Periphery* (Cambridge: Cambridge University Press, 2001).

60. John Kenneth Galbraith, "The Rush to Capitalism," *New York Review of Books,* October 25, 1990.

61. Jeffrey Sachs, "What Is to Be Done?" *Economist,* January 13, 1990, 23ff. Also Jeffrey Sachs and David Lipton, "Poland's Economic Reform," *Foreign Affairs* 69 (1990): 47–66; Jeffrey Sachs, *Poland's Jump to the Market Economy* (Cambridge, Mass.: MIT Press, 1993); Jeffrey Sachs, "Life in the Economic Emergency Room," in *The Political Economy of Reform,* ed. John Williamson (Washington, D.C.: Institute for International Economics, 1994). The MIT-based team headed by Olivier Blanchard and including Lawrence Summers and Paul Krugman agreed: "we have little choice but to move on all fronts at once—or not move at all." Olivier Blanchard et al., *Reform in Eastern Europe* (Cambridge, Mass.: MIT Press, 1991), xii.

62. David Lipton and Jeffrey Sachs, "Creating a Market Economy in Eastern Europe: The Case of Poland," *Brookings Papers on Economic Activity* 1990, no. 1 (1999), 75–147.

63. David M. Kotz and Fred Weir, *Russia's Path from Gorbachev to Putin: The Demise of the Soviet System and the New Russia* (London: Routledge, 2007), chap. 5. On the internal intellectual sources of neo-liberal economics: Johanna Bockman and Gil Eyal, "Eastern Europe as a Laboratory for Economic Knowledge: The Transnational Roots of Neoliberalism," *American Journal of Sociology* 108 (2002): 310–352; Mario I. Blejer and Fabrizio Coricelli, eds., *The Making of Economic Reform in Eastern Europe: Conversations with Leading Reformers in Poland, Hungary, and the Czech Republic* (Aldershot, UK: Edward Elgar, 1995).

64. Richard E. Ericson, "The Classical Soviet-Type Economy: Nature of the System and Implications for Reform," *Journal of Economic Perspectives* 5 (Fall 1991): 25, 26. On the Gaidar group: Anders Åslund, *How Russia Became a Market Economy* (Washington, D.C.: Brookings Institution, 1995), 17; Bockman and Eyal, "Eastern Europe as a Laboratory," 343.

65. Boris Yeltsin as quoted in Kotz and Weir, *Russia's Path from Gorbachev to Putin,* 161; International Monetary Fund, The World Bank, Organisation for Economic Co-operation and Development, and European Bank for Reconstruction and Development, *The Economy of the USSR: Summary and Recommendations* (Washington: World Bank, 1990), 18.

66. Sachs and Lipton, "Poland's Economic Reform," 47; Jeffrey Sachs as quoted

in John Lloyd, "The Russian Devolution," *New York Times Magazine,* August 15, 1999, SM37.

67. Peter Murrell, "Evolution in Economics and in the Economic Reform of the Centrally Planned Economies," in *The Emergence of Market Economies in Eastern Europe,* ed. Christopher Clague and Gordon C. Rausser (Cambridge: Basil Blackwell, 1992); Peter Murrell, "Evolutionary and Radical Approaches to Economic Reform," *Economic Planning* 25 (1992): 79–95; Peter Murrell, "The Transition According to Cambridge, Mass.," *Journal of Economic Literature* 33 (1995): 164–178. The leading American co-signers of the cautionary open letter to Boris Yeltsin on "shock therapy" in 1996, Kenneth Arrow, Robert Solow, and James Tobin, all spoke for a generation of economists that was now long in eclipse. "A New Economic Policy for Russia," *Economics of Transition* 5 (1997): 225–227.

68. Jerry F. Hough, *The Logic of Economic Reform in Russia* (Washington, D.C.: Brookings Institution, 2001), 254.

69. For the conservative debate over human rights policy: Walter Laquer, "The Issue of Human Rights," *Commentary,* May 1977, 29–35; Daniel P. Moynihan, "The Politics of Human Rights," *Commentary,* August 1977, 19–26; Peter L. Berger, "Are Human Rights Universal?" *Commentary,* September 1977, 60–63; "Human Rights and American Foreign Policy: A Symposium," *Commentary,* November 1981, 25–63; Irving Kristol, "Human Rights: The Hidden Agenda," *National Interest,* Winter 1986–1987, 3–11; Joshua Muravchik, *The Uncertain Crusade: Jimmy Carter and the Dilemmas of Human Rights Policy* (Lanham, Md.: Hamilton Press, 1986); Tamar Jacoby, "The Reagan Turnaround on Human Rights," *Foreign Affairs* 64 (1986): 1066–1086.

70. Sachs, "What Is to Be Done?"; David Lipton and Jeffrey Sachs, "Privatization in Eastern Europe: The Case of Poland," in *Reforming Central and Eastern European Economies,* ed. Vittorio Corbo et al. (Washington, D.C.: World Bank, 1991); Sachs, *Poland's Jump to the Market Economy,* 86; Maxim Boycko, Andrei Schleifer, and Robert Vishny, *Privatizing Russia* (Cambridge, Mass.: MIT Press, 1995). See also the IMF's former chief economist on the illusions of gradualism: Anne O. Krueger, "Institutions for the New Private Sector," in *Emergence of Market Economics,* ed. Clague and Rausser.

71. Joseph E. Stiglitz, "Preface" to Lawrence R. Klein and Marshall Pomer, eds., *The New Russia: Transition Gone Astray* (Stanford: Stanford University Press, 2001), xxii; Joseph Stiglitz, *Globalization and Its Discontents* (New York: Norton, 2002), chap. 5.

72. Jeffrey Sachs, "Economic Transformation of Eastern Europe: The Case of Poland," *American Economist* 36 (Fall 1992): 10.

73. David Lipton and Jeffrey D. Sachs, "Prospects for Russia's Economic Reforms," *Brookings Papers on Economic Activity,* 1, no. 2 (1992): 213–283; Pasell, "Dr. Jeffrey Sachs"; Åslund, *How Russia Became a Market Economy,* 313. At the still farther bounds of optimism: Richard Poe, *How to Profit from the Coming Russian Boom: The Insider's Guide to Business Profits and Survival on the Frontiers of*

Capitalism (New York: McGraw-Hill, 1993); Richard Layard and John Parker, *The Coming Russian Boom: A Guide to New Markets and Politics* (New York: Free Press, 1996).

74. Stanley Fischer and Ratna Sahay, "Taking Stock," *Finance and Development,* September 2000, 3; Peter Murrell, "How Far Has the Transition Progressed?" *Journal of Economic Perspectives* 10 (Spring 1996): 25–44; Kotz and Weir, *Russia's Path,* 239. On the construction of the new Russian oligarchy: Marshall Goldman, *The Piratization of Russia: Russian Reform Goes Awry* (New York: Routledge, 2003); Peter Reddaway and Dmitri Glinski, *The Tragedy of Russia's Reforms: Market Bolshevism against Democracy* (Washington, D.C.: U.S. Institute of Peace, 2001).

75. Olivier Blanchard, *The Economics of Post-Communist Transition* (Oxford: Clarendon Press, 1997); Surowiecki, "Dr. Shock," 73; Jeffrey Sachs, "Betrayal," *New Republic,* January 31, 1994, 14–18. For Sachs's earlier rejection of the idea that history or culture might play a role in delaying the Russian move to market capitalism: Lipton and Sachs, "Prospects for Russia's Economic Reforms." The most stinging critic of "transitionology" was Steven F. Cohen; his reports in the *Nation* and elsewhere were collected in *Failed Crusade: America and the Tragedy of Post-Communist Russia* (New York: Norton, 2000).

Epilogue 9/11

Epigraph: Andrew Sullivan, "This Is What a Day Means," *New York Times Magazine,* September 23, 2001, 61.

1. David Ansen, "Finding Our New Voice," *Newsweek,* October 1, 2001, 6.
2. Mitchell Fink and Lois Mathias, eds., *Never Forget: An Oral History of September 11, 2001* (New York: HarperCollins, 2002); Dean E. Murphy, ed., *September 11: An Oral History* (New York: Doubleday, 2002); Gail Sheehy, *Middletown, America: One Town's Passage from Trauma to Hope* (New York: Random House, 2003).
3. Sam Nunn is quoted in Amy Reynolds and Brooke Barnett, "'America under Attack': CNN's Verbal and Visual Framing of September 11," in *Media Representations of September 11,* ed. Steven Chermak, Frankie Y. Bailey, and Michelle Brown (Westport, Conn.: Praeger, 2003), 96; George W. Bush, Remarks at the National Day of Prayer and Remembrance, Sept. 14, 2001, accessed at John Woolley and Gerhard Peters, *The American Presidency Project* (online). Santa Barbara: University of California (hosted), http://www.presidency.ucsb.edu.ws. All subsequent citations to Bush's presidential speeches are from this source. George Packer, "Recapturing the Flag," *New York Times Magazine,* September 30, 2001, 16.
4. Marc Leepson, *Flag: An American Biography* (New York: St. Martin's Press, 2005), 253–265; Peter Elliott, *Home Front: American Flags from Across the United States* (Chicago: Lily Bay Press, 2002); Jonathan Alter, "The New Shape of Patriotism," *Newsweek,* October 1, 2001, 63.

5. Rachel Newman, "The Day the World Changed, I Did Too," *Newsweek*, October 1, 2001, 9.

6. Packer, "Recapturing the Flag," 16; George W. Bush, State of the Union Address, January 29, 2002.

7. Samuel P. Huntington, "Clash of Civilizations?" *Foreign Affairs* 72 (1993): 22–49; Samuel P. Huntington, *The Clash of Civilizations and the Remaking of World Order* (New York: Simon and Schuster, 1996); Thomas Carothers, "The End of the Transition Paradigm," *Journal of Democracy* 13 (January 2002): 5–21. Fukuyama himself was to write that he had never meant to say that there was a universal hunger for liberty pressing everywhere inevitably toward liberal democracy. Francis Fukuyama, *America at the Crossroads: Democracy, Power, and the Neoconservative Legacy* (New Haven: Yale University Press, 2006), especially 53–59.

8. Joyce Appleby quoted in John Meacham, "A Date with History," *Newsweek*, September 9, 2002, 65.

9. Fareed Zakaria, "The End of the End of History," *Newsweek*, September 24, 2001, 70.

10. Adam Piore, "Red, White, and What a Deal!" *Newsweek*, November 26, 2001, 59.

11. Chrisopher P. Campbell, "Commodifying September 11: Advertising, Myth, and Hegemony," in *Media Representations of September 11*, ed. Chermak et al.; Michael Elliott, "Don't Wear Out Old Glory," *Time*, February 18, 2002, 52.

12. Susan Faludi, *The Terror Dream: Fear and Fantasy in Post-9/11 America* (New York: Metropolitan Books, 2007).

13. Jerry Falwell as quoted in Dinesh D'Souza, *The Enemy at Home: The Cultural Left and Its Responsibility for 9/11* (New York: Doubleday, 2007), 4–5; Sean Hannity, *Let Freedom Ring: Winning the War of Liberty over Liberalism* (New York: Regan Books, 2002), 6, 11, 294.

14. Stanley Fish, "Condemnation without Absolutes," *New York Times*, October 15, 2001, A19. William J. Bennett, *Why We Fight: Moral Clarity and the War on Terrorism* (New York: Doubleday, 2002), 57–61.

15. Jeffrey Goldberg, "The Believer," *New Yorker*, February 13, 2006, 56–59; Michael Gerson, *Heroic Conservatism: Why Republicans Need to Embrace America's Ideals (And Why They Deserve to Fail If They Don't)* (New York: HarperOne, 2007). The quoted phrase is from p. 264. On the dynamics of the Bush speechwriting office: D. T. Max, "The Making of the Speech," *New York Times Magazine*, October 7, 2001, 32–37; Matthew Scully, "Present at the Creation," *Atlantic Monthly*, September 2007, 77–88.

16. George W. Bush, Inaugural Address, January 20, 2001; Hendrik Hertzberg, "The Word from W.," *New Yorker*, February 5, 2001, 29.

17. George W. Bush, Address before a Joint Session of the Congress on the United States Response to the Terrorist Attacks of September 11, September 20, 2001.

18. George W. Bush, State of the Union Address, January 29, 2002.

19. Ibid.; George W. Bush, Address to the Nation on Hurricane Katrina Recovery from New Orleans, Louisiana, September 15, 2005.

20. George W. Bush, State of the Union Address, January 29, 2002; David Frum and Richard Perle, *An End to Evil: How To Win the War on Terror* (New York: Random House, 2003), 9, 143–145.

21. Gerson, *Heroic Conservatism.*

22. Max, "Making of the Speech," 34.

23. George W. Bush, Inaugural Address, January 20, 2001; George W. Bush, Remarks at a Town Hall Meeting in Orlando, December 4, 2001; George W. Bush, Inaugural Address, January 20, 2005.

24. George W. Bush, Inaugural Address, January 20, 2005; George W. Bush, State of the Union Address, February 2, 2005.

25. Bob Woodward, *Plan of Attack* (New York: Simon and Schuster, 2004), 326.

26. Donald Rumsfeld, "Beyond Nation Building," Remarks at the Sea-Air-Space Museum, New York, February 14, 2003, www.defense.gov/Speeches/Speech.aspx?SpeechID=337; Bob Woodward, *State of Denial* (New York: Simon and Schuster, 2006). The most articulate insider's defense of the Bush war strategy, Douglas J. Feith, *War and Decision: Inside the Pentagon at the Dawn of the War on Terrorism* (New York: HarperCollins, 2008), does not essentially challenge these assumptions.

27. Larry Di Rita as quoted in George Packer, *The Assassin's Gate: America in Iraq* (New York: Farrar, Straus and Giroux, 2005), 133.

28. John Lewis Gaddis, "Grand Strategy in the Second Term," *Foreign Affairs* 84 (2005): 15.

29. Peggy Noonan, "Way Too Much God," *Wall Street Journal,* January 21, 2005, A8; Robert W. Tucker and David C. Hendrickson, "The Freedom Crusade," *National Interest,* Fall 2005, 12–21; "The Freedom Crusade, Revisited: A Symposium," *National Interest,* Winter 2005–2006, 9–17.

30. Peggy Noonan, *What I Saw at the Revolution: A Political Life in the Reagan Era* (New York: Random House, 1990), 103.

31. Thomas L. Friedman, *The World Is Flat: A Brief History of the Twenty-First Century* (New York: Farrar, Straus and Giroux, 2005), 345, 350; Steven D. Levitt and Stephen J. Dubner, *Freakonomics: A Rogue Economist Explores the Hidden Side of Everything* (New York: William Morrow, 2005).

32. Levitt and Dubner, *Freakonomics,* 13.

33. Rick Warren, *The Purpose-Driven Life* (Grand Rapids, Mich.: Zondervan, 2002); Jim Wallis, *God's Politics: Why the Right Gets It Wrong and the Left Doesn't Get It* (San Francisco: HarperSanFrancisco, 2005); Barack Obama, *The Audacity of Hope: Thoughts on Reclaiming the American Dream* (New York: Crown, 2006).

34. Zakaria, "The End of the End of History," 70.

Acknowledgments

Book writing is an intensely solitary activity that is, at the same time, a quintessentially social process, utterly dependent on the support, provocation, assistance, and criticism of others. Even in its most private moments, rewriting a sentence or watching one's thoughts skitter across a computer screen, it offers a lesson in social interdependence.

Acts of students, friends, and strangers have shaped this project from the beginning. Many of the themes of *Age of Fracture* trace back to my efforts, haltingly improvised at first, to make historical sense of contemporary cultural and intellectual life for undergraduate students first at the University of Wisconsin and later at Princeton. If I could name all of those students, along with the dozens of co-teachers who undertook the task with me as the times cracked and shifted beneath us, they would have pride of place in these acknowledgments.

The book itself was assisted by other hands. It was launched with a fellowship at the Woodrow Wilson Center for International Scholars in Washington, D.C., and aided by the generous resources of the Center's staff and fellows. Much of the book's initial drafting took place at the University of Cambridge, where as Pitt Professor of American History and Institutions I found myself drawn into an immensely stimulating circle of conversations among colleagues young and old. The last chapters of the book were written with the generous support of a Guggenheim Fellowship and an Old Dominion Fellowship from Princeton University. To all of these institutions, I am extremely grateful.

I am grateful, too, for the opportunities to present early drafts of the book. From those occasions I became the beneficiary of many a helpful conversation, unanticipated lead, and tough, valuably skeptical question.

My thanks to inviters and interlocutors at the Universities of Cambridge, East Anglia, Glasgow, Nottingham, and Oxford, the University of California at Santa Barbara and UCLA, the Miller Center of Public Affairs at the University of Virginia, Brandeis University, Harvard University, Columbia University, Princeton University, the École des hautes études en sciences sociales in Paris, and the Maine Town Meeting at Skowhegan. The Commonwealth Fund Lecture at the University of London provided a valuable opportunity to try to put together an early version of the whole.

Readers and listeners make books as well. This one is deeply indebted to the friends and colleagues, too numerous to be individually acknowledged here, whose conversations or responses to early drafts and proposals helped to shape the project into something better. Jonathan Aldred, Thomas Bender, Alan Brinkley, Eduardo Canedo, Stefan Collini, Fernando Fasce, Marion Fourcade-Gourinchas, Dirk Hartog, Sarah Igo, Richard King, Walter Johnson, Arno Mayer, Lee Mitchell, Jocelyn Olcott, Jonathan Rieder, the late Michael Rogin, Emma Rothschild, Nicole Sackley, Christine Stansell, John Thompson, and Eric Yellin all gave helpful, critical readings of parts of the manuscript. The fellows of Princeton University's Davis Seminar in Historical Studies worked over the epilogue. Brooke Blower, Benjamin Schmidt, and James Kloppenberg went out of their way to share their critical reactions to the book as a whole. None bears responsibility for the result, but without their prodding and patience it would be a different enterprise.

As the early drafts moved toward book form, Joyce Seltzer gave the manuscript a very smart reception and a home at Harvard University Press. Christine Thorsteinsson edited the manuscript with scrupulous care. Benjamin Schmidt, Dov Weinryb-Grohsgal, and Stephen Feldman chased down many a stray fact.

Of all this project's many wise and generous readers, however, one never ceases to matter most of all. This book belongs, once more, to Rene, for a lifetime's reasons.

Index